The Kingdom at Work Project

An environmentally friendly book printed and bound in England by
www.printondemand-worldwide.com

Commendations

'This project challenges all to relate good faith to the theological resonances in everyday tasks throughout our economic system. This profoundly applicable study will enable the expression of faith at work through a vibrant rediscovery of the incarnational truths of our Christian scriptures, tradition and understanding of chaplaincy. A brilliant work-book for the servant leader who genuinely starts where others are in their work - thus enhancing bold witness through the household of God made apparent in the public realm and furthering a moral and ethical political economy.'

Peter Challen was for many years a chaplain with the South London Industrial Mission. He is a Sloan Fellow of the London Business School and Chair of the Christian Council for Monetary Justice. He is a Canon of the Church of England.

'Christians are charged with the mission to "go out" - yet many of us seem reluctant to take our faith actively into the world of work. David Clark has developed an innovative communal model of mission in the workplace. The book is a valuable mission resource which explores context, theology and intervention at depth. His methodology encourages Christians to discern the gifts of the kingdom present in their workplace and to build on them for its transformation. The role of mentors in this process is rightly to the fore. The task is an urgent one and the project much to be commended.'

Jennifer Tann was a former Professor of Innovation Studies and member of the Business School at Birmingham University. She is currently working as a process consultant. She is a member of the General Synod of the Church of England.

'We spend much of our lives at work. We learn from and give to this community. However David Clark is ambitious for more than this. For him, as for the project behind this book, the world of work needs radical transformation of a communal character. I believe that enabling lay people to understand and enter into this kind of communal mission in the workplace is extremely important and widely neglected. I welcome this detailed and helpful study on which people can draw in many different ways.'

Ruth McCurry was a former Commissioning Editor with SPCK.

'In recent years various resources have appeared to help us relate our faith to our work. What sets the Kingdom at Work Project apart is its truly holistic approach. While other resources offer advice on witness at work, this project recognises that God and his kingdom are there before we are. The project is built around God *in* Monday - and every day. Our workplace is seen not as alien to our faith but as closely related to it as is our Sunday worship.'

Robert Fox is Customer Relationship Manager at HM Revenue and Customs. He is an ordained minister in the Church of England and editor of *Ministers-at-Work*.

The Kingdom at Work Project

*A communal approach
to mission in the workplace*

David Clark

www.fast-print.net/store.php

THE KINGDOM AT WORK PROJECT:
A Communal Approach To Mission In The Workplace
Copyright © David Clark 2014

ISBN 978-178456-115-4

First Published 2014 by
Fast-Print Publishing of Peterborough, England

Contents

Part 2 Discernment and intervention

Part 4 Review

To Bill Gowland and Mollie Batten -

pioneers in enabling faith to
transform the world of work

Foreword

The church in the west has for most of its history remained institutionally moulded by the norms of Christendom. Those norms maintained forms of community which were shaped by the sharing of a common territory, bonded by kinship and sustained by human-scale collective economic endeavour. Over recent years, the emergence of a global economy driven by competition and market forces, the accelerating ease and rapidity of travel and the increasing speed of communication, given an enormous boost by the rise of information technology, have led to the collapse of traditional communal bonds.

It is imperative, therefore, that to meet the immense challenges of a new millennium different and sustainable forms of community be found. In this book I describe an endeavour, called the Kingdom at Work Project, which sets out, in the context of Christian faith and the world of work, to address that task.

In the creation and maintenance of community, the world of work in general, and the workplace in particular, have had a key part to play. For many centuries the workplace - farm and market, mine and mill, shop and warehouse, office and factory, school and hospital, board room and council chamber - has fostered powerful communal ties which have enriched relationships, facilitated decision-making, humanized the delivery of services, enhanced processes of production and furthered the common good. In this project I contend that, though its nature and form are ever changing, the workplace continues to have an invaluable contribution to make to the quest for community.

However, this project goes further. My contention is that the workplace can be communally transformed by an ongoing engagement with Christian faith through what I call the gifts of 'the kingdom community' - life, liberation, love and learning - gifts which, taken together, exemplify community at its zenith. The project explores the potential of the workplace as a kingdom-empowered manifestation of community and as a means of communal transformation both within and beyond the world of work.

In what follows I argue that the church is first and foremost the servant of the kingdom community. Thus one vital aspect of its mission, in recent years barely addressed let alone fulfilled, is to help bring into being a world of work, and the multitude of workplaces it embraces, transformed by the gifts of that community. The Kingdom at Work Project describes a communal theology, spirituality, economy and communal structures able to give impetus to such a mission and offers an innovative and comprehensive process of discernment and intervention through which that mission might be accomplished.

David Clark

Bakewell, Derbyshire

October 2014

Preface

The recent collapse of the global financial system, as well as the undermining of trust in other institutions of public life from government to the police service, reveals an acute ethical deficit within the working world. The past few years have also demonstrated that the economic models which have been taken for granted for so long are in need of radical renewal, if not eventual replacement. The impact of these ethical and economic failures on the lives of many ordinary citizens, not least those on limited incomes, brings home yet again that the world of work has the potential not only to enrich but to undermine human well-being. However, so entrenched is the existing exploitation and manipulation of market forces that change will be no easy matter to achieve. Thus the question as to how the world of work might be transformed so that its potential for the enrichment of human life is realized is an urgent one.

Faith, work and community - my story

My own conviction that the Christian contribution to the world of work is of vital importance goes back many years. My father, a Methodist layman, was the first personnel manager to be appointed by Boots the Chemist, the pharmaceutical company based in Nottingham. In my youth he used to recount to me stories of his dealing with the ups and downs of life in that company. It was his deep commitment to expressing his faith through his involvement in the world of work which in large part inspired me to take a life-long interest in the contribution of Christian faith to public life in its many different facets.

Whilst training for the Methodist ministry, I made a number of visits to Luton Industrial College. The latter was established in 1955 to bring together groups of workers from all walks of industry to reflect on the implications of Christian faith for their working lives. I have for ever been indebted to its inspirational founder William Gowland, a Methodist minister. I also was privileged to be the first Methodist ordinand to study for a year at the William Temple College in Rugby, a centre led by a formidable civil servant, Mollie Batten. Through residential studies and short courses, the college sought to bring the insights of theology to bear on many aspects of the life of society, especially on the world of work.

Some years later as a Methodist minister I was able to gain first-hand experience of the working world through teaching part-time in inner London, first in a girls secondary school and then in a newly established social education department of a large London comprehensive (Clark, 1973b; 1975; 1976). In 1973, I became a 'sector minister' and for the next twenty-five years was engaged in training community and youth workers and, later, community educators (1996) at Westhill College, Birmingham, a Free Church foundation and part of the Selly Oak Federation of Colleges. That role involved me in supervising students engaged in youth work, social work, community work and teaching throughout Birmingham, often in very deprived areas of that city.

Between 1992 and 2000, I initiated and managed the Christians in Public Life Programme, the main achievement of which was the publication of over 200 short papers written by a wide diversity of authors. Together these formed a comprehensive agenda for the mission of the church in public life (2005, pp. 170-187). In order to earth this agenda in the real world, from the mid-1990s until the early 2000s, I was involved in Birmingham in setting up and directing what was initially known as the Human City Initiative, later to become the Human City Institute (2005, pp. 188-209; 2012). The mission statement of the Institute was: 'To enable those who share a vision of the human city to work together with others to make that vision a reality'. Many hundreds of people were involved in this venture which involved, amongst other activities, promoting the concept of the human business.

Alongside my commitment to exploring the relation between Christian faith and public life was a life-long fascination with the concept of community. This interest was sparked during my first appointment as a Methodist minister in Woodhouse, formerly a farming and mining village but in my time a largely working-class suburb on the outskirts of Sheffield. The fluctuating fortunes of the village between 1912 and 1966 became the subject of a doctorate in urban sociology which I undertook with the University of Sheffield (1969). My study of and writing about the concept of community has continued from that time onwards, in particular informed by my involvement with the Christian Community Movement from the early 1970s until the late 1980s (2005, pp. 150-169).

My research into the nature and forms of community led me to develop a theology of community which was built on firm sociological foundations (1973a, 2005 pp. 14-18). The concept of what I called 'the kingdom community' was the result. The concept was coined by me in the 1980s and developed in the years following (1987, 1996 pp. 53-55; 2005 pp. 20-27). In recent years, I have sought to apply a theology of the kingdom community, as in this project, to many aspects of the church's mission (2010, 2012, 2013).

The communal transformation of the workplace

The Kingdom at Work Project reflects my conviction that the world of work not only needs radical transformation but that *such transformation has to be communal in character*. However, to get to grips with its mission in the world of work, the church needs an entry point. One such entry point is intervention on the societal or global stage. However, taking up that challenge can only be undertaken by major denominations whose representatives have considerable influence in the public realm.

The entry point for the Kingdom at Work Project is deliberately chosen as being at the other end of the scale. Thus *the project's focus is the communal transformation of the workplace*. The project seeks entry into the world of work at this point for a number of reasons. First, within the world of work it is within the workplace where relationships which determine the strength of community are created or destroyed. Without the communal transformation of the workplace there can be no transformation of the world of work. Secondly, the workplace is where many lay people, the church's primary resource for mission, are actively engaged. Thirdly, there are a growing number of initiatives being taken by agencies within a secular society to promote 'the good workplace'. Christians at work will thus find that there are others with similar concerns with whom they can work in partnership.

The Kingdom at Work Project

The purpose of the Kingdom at Work Project is to enable Christians to create workplaces transformed by the gifts of the kingdom community. There are three requirements if this purpose is to be fulfilled.

First and foremost, there is the need to develop a communal model of mission for the world of work. The Kingdom at Work Project sets out the key components of such a model in some detail.

A second requirement is the need for the training of 'mission mentors'. Mentors will need the experience and skills to enable lay people to engage in mission at work and to facilitate the church as a whole in supporting the laity in that task. The project is a major resource for such an undertaking and can be regarded as 'a manual for mentors'.

Thirdly, if the project is to succeed, the gathered church will need to play a much more pro-active role in supporting its members engaged in mission within the workplace.

Origins of the project

The Kingdom at Work Project has developed out of the endeavours of the Methodist Diaconal Order's Faith and Work Group, of which I was until recently the convenor. I entered the Methodist Diaconal Order in 2005. A year later I was invited by the then Warden of the Order to set up a group of deacons to explore the nature of diaconal ministry in relation to the world of work. The group's programme focused on raising the awareness of members of the Order to the importance of ministry and mission at work. The group was also concerned to support the growing number of deacons undertaking the role of chaplain.

In 2009, members of the Faith and Work Group produced a series of short worksheets to facilitate mission in the world of work (Methodist Diaconal Order, 2009). Following this venture, the group decided to launch a new initiative, the Kingdom at Work Project, to help facilitate Christian engagement within the workplace. As the convenor of the group, I took on the task of drafting the documentation for the project. After ending my time as convenor, I continued with that task. The project's current strengths and weaknesses are thus my own.

The future of the project

At the same time as the project was being developed, St Peter's Saltley Trust, based in Birmingham, was undertaking research into the ways in which theological colleges and training agencies in the West Midlands were equipping ordinands with the skills to support lay people in their ministry within the world of work (Hannah Matthews, 2013). The findings of this research demonstrated that very few such colleges and agencies were explicitly addressing that task and, in many cases, the subject hardly ever appeared on their training agendas. Thus the concern of the trust and of the project to further mission in the world of work came together.

The openness of the Saltley Trust, under its Director Ian Jones, to pursue these common interests facilitated the establishment of a partnership with the project which was committed to moving mission in the world of work much further up the church's agenda. The partnership has already led to a number of important developments. In February 2014, a project *Bulletin* was produced which identified a range of agencies and individuals taking creative initiatives in this field, including details of how to obtain copies of Hannah Matthews' report. This was circulated to over a hundred of the project's contacts. The *Bulletin*, together with Hannah Matthews' report, was also made available through St Peter's Saltley Trust's website. The project and the trust have set up a day consultation to be held in Birmingham in November, 2014, on the topic of 'Educating for mission in the world of work'.

Introduction

A brief history

For a good part of the twentieth century the church in the UK was actively engaged with the world of work. At the helm in the early years of that century was the towering figure of William Temple. He was the instigator and animator of a number of high profile conferences on the church and a new social order, notably the Malvern Conference of 1941 which expressed the church's concern to promote the common good defined as 'freedom, fellowship and service'. One of his last books, *Christianity and the Social Order* (1942), remains a classic on the relationship between faith and public life.

The 1940s saw the setting up of the South London Industrial Mission and the Sheffield Industrial Mission, the latter under the inspirational leadership of Ted Wickham. In 1947, the William Temple College was founded at Hawarden near Chester (it moved to Rugby in 1954) to engage sectors such as industry and business in discussions about the contribution of Christian faith to the life of post-war society. In 1955, the Luton Industrial College was established, the result of the unflagging enthusiasm and endeavours of William Gowland, a Methodist minister.

In the early 1960s, Mark Gibbs, a layman deeply committed to supporting the contribution of the laity to the life of society, set up the Audenshaw Foundation which published a well-informed series of papers on that theme. In 1964, together with Ralph Morton, he published a ground-breaking book, *God's Frozen People*, which sought to goad the church to support lay people engaged in the public arena more effectively. In 1966, St George's House Windsor was opened to offer an opportunity for those with major responsibilities in public life to debate issues of common concern in a Christian context. 1968 saw the formation of the Christian Organizations Research and Advisory Truest (CORAT) to assist the church in the fields of management and development. (CORAT eventually became MODEM, the latter now giving particular attention to the nature of church leadership.)

In 1960, the Southwark Ordination Course was established, the first course to train Anglicans in secular occupations for a part-time non-stipendiary priesthood. In the late 1960s, Methodism affirmed the importance of its ministers in secular employment and appointed a full-time officer to support this form of ministry.

The decline of faith and work initiatives

By the 1970s, however, the church was beginning to feel the pinch of numerical and financial decline. Because the church regarded the equipping of its members for mission in public life, especially within the world of work, as of secondary concern, many of the initiatives mentioned above have borne the brunt of retrenchment. In 1971, the William Temple College was closed. The proceeds from its sale were used to set up the William Temple Foundation in Manchester, an important development but with nothing like the impact on wider society once enjoyed by the college. Industrial mission continued but full-time industrial chaplaincies steadily declined. Its ministry has been steadily dispersed across a growing diversity of sectors, in particular the retail trade, and the role of chaplain has become increasingly pastoral.

Luton Industrial College was closed in 1996 due to declining support from the Methodist Church as well as lack of funding. Though Anglican and Methodist ministers in secular employment both set up associations to support their members in workplace ministry during this period, the former has gradually dwindled in numbers and the latter failed to survive beyond the early 1990s.

During the second half of the twentieth century, a number of evangelical bodies, notably the London Institute for Contemporary Christianity founded by John Stott in 1982, were active in this field. However, despite their endeavours, the church in the UK has made faith at work an increasingly low priority.

The consequences of disengagement

A research project by Hannah Matthews, carried out between 2010 and 2011 for the Saltley Trust, Birmingham, reports that training institutions of all denominations continue to give little or no attention to preparing clergy and ministers for the task of affirming, supporting and equipping their members for mission in the world of work. Trevor Beeson (2013), for many decades an astute commentator on the mission of the church in the public realm, has recently expressed the view that 'the church is no nearer (than in the days of Industrial Mission) to bridging the gulf between its own life and that of industrial and commercial Britain' (p. 187).

The consequences of the church's disengagement from the world of work are extremely serious, a matter to which this project returns many times in the pages that follow. For good or ill, the world of work is of crucial importance to the future of humankind. The failure of the church to see the working world as a priority in its missionary endeavours means that both the world of work and the church are massive losers.

A church that fails to engage with the working world also has its vision of a society redeemed by the good news of the kingdom fatally narrowed. Withdrawal from such a key aspect of daily life deprives its members of that world's influence on its worship, not least its preaching and praying, its learning and pastoral care. Disengagement means church members are left ill-equipped for mission in their places of work. Thus they can only struggle as isolated individuals to witness to their faith convictions in a challenging and complex environment with little affirmation or guidance.

Disengagement also means that the working world is left to its own devices, deprived of the spiritual energy and values that could affirm its creativity and production of life-enhancing goods and services yet, at the same time, challenge its inhumanity and selfishness. Left untouched by Christian faith, the working world can easily pervert the God-given purposes for which work was intended, as has been witnessed only too clearly in recent years. As a consequence, the working world's vital role in furthering the common good, and its contribution to building that global community so essential to the survival of humankind is negated.

Theologies of work

Despite the disengagement of churches in the UK from the world of work, over recent years there have been a number of attempts by theologians, including some from the USA, to explore the meaning of work. For example, Miroslav Volf (1991) emphasises that the Christian's calling is that of undertaking the kind of work for which God's Spirit has gifted him or her. Darrell Cosden (2004; 2006) seeks to give daily work deeper meaning by setting it in an eschatological context. David Jensen (2006) sees good work as our response to a God who labours on our behalf and requires that work and any abundance it produces is shared. John Hughes (2007) stresses the nature of work as art, akin to God's work in creation, over against 'the spirit of utility'. Esther Reed (2010) sees work as an integral part of the biblical pattern of 'repair, restoration and renewal' (p. 108). In *Crucible* (January - March, 2011), a group of academic theologians (including John Hughes and Esther Reed) offer further views on a theology of work for our time.

These approaches to the meaning of work from a theological perspective are helpful, yet only as far as they go. One problem is that they often appear to be removed from the cut and thrust of everyday working life. They may be strong on theory but remain weak on practice. Margaret Whipp (2008) states: 'Losing touch with any concrete foundations of working life... has been a recurring problem for theologies of work which are typically constructed by academic theologians... placed at some remove from the ordinary pressures and realities of working life' (pp. 28-9). A further problem is that whilst there has been a good deal of attention given to the meaning of *work*, the importance of *the workplace* as a key component in the transformation of the world of work has been largely neglected. The Kingdom at Work Project draws on this material concerning the theology of work but seeks to give it stronger practical application.

The foundations of the project

The purpose of the Kingdom at Work Project is to enable Christians to create workplaces transformed by the gifts of the kingdom community.

To help the church actively re-engage with the world of work, the Kingdom at Work project sets out a *communal* vision of mission within the workplace. It pays careful attention to the kind of theology and spirituality needed to underpin mission in that context. It explores at some depth the implications of such a theology and spirituality for the principles of an economy and the nature of organizations which would shape that field of mission. It then applies this academic underpinning to practice, notably through a model of discernment where the kingdom is seen as already present within the workplace and intervention undertaken in the light of such discernment. The project then attends to the matter of how to equip Christians for mission at work and to the role of the gathered church and the ordained ministry in that undertaking. The project as a whole is set out in a series of stages depicted in *Diagram 2* at the end of this Introduction.

The project's vision of mission is based on a number of foundations, academic and practical, as follows:

1. A key foundation of the project is *the necessity of creating strong and open forms of community*.

Over the next millennium humankind faces many challenges which could call its very survival into question. There are the ever-present problems of poverty, homelessness, hunger and disease. To these can be added concerns about weapons of mass destruction, an exploding world population, the squandering of the planet's resources and rapid climate change, all issues well documented in Al Gore's impressive survey of *The Future* (2013). Thus, the project's stance is that only through the emergence of our world as a genuine community of communities, together with a new quality of global leadership to bring that about, is there any hope of such problems being solved.

The quest for community is not new. Nevertheless, in a world that is increasingly becoming 'a global village', its creation and sustainability have become literally a matter of life or death (Clark, 2005, pp. 3-12). 'Community', wrote Parker Palmer some years ago (1987) 'means more than the comfort of souls. It means, and has always meant, the survival of the species' (p. 15). And it is 'the survival of the species' that is coming ever more to the fore. 'At no other time has the keen search for common humanity, and a practice that follows... been as imperative and urgent at it is now', writes Zygmunt Bauman (2001, p.140).

2. A second essential foundation of the project is *a theology of the kingdom community*, and what are identified later as the latter's *inclusive* and *universal gifts of life, liberation, love and learning*. The concept of the kingdom community offers the supreme exemplification of what it means to be a community.

Pope Francis in *The Joy of the Gospel: Evangelii Gaudium* (2013), states: 'The kerygma has a clear social content: at the very heart of the Gospel is life in community and engagement with others' (p. 55, para. 177). The project's vision of mission, now of global significance, is that of a world transformed from potential chaos into a community of communities. That vision is defined and given impetus by a theology embracing the images of Trinity and kingdom. Knit together these form the project's key concept of 'the kingdom community'.

The project contends that a theology of the kingdom community offers humankind the inclusive and universal gifts of life (God as Creator), liberation (Christ as Liberator), love (the Holy Spirit as Unifier) and learning (the Trinity as a learning community), all described more fully in Stage 2. These four inclusive and universal gifts are seen as forming the hall-marks and power-house of mission.

In this project, the theology of the kingdom community also informs and inspires the communal spirituality presented in Stage 3. Likewise it undergirds the principles of a communal economy and the organization of communal institutions, including the institutional church, set out in Stages 4 and 5.

3. A third foundation of the project is *the importance of the human scale*.

Stage 6 of the project argues that the process of communal transformation cannot depend simply on large-scale or high profile endeavours, though these are essential. As is frequently emphasized in the New Testament, transformation can as often be triggered by the endeavours of those who appear relatively powerless. Small is not only beautiful but has the potential to initiate significant communal change.

4. The project's fourth foundation is *the art of discernment* and, in response, the ability to engage in *appropriate forms of intervention*.

The art of discernment

The kingdom community is an inclusive and universal phenomenon. Thus it is present 'in the midst of life' (Lk 17: 21). Because God goes before us in seeking the redemption and transformation of the world, the kingdom community's gifts are on offer to any who will receive and use them. As described in Stages 7 and 8, the task of the Christian is first and foremost to discern the signs of the kingdom community within daily life and then to intervene in appropriate ways to enable those signs to be given their fullest possible expression. Mission is not about taking a pre-packaged version of Christian faith into the world and attempting to get people to buy into it.

The art of discerning the presence of the kingdom community in daily life is itself a divine gift, closely linked to the kingdom community's gift of learning. But discernment also depends on 'the practice of the presence of God' and our openness to revelation. As Christ put it on more than one occasion: 'He who has ears to hear, let him hear' (Mk 4: 9). Stage 3 of the project explores how the art of discernment is facilitated by four forms of spirituality. These reflect the communal character of Trinity and kingdom: Celtic spirituality (particularly attuned to the gift of life), Ignatian spirituality (focussing on the gift of liberation), Methodist spirituality (expressing the gift of love) and Quaker spirituality (nurturing the gift of learning).

Appropriate forms of intervention

Discernment is not an end in itself. It is the gateway to the identification of a mission task which can further the communal transformation of the group or larger social collective with which the Christian is involved.

Any approach to mission needs to be shaped by the constraints of those real-life situations in which Christians find themselves. However, it is even more important that mission embraces a vision of ways in which those situations might be communally transformed. In an economic context, for example, the mission task must take seriously the economic model which currently shapes the organization concerned. However that task *also* needs to be shaped by a vision embracing economic principles which might more fully reflect the character of the kingdom community. Similarly, in an organizational context, any mission task needs to take on board the actual structures and leadership styles of the social collective to which the task is related. However, it should *also* embrace a vision of organizational forms and leadership styles which might more effectively further the coming of the kingdom community.

In Stage 8 of the project, possible forms of intervention are fully discussed. It is argued there that intervention can be implicit (with no overt reference to Christian concepts) or explicit (where Christian concepts are employed as and when appropriate). Intervention can also be undertaken on an individual or collective basis. In the latter case it should be in partnership with those, Christian or otherwise, who have a commitment to the outcomes of the mission task chosen. The project also discusses intervention as dialogue, as symbols or messages and, finally, as prayer or worship.

5. A fifth foundation of the project is **the primacy of lay people in the mission of the church.**

There is no shortage of exhortation that lay people engage in mission. However, in practice, they are often poorly prepared by the church for mission in a day and age when to be an advocate for the Christian way of life is no easy or simple matter. At the same time, the ordained ministry frequently appears ill-equipped with the skills of enabling and encouraging lay people to understand the nature of and engage in the practice of mission in to-day's world.

6. The project's sixth foundation is the conviction that *the gathered church has an essential part to play in equipping its members for mission* in today's world.

This foundation might appear so obvious that there is no need to make any reference to it. However, many gathered churches do little to raise the awareness of their members to the meaning and importance of mission in some of the most significant spheres of life and even less to equip their people as to how to engage in mission in those arenas.

7. The seventh foundation of the project is the belief that *the role of mentor is a vital one* in the task of equipping lay people for mission in daily life.

This conviction springs directly from the project's fifth and sixth foundations. The role of mentoring for mission is currently on the agenda of very few theological colleges or courses set up by church training agencies. In the few situations where mentoring is being developed, the emphasis is almost invariably on preparing people to be counsellors or pastors rather than being able to equip Christians to engage in mission. This project is based on the belief that because of the many challenges facing the mission of the church in daily life, equipping people, ordained or lay, with the knowledge and skills to undertake the role of mentoring for mission is a matter of urgency.

Mission in the world of work

The Kingdom at Work Project assumes that the quest for community and a theology and spirituality to guide that search, the power of the human scale, the art of discernment and engaging in appropriate forms of intervention, the primacy of lay people in any missionary endeavour, the responsibilities of the gathered church in this respect and developing the role of mentor for mission, should be at the forefront of the church's missionary agenda. They are foundations which should be the basis for mission in *all* contexts from the local to the global - within family life, in neighbourhoods, across cities and throughout societies.

However, because of the concerns raised at the outset of this Introduction, the project takes the stance that the communal transformation of the working world must come much higher on the church's agenda than is currently the case. In what follows, therefore, the vision of mission set out above is brought to bear *explicitly on the world of work*.

The centrality of the workplace as a community

Because the Kingdom at Work Project places the quest for community at the heart of mission, it is assumed that the workplace is a key point of entry for mission within the world of work. Thus the project focuses attention on the strength or weakness of the workplace as a community. The hope is that the communal transformation of many workplaces will in time act as a catalyst for the communal transformation of the world of work as a whole.

Internally, it is assumed that the communal strength of the workplace transforms the quality of work itself. Etienne Wenger (1998) believes that 'communities of practice' make an essential contribution to the quality of products produced or services offered. Michael Burchell and Jennifer Robin (2011) contend that, unless the workplace embodies communal virtues such as credibility, respect, fairness, pride and camaraderie, its productivity and sustainability will suffer. When Nikil Saval in his study of the office (2014) asked a Google representative whether that firm permitted workers to telecommute the reply was 'No - and we discourage it' (p. 288). The reason given was that Google believed that trying to liaise with workers beyond the office was unhelpful in terms of personal relationships and consequently of productivity. Elsewhere (1996), I have argued that education can never reach its full potential unless schools become strong and open learning communities.

Those factors which enable the workplace to become a strong and open community also enhance the well-being of workers. Marissa Mayer, Chief Executive of Yahoo, insists that all 11,500 of Yahoo's employees should find time to work together on a regular face-to-face basis because she is convinced that the communal dynamism of her company is being eroded by a dispersed workforce. Alexandra Shulman, the editor of *British Vogue*, writes in support of Mayer's stand, believing strongly in 'the collective creativity of an office' (*Guardian*, 2/3/13, p. 38). A communally strong workplace will also be one in which the well-being of workers' families and friends is seen as of major concern. Thus amongst the signs of the communal workplace will be facilities, pastoral provision and material support which add to the health, welfare and enjoyment of employees' relations and colleagues.

The *external* impact of the work undertaken or the services rendered will be enhanced if the workplace is communally strong. Such workplaces will also be to the fore in promoting the well-being of society and world. For example, a communal workplace will be ready to open its doors to young people seeking work experience or employment opportunities. It is likely that it will be engaged in offering grants and sponsorship in support of charities and good causes. It may well be a community which encourages its workers to become involved in voluntary service beyond the workplace. It will be to the fore in its concern about the pollution of the planet and in making its contribution to the latter's sustainability. It will be a workplace committed to co-operation and partnership with other social collectives within and beyond the world of work.

The workplace as a reflection of the kingdom community

The Kingdom at Work Project contends that the workplace which is communally transformed will manifest the gifts of life, liberation, love and learning through both the nature of the work it undertakes and through the strength of workplace relationships. It will draw on the spiritual power behind the kingdom community's gifts to enable its life and work to flourish. Such workplaces will make a significant contribution to the common good. In pursuit of the latter, they will give special attention to the needs of the poor, vulnerable and marginalized. Through attention to the gift of learning, they will be constantly open to new means of communal transformation.

Definitions

The world of work

In the Kingdom at Work Project 'the world of work' is taken to be that sphere of life where people are *in paid employment*. The world of work is often assumed to be primarily concerned with manufacturing, commerce and finance. However, in this project it is seen as embracing *every* sphere of life where people are in paid employment - education, the service sector, health and welfare, government and administration and so on. This comprehensive definition of the world of work is important because each form of employment has a distinctive and significant part to play in the communal transformation of society and world.

The workplace

This project regards 'the workplace' as the primary focus of the church's mission in the world of work. The workplace is defined as *that network of relationships which links those involved in a shared occupational endeavour usually focused on or emanating from some identifiable location*.

The rapidly changing nature of to-day's workplace means that it is a concept which needs some clarification. One problem in defining 'the workplace' is that people are moving ever more rapidly between jobs and thus between workplaces. Margaret Whipp (2008) writes: 'With the duration of work contracts in the most advanced and high-tech corporations averaging at around eight months, the loss of social anchor-points and group solidarity produces the disconcerting sense that "a flexible workplace is unlikely to be a spot in which one would wish to build a nest!" ' (p. 36).

Another challenge to the concept of the workplace is that even when people are engaged in a shared occupational endeavour they often work on their own, are geographically mobile and/or are widely dispersed. Such situations are becoming ever more common as the digital revolution reduces the necessity for people to work together within a shared physical location. The Towers Watson's *Global Workforce Study* for 2012 states that 'nearly half of our global sample work remotely or in some kind of flexible arrangement' (p. 6). Indeed hardware providers now boast that work can be performed in such places as 'a bus stop… the bus itself… a cliff face… the beach… a catamaran… a building site… a park… a café… a hairdressers… and even nude!' (Gregg, 2011, p. 32). Notions such as 'flexible working', 'home offices' (pp. 121-165) and 'transit time' are just a few of the concepts emerging as a cyber-culture steadily transforms the nature of the traditional workplace. It is because of this changing scene that the project's definition of the workplace emphasizes the network of relationships existing between those involved in a shared occupational endeavour as well any physical location on which that endeavour might be focused.

Nevertheless, many workplaces continue to be important locations for the production of goods, the provision of services and overall administration. They remain places where many workers congregate and interact. Even when a workforce is widely dispersed, the workplace as a location can, and arguably should facilitate the creation of a real and not just virtual community and become a genuine 'home-base' (note the term). Rowan Williams (2012) writes: 'Functioning communities need to develop a sense of place, and that means developing variety, a real landscape, not just a territory covered with "machines for living" ' (p. 236). This only occurs when the workplace is recognized as an important meeting ground - for the frequent-flyer returning home to be briefed, the commercial traveller reporting on sales, the long-distance lorry driver picking up a consignment of goods, the farmer meeting colleagues at market or postal workers collecting their delivery from the sorting office. In such cases, face-to-face interaction may be relatively short-lived but, over an extended period, its frequency and intensity can help to foster a strong sense of community across the wider network of working relationships.

Discipleship and kingdom models of mission at work

Before ending this Introduction, it is important to note that in recent years a discipleship model of mission has come to dominate the agenda of many churches, national, regional and local. As a model of mission for Christians seeking to communicate the meaning of faith to those they encounter in everyday life, it is of some consequence. Nevertheless, for mission within the global, complex and often faith-averse world of work, a discipleship model has some major theological and sociological limitations.

The concept of model brings together key features from a range of sources, theoretical and practical, to offer an overview of the phenomenon concerned. This project argues that for the church to engage effectively with the world of work nothing less than a communal model of mission rooted in the images of Trinity and kingdom can suffice. *Diagram 1* below contrasts some key features of, on the one hand, a discipleship model and, on the other, a kingdom model of mission at work.

The material for a discipleship model of mission at work comes largely from faith and work publications underpinned by an evangelical theology. These include books by Mark Greene (2005); David Oliver (2006); Tom Chester (2006); Ken Costa (2007); Paul Valler (2008); Ian Coffee (2008); Jago Wynne (2009) and Chick Yuill (2011). Though writers such as Mark Greene and Ken Costa clearly have a concern for the redemption of the workplace as an entity, the emphasis is normatively on discipleship as a personal undertaking by Christians at work ultimately concerned with the conversion of their colleagues.

The material for a kingdom model of mission at work is presented throughout the various stages of this project (see *Diagram 2* at the end of this Introduction). The project offers a kingdom-focused and world-centred model of mission concerned with the communal transformation of the workplace. The model embraces a diaconal understanding of the nature of the church and its mission. It places the laity at the forefront of any missionary endeavour. A kingdom model stresses the importance of discernment and intervention, individual and collective, based on insights gained from such discernment. The model assumes dialogue not monologue to be at the heart of mission. It takes mission to be a partnership with all those, Christian or otherwise with similar concerns. A kingdom model of mission at work takes the role of mentor to be of major importance.

Diagram 1

Discipleship and kingdom models of mission at work

A discipleship model of mission	A kingdom model of mission
Theology Centred on Christ and 'the Great Commission'	Centred on the Trinity and kingdom and their inclusive and universal gifts of life, liberation, love and learning - in this project termed the gifts of 'the kingdom community'
Focus of mission - the transformation of the individual at work	The transformation of the workplace through the gifts of the kingdom community
The world transformed through the conversion of a multitude of individuals	The world transformed into the kingdom community through the communal transformation of a multitude of workplaces
Spirituality A personal spirituality	A communal spirituality
Societal and economic context The hall-marks of 'a Christian society' focused on individual morality and personal ethics	The hall-marks of 'a Christian society' shaped by what it means to be holistic and open communities and by the principles of the common good
Acceptance of the capitalist economic model as normative	Critique of the capitalist economic model as normative

The church	
The gathered church as the ideal-type community	The kingdom as the ideal-type community
The gathered church as representing the kingdom	The church - gathered and dispersed - as the servant of the kingdom community
Limited awareness of the kingdom's presence in the world	The kingdom omnipresent in the world
The Christendom church taken as the model for institutions, sacred and secular	The diaconal church taken as the model for institutions, sacred and secular
Approach to mission	
Entry *into* the workplace in order to draw individuals *out* of the workplace and recruit them into the gathered church	Building workplaces that manifest the gifts of the kingdom community *from within*
Mission as an individual endeavour	Mission through individual and collective endeavour
The Christian living out his or her faith at work as an individual calling	The Christian at work inviting all to play their part in the communal transformation of the workplace
Partnerships not a major concern	Partnerships sought with anyone seeking the communal transformation of the workplace
Involvement with those of other faiths or convictions tolerated - parallel relationships	Engagement with those of other faiths or convictions vital - integrated relationships
Method	
Preparing the ground through individual initiatives - Presence - 'being there'	*Discernment* - Practising the art of identifying the gifts of the kingdom community within the

Example - personally living out the gospel Pastoral care and counselling Service - acts of kindness	workplace - leading to: *Intervention* - Taking a diversity of initiatives - individual and collective - to harness the gifts of the kingdom community for the communal transformation of the workplace
Mission as proclamation - engaging in pre-determined and explicit reference to the nature and means of pursuing the Christian way of life	Mission as facilitation - all those interested invited to participate in harnessing the gifts of the kingdom community for the communal transformation of the workplace
Mission as monologue - often 'closed-to-learning' from others	Mission as dialogue - being 'open-to-learning' from others
Christian symbols as magnets - attracting people to the faith	Christian symbols as doors - promoting dialogue about the faith
Prayers for the conversion of individuals and the well-being of the workforce	Prayers for personal enlightenment and the communal transformation of the workplace
Leadership The ordained ministry dominant in mission - the laity as followers	The laity as the primary missionary resource - the ordained ministry as enablers
Chaplains and MSEs as the key representatives of the church at work	All the people of God as representatives of the church at work
The pastoral leadership style of the gathered church imported into the workplace	The transformational leadership style of the kingdom community exercised in the workplace
Mentoring lay people for mission at work not on the agenda	Mentoring lay people for mission at work essential

Roger Walton in his book *The Reflective Disciple* (2012) makes a noteworthy attempt to bridge the gap between an individual (discipleship) and communal (kingdom) approach to mission. Advocating the latter, he commends John Hull's (2006) critique of *Mission-shaped Church* (2004) as being a model of mission too concerned with what is in reality 'church-shaped mission' (pp. 67-69). He stresses the importance of mission as community building, frequently using the concept of 'the kingdom community' (see especially pp. 147-181). He is critical of a 'one-way traffic' concept of mission, a form of evangelism which focuses on what Christians take into the world rather than learn from it. He is insistent on the need for Christians to be reflective in their approach to mission - echoing this project's concern with discernment as a crucial stage before any intervention is attempted (pp. 111-142). He also recognizes that mission within the workplace has been neglected for too long, though he spends only a couple of pages explicitly on this sphere of mission (pp. 65-66).

However, ultimately, Walton ends up focusing on the preparation and equipping of the Christian for mission as an individual and personal undertaking. He says little about how the communal transformation of social collectives might be approached, let alone accomplished. In practice if not in theory, therefore, the discipleship model of mission remains to the fore.

Potential users of the project

Mentors

The group of users essential for the development of mission at work are those the project describes as 'mentors'. Their role is discussed in Stage 9. The skills of the mentor are necessary because the workplace can be a very difficult and stressful place in which to try to bear witness to Christian convictions. Thus equipping lay people for this kind of ministry is a demanding undertaking. Because 'mission mentors' to support those engaged in the world of work are not at present in evidence within the life of the church, from where are they to come?

The project sees the most productive source of mentors as being from amongst chaplains and self-supporting ministers, especially ministers in secular employment, who would be committed to employing their experience and skills to prepare Christians for mission within the workplace. Deacons, especially in the form in which the diaconate exists within the Methodist Church, would likewise be well suited to undertake the role of mentors to Christians at work (Clark, 2005, pp. 273-295). Mentors might also come from the ranks of early retired lay people who have considerable experience of the world of work. In the longer-term, however, all church leaders who have responsibility for the life of a gathered church should be equipped as mission mentors or at least ensure that members of their congregations possess these skills.

The emergence of those with mentoring experience and skills for this sphere of mission will require something of a Copernican revolution in the training of ministers and deacons, pre-ordination and post-ordination, as Hannah Matthews' research (2013) into the current curricula of theological institutions clearly demonstrates. How this revolution might be triggered is discussed in Stage 9.

Lay people at work

All the material set out in the project is relevant to those lay people who have the opportunity and energy to study it. However, it is appreciated that many lay people at work will not have the time to take on board the project as a whole. In their case the discernment and intervention stages (Stages 7 and 8) should take precedence, though the importance of the project's holistic nature still needs to be recognized. Where possible lay people should try to dip into the earlier stages of the project to help them reflect on and debate the communal foundations on which the discernment and intervention processes are built. Stage 10 of the project will also offer lay people some ideas as to how their local church can affirm and support mission at work.

Ordained leaders of gathered churches

For most clergy and ministers the location of the gathered church is their actual place of work, the focus of their paid employment. In this respect, the project has as much relevance to the gathered church as a workplace and to its employees as to workplaces in the secular world. If the medium is to be the message, therefore, it is just as important for ministers and clergy to apply the discernment and intervention process to the life of the gathered church in which they are employed as it is for church members in paid employment to apply the process to their secular places of work.

Other than as mentors, there are numerous initiatives that the ordained leaders of gathered churches can take to support their members at work. As Stage 10 indicates, these include ensuring that awareness raising, worship and prayer, education and pastoral care in the context of the world of work, are an integral part of congregational life. Church leaders should also be looking for ways of initiating some form of mission to places of work in the neighbourhood in which the gathered church is located.

Chaplains and ministers in secular employment

In addition to drawing attention to the importance of their training as mentors, chaplains and ministers in secular employment should find the project of value in throwing light on the extent to which the organizations or institutions which they serve manifest the gifts of the kingdom community. This should prompt them to reflect on whether or not their role as chaplain or as minister in secular employment would be enhanced by their own involvement in discernment and intervention initiatives which could further the communal transformation of the place in which they work.

Christian organizations and agencies

The project could be of considerable value to Christian organizations and agencies (other than gathered churches) which, as workplaces, are called to manifest the gifts of the kingdom community. Such collectives would include theological colleges, church schools, Christian welfare agencies and voluntary organizations, and Christian residential homes and hospices.

In this context, the discernment and intervention stages of the project are particularly important. It is worth noting here that the discernment stage has already been used by one church school seeking to identify what it means to be 'a *Christian* school'. In this case, the discernment process was undertaken by the school staff and the findings used to determine what kind of intervention might enrich the life and work of the school as a community.

Those with other beliefs or convictions

The gifts of the kingdom community do not exist in some kind of spiritual vacuum removed from the experiences of everyday life. They are revealed in the realities of all workplaces. Thus it is possible for Christian and non-Christian alike to recognize the communal significance of the gifts of the kingdom, even though the non-Christian may interpret the latter as human virtues rather than divine gifts. There is no reason, therefore, why those who are committed to furthering life, liberation, love and learning as human virtues should not enter into active partnership with Christians who regard them as divine gifts.

The conviction that Christians and non-Christians may have much in common in working for a communally transformed workplace is borne out by the fact that many signs of the kingdom community suggested in the discernment and leadership stages of this project mirror indices mentioned in secular studies of 'the good workplace' [Stage 7(Introduction)]. Indeed given that the signs of the kingdom community are earthed in the realities of working life, it would be surprising if this were not the case. It follows that the discernment and intervention stages in particular could be of value to *anyone* committed to the communal transformation of the workplace.

Taking the project forward

The Kingdom at Work Project has been and remains a work in process. Thus its stages and their content remain open to debate and revision as and when needed. However, the immediate task is to raise the awareness of the whole church to the importance of mission within the world of work.

To help address that task, a project *Handbook* has been produced and is available in hard copy and digital form. This is intended to give readers a taste of the project's more practical aspects. However, because the *Handbook* includes very little material relating to the early foundational stages of the project, there is some danger that those who only use that form of the project may get a superficial view of the foundations on which the discernment and intervention process rests. The *Handbook* has been revised once (December 2013) and ongoing revisions will be made.

It is hoped that those agencies and associations concerned with mission at work will feel able to share their experience, concerns and insights to enhance the content and design of the project. In the process, it would be very encouraging if, despite differing theological views about the nature of mission at work, networking between such bodies could become more frequent and open. An occasional project *Bulletin* (2014) has already begun this task. It would also be a step forward if, as a consequence of such networking, occasional consultations of representative of these bodies could be regularly held. Such a development would be even further enhanced if the institutional church were prepared to establish some form of national and ecumenical resource base to gather and disseminate material relating to the nature and methodology of mission at work.

Diagram 2

The Kingdom at Work Project

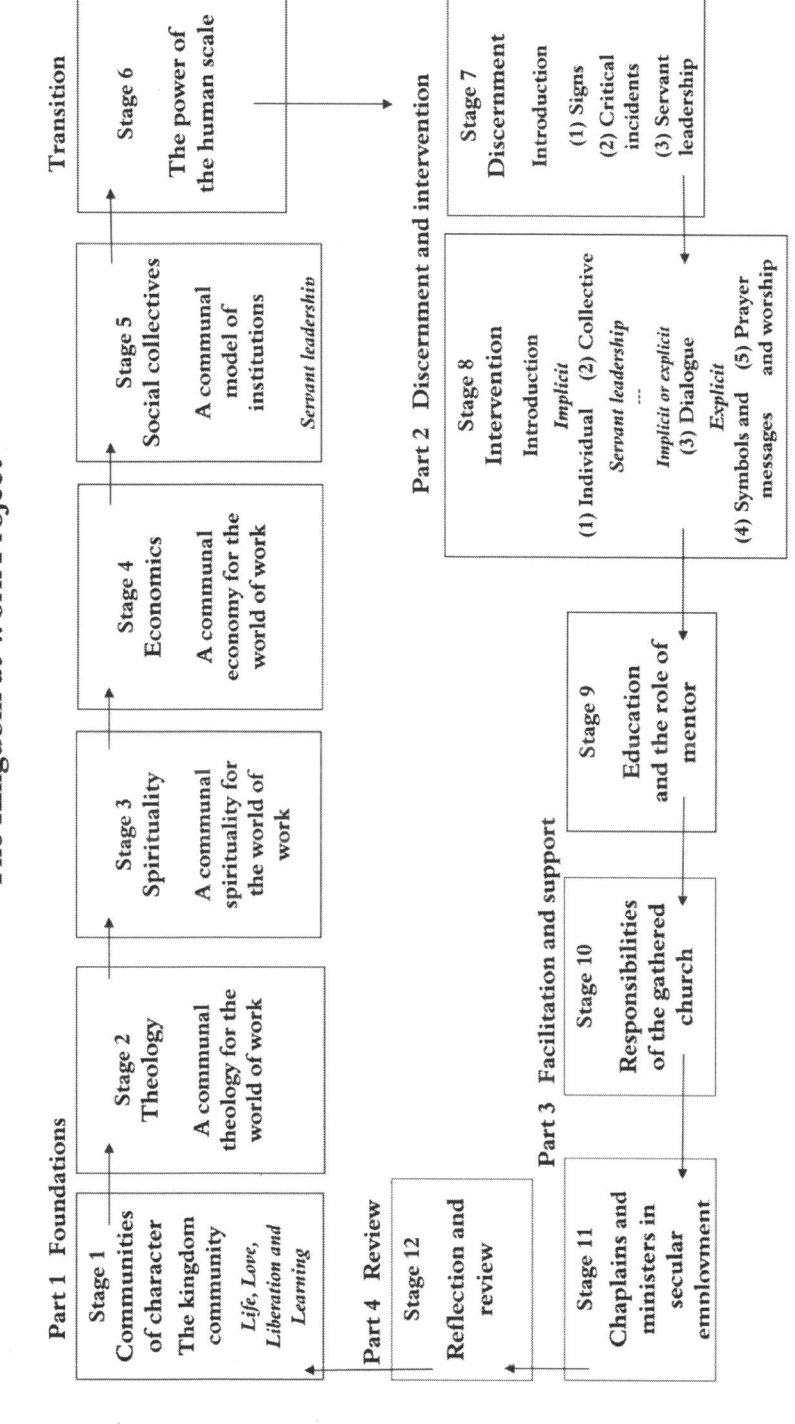

Part 1 Foundations

Stage 1	Stage 2	Stage 3	Stage 4	Stage 5	Stage 6
Communities of character	Theology	Spirituality	Economics	Social collectives	The power of the human scale
The kingdom community	A communal theology for the world of work	A communal spirituality for the world of work	A communal economy for the world of work	A communal model of institutions	
Life, Love, Liberation and Learning				*Servant leadership*	

Transition

Part 2 Discernment and intervention

Stage 7	Stage 8
Discernment	Intervention
Introduction	Introduction
(1) Signs	*Implicit*
(2) Critical incidents	(1) Individual (2) Collective
(3) Servant leadership	*Servant leadership* ...
	Implicit or explicit
	(3) Dialogue
	Explicit
	(4) Symbols and (5) Prayer and worship
	messages

Part 3 Facilitation and support

Stage 9	Stage 10	Stage 11
Education and the role of mentor	Responsibilities of the gathered church	Chaplains and ministers in secular employment

Part 4 Review

Stage 12
Reflection and review

21

Part 1
Foundations

Stage 1
Communities of character

This first stage of the Kingdom at Work Project describes some of my personal experiences which have informed the academic foundations on which the project is built. In particular, I note those experiences which have led to my understanding of what I call 'communities of character'. I define the latter as *social collectives that manifest one or more of the kingdom community's universal and inclusive gifts of, life, liberation, love and learning.* In Stages 2 to 5 of this project, these gifts are defined and discussed more fully and their implications for the transformation of the world of work addressed. Here I explain why I have chosen the concept of communities of character to represent community at its zenith, and the personal experiences that have led me to an appreciation of its components.

The significance of communities of character for mission in the world of work

Alistair MacIntyre (1985) argues that 'morality and civility' will not survive 'the new dark ages' (p. 263), which he believes the world has currently entered, unless such virtues are sustained and renewed by the power of community expressed in interpersonal, tangible and sustainable forms. In seeking to point to a model of the kind of community he is searching after, MacIntyre suggests that we are not waiting 'for a Godot, but for another – doubtless very different – St. Benedict' to show us the way (p. 263).

If MacIntyre is right, I believe his convictions have two important implications. The first is that *all attempts to bring about creative change within the world of work need to be rooted in a theology of community.* Secondly, *the credibility of any such theology for the world of work will depend on the degree to which it is derived from first-hand experience of what I define below as 'communities of character'.* In this respect, the theology which informs this project [Stage 2] is better described as a theology *for* the world of work than a theology *of* the world of work.

25

The meaning and nature of communities of character

The sort of social collectives that it seems Alistair MacIntyre is looking for are what I call here 'communities of character', a phrase first coined by Stanley Hauerwas (1981). As noted above, I define such communities as social collectives that manifest one or more of the kingdom community's universal and inclusive gifts of, life, liberation, love and learning.

Stanley Hauerwas contends that it is, first and foremost, to the church that we must look if we want to understand the true nature of communities of character. He sees the church as made up of 'virtuous people' drawn together within diverse 'communities of character' (p. 3). Furthermore, he believes that 'the church is the truest possible human community' (p. 2) and, because of this, 'stands as a political alternative to every nation, witnessing to the kind of social life possible for those that have been formed by the story of Christ' (p. 12). For Hauerwas, the church is a counter-cultural *polis* or *civitas* shaped by the new reality of the kingdom of God (Frank Kirkpatrick, 2001, p. 106).

I agree with Stanley Hauerwas that the church as a community of character can offer us a compelling vision of community in practice, a vision rooted in the spiritual dynamic of Christian faith, informed by biblical insights and enriched by tradition. However, I take issue with Hauerwas when he suggests that the church is the *only* form of social collective genuinely able to reflect the true nature of the kingdom community.

It is my conviction that the kingdom community is omnipresent. I believe that its gifts are discernable within *all* sectors of society, including the world of work [Stage 7]. I also agree with Frank Kirkpatrick (2001) that the so-called 'secular world' may, 'in its own various ways, be doing more things to realize God's intentions than the church itself has done or has been able to appreciate' (p. 110). I offer just three examples here. Dawn Waterton, a minister in secular employment working in the construction industry writes (*Reflections on Ministry in Secular Employment*, 2010, p. 17):

> (In my company) people care about each other. I celebrate good things, new homes, new jobs, new relationships and I mourn the bad things and the sad things, the loss of a colleague through illness perhaps or the loss of a relationship or a bereavement. The conversations I have may be at the tea machine instead of

the back of the church but they are no less a building up of fellowship and community for all that. The silence following a discussion in the office about any one of a number of issues currently affecting people, may not be prefaced by 'Let us pray' but it happens, there in the silence. And the support offered to one another through listening and sometimes grumbling together is vital because for many this community is their primary community. The place where someone notices if they are not there and cares enough to find out if they are OK. The people I work with may not attend church, may not know the liturgy or theology of sacrifice or redemption, but make no mistake, they 'do' theology every day.

Richard Dobell (p. 23) writes in a similar vein of the school where he teaches music.

In its mission statement, my school sets out to value each individual student for him or herself, to keep doors open so that students, parents, teachers and non-teachers alike can communicate together. It treats mistakes as learning opportunities and rarely removes a difficult student. It tries hard to express loving care for each person, each student in the school. In other words, it is trying to express the values of God's kingdom in today's life. Many of my colleagues are working for God's kingdom without realizing it and do better than me.

David Helms (2013), one time chaplain with Kent Workplace Mission, writes (p. 21):

The world of work is a wonderful and sometimes terrible place to be. Yes, it is a world of pressures and stress and the proverbial bottom line, but it is also a glorious world of human ingenuity and invention, complex productive systems and most important of all a world of people working hard, long hours, attending often long tedious meetings and trying to meet impossible deadlines. What long term workplace missioners like myself learned was that God was already at work in the world before we arrived and still working when we left. We were just fools for Christ raising questions about the possibility of God's presence in the so called dark satanic mills and brightly lit and hanger-like possibly satanic call centres. But every one of us knew then and knows now God was there when we arrived and is still there now working alongside Christians and people of other faiths and people of no faith…

I would argue, with Kirkpatrick (2001), that church *and* world each performs its own 'distinctive work in furthering the advent of universal community, the kingdom of God' (p. 112). In this project, therefore, *the concept of communities of character embraces secular as well as religious communities, from the local to the global.*

Nevertheless, for any community of character to be authentic and its message credible, the medium must be the message. A sense of community cannot be experienced at any depth unless the social collective concerned practises what it preaches. This is why mission statements, secular or sacred, which remain merely verbal expressions of intent are communally worthless. Chris Argyris describes such a disjuncture between intent and practice as that between 'espoused theories' and 'theories-in-use' (1974, pp. 6-7). It follows that any authentic theology for the world of work must be founded on first-hand experience of social collectives, religious and secular, which now and then offer 'peak experiences' that not only espouse but manifest in everyday practice the gifts of the kingdom community (Clark 1987, pp. 14-19).

In daily practice, some communities of character are likely to manifest certain gifts of the kingdom community more fully than others. Thus some communities of character may give clear expression to the gift of life, whilst others are better equipped to making manifest the gifts of liberation, love or learning. This means that an understanding and development of an adequate theology of community will depend in large part on the theologian's first-hand experience of a wide diversity of communities of character, religious *and* secular. For theologians to rely on their experience of the church alone as a community of character cannot, despite the case made by Stanley Hauerwas, offer us adequate insights and resources to develop a holistic communal theology.

Personal experiences of communities of character

The communal theology, communal spirituality, principles of a communal economy and diaconal model for social collectives set out later [Stages 2 to 5] are based on my own experience of a wide diversity of communities of character. To illustrate more clearly the character of these communities I offer examples below of a number of these, some associated with the church, others not, which have in my experience revealed one or more of the gifts of the kingdom community: life, liberation, love and learning.[1]

The gift of life

My awareness of God the Creator, and the gift of life offered to us by him (her), have come very powerfully through those communities which have enabled me to experience the wonder and beauty of the natural world. From the age of seven onwards I was introduced to walking and climbing through what was at that time known as the Holiday Fellowship (now HF), a body originally set up in 1913 by T. A. Leonard: 'To… provide for the healthy enjoyment of leisure, to encourage the love of the open air, and to promote social and international fellowship', especially for those of very limited financial means. Over succeeding years, I have often walked and climbed with groups from the Holiday Fellowship, Co-operative Holiday Association and Ramblers Association in Britain and abroad. My experience of these leisure communities has necessarily been short lived. Nonetheless, I was made fully aware that their members enjoyed and shared a rich experience of the gift of life through their many vivid experiences of the natural world.

Another facet of the gift of life has come through those communities of character which have enabled me to be physically active in the world of sport. One of these communities was my school, Nottingham High School, where I was actively involved with fellow students in cricket, rugby and athletics. Likewise at Oxford University I was actively engaged with others in cricket and rugby at both college and university levels. In retirement, though I would never have believed it in earlier years, I have found the gift of life still on offer through my membership of a local bowls club!

In a very different way, my appreciation of the gift of life, as of the other three gifts indicated below, has come through nearly twenty years involvement with the Christian Community Movement. Here I single out just one such experience mediated by the Iona Community during

---

[1] For more details about such communities the reader is referred to the Bibliography for this project under my name, especially to *Basic Communities* (1977), *Yes to Life* (1987), a number of the case-studies in *Breaking the Mould of Christendom* (2005) and in *Building the Human City* (2012).

the 1970s, in particular through its association with the Island of Iona. In *Yes to Life* (1987, p. 92), I wrote:

> What enthralled me on my first visit to Iona was the certainty that 'some God was in this place'; not cooped up in a holy building, but exhilaratingly alive in the pounding seas, the white sands, the brilliant green of the machair and the dark mountains of Mull. In this setting the abbey does not contain God, but simply focuses his presence like a magnifying glass held to catch the rays of the sun. Thus for the community and its many visitors the whole of Iona becomes a truly symbolic place, bringing men and women to a vivid awareness of the omni-presence of God the Creator.

The gift of liberation

The meaning of the gift of Christ as Liberator first dawned on me through the ministry of my home church in Beeston, Nottingham, which was at that time a dynamic worshipping and social fellowship, embodying many attributes of a community of character. At the age of fifteen I had what is traditionally called 'a conversion experience' during a service led by the Reverend William Gowland, then minister of the Albert Hall in Manchester, and deeply involved in preaching and practising the social gospel at the heart of that city. For me that experience was a life-changing encounter with Christ the Liberator and one which has remained a powerful driving force in my life ever since.

A second experience of the gift of liberation came very much later in life. In 2005, I felt moved to relinquish my role as a Methodist presbyter and become a member of the Methodist Diaconal Order. I was ordained as a presbyter in 1962. When I became a full-time lecturer at Westhill College in Birmingham, from 1973 until 1995, I retained that status but as a 'sector minister'. However, in early retirement I felt that because most of my life's work had been undertaken largely on the edge of the institutional church, I ought to seek membership of the Methodist Diaconal Order. Joining that Order and sharing in its ongoing search to deepen its own life as a community of character has been for me an experience of genuine liberation and fulfilment.

Other experiences have offered me a particularly vivid glimpse of the meaning of the gift of liberation. In 1967, I became the Methodist minister (presbyter) in West Greenwich, south-east London. The church there, once a dynamic congregation, was by then a faint shadow of its former self. After eighteen months of often difficult negotiations, the small congregation took the brave decision to close its premises and move across the road to become a partner in the first united Presbyterian-Methodist church in the UK (Clark, 2005, pp. 137-149). For me and my Methodist members, and indeed the Presbyterian congregation which had suddenly to accept so many strangers into its life and worship, this initiative heralded the emergence of a dynamic community of character and, with that, a hope-inspiring sense of liberation.

Another experience of liberation came through my contacts with and visits to the Corrymeela Community in Northern Ireland. In the 1970s and 1980s, when the Irish 'troubles' were at their height, the Corrymeela Community, from its base in Belfast and residential centre in Ballycastle, worked with courageous commitment to heal the many social, religious and political divisions in that part of the United Kingdom. At considerable cost in terms of personal safety and social acceptance, its members established an impressive community of character sacrificially engaged in the demanding task of reconciliation and peace-making.

A final example of the gift of liberation in which I was personally involved was, and still remains known as the Human City Institute (Clark, 2005, pp.188-209; 2012). I set up the Human City Initiative in Birmingham in the mid-1990s, a venture which led to the creation of the Human City Institute in 1997. The latter's mission statement was 'to enable those who share a vision of the human city to work together with others to make that vision a reality'. Its shorter mission statement was: 'All matter; each counts' (2005, p. 193). The Institute sought to operationalize these statements of intent through a city-wide *Bulletin* and *Futures Papers*, public *Hearings* and a range of human-scale projects in Birmingham and two other cities, Bradford and Swindon. During those years, the Institute became an innovative community of character seeking to offer a liberating alternative to the inhumanity of many cities in the UK, a situation exacerbated by the economic and political culture of the time.

The gift of love

I have to thank family life for offering me a deep experience of the gift of love. Both my community of birth and that of marriage have been profoundly influential communities of character in this respect. My parents (1987, pp. 37-39) provided a Christian community of fun and laughter as well as of affirmation and love which, amongst other important happenings in my life, saw me through a serious nervous breakdown during my student days in Oxford (pp. 40-41). My marital family has also been a rich community of character, a source of joy and a tower of strength for fifty years which has never ceased to lead me into new experiences and an ever deeper understanding of the gift of love (pp. 57-59).

Beyond family life, the meaning of the gift of love has been revealed to me by many other communities of character. One of these was my school, already mentioned, where everyday colleagueship taught me much about the real meaning of friendship. At Oxford University, I belonged for four years to a small group, one of over twenty such groups which made up what was then known as the John Wesley Society. The group became for me a strong community of character creating friendships which have lasted to the present day.

Beyond home and student life, my many years of active involvement in the Christian Community Movement (Clark, 2005, pp. 150-169) brought me into contact with numerous communities of character of all denominations which embodied the gift of love. The only example there is space to mention here is the l'Arche communities, founded in the early 1960s by Jean Vanier, which seek to provide a strong home-life and working environment for adults with learning disabilities. When I was involved with the Christian Community Movement, I visited several l'Arche communities always coming away deeply impressed by their quality of caring and moved by the way in which every member, whatever their abilities, was constantly affirmed.

The gift of learning

Life for me has always been an ongoing journey of discovery (1987, pp. 25-28, 56-60 and 81-83). However, there have been certain communities of character which have taken such learning to a new level.

I was privileged to spend my final year training for the Methodist ministry at the William Temple College, Rugby (1987, pp. 165-166 and 2005, pp. 134 and 298). The college was set up as a lay academy in 1949 to engage in the study of the natural and social sciences, as well as of political and economic issues of the day, in the light of Christian faith. I was part of a residential community of some twenty people, though hundreds more people attended short courses at the college during the year. The college opened my eyes to a radically new understanding of the unique contribution of Christian faith to key issues facing the contemporary world. Though it is now long since closed, the college remains for me an outstanding example of the gift of learning in practice and how communities of character can further the creative engagement of Christians and others in reflecting together on major concerns relating to the world of work.

A second community of character which in the early 'seventies took my learning into a new orbit was the Social Education Department of Eltham Green Comprehensive School in south-east London (Dawson, 1981 and Clark, 1987, pp. 181-191). I spent two years there as a part-time member of staff from 1971 to 1973. It was a period which coincided with the raising of the school-leaving age from fifteen to sixteen. In response to that development, the school, under the leadership of a recently appointed and dynamic headmaster, took the bold step of creating a self-contained Social Education Department, of which I was a staff member, for what was a very large group of so-called 'early school-leavers'. As a new team, the staff of the department quickly moulded themselves into a lively and innovative community of character. In the process they fashioned an imaginative student-centred curriculum, delivered on and beyond school premises, to meet the demanding needs of the pupils, many from disadvantaged backgrounds, whom they served (1973b, 1975, 1976). Though the world of education has gone through numerous metamorphoses since then, in my view it has rarely come near to providing the vitality and quality of learning offered by that department to its pupils.

Another learning experience which broke new communal ground for me was the thirteen years (1982 - 1995) I spent as leader of the post-graduate degree course on community education at Westhill College, Birmingham (1987, pp. 191-194). I describe the *raison d'être* and content of that course, including its theological underpinning, in *Transforming Education - The school as a learning community*, a book I wrote in 1996. The course sought to introduce those from a wide diversity of professions engaged in education - teachers, adult educators, youth workers, community workers, probation officers, clergy, police officers and so on – to the importance of transforming the groups in which they were involved into dynamic learning communities. Over the years, staff and students involved in many of the courses welded themselves into communities of character which clearly manifested the gift of learning.

Finally, since becoming a member of the Society of Friends in 2012, I have experienced my local Quaker meeting in Bakewell as a strong community of character, particularly energized and inspired by the gift of learning. The meeting for worship each Sunday morning is attended by some 30 people and follows the normal Quaker practice of an hour's quiet reflection, though anyone can speak if they feel so moved. These 'ministries' as they are called are invariably insightful, stimulating and challenging learning experiences. They frequently call into question my assumptions but do so in a spirit of seeking 'the light', as Quakers describe it.

'The ecumenical imperative'

These and many other communities of character with which I have been involved over the years have been extremely diverse. Their members have often held strong convictions but, where such communities were Christian in character, they invariably remained appreciative of their own denominational heritage. However, all were committed to 'the ecumenical imperative' in the fullest sense of that phrase Though people of very different backgrounds, they were dedicated to working together to create one world and, in the case of Christian communities, one church. All made manifest, though often unaware of the fact, what the gifts of life, liberation, love and learning mean in practice.

Stage 2

A communal theology for the world of work

Introduction

The Future, as Al Gore (2013) impressively surveys it, presents humankind with as daunting a task as it has ever faced. At the top of the agenda are issues concerning how to preserve the natural resources of planet earth, manage the destructive consequences of climate change, resolve the problems of an exploding global population, overcome new endemic diseases and handle nuclear power responsibly. Along with these immediate challenges, there is the ever-present task of lifting billions out of poverty and hunger and of creating a just and peaceful world.

Humankind also enters a new century facing the task of achieving economic sustainability and social justice. The demise of communism, and the apparent triumph of capitalism, is not proving to be the end-game which many predicted. The collapse of the banking system in 2008, revelations of malpractice within the financial markets then and since, and the rising tide of unemployment in many countries, has re-opened the debate as to what sort of economic model can sustain the well-being of humanity in the century ahead.

To these issues must be added a digital revolution which is creating exciting new possibilities and challenges for humankind, not least within the world of work, and profoundly changing the way in which people relate to one another. This raises many questions as to how human beings, from the family to the nation and beyond, can build and sustain relationships of an enduring and creative kind.

Furthermore, humankind is attempting to address this massive agenda in the context of a world which has relatively recently experienced what Charles Taylor calls 'the great disembedding' (2007, pp. 146-58, 270-95). 'Disembedding' refers to the processes of privatization (the individualization of life and its meaning), of societalization (where large and impersonal collectives take over from local and interpersonal ones) and of rationalization (where naturalistic and scientific interpretations of reality displace religious and spiritual ones). Disembedding is a phenomenon which has led to the creation of an increasingly functional and individualistic understanding of human existence, one in which 'the ontological relations that bound the physical, the political, and the cosmic together no longer hold' (Ward, 2009, p. 229).

The Kingdom at Work Project is founded on the conviction that none of these challenges can be addressed effectively unless we recognize that the survival of human civilization is dependent upon our creating a world which learns to live together as what we have called a community of character [Stage 1]. Thus the building of community, from the local to the global, is an issue of paramount importance.

In the communal transformation of humankind, the world of work has a vital part to play. Its first responsibility is to provide for the physical and material welfare of the whole of humankind. It second, and equally important responsibility, is to foster relationships within and beyond the workplace which exemplify what it means for all social collectives to become communities of character.

The church and the world of work

In enabling the world of work to make its contribution to the building of a global community of character, the church has an essential part to play. As Margaret Whipp (2008) states: 'Within the complex force fields of the workplace… the need for Christians to express their calling with tenacity, compassion and wisdom has never been greater' (p. 72). The problem is that for too long the church has been captive to theological assumptions which have led to its neglect of the working world.

Armand Larive (2004, pp. 149-155) identifies a number of these assumptions as follows (Whipp's summary, 2008, p. 177):

> A concept of perfection which elevates the detached and contemplative life above the engaged and working life
>
> An approach to spirituality which denigrates, or at least fails to appreciate, the efforts of daily work
>
> A Reformation emphasis on *sola gratia* ('by grace alone') which devalues the significance of daily work
>
> A neo-orthodox neglect of natural theology and the theology of culture

A tacit assumption that the Kingdom of God is coextensive with the church

A pietist mentality which fails to name, unmask and engage the Powers that be

An individualistic atonement theology

A clericalist mindset which fails to honour the lay vocation

A church-centred ecclesiology which, to the extent that the lay vocation is honoured at all, constructs laity as helpers to the clergy

The Kingdom at Work Project challenges these assumptions. To that end, it offers a communal theology, spirituality, communal principles for the economy and a diaconal model of social collectives, along with a process of discernment and intervention based on the former, which is intended to inspire and empower Christians to transform their workplaces into communities of character. The immediate task, therefore, is to set out a communal theology which can undergird and inform that undertaking.

The meaning of community

The word 'community', like aerosol, has been sprayed onto so many human activities to try and give them a pleasant aroma – community development, community care, community health, community policing, community newspapers, community schools, community businesses, the European Economic Community itself – that it has come to mean all things to all people and thus little to anyone. This casual use of the concept of community has led to what Jonathan Boswell (1990) calls 'a gigantic omission' (p. 3). It is an omission of which we need to be acutely aware and speedily address if any kind of global order is to come out of potential chaos. To appreciate the full implications of this 'omission' we must also explore what lies at the heart of the concept of community, by which this project lays so much store.

Many linguistic usages of the concept conceal rather than reveal the dynamic nature of community. For example:

- the power of community appears as very weak when the word is used to refer to some vague *social collective* described as '*the* community'.

- its power is also minimal when the concept is used to describe a social collective situated in an ill-defined form of *place* - such as 'a suburban community' or 'a rural community'.

- its power increases when the word is used to describe a social collective drawn together by *shared interests* - such as 'a mining community' or 'a school community'.

- its power is even stronger when the concept is used to describe those *relationships* characterizing a social collective connected by kinship or cultural bonds - such as 'the extended family' or 'a Moslem community'.

However, for the power of community to reveal its full potential, attention must be focused first and foremost on communal *feelings*. This happens when a phrase such as *a sense of community* is employed. This offers an understanding of community founded on the passions and power that *feelings* can generate. What, then, are the feelings which give particular dynamism to 'a sense of community'?

Robert MacIver and Charles Page (1950, pp. 291-296; see also Clark, 2005, pp. 16-18) call such feelings 'community sentiments'. They identify three such sentiments as of paramount importance. Here we build on their work. The first essential communal feeling or sentiment is ***a sense of security***, where security refers to adequate physical and material well-being, as well as freedom from the fear of natural forces or human agencies which might threaten life or limb.

The second essential feeling is ***a sense of significance***. This is the sentiment which is engendered when people feel they have a role to play, formal or informal, which carries public recognition and/or which offers personal fulfilment.

The third essential feeling is ***a sense of solidarity***. This is the sentiment experienced when people feel that they belong to and are an integral part of some social collective.

I would argue that a fourth essential communal characteristic should be added here, that of ***socialization***. This is the process of induction whereby, beginning with the family, members of social collectives are nurtured, instructed and trained within a particular culture that gives social collectives associated with it clear boundaries and a distinctive identity (Clark, 2005, pp. 34-35).

These four fundamental *sociological* communal components I term **the 4Ss**. When such communal feelings are strong and socialization intense, those concerned will experience a strong sense of community; when they are weak, their sense of community will also be weak.

The communal dilemma

All human beings need to experience a sense of community within a bounded social collective before they are able to experience similar sentiments within larger and more open ones. The problem is that social collectives often remain bounded, self-protective and exclusive for too long. Such insulation is so commonplace that it can be called the default condition of all societies (Clark, 2005, pp. 18-20). For fear of weakening their sense of security, significance and solidarity, people become victims of cognitive, geographic, social or cultural immobility. They remain closed to any experience that is not familiar and seems to threaten their established way of life. This faces a world which needs to become a global community of character if it is to survive with the difficulty of resolving what I call 'the communal dilemma'.

This dilemma is typified by social collectives (especially those with a very strong sense of community) which remain insular and exclusive, and normatively suspicious of and hostile towards other social collectives. As David Jenkins (1976, pp. 14-16) puts it: 'That by which we identify ourselves and gain our sense of identity, significance and belonging is also that by which we dehumanize others'. In more recent history, such exclusive communal collectives have been exemplified by small groups (such as fundamentalist religious sects), by movements (the Ku Klux Klan and al-Qaida), as well as by entire nations (Nazi Germany and Mao's China).

It is this propensity for social collectives to strengthen their sense of community at the expense of others which presents humankind with the communal dilemma - *the problem social collectives face when attempting to become increasingly open to one another without undermining or weakening their own sense of community or that of others*. Unless the communal dilemma is resolved we will never be able to create a global community of character. The power of community will then, at best, go to waste and, at worst, become incestuous, exclusive and eventually destroy us. Alastair McFadyen (1990) recognizes this problem when he comments: 'Given that so much of our present social and political situation can be described as a reversal of the values of true community, our situation is one of immense seriousness and urgency' (p. 270).

A theology of community

Breaking the stranglehold of the communal dilemma

Breaking the stranglehold of the communal dilemma is an immensely difficult task. Even when we are aware of the dire consequences of that dilemma and wish to resolve it, we still need an understanding of the tools needed to address such a challenging task.

Learning as education

The key to breaking the grip of the communal dilemma lies in moving beyond the constraints of socialization. It is imperative that humankind acquires the motivation and the ability to question the assumption that the culture into which one has been socialized is the only possible source of one's communal identity. We have to learn how to build positive communal relationships not only with those with whom we have a cultural affinity but with strangers and even enemies. This necessitates us going beyond an experience of learning shaped by nurture, instruction and training, and becoming open to learning as education, in its fullest and richest sense.

Only learning as openness to new vistas can offer us experiences that question the received wisdom into which we have been socialized, enable us to gain a deeper understanding of what it means to be human and engage with life as a journey of discovery (Clark, 2005, pp. 32-37). It is only a shift from closed to open learning, that which genuine education should be all about, that can offer us the opportunity to break the stranglehold of the communal dilemma, enable us to become 'dialogue-partners' (McFadyen, p. 269) with the wider world and make possible the creation of a global community of character.

Chris Argyris and Donald Schön (1978) refer to learning of this kind as 'double-loop' learning. It brings experiences which expand our conceptual frame of reference to identify and then challenge those underlying assumptions that maintain exclusive goals, values and convictions. Argyris and Schön see double-loop learning as the antithesis of 'single-loop learning', or closed learning, which never questions deeply embedded social and cultural assumptions.

Peter Hawkins (1991) goes even further (pp. 172-187). He is convinced that we can have an experience and discover the art of learning which he calls 'triple-loop learning', learning that is even more open-ended than double-loop learning. Hawkins argues that if we want to resolve the communal dilemma, double-loop learning has limitations because it remains conditioned by an implicit 'philosophy of effectiveness' emanating from a competitive and dominating materialistic market-place culture. He believes that the most important questions arise out of our being engaged in a form of learning, triple-loop learning, which requires that the learner faces up to his or her mortality and the profound issues of life's meaning and purpose. Hawkins also claims that triple-loop learning opens our eyes to envisaging not only our own planet but the entire cosmos as a physical, communal and spiritual whole, and to the importance of discovering our place within it.

We interpret Hawkins as talking about learning as a journey of *spiritual* discovery. We see such learning as not only a human endeavour but as a divine gift through which we are privileged to grasp something of the purposes of God in creation and redemption. Triple-loop learning, as we understand it, is inspired and informed by revelation and discernment [see Stages 3 and 7].

By helping us to move beyond closed social collectives held captive by the communal dilemma, double-loop learning and, if we follow Hawkins, triple-loop learning in particular, open up a theological vision of community greater than that encompassed by the 4Ss on their own, the sociological dimension of community, though a sense of security, significance and solidarity, and the process of socialization, remain the experiential foundations for any deeper understanding of the meaning of community.

Symbolic universes

A vision of community in its fullest and richest sense is always informed by some kind of 'symbolic universe', a nexus of all-embracing values and the beliefs from which these are derived (Berger and Luckmann, 1984). At their best, symbolic universes present a vision of community which is open not closed, inclusive not exclusive, universal and not circumscribed by culture, race, gender or nationality.

Symbolic universes are clearly manifest within the world's great religions. As a symbolic universe, Christian faith offers us two dynamic communal images, that of the Trinity and that of the kingdom of God. Both embody a vision of community as an open, inclusive and universal phenomenon. Both build on the 4Ss, a sense of security, significance, solidarity and the process of socialization - but go much further. Both embrace a triple-loop, a cosmic vision of community and offer the power to make that vision a reality.

I maintain that this transformative vision of community embraces four universal and inclusive gifts of grace; *the gifts of life, of liberation, of love and of learning* (*Diagram 3*). We call these gifts *the 4Ls*. The first three gifts, life, liberation and love, build on the experiences of security, significance and solidarity respectively but, as indicated below, add a radically new dimension to them. The fourth gift, learning as education, builds on the process of socialization but goes a good deal further. It inspires, informs and guides our spiritual journey of discovery and is paramount in enabling us to break the stranglehold of the communal dilemma.

Diagram 3

The kingdom community

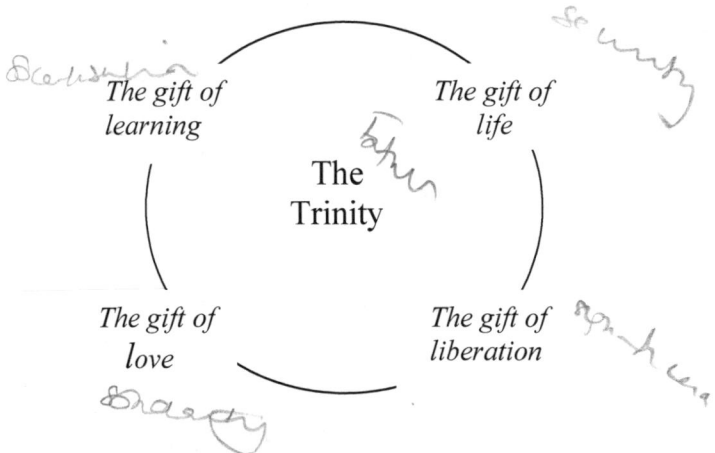

To begin to understand the full meaning and implications of these four communal gifts, it is to the images of the Trinity and the kingdom that attention must be given. The Trinity portrays the essence and interdependence of the 4Ls; the image of the kingdom illustrates how these gifts are grounded in everyday living, with the life and teaching of Christ as the supreme exemplification of this grounding.

The Trinity

Alastair McFadyen (1990, p. 166) writes:

> The conditions of fallen human interaction are such that expectation, love, hope and trust are continually disappointed. The hope of reaching a genuine mutuality of understanding can be sustained by faith neither in oneself nor in the other, much less in mutual trustworthiness, but only in the empowering co-inherence of Father, Son and Spirit - that is, in God as the one hoped for.

'The full beauty of Trinitarian grace can only be discerned when human beings live and work together in community' writes Mikhail Bakhtin (in Cunningham, 1998, pp. 155-164). The Trinity, above all religious images, embodies the divine gifts of life, liberation, love and learning. It is no surprise, therefore, that these four gifts reveal the essence of community at its zenith. They are gifts offered by 'a holy community of Persons' (Ecclestone, 1975, p. 112), distinctive gifts yet intimately and dynamically interrelated.

The first Person of the Trinity, God as Creator, Provider and Sustainer, offers us *the gift of life*. It is a gift which gives far greater depth and much greater strength to any sense of security we may experience, the first of the 4Ss. The gift of life embraces the power and glory of the whole created universe and offers humankind, as Matthew Fox (1994) contends, a part in ' "the Great Work" of creation itself' (p. 61). It is a gift which reminds us that our lives and our destiny are intimately linked to the preservation and sustainability of the planet. The gift of life also promises human flourishing. 'The glory of God is man fully alive', as Irenaeus puts it.

The gift of life embraces *a sense of security*. However, it also offers us such gifts as:

vitality and energy;
health and healing;
enjoyment and well-being;
beauty, awe and wonder;
reverence and respect;
vision and inspiration.

Our response might be that of *adoration, gratitude and devotion*. It might also include:

thanksgiving and celebration;
delight and pleasure;
fun and laughter;
generosity and munificence;
responsibility for the preservation of life;
the fight against ugliness, squalor and disease;
concern for all those materially and physically in need;
faithful stewardship of the earth's resources.

The second Person of the Trinity, Christ as Redeemer and Liberator, offers us **the gift of liberation**. As a gift which affirms that we are not only of human but of divine worth, it greatly deepens and enriches our sense of significance, the second of the 4Ss.

The gift of liberation is so unexpected and unwarranted because the assurance of our divine worth comes to a world which, in Francis Spufford's (2012) words, has 'a crack in everything' (pp. 24-53). More often than not, responsible for the creation and perpetuation of that crack, as Spufford frankly describes it, is 'the human propensity to fuck things up' (p. 27). We may strive to build a world which is a global community of character, but time and again we end up with a world which is unjust, divided and inhuman.

Accessing the gift of liberation depends on our recognition and acceptance of 'what God has wrought in us and not what we deserve'. On a personal level, it is a gift which liberates us *from* whatever destroys the divine image within us and *for* the service of One 'whose service is perfect freedom'. However, as the Old Testament and New Testament indicate, from the Exodus ('Let my people go!' - Exodus 5: 1-7, 16; 8: 1, 20; 9: 1, 13; 10: 3) to the promise of a new Jerusalem (Rev 3: 12; 21: 2), the gift of liberation also has a corporate dimension. It offers social collectives the means and the power to break free *from* the destructive forces of a 'cracked' world, be those forces political, social or economic, and *for* the task of building a just and peaceful global community of character.

The gift of liberation embraces *a sense of significance*. However, it also offers such gifts as:

affirmation;
forgiveness and renewal;
joy;
self-confidence and fulfilment;

courage.

On a personal level, our response might include:

the affirmation of others;
the forgiveness and restoration of others;
humility;
gratitude and thanksgiving.

On a collective level, our response might include:

the pursuit of justice and peace;
the empowering of the powerless;
the inclusion of the marginalized.

The third Person of the Trinity, the Holy Spirit as Unifier, Reconciler and Comforter offers us **the gift of love** (*agape*). 'Love is the cosmic energy that flames from the constellations and is concealed in the abyss of the atom: is whispered by the Holy Spirit in the heart and placarded before men's eyes on the Cross', writes Bishop Lumsden Barkway (1953, p. 23). The gift of love promises humankind a profound experience of interdependence and togetherness which transcends the forces of fragmentation, conflict and division. By inviting us to enter into 'the fellowship (or unity) of the Holy Spirit', the Spirit not only gives depth and strength to any sense of solidarity, the third of the 4Ss, but goes far beyond that experience. That invitation requires of us a readiness to place the two great commandments, love of God and love of our neighbour, at the very heart of what is means to be human, for ourselves, our families, our society and our world.

The gift of love embraces *a sense of solidarity.* However, it also offers us the gifts of:

compassion and kindness;
honesty and integrity;
empathy and reconciliation;
fellowship and friendship;
belonging and unity.

Our response might include:

trust and loyalty;
generosity and kindness;
caring and hospitality;
respect and courtesy;

sharing and co-operation.

The Trinity also offers us **the gift of learning**, that is, learning as a journey of *spiritual* discovery. As a holy or whole community, the Trinity is open to learning not closed, inclusive not exclusive, universal not circumscribed. It is the supreme exemplification of the learning community (Clark, 2005, pp. 37-40). The gift of learning embraces the fourth of the 4Ss, socialization, which includes nurture, instruction and training. However, it breaks the stranglehold of what we have called single-loop forms of learning, not least nurture, and involves us in an educational engagement with life and experience which is truly open. It inspires, energizes and guides us on a journey of spiritual discovery enlightened by revelation and informed by discernment. It is a gift which enables us to break the fetters of the communal dilemma.

The gift of learning begins with socialization, the fourth of the 4Ss. However, it goes far beyond the latter and embraces the gifts of:

curiosity;
revelation;
discernment and insight;
imagination;
wisdom.

Our response might include:

openness and eagerness to widen out experience;
dialogue and debate;
inquiry and questioning;
listening and reflection;
perseverance and life-long engagement.

The Trinity embraces the gifts of life, liberation, love and learning within *a dynamic and holy, or living and holistic learning community.* In a Methodist context, we have elsewhere described these four gifts as integral components of 'the gift of communal holiness' or wholeness (Clark, 2010, pp. 172-82). They are gifts of grace offered in order that humankind might become one: whole individuals, families, neighbourhoods, workplaces (as we explore in the rest of this project), cities and nations, all contributing to the emergence of one world and 'the integrity of creation'. As Charles Elliott puts it (1985), 'The good news of social and individual wholeness is cosmic in its extent' (p. 120).

The four gifts of the kingdom, as with the Persons of the Trinity, are distinctive communal dimensions of an integral whole. Where one exists, others will inevitably be present. Their attributes overlap and often merge. However, we identify these four gifts' particular contribution to the communal whole in order that the depth and richness of that whole can be recognized.

The kingdom

The second great communal image, the kingdom, lies at the very heart of Christ's life and teaching. If it was so central to the ministry of Christ, it can be no less so for us today. Charles Elliott (1985) believes that 'the kingdom implies the transformation of human society – its politics, its economics, (and) its personal, group, institutional and international relationships... (The kingdom is about) the real potential of the whole created order for the fullness of life in community' (p. 1). Hendrik Kraemer writes (1958), the kingdom is 'the order of existence for which the whole world unconsciously yearns' (p. 171). Thus we neglect what Alan Ecclestone (1975) refers to as 'the great tidal wave of His oncoming kingdom' (p. 125) at great cost.

The kingdom is an image supremely personified in the life and teaching of Christ. As Lesslie Newbigin (1980) puts it: 'The presence of the Kingdom is the presence of Jesus himself' (p. 19). His ministry manifests the gifts of life, liberation, love and learning, all attributes of the Trinity, and earths them in everyday human experiences and happenings.

The gift of life is revealed in the dynamic power of the tiny mustard seed (Mt 4: 30-32), the leaven (Mt 13: 33) and the seed growing unnoticed (Mk 4: 26-29). 'The kingdom depends on the invisible but unstoppable processes of God', Elliott observes (1985, p. 88). We are offered a gift which enables us not only to live life but to live it 'abundantly', here and hereafter (Jn 10: 10 and 11: 25).

The gift of liberation on a personal level brings liberation *from* self, sin and failure, a gift earthed in Christ's call to repentance (Mk 1: 15), offering the assurance that all things work together for good for those who put God's kingdom first (Mt 6: 33). Collectively, it is a gift bringing 'good news to the poor... release to the captives... recovery of sight to the blind... and liberty (for) those who are oppressed' (Lk 4: 18). Individually, it is gift about liberation *for* the redemption of others, as witnessed in the parable of the king who forgave his servant's debts

(Mt 18: 23-25). Collectively, it is a call to strive *for* liberty, justice and peace (Mt 5: 6, 9 and 10).

The image of the kingdom grounds *the gift of love* in everyday life. The kingdom is inherited by any who, even if unconsciously, become channels of the gift of love: by feeding the hungry, giving water to the thirsty, offering hospitality to the stranger, providing clothes for the naked, visiting the sick or befriending the prisoner (Mt 25: 34-36). The gift of love is exemplified by the counter-cultural generosity of the owner in the parable of the labourers in the vineyard (Mt 20: 1-16). It is a gift which embraces everyone, as witnessed in the story of the great banquet (Lk 14: 16-24).

The ministry of Christ gives profound meaning to *the gift of learning*. He repeatedly referred to the latter as a spiritual journey of the utmost importance (Mt 6: 33). He taught that learning is a gift which requires discernment and wisdom (Mk 4: 11). He stressed that learning what membership of the kingdom entails is a life-long task which rules out those who put their hand to the plough and then look back (Lk 9: 62).

The gifts of the kingdom, life, liberation, love and learning, are offered to all, righteous and unrighteous, just and unjust alike (Mt 22: 2-10). Thus the kingdom is *an inclusive and universal,* indeed *cosmic kingdom* (Elliott, 1985, p. 120).

Though the fullness of 'the kingdom is not yet and therefore remains incomplete, nevertheless it persists, perdures' (Ward, 2009, p. 171). At the same time, the gifts of the kingdom are 'an index of the mysterious – that is, the sacramental excess that invests the everyday realities of things' (p. 170). Or, as Elliott puts it, the gifts of the kingdom are about 'changing water into wine', the transformation of the ordinary into the extraordinary (1985, p. 99).

An upside-down kingdom

The gifts of the kingdom are not innocuous gift because Christ overturns accepted standards. 'He does put down the mighty from their seats, and raises up the humble and meek' states Lesslie Newbigin (1958, p. 19). Christ gives 'priority in the announcement of the kingdom to the poor, the outcasts, the marginal, the "little ones," the sick, the despised and rejected - the *sinned-against...* (The harshest words of judgement are addressed) to the strong, the arrogant, the pious, the self-righteous, the supposed owners of the kingdom', writes Mortimer Arias (1984, p. 79). If the gifts of the kingdom are brought to bear on the life of society, they inevitably clash with those forces which encourage greed and the exploitation of the planet, foster injustice and violence, debase and devalue compassion, condone ignorance and promote indoctrination. Because of this, to live in accordance with the gifts of the kingdom is a very costly endeavour. It is to take up the cross on behalf of the King (Mk 8: 34-35).

The kingdom community

The kingdom is about a Sovereign whose rule extends throughout the created universe. It embraces those who, Christian or otherwise, have come to treasure the Trinity's gifts of life, liberation, love and learning, and have committed themselves to making those gifts manifest. Thus the kingdom is not only about a Sovereign, however important, it points to *a divinely ordained and ordered community*. We call this '*the kingdom community*' (Clark, 1987, 2005, pp. 13-53; Snyder, 1991, pp. 145-156).

The kingdom community, through its universal gifts of life, liberation, love and learning, becomes the supreme expression of and model for all forms of human community, as I shall argue below, not least within the world of work. Because these gifts are embodied in the Trinity (its communal essence) and the kingdom (its communal practice), essence and practice here come together in a unique and exemplary way.

The gifts of the kingdom community embody the offer of transformational grace to a world that all too often makes a mess of things because it ignores or refuses the divine generosity. 'As long as we imagine that the world can be changed by our activities, our good works, our energy, we substitute our effort for the power of God. That is as ineffective as it is blasphemous... Our power to transform the world is God's power', writes Charles Elliott (1985, pp. 19, 20). Evelyn Underhill (1953) reflects on the unique nature of the kingdom community as follows (p. 58):

> What we look for... is not (an earthly) Utopia, but for something which is given from beyond: Emmanuel, God with us, the whole creation won from rebellion and consecrated to the creative purposes of Christ. This means something far more drastic than the triumph of international justice and good social

conditions. It means the transfiguration of the natural order by the supernatural; by the Eternal Charity. Though we achieve social justice, liberty, peace itself, though we give our bodies to be burned for these admirable causes, if we lack charity we are nothing. For the Kingdom is the Holy, not the moral; the Beautiful not the correct; the Perfect not the adequate; Charity not law.

The gifts of the kingdom community are indispensable. *The endemic problem is that we are still operating with an impoverished understanding of the nature and power of community.* That understanding remains captive to social and economic myths which can never bring us salvation. If the communal transformation of humankind is to become a reality, then a new communal vision, that of the kingdom community is needed. 'Without (such) a vision the people perish' (Proverbs 29: 18).

This means that *for the transformation of society and world to become a reality, secular as well as religious collectives will need to become communities of character, that is social collectives that clearly manifest one or more of the kingdom community's universal and inclusive gifts of life, liberation, love and learning.* Not least among such collectives are those associated with the world of work, the particular concern of the Kingdom at Work Project.

Diagram 4 sets out the key components of the project's theology of community.

Diagram 4
A theology of community
The Kingdom Community

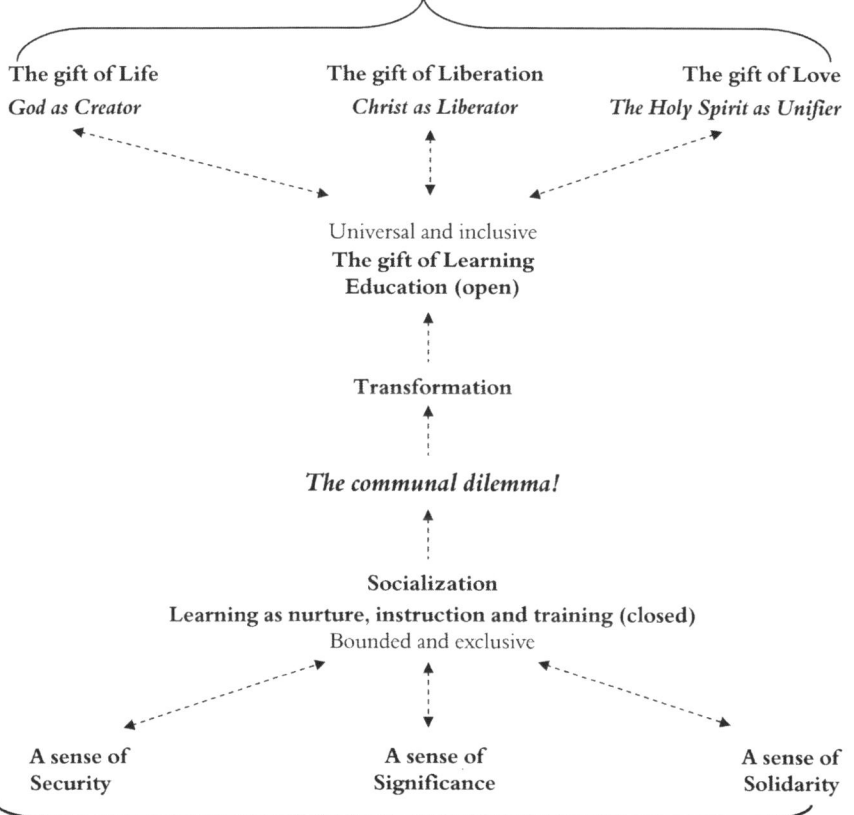

Whole persons - whole workplaces and work organizations
- whole cities - whole societies - one world -
'the integrity of creation'

The Trinity

The gift of Life	The gift of Liberation	The gift of Love
God as Creator	*Christ as Liberator*	*The Holy Spirit as Unifier*

Universal and inclusive
The gift of Learning
Education (open)

Transformation

The communal dilemma!

Socialization
Learning as nurture, instruction and training (closed)
Bounded and exclusive

A sense of Security	A sense of Significance	A sense of Solidarity

A sociology of community

A communal theology for the world of work

'The Christian mission is to proclaim and live the kingdom of God,' writes Jim Wallis (2013, p. 22), the prophetic American activist. The Kingdom at Work Project rests on the conviction that the world of work has a vital part to play in enabling humankind to become a global community of character. The contribution of the working world to that undertaking lies not only in ensuring the physical and material well-being of humankind, but in humankind modelling within every workplace what it means to manifest the gifts of the kingdom community. For the world of work to address this task it has to be shaped by a communal theology and empowered by a communal spirituality [Stage 3].

Transformation at every level

The world of work should be able to make manifest the gifts of the kingdom community from the local to the global dimensions of human endeavour. However, Margaret Whipp wisely states that 'it would not be realistic for Christians engaged at the grass roots level of working institutions to try to voice a comprehensive critique of the powers which have shaped, and continue to sponsor, the climate of modernism in work and economic life which is so powerfully challenging to the discourses of traditional Christianity' (p. 70). We accept, with her, that engagement with 'the powers that be' on a national or international level is 'the proper responsibility of public representatives of the church (lay and ordained) and academic theologians' (p. 70). However, we agree with her that 'within this wider reflective community, it is essential that a robust critique of ideologically driven secularist thinking should challenge the hegemony of those academic, bureaucratic and economic élites who stand to gain through a process which does not merely describe, but actively promotes, the marginalization of religious discourse and influence' (p. 71).

In practice, therefore, the responsibility of most working Christians has to be specific and immediate. It is to discern the presence of the gifts of the kingdom community within their places of work and then to be committed and equipped to intervene in ways that enable the latter to be communally transformed by those gifts.

We turn to the matter of discernment and intervention in Stages 7 and 8 of this project. Without the transformation of macro-economic systems, transformation at the level of the workplace might appear a vain hope. Nevertheless, as Charles Elliott (1985) states, 'Throughout the Old Testament and the New, the kingdom changes systems by changing people' (p. 109). As is argued in Stage 6, the significance of small and incremental change must not be underestimated.

A communal theology is an essential foundation for the Christian's attempt to further the transformation of the world of work. However, a communal theology offers only one frame of reference. To promote practical and effective action, a communal theology needs to be complemented by a communal spirituality, principles of a communal economy - and a diaconal model of institutions derived from them. Stages 3 to 5 of the project explore these other foundational dimensions of mission.

Appendix 1

A Roman Catholic contribution to a communal theology for the world of work

'The call to love our neighbour is the foundation for re-establishing and reclaiming the common good, which has fallen into cultural and political - and even religious - neglect... The common good is quite *uncommon* today. We seem to have lost this unifying vision in our community and public life, and especially in our politics,' writes Jim Wallis (2013, p. 4).

Roman Catholic Social Teaching has been one of the most outstanding examples of the church wrestling with the social, economic and political issues of our day. One of its particular concerns has been with how the concept of the common good gives direction and hope to a society facing social and economic upheaval. In this Appendix we explore how Roman Catholic Social Teaching, especially that which is related to the concept of the common good and the communal theology set out in Stage 2 complement one another.

The common good

In the words of many papal encyclicals addressing that which threatens humankind as a global community of character, Roman Catholic social engagement, with the world of work as well as other sectors, is described as the quest for 'the common good', akin to what has been described above as the quest for community. In Catholic Social Teaching, the common good is defined as 'the total of all those conditions of social living - economic, political, sociological and cultural - which make it possible for men and women readily and fully to achieve the perfection of their humanity' (DeBerri, p. 23). *The Compendium of the Social Doctrine of the Church* (2005, para. 165) states that:

> A society that wishes and intends to remain at the service of the human being at every level is a society that has the common good - the good of all people and of the whole person - as its primary goal... No expression of social life - from the family to intermediate social groups, associations, enterprises of an economic nature, cities, regions, states, up to the community of people and nations - can escape the issue of its own common

good, in that this is a constitutive element of its significance and the authentic reason for its very existence.

However, 'the common good of society is not an end in itself; it has value only in reference to attaining the ultimate ends of the person and the universal common good of the whole of creation. God is the ultimate end of his creatures and for no reason may the common good be deprived of its transcendent dimension, which moves beyond the historical dimension while at the same time fulfilling it' (para. 170).

It is in this context that Catholic Social Teaching stresses 'the universal vocation of Christianity' in furthering the common good (para. 432).

> The world community must be presented, over and over again with ever increasing clarity, as the concrete figure of unity willed by the Creator. The unity of the human family has always existed, because its members are human beings all equal by virtue of their natural dignity. Hence there will always exist the objective need to promote, in sufficient measure, the *universal* common good, which is the common good of the entire human family.

The Trinity as an image of the universal common good

The Catholic Bishops' Conference of England and Wales (*The Common Good*, 1996) speaks of 'the human race' being 'a community of communities... existing at international, national, regional and local level' (para. 21). The task of Christians is seen as building 'a true international community, the ordering of which must aim at guaranteeing the effective universal common good' (*Compendium*, para. 433).

That task is intimately associated with what Catholic Social Teaching calls 'the life and destiny of men and women, called to Trinitarian communion' (para. 74)... 'because the image and likeness of the Trinitarian God are the basis of the whole of "*human ethos*" ' (para. 33). Thus 'there is a certain parallel between the union existing among the divine Persons and the union of the children of God in truth and love' (para. 34). Indeed, the unity of the human family 'is the result of that "supreme model of unity, which is a reflection of the intimate life of God, one God in three Persons,... what we Christians mean by the word communion' (para. 432).

Communal gifts

Catholic Social Teaching frequently emphasises what we have identified above as the universal Trinitarian gifts of life, liberation, love and learning.

The gift of life

Those facing material deprivation 'have a right to food security, the ability to produce their own food or to buy it' (*Catholic Social Teaching*, p. 34). Catholic Social Teaching argues for 'the right to a safe environment'. However, life is far more than a sense of physical and material security. Life is 'the gift of God' (para. 231) and the kingdom is a 'kingdom of truth and life' (para. 57). 'The deepest meaning of human existence… is revealed in the free quest for that truth capable of giving direction and fullness to life' (para. 15). Thus a people 'exists in the fullness of the lives of men and women by whom it is made up…' (para. 385).

The gift of liberation

As with this project, in Catholic Social Teaching 'the liberating mercy of God' (para. 135) is understood as a gift. It is a gift which, first and foremost, acknowledges and affirms 'the inviolable dignity of the human person' (para. 107). 'Man exists as a unique and unrepeatable human being' (para.131). In *The Common Good* the English bishops state: 'We believe each person possesses a basic human dignity that comes from God, not from any human quality of accomplishment, not from race or gender, age or economic status' (para 13). Furthermore, 'man and woman have the same dignity and are of equal value' (para. 111).

Liberation concerns how the full human dignity of women and men can be achieved. It 'must encompass the entire human person' (*Catholic Social Teaching*, p. 24). On a personal level, liberation is freedom from sin, guilt and fear. Once forgiven and 'bearing witness to the grandeur and goodness of the Creator, (man) walks towards the fullness of freedom to which God calls him' (326). However, liberation is also a collective phenomenon 'beginning with the poor, the marginalized, the sinners' (para. 29), and rooted in the experience of the Exodus (para. 21). It works for 'a just society (which) can become a reality only when it is based on the respect of the transcendent dignity of the human person' (para. 132).

The gift of love

Catholic Social Teaching offers two concepts which relate closely to this heading - that of solidarity and that of love as such.

Solidarity

In the case of Catholic Social Teaching solidarity is seen as a key concept possessing two facets. On the one hand, there are 'de facto forms of solidarity' (para. 193) which would seem to come nearest to our sociological interpretation of solidarity (as one of the 4Ss).

On the other hand, there is an 'ethical-social (form of) solidarity' (para. 193), seen by the *Compendium* as one of a number of key 'principles' (paras. 192-196). As such, solidarity is taken to be 'an authentic moral virtue, not a feeling of vague compassion or shallow distress at the misfortunes of so many people, both near and far' (para. 193). The ethical characteristics of this virtue highlight 'in a particular way the intrinsic social nature of the human person, the equality of all in dignity and rights and the common path of individuals and peoples towards an ever more committed unity' (para. 192). 'There exists an intimate bond between solidarity and the common good, between solidarity and the universal destination of goods, between solidarity and the equality among men and peoples, between solidarity and peace in the world' (para. 194).

However, although 'in the light of faith, solidarity seeks to go beyond itself, to take on the specifically Christian dimensions of total gratuity, forgiveness and reconciliation' (para. 196), in Catholic Social Teaching the concept appears to retain more of an ethical than theological character.

Love

In Catholic Social Teaching, love is regarded as a Trinitarian attribute. 'In the communion of love that is God, and in which the Three Divine Persons mutually love one another and are the One God, the human person is called to discover the origin and goal of his existence and of history' (para. 34). As a consequence, 'Mutual love, in fact sharing in the infinite love of God, is humanity's authentic purpose, both historical and transcendent' (para. 55). That purpose is to be perfect in love: 'The fundamental law of human perfection, and consequently of the transformation of the world, is the new commandment of love' (para. 54).

Love transforms people as individuals. 'Only love can completely transform the human person' (para. 583). 'Personal behaviour is fully human when it is born of love, manifests love and is ordered to love... love is the only force that can lead to personal and social perfection' (para. 580). However, ' "Social love" is the antithesis of egoism and individualism... and must embrace the entire human race' (para. 581). Thus love also has immediate relevance to any vision of a new global order. 'In order to make society more human, more worthy of the human person, love in social life - political, economic and cultural - must be given renewed value, becoming the constant and highest norm for all activity' (para. 582). 'It is from the inner wellspring of love that the values of truth, freedom and justice are born' (para. 205). In fact, 'love presupposes and transcends justice' (para 2006). 'No legislation, no system of rules or negotiation will ever succeed in persuading men and peoples to live in unity, brotherhood and peace; no line of reasoning will ever be able to surpass the appeal of love' (para. 207).

'In recent decades... the Social Teaching (of the Catholic Church) has been increasingly shaped by the primacy of love' states *Catholic Social Teaching* (Deberri, p. 17). 'Charity (becomes) the mistress and the queen of virtues' (*Compendium*, para. 581), for love is 'the highest and universal criterion of the whole of social ethics' (para. 204). Building 'a civilization of love' is thus humankind's quest here on earth (paras. 575-583), though it must always be remembered that 'love (cannot) find its full expression solely in the earthly dimension of human relationships and social relations, because it is in relation to God that it finds full effectiveness' (para. 583).

The gift of learning

The concept of learning as such is not so clearly to the fore within Catholic Social Teaching. However, that of 'development' - personal and collective - is prominent. On an individual level, *The Common Good* states that the 'notion of development, understood in Christian terms, is the heart of the Christian social message. Every person is called to develop and fulfil themselves, for life itself is a vocation, a summons which finds its final fulfilment only in the mystery of God... Development must always include... spiritual growth, with openness to God' (p. 9). 'The truth of development consists in its completeness: if it does not involve the whole man and every man, it is not true development' writes Pope Benedict XVI (*Caritas in Veritate*, p. 34).

On a global level, development requires 'a person-based and community-oriented cultural process of worldwide integration that is open to transcendence' (*Caritas in Veritate*, p. 85). This means 'the ongoing promotion - even in the midst of economic crisis - of greater access to education, which is at the same time an essential precondition for effective international cooperation. The term "education" refers not only to classroom teaching and vocational training - but to the complete formation of the person' and 'assisting people in realizing their full human potential' (pp. 125-126). However, 'man cannot bring about his own progress unaided, because by himself he cannot establish an authentic humanism. Only if we are aware of our calling, as individuals and as a community, to be part of God's family as his sons and daughters will we be able to generate a new vision and muster new energy in the service of a truly integral humanism. The greatest service to development, then, is a Christian humanism' (p. 153).

On a pragmatic level, Catholic Social Teaching is often associated with the role of the church as instructor, and the importance of catechesis (*Compendium*, para. 529). 'Catholic educational institutions can and indeed must carry out a precious formative service, dedicating themselves in a particular way to the inculcation of the Christian message, that is to say, to the productive encounter between the Gospel and the various branches of knowledge' (para. 532). Furthermore, it is urged that 'the church's social doctrine must be the basis of an intense and constant work of formation, especially of the lay faithful. Such a formation should take into account their obligations in civil society' (para. 531).

The kingdom of God

In Catholic Social Teaching, the kingdom of God reflects important aspects of the image of the kingdom community developed within this stage of the project. First and foremost, as with the kingdom community, Catholic teaching asserts that 'the Kingdom... (is) a free gift of God' (para. 58). The foremost characteristics of the kingdom of God in Catholic Social Teaching include life, liberation and love (learning is not so evident), amongst others. Thus it is a 'Kingdom of truth and life, of holiness and grace, of justice, of love and of peace' (para. 57); 'freedom and redemption... (are integral to) the Gospel of the Kingdom' (para. 63).

Mirroring how the gifts of the kingdom community transform human values and virtues, in Catholic teaching the kingdom of God is described as transforming life: 'Through the gift of his Spirit and the conversion of hearts, (Christ) comes to establish the "Kingdom of God", so that a new manner of social life is made possible, in justice, brotherhood, solidarity and sharing. The Kingdom inaugurated by Christ perfects the original goodness of the created order and of human activity, which were compromised by sin' (para. 325).

The kingdom of God is not synonymous with any human collective. 'At the level of concrete historical dynamics… the coming of the Kingdom of God cannot be discerned in the perspective of a determined and definitive social, economic or political organization' (para. 51). However, 'the divine promise guarantees that the world does not remain closed in upon itself but is open to the Kingdom of God' (para. 578). The signs of the Kingdom of God are ubiquitous. Thus 'the inchoate reality of the Kingdom can… be found beyond the confines of the Church among peoples everywhere, to the extent that they live "Gospel values" and are open to the working of the Spirit who breathes when and where he wills' (para. 50). 'The goal of salvation, the Kingdom of God embraces all people and is fully realized beyond history, in God' (para. 51).

In Catholic Social Teaching, as in Stage 5 of this project, the church is seen as the servant of the kingdom community for 'the Church places herself concretely at the service of the Kingdom of God above all by announcing and communicating the Gospel of salvation and by establishing new Christian communities' (para. 51). However, diverging somewhat from the stance taken in this project, it is argued that the church is uniquely the origin and embodiment of the kingdom. Hence 'it must immediately be added (in Catholic Social Teaching) that this temporal dimension of the Kingdom remains incomplete unless it is related to the Kingdom of Christ present in the Church' (para. 50). It is 'the Church (which) has received the mission of proclaiming and establishing among all people the Kingdom of Christ and of God, and she is, on earth, the seed and beginning of that Kingdom' (para.49).

Stage 3

A communal spirituality for the world of work

Any spirituality for the world of work without a communal theology to give it form and purpose is rudderless. However, a communal theology for the world of work without a communal spirituality to empower and earth it remains a dead letter. In Stage 3 of the project, therefore, we explore the nature of a communal spirituality.

How does a communal spirituality enable us to become more effective in building workplaces transformed by the gifts of the kingdom community? In Stage 2 we offered a communal theology for the world of work founded on the image of the Trinity, and its inclusive gifts of life, liberation, love and learning, made manifest and earthed through the universal presence of the kingdom community. In Stage 3, we seek to show how these gifts are expressed through four major forms of spirituality: *Celtic (the gift of life)*, *Ignatian (the gift of liberation)*, *Methodist (the gift of love)* and *Quaker (the gift of learning)*. Each of these spiritualities can be seen as having a particular affinity with the gift indicated, though all embrace other gifts of the kingdom community in a less explicit way. All offer the Christian essential resources for mission within the workplace.

In the first part of this stage, we look at how these four spiritualities reflect and inform the gifts of the kingdom community. In the second part, we discuss the implications of such a communal spirituality for mission in the world of work.

A communal spirituality and the gifts of the kingdom community

A Trinitarian Reality

'Spirituality is concerned with seeking out what is real in life', writes Alan Ecclestone (1999, p. 36). Evelyn Underhill (1937) gives the search for what is real a spiritual orientation when, in her classic meditation on *The Spiritual Life,* she quotes the words of Augustine: 'God is the only Reality, and we are only real in so far as we are in His order and He in us' (p. 122). *It is the quest to engage with, learn from and share with others our experience of Reality that gives meaning and purpose to the engagement of Christians with the working world.*

We have identified the Reality on which a communal theology for the world of work is founded as that of the Trinity. The same holds true for a communal spirituality. In this context **Celtic spirituality** has a great deal to offer us. The Celtic spiritual tradition is grounded in 'a profound awareness and belief in the Holy Trinity... (It) sees all relationships as inherently reflecting our being made in the image of a relation-based Triune God in whom we live and move and have our being' (Timothy Joyce in de Waal, 2001, p. viii). For Celtic Christianity, the Trinity was an intensely personal *and* corporate reality. The Celts lived and worked at ease with a deep awareness of and an intimate relationship with the Trinity, in one evening prayer, God, Son and Holy Spirit being invoked as 'the Three of my love' (Esther de Waal, 1996, p. 85). For the Celts, 'It is always to the Three-as-One that prayer is made' but also 'prayer which sees the Godhead in its cosmic context' (de Waal.1996, p. 44).

Celtic spirituality and the gift of life

Charles Elliott in his book *Praying the Kingdom* (1985) notes that 'Many of Jesus' *acts* (his italics) are prophetic demonstrations of the new life, the new quality of life, that the Kingdom offers' (p. 93). It is perhaps **Celtic spirituality** which has most fully grasped the all-embracing power of the divine gift of life and the beneficence and generosity of God as Creator.

The Celts had a profound awareness of 'the great God of life, the Father of all living' (de Waal, 1996, p. 85). 'O Lord and God of life' and 'O Father everlasting and God of life' (p. 175) are typical of the ways God is addressed in Celtic literature. The Celts believed that 'the very nature of God is to create and that the entire universe is in some senses an overflowing of his being,' writes Ian Bradley (1993, p. 68).

'The God whom they (the Celts) worshipped was not conceived primarily as the Lord of history... but rather as the Lord of Creation, the one who revealed himself most fully and characteristically in the wonders and splendours of the natural world' (Bradley, p. 52). He was described as 'the Craftsman of the Heavens' (de Waal, p. 170). 'Understand the creation if you wish to know the Creator... For those who wish to know the great deep must first review the natural world,' said Saint Columbanus (p. 59).

To the Celtic saints, 'human life is contained within, and unfolds within, the dimension of the eternal' (p. 160). Thus rising each morning from sleep to the responsibilities of daily life was always a kind of resurrection:

> Thanks to Thee, O God, that I have risen to-day,
>   To the rising of this life itself;
> May it be to Thine own glory, O God of every gift...

(de Waal, p. 175).

The Celts also experienced a providential rhythm to life in the changing seasons which for them represented 'the alternation of opposites: light and dark, warmth and cold, life and death' (p. 54). 'The dark and light are themselves symbols of the Celtic refusal to deny darkness, pain, suffering and yet exult in rejoicing, celebration, in the fullness and goodness of life,' states Esther de Waal (p. 2). Although nature was recognized as often cruel, menacing and uncertain, Celtic Christianity was sustained by a belief in the power of 'light in darkness, hope in despair, life in death' (p. 106).

'When life is seen as the gift of God praise and thanksgiving is inevitable', writes Esther de Waal (p. 177). Euros Bowen, a modern Welsh poet, reflecting the Celtic tradition, speaks of a 'sense of unity with all creation, both human and non-human, that transcends time and space and brings the whole world together as participants in the singing of one great hymn of praise' (p. 173). Alexander Carmichael, the famous collector of Celtic prayers, provides many examples of this profound sense of gratitude for the gift of life. For example:

> Thanks be to Thee, Jesus Christ
> Who brought'st me up from last night,
> To the gladsome light of this day,
> To win everlasting life for my soul,
> Through the blood Thou didst shed for me.
> Praise be to Thee, O God, for ever,
> For the blessings Thou didst bestow on me -
> My food, my speech, my work, my health... (p. 16)

and

> I believe, O God of all gods,
>   That Thou are the eternal Father of life...
> I am giving Thee worship with my whole life,
>   I am giving Thee assent with my whole power,

I am giving Thee praise with my whole tongue,
I am giving Thee honour with my whole utterance. (pp. 176-177)

The Celts believed that they were co-workers with God the Creator. 'Everything they touched, every tool they handled, was done with respect and reverence; every activity performed with a sense of the presence of God, indeed done in partnership with him' (de Waal, p. 70).

Ignatian spirituality and the gift of liberation

The Celts had a genuine awareness of a fallen and fearful world. For them 'creation (came) with pain' (p. 59). How could it be otherwise when they were subjected to the destructiveness and unpredictability of the natural elements, as well as to the violence of marauding invaders? It is no surprise, therefore, that the cross was at the heart of their faith, a sign and symbol of the triumph of light over darkness, good over evil. 'In a Celtic cross we see that great round O, the circle of the globe itself, held in tension by the two arms of the cross – creation and redemption together' (de Waal. 1996, p. 125). 'There is no divide here between this world and the next. Heaven and earth are interconnected and interacting' (de Waal, 2001, p. xxvi). At the same time, theirs was a belief in 'Christ as liberator and enabler, rather than judge and reprover' (Bradley, 1993, p. 61).

Nevertheless, it is to **Ignatian spirituality** that it is particularly helpful to turn to enrich our understanding of the meaning of the gift of liberation, a spirituality forged within the more complex world of the sixteenth century. In 1548, well before he founded the Society of Jesus, the Jesuits, Ignatius Loyola drew up his *Spiritual Exercises* which are today as widely a used spiritual resource as at any time in history. At the heart of the *Exercises* is his experience as an ex-soldier who, increasingly aware of his own failures, 'wrestled with God and won emancipation at tremendous cost' (James Brodrick, 1942, p. 20). Behind its many rules, annotations and additions is the experience of 'the survivor of a grim battlefield, a war-torn veteran, stiff-jointed indeed, but wise beyond the fashion of many more graceful counsellors' (p. 20). Ignatius believed the Christian to be engaged in a life or death struggle with what he called 'the enemy' (*Spiritual Exercises*, para. 350, p. 106).

For Ignatius, therefore, the Christian life was a journey from captivity to liberty. His Exercises start with a wholehearted acknowledgement of sin and the need for repentance. The first 'week' of the Exercises begins with meditations on the themes of death, judgment and hell, which bring 'the soul through its valley of troubling to Christ, its door of hope' (p. 23). Thereafter, the life of Christ (whom in this project's communal theology is called 'the Liberator') forms the entire content of the *Exercises*. At the end of the fourth 'week', the *Exercises* are meant to lead those engaged in them to 'rejoice in the great joy and gladness of Christ our Lord', 'to call to mind and think about those things which cause happiness, gladness, and spiritual joy, such as final glory' and, in a more everyday context, 'to make use of the light and pleasures of the seasons' (*Spiritual Exercises*, para. 229, p. 67).

Ignatius believed that his *Exercises* should lead to a definitive choice between good and evil. The purpose of the *Exercises* is 'the overcoming of self and the ordering or one's life on the basis of a decision made in freedom from any disordered attachment' (para. 21, p. 11). He sees the Christian as needing to be liberated from feelings which distract, in order to be able to engage in 'effective not affective love'.

Nevertheless, liberation is not an end in itself. In the fourth 'week' of the *Exercises* these memorable words appear:

> *Take Lord and receive all my liberty* (our italics), my memory, my understanding and my entire will, all that I have and possess. You gave it all to me; to you I return it. All is yours, dispose of it entirely according to your will. Give me only love of you, together with your grace for that is enough for me. (para. 234, p. 68)

In more recent years, a much shorter version of the *Exercises* has emerged in the form of the *Examen of Conscience*. This is meant to be a regular review of how the participant is living out the Christian life. It has two aspects – the *Particular Examen* (often undertaken in the middle of the day) which focuses on some detrimental practice or habit which needs to be changed; and the *General Examen* (undertaken at the end of the day) which reviews the day's doings in the context of thanksgiving, forgiveness, renewal and commitment. We look later in this section at the value of the *Examen* as a resource for discernment in the context of the workplace.

However, a qualification must be made in taking the *Spiritual Exercises* and the *Examen* as exemplifying a spirituality reflecting the kingdom community's gift of liberation. Although retreatants are exhorted to put love into action (para. 230, p. 68), the *Exercises* and *Examen* are essentially individualistic in nature. The gift of liberation, and any spirituality associated with it, is treated very much as a personal matter. In contrast, this project's communal theology for the world of work [Stage 2] is not only about the liberation of the individual but the redemption of the whole creation (Romans 8: 18-25). It thus concerns the liberation of all social collectives from the local to the global, including those of all shapes and sizes operating within the world of work.

Methodist spirituality and the gift of love

All four of the spiritualities we are considering are closely associated with the kingdom community's gift of love. However, it is **Methodist spirituality** which, as fully as any, manifests the passion which empowers this particular gift. In the early twentieth century, William Fitzgerald (1903) summarized the mission statement of the early Methodists in the words: 'All need to be saved, all can be saved, all can know that they are saved and all can be saved to the uttermost'. This affirmation, which in the language of Methodism brings a 'heart-warming' experience of the all-embracing love of God, has become something of a Methodist mantra. The phrase 'saved to the uttermost' represents Wesley's conviction that the goal of the Christian life was a state of sanctification or holiness, a state which he also described as one of 'Christian perfection' or 'perfect love,' writes Gordon Wakefield (1999, p. 24). It was this 'emphasis on holiness as perfect love (which) gave Methodist spirituality its own distinctive character' (*Called to Love and Praise,* 1999, 4.3.19).

In what has come to be regarded as a classic exposition of Methodist faith and practice, *Called to Love and Praise* (note the title) (1999, 4.3.10), John Wesley's words in *A Plain Account of Genuine Christianity*, written in 1753, are quoted as being at the heart of a Methodist spirituality grounded in the love of God.

> Above all, remembering that God is love, he (the Christian) is conformed to the same likeness. He is full of love to his neighbour: of universal love, not confined to one sect or party, not restrained to those who are allied to him by blood or recommended by nearness of place. Neither does he love those only that love him, or that are endeared to him by intimacy of acquaintance. But his love resembles that of him whose mercy is over all works.

For Wesley the outworking of the gift of love in the life of the Christian was 'the work of the Holy Spirit, whom Christ has sent to transform us into his (Christ's) likeness' (Williams, 1960, p. 100). The Spirit within gave the Christian the assurance of sins forgiven, and the power and passion to live out their liberation by witnessing to the transforming nature of the love of God, an experience Wesley described as a 'religion of the heart'. A hymn of Charles Wesley illustrates this heart-warming religion (*Singing the Faith*, 2011, 564):

O thou who camest from above
the pure celestial fire to impart,
kindle a flame of sacred love
on the mean altar of my heart!

There let it for thy glory burn
with inextinguishable blaze,
and trembling to its source return
in humble prayer and fervent praise.

Methodist spirituality grounded the gift of love in what Methodism came to call 'fellowship'. 'Fellowship was the spiritual cement of early Methodism…' (*Called to Love and Praise*, 1999, 4.2.14). It was given distinctive expression within small groups known as bands and classes (Martyn Atkins, 2010, p. 28). Though bands, for the particularly devout, and classes for all other members declined in number during the nineteenth century (Munsey Turner, 2005, p. 52), the experience of fellowship within Sunday Schools, women's meetings, the Wesley Guild movement and, in the twentieth century, a multitude of youth clubs and university societies, took their place and remained at the heart of what it meant to be a Methodist.

Methodist worship, with its focus on the exhortatory sermon and '*Singing the Faith*' (2011), also nurtured and deepened an experience of fellowship rooted in the gift of love. Methodism's *Hymns and Psalms* (1983), until 2011 its official hymnbook, retained a section on 'Fellowship' including many hymns of Charles Wesley with verses such as:

He builds us build each other up;
And, gathered into one,
To our high calling's glorious hope
We hand in hand go on.

The gift which he on one bestows,
We all delight to prove;
The grace through every vessel flows,
In purest streams of love. (753)

Methodism also demonstrates loving commitment to the divine fellowship of the Trinity in its annual Covenant Service which includes the following vow:

I am no longer my own, but thine.
Put me to what thou wilt, rank me with whom thou wilt:
put me to doing, put me to suffering;
let me employed for thee or laid aside for thee;
exalted for thee or brought low for thee...
And now, glorious and blessed God, Father, Son and Holy Spirit,
Thou art mine and I am thine. So be it.
And the covenant which I have made on earth,
let it be ratified in heaven.

However, for Methodism, 'holiness was never understood as an individualistic affair. In Wesley's own words, "the gospel of Christ knows no religion but social: no holiness but social holiness" ' (*Called to Love and* Praise, 1999, 4.3.9). In the nineteenth century, love for one's neighbour came increasingly to be focused on the preaching and practice of the 'social gospel'. This was manifest in the so-called 'Forward Movement' when, towards the end of that century, over a hundred Methodist 'central halls' were built to address the needs of the destitute and needy within the inner city. At that time Methodism also exercised a vigorous campaign against the social evils of drinking and gambling. A century later, from 1983 to 1996, Methodism was still actively engaged in a programme entitled 'Mission alongside the poor'.

Methodism's passionate witness to the kingdom community's gift of love, to the latter's power to change lives, to the importance of fellowship in making that gift manifest and to its expression through an ongoing concern to create a world founded on social and economic justice, remains an important contribution to a communal spirituality concerned with transforming the world of work.

Quaker spirituality and the gift of learning

Judith Jenner, then a tutor in Quaker Studies at Woodbrooke Quaker Study Centre, Birmingham, writes (2008): 'The Society of Friends exemplifies what it means to be a learning community, with deep roots in the kingdom community' (p. 147).

Life as a learning community is a vital aspect of **Quaker spirituality** and is well documented in their 'bible', *Quaker Faith and Practice* (QFP, 2005). The latter has two main sections. The first is *Advices and Queries*. Jenner describes these as 'the ground from which our faith and life spring and (which) are fundamental in shaping the Society of Friends as a learning community' (p. 150). The second part of *Quaker Faith and Practice* is by far the longer. It contains personal reflections recorded over many centuries intended to help Quakers discover what it means to live out their faith in daily life, as well as major sections on how the Society of Friends should conduct its internal business. Here we focus mainly on *Advices and Queries*.

'The Religious Society of Friends is rooted in Christianity and has always found inspiration in the life and teaching of Jesus' (*QFP*, 1.02.4). Thus Quakers continue to be prompted to consider how Jesus is speaking to them and whether they are following his example of love in action (1.02.4). However, for Quakers, 'Christianity is not a notion but a way' (1.02.2).

Advices and Queries places Quaker worship at the heart of what it means to be a learning community. It states: 'As Friends we commit ourselves to a way of worship which allows God to teach and transform us. We have found corporately that the Spirit, if rightly followed, will lead us into truth, unity and love' (1.01). Quakers are urged to let worship and everyday life enrich one another (1.02.1).

The life and work of the Society of Friends, is rooted in the conviction that Quakers are called to a life-long journey of spiritual discovery.

> Be aware of the spirit of God at work in the ordinary experience of your daily life. Spiritual learning continues throughout life, and often in unexpected ways. There is inspiration to be found all around us, in the natural world, in the sciences and arts, in our work and friendships, in our sorrows as well as in our joys (1.02.7).

For Quakers, learning requires the discipline of being open to 'God whose Light shows us our darkness and brings us to new life' (1.02). It is a 'Light that is in all of us' and a *Light to Live By* (Rex Ambler, 2002). Thus we need to 'take time to learn about other people's experiences of the Light' (*Advices and* Queries, 1.02.7). This means a readiness to 'respect that of God in everyone' and to 'listen patiently and seek the truth which other people's opinions may contain' (1.02.17). *Advices and Queries* prompts Quakers to respect the wide diversity of people who make up their Society and to 'foster the spirit of mutual understanding and forgiveness which (their) discipleship asks of (them)' (1.02.22).

Being prepared to question hitherto unquestioned assumptions is an essential aspect of the spirituality of the Society of Friends as a learning community. Quakers are urged to 'appreciate that doubt and questioning can... lead to spiritual growth and to greater awareness' of the Light (1.02.7). Such questioning is not to be undertaken in a critical or aggressive spirit, but by joining with others 'in expectant waiting' (1.02.8). Those involved are to 'think it possible that (they) may be mistaken' and 'listen patiently and seek the truth which other people's opinions may contain' (1.02.17).

Quakers believe that their life as a learning community should bear fruit in the way they conduct their internal business, especially in the way they approach decision-making. In that process, they should 'wait patiently for divine guidance' as to 'the right way' rather than 'seek a majority decision (or) even consensus' (1.02.14).

Quakers' experience as a learning community must be manifest in daily life. *Advices and Queries* urges them to 'live adventurously' and let their lives speak for themselves. Quakers should 'seek to understand the causes of injustice, social unrest and fear'. Their learning needs to 'bear witness to the humanity of all people' and help create 'a just and compassionate society' (1.02.33). Living simply (1.02.41), temperance (1.02.40), a loving home life (1.02.26), integrity in business (1.02.37), working for peace (1.02.31 and 32) and concern for the planet (1.02. 42) are all manifestations of their commitment to be constantly 'in the light walking and abiding' (1.01).

Inclusive and universal

A communal spirituality is an inclusive and universal spirituality. It is underpinned by the conviction that the gifts of the kingdom community are latent within every person. Ian Bradley writes that 'in finding God's presence in everybody and everything, however high and however lowly, Celtic Christianity... found the most fundamental reasons for loving and serving others' (1993, p. 50). Methodist spirituality likewise is rooted in the conviction that God's love, as 'prevenient grace', is available to all ('All can be saved') and not just to the chosen few (Colin Williams, 1960, pp. 39-46). Both Celtic and Methodist spirituality reflect the heart of Quaker spirituality that 'the Light of the Christ-like God shines in every person' (*Quaker Faith and Practice*, 2005, 26.65). In particular, the gifts of the kingdom community are on offer to the poor, marginalized and vulnerable. 'For the Kingdom is for them first... (It is) the triumph of the last over the first, of the humble over the proud, the ordinary over the exotic' (Elliott, 1985, p. 28).

Communal spirituality reminds us of our inherent inter-dependence. Esther de Waal notes that 'Celtic spirituality is corporate spirituality with a deep sense of connectedness to the earth itself and the natural elements, to the human family, not only the present immediate family... but the extended family as it stretches back in time through many generations' (1996, p. 39). Richard Andrew (1999) argues that Methodism too has what he calls 'a catholic vision (which)... entails embracing the unity of *all* humanity' (p. 22). Meg Maslin, a Quaker, comments: 'Personality, sex, race, culture and experience are God's gifts. We need one another and differences shared become enrichments, not reasons to be afraid, to dominate or condemn' (*QFP*, 23.33).

A communal spirituality transcends human divides. Celtic spirituality regards women and men as whole persons and many of their prayers place body, mind and spirit under God's protection. Methodist hymnology sees God's grace as transcending every social division. From Charles Wesley's pen:

> Thy sovereign grace to all extends,
> > Immense and unconfined;
> From age to age it never ends;
> > It reaches all mankind.

> Throughout the world its breadth is known,
> > Wide as infinity;
> So wide it never passed by one,
> > Or it has passed by me. (*Hymns and Psalms*, 46)

A communal spirituality recognizes no sacred-secular dualism. The Celts believed that God was present throughout the whole of creation. Even so, 'there (was) no blurring of the distinction between Creator and created, no worship of nature for its own sake but rather a wonderful sense of the whole creation as a theophany – a marvellous revelation of the goodness and wonder and creativity of God' (Bradley, 1993, p. 35). Ignatian spirituality operates on the premise of 'finding God in all things', hence Jesuits have always been active in the arts, literature and science. In 1989, a group of Quaker scientists wrote that 'science and religion have much in common. They are communal activities and involve a search for some greater truth' (*QFP* 26.24).

A transformational spirituality

Because a communal spirituality which is inclusive and universal faces a world that remains exclusive and divided, it inevitably takes on the character of a transformational spirituality. It gives humanity a new impetus towards wholeness, or 'communal holiness' as I have called this phenomenon elsewhere (Clark, 2010, pp. 172-82). It is a spirituality which possesses an energy epitomised by St. Patrick's breast-plate, a classic prayer from the Celtic tradition. The latter invokes a vibrant and life-giving power which pilgrims can access in their quest for a deeper vision and experience of what the Christian life is all about.

Alan Ecclestone (1975, pp. 96-97), reflecting on the lessons to be learnt from a communal spirituality which inspired earlier generations to embark on the construction of majestic cathedrals, believes that:

> Men and women today (need) to discover for themselves a life energising principle, an impulse of spirituality commensurate with the needs of the time. It (has) to be, like its forerunners, grounded deep in the earth, in the consciousness of men and women, and it (has) to soar towards the heavens in a growing unity of purpose, a consciousness of community, of mankind unified, divinised and expectant of the Christ.

A communal spirituality, however, can never ignore the reality of a world of pain, suffering and sinfulness. The Celts lived close to the violence and destructiveness of nature and what they often felt to be evil and mysterious powers. Many of their prayers were for protection and strength against the forces of darkness, human and satanic. The Ignatian *Exercises* show a profound awareness of a fallen world, the whole of the 'first week' being given to furthering recognition of human sinfulness and the cost of our redemption. John Wesley's understanding of holiness 'was far deeper than the absence of "wilful transgressions of a known law" (his definition of actual sin). Rather, perfection meant perfect love, including freedom not just from evil actions, but evil thoughts and "tempers" ' (*Called to Love and Praise*,

1999, 4.3.8). In 1904, John William Rowntree, a Quaker, wrote (*QFP*, 26.49):

> No legal bargain, but a spiritual conflict, an inward change, the rejection of the living death of sin, the choice of the new birth, of the purified self, the conversion from a low and earthly to a high and spiritual standard of life and conduct – here you have the practical conditions of salvation, and in the active, free and holy love of God, ever seeking entrance, ever powerful if we but yield the gateway of our hearts, is the substance of the Gospel.

Discernment and its implications for mission in the world of work

The four spiritualities considered above throw fresh light on the nature of the gifts of the kingdom community. It is these gifts that need to be accessed and employed in order to further mission within the world of work [Stages 7 and 8]. Thus there is a need for:

- *recognition of* **the omnipresence of the gifts of the kingdom community**;

- *practice in discerning the presence of the gifts of the kingdom community -* **the art of discernment**;

- **means of aiding the art of discernment**;

- *awareness of the potential for communal transformation that the gifts of the kingdom community offer -* **the power of transformation**.

These gateways into a communal spirituality and their implications for the world of work are explored below.

The omnipresence of the gifts of the kingdom community

The Celts possessed an ever-present and intimate experience of the Trinity. They possessed 'a deep sense of the presence of God… here and now, with me, close at hand, a God present in life and in work, immediate and accessible' (de Waal, 1996, p. 65). For them 'God is companion, guest, fellow-traveller, friend, fellow-worker', writes Esther de Waal (p. 66). That experience 'flows from their real, lived-out grasp of the centrality of the incarnation… "God with us" is true!' (p. 66). At the same time, 'the Celts felt the presence of Christ almost physically woven around their lives' (Bradley, 1993, p. 33). The Holy Spirit was invoked as the ever-present source of comfort and power:

God with me protecting,
The Lord with me directing,
The Spirit with me strengthening,
For ever and for evermore,
    Ever and evermore. Amen. (de Waal, 1996, p. 71)

Alongside a sense of the ever-present Trinity, Celtic spirituality constantly sought the help of Mary the Mother of Christ and of many of the saints. All 'are approachable, close at hand, woven quite naturally into life just as would be any other member of an extended family' (p. 143).

The Celts did not have any need to bring the Trinity into their daily lives 'from beyond'. God was already at work as Creator, Liberator, Lover and Teacher in every moment of the day. Thus the gifts of the kingdom community were evident in their rising and sleeping, in homemaking and farming, in hunting and fishing, in rest and in travel, in health and in sickness and in childbirth and death.

Quaker spirituality likewise embodies a deep sense of the omnipresence of God. Since the time of George Fox, Quakers have believed that 'the Light' exists within everyone. 'For a Quaker', writes Harvey Gillman, 'religion is not an external activity, concerning a special "holy" part of the self. It is an openness to the world in the here and the now with the whole of the self... In short... there is no part of ourselves and of our relationships where God is not present' (*QFP*, 20.20). In 1986 the London Yearly Meeting commented: 'The whole of our everyday experience is the stuff of our religious awareness: it is here that God is best known to us' (*QFP*, 27.38).

A classic work of spirituality not yet mentioned is *The Practice of the Presence of God* by Brother Lawrence (2008). This also bears witness to the presence of God within us and around us. Brother Lawrence, a sandal maker and kitchen servant, believed that 'God (was) always in the depth of the soul, no matter what (a man) does or what happens to him' (p. 74). Lawrence also felt God to be powerfully present in the whole of life. He spoke of his 'soul's secret experience of the actual unceasing presence of God' (p. 85). This enabled him 'to become involved in a continuous conversation with Him in a simple and unhindered manner' (p.71) and thereby experience a mutual 'exchange of love' (p. 80).

A sacramental communal spirituality

The communal spirituality we have described above is regarded by many as a profoundly sacramental experience. Evelyn Underhill calls it 'the sacrament of the present moment' (1934, p. 108). The gifts of the kingdom community are also just that - gifts. As Underhill (1953) puts it: 'That which we really know about God is not what we have been clever enough to find out, but what Divine Charity has secretly revealed to us (p. 42)... (God) inspires and supports the adventure of which he is the goal' (p. 107).

For the Celts 'the real presence' of God, Father, Son and Holy Spirit, was manifest and accessible within and throughout the whole of life. Ian Bradley (1993) writes that '(the Celts) had the ability to invest the ordinary and the commonplace with sacramental significance, to find glimpses of God's glory throughout creation and to paint pictures in words, signs and music that acted as icons opening windows on heaven and pathways to eternity' (p. 84). Theirs was an experience illustrated by the following prayer (de Waal, 1996):

> Each day may I remember the sources of the mercies
>   Thou hast bestowed on me gently and generously:
> Each day may I be fuller in love to Thyself.
>
> Each thing I have received from Thee it came,
> Each thing for which I hope, from Thy love it will come,
> Each thing I enjoy, it is of Thy bounty;
> Each thing I ask, comes of Thy disposing. (p. 178)

Every moment of the working day or of the night, of the changing seasons and of the passing years, becomes a means of grace, enriched 'by a succession of rituals (which) upheld and sacramentalized (them)' (de Waal, 1996, p. 59).

In the *Spiritual Exercises* of Ignatius there is no specific reference to sacramental grace other than in the context of the mass, though the grace of God is clearly communicated to the penitent through his or her many acts of devotion.

Methodism's understanding of sacramental grace reflects its Anglican inheritance, with baptism and holy communion being to the fore, though communion services were originally more 'gospel feasts than holy mysteries' (Wakefield, 1999, p. 34). At the same time, John Wesley also identified what he called 'extraordinary' means of grace.

These could be public (love feasts, watch-night and covenant services, band and class meetings), private (bible reading, prayer, devotional reading, self-denial) or 'works of mercy' (Jones, 2004, p. 160). Many of Charles Wesley's hymns likewise convey a deep sense of the sacramental or 'real presence' of God as Father, Son and Holy Spirit.

> Open, Lord my inward ear,
> And bid my heart rejoice;
> Bid my quiet spirit hear
> Thy comfortable voice;
> Never in the whirlwind found,
> Or where earthquakes rock the place,
> Still and silent is the sound.
> The whisper of thy grace. *(Hymns and Psalms, 540)*

'To (George) Fox and the early Friends the whole of life seemed sacramental, and they refused to mark off any one particular practice or observance as more sacred than others... Their whole attitude was gloriously positive, not negative. They were "alive unto God" and sensed him everywhere' (*QFP*, 27.39). Barratt Brown, a Quaker, comments (*QFP*, 27.43):

> It is a bold and colossal claim that we put forward – that the whole of life is sacramental, that there are innumerable 'means of grace' by which God is revealed and communicated – through nature and through human fellowship and through a thousand things that may become the 'outward and visible sign' of 'an inward and spiritual grace'.

Implications for mission in the world of work

The ever-present and intimate experience of the Trinity and its gifts which typify a communal spirituality is highly relevant to mission within the world of work. It is an experience which shows us that the kingdom community's inclusive and universal gifts of life, liberation, love and learning are ever present within the workplace. From the production line to the office, from the school to the hospital ward, from the bank to the town hall, the gifts of the kingdom community are on offer and ours for the taking. Whether we are based in the same location each day or constantly on the move, whether at our desk or doing business on our iPhones or iPads, the gifts of the kingdom community are intimately to hand. Thus at any moment of day or night, the world of work can become a means of grace, a way of enabling work and the workplace to be transformed by and manifest the gifts of the kingdom community.

Our first responsibility as Christians active within the world of work is to discern where the gifts of the kingdom community are in evidence or where they are being neglected or negated [Stage 7]. Our second responsibility is to use the signs of the kingdom community discerned to inform and shape the kind of intervention we engage in to enable the workplace to manifest the gifts of the kingdom community more fully [Stage 8].

The art of discernment

'Seeing is no simple matter. Even to claim to see things of God is a dangerous business, yet, says the Christ, men must be on the watch, prepared to see, looking for the coming of their Lord, awaiting the onset of His Kingdom' writes Alan Ecclestone (1975, pp. 42-43). Charles Elliott (1985) states:

> People do not look for the Kingdom to break in around them, because they do not expect to find anything if they do. And yet when they do look, they are astonished and delighted at what they discover. This is not to say that if you go to Wigan or Wichita, your will find the Beatitudes fulfilled in the High Street. The process is more subtle, more ambiguous, more provisional: it needs discernment and the eye of faith to see where God is working' (p. 128).

Here, as Jonathan Sacks (2011) puts it, we share in the experience of Elijah listening to the 'still small voice', of Paul looking 'through a glass darkly' and of Wordsworth's 'sense of something far more deeply infused' (p. 285).

Discernment of the kingdom community's gifts of life, liberation, love and learning requires what the Celts call 'rinsed eyes' (de Waal, 1996, p. 88) and Benedict calls 'the ear of your heart' (Parry, 1990, p. xviii). Brother Lawrence describes such awareness as 'the practice of the presence of God'. For Brother Lawrence such 'practice' was a matter of 'train(ing) yourself to dwell in His presence all day long' (2008, p. 90). However, states Alan Ecclestone (1975), 'It is not the job of spirituality today to turn men and women into second and third rate mystics' (p. 41). Its job is to enable us, with all our sinfulness and limitations, to become as aware as possible of the presence of the gifts of the kingdom community so that, by accessing what they offer, we can make our modest contribution to the transformation of the workplace and the world beyond.

The journey in and the journey out

The art of discernment can be enhanced in a number of ways. Prominent amongst these are prayer and worship [Stage 8(5)]. However, here attention is focused more explicitly on the *practice* of discernment. The practice of discernment can operate at a number of levels of human experience. One is that of the self-awareness. This can be called 'the journey in'. Another is that of human relationships. A third is our experience of the natural world. The last two can be called 'the journey out' (Clark, 1997, pp. 78-81).

The journey in

Eckhart Tolle describes the journey in as shaped by 'the shift from thinking to awareness' (2005, p. 117). It is the art, recognized within many forms of spiritual direction, of freeing our minds from their constant preoccupation with past or future, and allowing ourselves to become fully aware of the present. Tolle puts it succinctly: 'Life is now' (2002, p. 23). All four forms of spirituality discussed earlier offer ways in which this journey in can be nurtured and enriched. They suggest means of discernment through which we can be empowered by the presence of the Trinity and transformed by its communal gifts.

The journey out

Unless we are committed to the journey in we will be unable to discern the kingdom community's gifts of life, liberation, love and learning, in our relationships with others or with the natural world. However, the journey in needs to be complemented by the journey out if we are to access and employ the gifts of the kingdom community for that purpose for which they were intended.

Like the journey in, the journey out is about the practice of discernment. That means becoming more aware of the presence of the gifts of the kingdom community in what is commonplace. 'The most effective way Brother Lawrence had for communicating with God was simply to do his ordinary work' (2008, p. 72). In his case, this meant working for many years in the monastery kitchen and, in later life, repairing sandals. Much of Celtic and Quaker spirituality likewise indicates that the journey out entails our learning to become aware of the presence of God in the daily encounters and events of life and work. Nevertheless, the journey out should spur us on to look for the gifts of the kingdom community in the midst of poverty and deprivation, conflict and violence.

The journey out can also involve us in a deeper relationship with the natural world. This means that we seek to align ourselves with what Matthew Fox (1994) calls 'the "Great Work" of creation itself – the work of creation unfolding, the work of evolution or creativity in the universe' (p. 61), of which God is the instigator and sustainer. That journey may also take us onto 'the high ground' of the theological and philosophical quest for meaning and truth.

Implications for mission in the world of work

If we are to be involved in the task of transforming the world of work we first need to practice the art of discerning the hall-marks of the kingdom community already present within the workplace [Stage 7]. What ways are there of equipping ourselves for this undertaking?

Means of aiding the art of discernment

There are a number of means available to aid the Christian in the art of discernment within the workplace. We mention four of these below.

Celtic and Quaker approaches

The kind of spirituality represented by the Celtic and Quaker traditions, as well as that espoused by Bother Lawrence, is one way of helping us to engage more fully in 'the practice of the presence of God' in working life. At first sight, this form of discernment may seem unstructured and informal. However, we know that 'the Celtic way of prayer was learnt from the monasteries; (and that) it was from its religious communities that the people learnt to pray. As a result they learnt that there was no separation of praying and living; praying and working flow into one another' (de Waal, 1996, p. 3). This also meant that the prayer life of the people followed the rhythm of the monastic day. It was likewise for Brother Lawrence. Although his letters and conversations imply a spontaneous approach to practising the presence of God, his membership of the Carmelite Brotherhood offered him an important training ground and the daily practice of corporate prayer. Reflecting this need for discipline, a minister in secular employment speaks of following 'a personal rule, using my cellphone's reminder feature to set times for prayer during the day' (*Spiritual Direction*, 2011, p. 17).

For Quakers, their meeting for worship, which Thomas Kelly describes as grounded in and founded on 'the Real Presence of God' (*QFP*, 2.40), is their school for discernment. Their *Advices and Queries* state that their meeting for worship 'is our response to an awareness of God... When we join with others in expectant waiting we may discover a deeper sense of God's presence... and the power of God's love drawing us together and leading us' (*QFP*, 1.08). Thus behind the apparent informality of Quaker practice, there lies a form of communal discernment which equips them well for their ministry within the working world.

The Examen - an Ignatian approach

Ignatian spirituality provides a more overtly structured approach to discernment and developing an awareness of the gifts of the kingdom community in the workplace. One method it offers is known as 'the examination of conscience' or 'Examen' (*Spiritual Exercises*, 2004, paras. 24-44, pp. 12-18). As a rule, 'the General Examen' takes place at the end of each day and 'the Particular Examen', which focuses on a particular fault to be addressed over days or weeks, in the middle of the day. The forms for the Particular and General Examen, as set out in the *Spiritual Exercises*, have in many cases been adapted to working life. The *Exercises*, and in some cases the Examen, are often facilitated by a mentor.

The General Examen suggests five matters for recollection and prayer which can be summarized as follows:

- recalling one is in the presence of God
- looking back over the day with gratitude
- reviewing how one has lived the day
- asking for forgiveness
- resolutions for the future and a prayer of commitment.

The General Examen offers a structured approach for discerning the gifts of kingdom community in the workplace. However, it focuses more on the individual than Celtic or Quaker spirituality and on the way in which he or she is living out their faith in daily life.

Theological auditing

In the 1990s, the South London Industrial Mission was involved in facilitating an approach to discernment in the workplace called 'theological auditing'. Peter Challen, who developed this method, describes its three main stages (in Clark 1997, pp. 115-116) as:

- an exploration by 'the client' (the lay person at work) of comprehensive themes of faith relevant to daily life: such as creation (ecological issues), jubilee (justice implications) and covenant (in contrast to contract), etc;

- examining where these themes are experienced in the workplace and how they might suggest a new approach to mission;

- examining where these themes are being blocked or negated and how the client might prevent this situation continuing.

The theological audit is facilitated by an 'auditor'. Challen stresses that the value of the audit depends on the building of trust between client and auditor. Such theological auditing has also been undertaken with groups and not only as a one-to-one exercise.

The means of discernment outlined above are 'open-ended'. That is, they are not associated with specific signs or incidents which might suggest the presence of the gifts of the kingdom community at work. In Stage 7 of the Kingdom at Work Project, another approach to discernment is offered. This focuses on signs and/or critical incidents as a resource for seeking out the gifts of the kingdom community within the workplace.

The power of transformation

'Awareness is the power that is concealed within the present moment' (Eckhart Tolle, 2005, p. 78). A communal spirituality which discerns the presence of and is able to accesses the gifts at the heart of the kingdom community is an immensely powerful resource. 'For the kingdom, the power and the glory are yours' - the doxology to the Lord's Prayer reminds us that 'the kingdom' and 'the power' go hand in hand. However, such power is never coercive or destructive, as one particular paraphrase of the Lord's Prayer seeks to emphasize (Clark, 2008):

Your kingdom is always with us.
We are humbled and thankful to be members of it.
Yours is the power that never crushes and the glory that never dazzles.
You love and care for us – beyond life and death, time and space.
For all you are to us, we praise you and thank you.

Their communal spirituality enabled the Celts to tap into the power of the Trinity's gifts from rising up to going to bed, and throughout every season. They regarded this power as given for their protection, as epitomized by St. Patrick's breastplate, or lorica:

For my shield this day
   A mighty power:
   The Holy Trinity!
Affirming threeness,
Confessing oneness,
In the making of all
Through love… (de Waal. 1996, pp. 22-23)

However, the power of a spirituality which embodies the kingdom community's gifts of life, liberation, love and learning is not only concerned with providence and protection. It is a power far beyond human power offered as a means of transformation, as reflected in the Methodist spirituality of Charles Wesley:

Give me the faith which can remove
   And sink the mountain to a plain;
Give the childlike praying love,
   Which longs to build they house again;
Thy love, let it my heart o'erpower,
   And all my simple soul devour.

Only the power offered by a communal spirituality can break the mould of those customs and structures which would negate or ignore the gifts of the kingdom community. Celtic and Ignatian spirituality, in particular, saw accessing this power as the way to overcome what they regarded as 'the enemy' (*Exercises*, paras. 324-326, pp. 97-98) - those tenacious forces of evil which annihilate love and compassion and perpetuate injustice and violence.

Implications for the world of work

Discernment of the presence of the gifts of the kingdom community, and the power which these gifts offer, brings with it the promise of, as well as our responsibility for the communal transformation of the world of work. It is a commission at the heart of which is a quest for communal wholeness. As Esther de Waal puts it in her reflections on Celtic spirituality, it is a call to move away from 'the highly individualistic, competitive, inward-looking approach common in today's society' towards 'the promise... of (the) healing of the many fractures that maim and corrupt each of us and the world in which we live' (1996, p. 6).

It must be stressed that a communal spirituality for the world of work is not about pouring oil on troubled waters. It is a spirituality which has no truck with a global culture that exalts utility but devalues creativity, promotes the accumulation of wealth and possessions but neglects what it means to be human, furthers vested interests yet turns a blind eye to injustice and exploitation, seeks to indoctrinate not educate, and squanders the resources of the planet at the expense of generations to come. The purpose of a communal spirituality is to raise searching questions about how, when and where the kingdom community's gifts of life, liberation, love and learning are being denied as well as affirmed at every level of economic endeavour, from a particular workplace to the global economy.

Because a communal spirituality for the working world is about the task of transformation, it is a political spirituality. Charles Elliott writes: 'There can be no spirituality without... politics' (1985, p. 146). That sentiment is echoed by Graham Ward in his thesis on the nature of discipleship when he states: 'Praying is... the most political act any Christian can engage in' (2009, p. 281). The Kingdom at Work Project is not about moving the deck-chairs on the Titanic. It is about transforming the world of work into a community of character which can blaze a trail for the transformation of every aspect of life. The contribution of a communal spirituality is to give meaning and purpose to, as well as empower the Christian for that endeavour.

Stage 4

A communal economy for the world of work

Introduction

There have been a number of endeavours over recent years to engage in a Christian critique of the economic model which now shapes our world [for example: Preston (1991); Selby (1997); Jenkins (2000); Atherton (2003); Larive (2004); Tanner (2005); Atherton and Skinner (2007); Sedgewick (2008); Ward (2009), Poole (2010), Higginson (2012) and Williams (2012)]. Many of these writers make pertinent criticisms of the nature and form of our global economy. Some of these have been in a position to respond to the destructive nature of the forces which triggered the banking crisis of 2007 – 2008 and led to the subsequent worldwide recession. However, all are stronger on diagnosis than prognosis. Nobody is as yet clear as to the kind of economic and political model which could bring into being a more just and peaceful world. As Peter Selby comments: 'The task of serious and radical theological engagement with the economic realities of our time remains to be accomplished' (*Church Times*, 11/3/11).

Nevertheless, if the signs of the kingdom community within the world of work are to be discerned [Stage 7], some guidelines as to the nature of a communal economy are essential, not least because no business, small or large, can be 'an island unto itself'. We need, therefore, to have some idea as to the ways in which a communal economy informs or calls into question the principles underpinning the market model which currently dominates the global scene. As Rowan Williams (2012) argues: 'The non-economist is bound to be intimidated by the complexity of what we confront, but, as has been said, "we are all economists now"; the specialists are not more conspicuously successful than others in mapping the territory, and this at least encourages some tentative proposals from the side lines, however broad and aspirational (p. 219)'.

In Stage 2, it was stated that a communal theology for the world of work needed to be grounded within some form of symbolic universe, 'a nexus of all-embracing communal values and the beliefs from which they are derived'. We contended that such a symbolic universe must give us 'a vision of community which is open not closed, inclusive not exclusive, universal and not circumscribed by culture, race, gender or nationality'. We argued that the Christian faith - notably through the images of Trinity and kingdom - offers us such a vision. What holds for a communal theology also holds for a communal economy. Consequently the main features of a communal economy described below are closely associated with the communal theology set out in Stage 2. The gifts of the kingdom community - life, liberation, love and learning - remain the hall-marks of both.

The project's description of what the economic characteristics of these gifts of the kingdom community might look like in practice draws largely, though not exclusively, on what has been called 'the rich heritage of Catholic Social Teaching' (*Our Best Kept Secret*, 2003). It is a heritage peculiar to the Roman Catholic Church, no other denomination having attempted such a comprehensive, coherent, in-depth and developmental approach to economic and work-related issues.

In the Appendix to Stage 2, we looked at the Catholic Social Teaching relating to 'the common good' and how that has helped to elucidate and enrich our *theological* understanding of the kingdom community. In this stage of the project we draw again on Catholic Social Teaching to help deepen our understanding of the *economic* characteristics of the kingdom community's four gifts.

Catholic Social Teaching is usually seen as beginning with Pope Leo XII's papal encyclical *Rerum Novarum* (The Condition of Labour), in 1891, and has been ongoing up to and including Pope Benedict's encyclical *Caritas in Veritate* (Charity in Truth) published in 2009. The teaching is exhaustively summarized and indexed in the *Compendium of the Social Doctrine of the Church* (2005). Even so, Catholics would be the first to accept that 'the Church has neither immediate nor universally valid solutions to all the complex and pressing problems of society' (*Our Best Kept Secret*, p. 8). Nor is 'the body of Catholic Social Teaching... a fixed set of tightly developed doctrine. Rather, it is a collection of key principles which has evolved in response to the challenges of the day' (p. 14). Its value to us lies in the identification of a number of such principles which, reflecting our 4Ls, help to elucidate the nature of a communal economy.

Reflections on a market economy

We live in an age in which economics has long since ousted theology as the queen of the sciences. In the words of Michael Sandel (2012), 'Economics has become an imperial domain' (p. 6). Like ivy taking over an ancient building, the all-pervasive growth of 'economics' has come about not by some clear-cut popular acclaim but by the slow and, at times, almost imperceptible colonization of previously dominant interpretations of the meaning of human existence (in Stage 2 we called these 'symbolic universes').

The current form which the sovereignty of economics assumes is that of global capitalism. Lesslie Newbigin brooks no compromise here (1980, p. 31). He writes:

> How can the church become a credible sign to all peoples of every kind, a sign of the kingship of God as it is set forth in the bible - a kingship which *offers* the fullness of life, peace, justice and holiness; and at the same time *requires* the total obedience of every creature?... I think the first implication (of any answer) must be a radical break with the ideology of capitalism. Our timid compromise with this ideology has persisted too long.

Graham Ward (2009) argues that, for all its achievements, global capitalism now holds us captive to two complementary myths. The first is the assumption that monetary value is the measure of 'reality'. He writes: 'Capitalism generates virtual realities… The reality of things and their value are screened from us by money and what the market will bear, creating a false consciousness' (p. 94). The second myth is the promise of salvation though economic globalization. Ward thinks that globalization colludes with capitalism in holding out the false hope of a new and harmonious universalism brought about by collective engagement in a worldwide market. He believes that we now live in a world where 'the dominance of economic relations distorts all social relations' (p. 94).

To the false nirvana that capitalism often offers must be added the abuses of the market that have been evident since the collapse of the banking system in 2008. Here we have not simply an economic model that is revealing inherent flaws, but the problems that arise when what the Skidelskys (2012) call 'an ethic of acquisitiveness' rules the roost. The abuse of lending and the failures still emerging, such as the libor-rigging scandal, have profoundly undermined trust. They have also played havoc with people's lives as the repossession of homes and long-term unemployment have come to dominate the recent experience of millions in the western world.

It is no surprise, therefore, that what many are searching for is an alternative economic model. Of late, there has emerged a consensus amongst a growing number of economists that any such alternative must address the issue of 'soaring inequality' as Polly Toynbee describes it (*The Guardian*, 2/5/14). Two books have led the way here, Richard Wilkinson's and Kate Pickett's *The Spirit Level* (2010) and Thomas Picketty's *Capital in the Twenty-first Century* (2014), though numerous other works have contributed to the debate. Picketty's book in particular documents historically the fact that where the rate of return on capital outstrips the rate of growth, inherited wealth, in the form of land, property or shares, will always grow faster than earned wealth. He believes that because of this inequality inevitably grows under an unfettered capitalism. Democracy as well as social justice are the victims. This situation, he argues, is ultimately unsustainable for society and world alike, both socially and economically. Picketty's analysis and suggestions for addressing this crisis are already being hotly debated but there is little doubt that the need for a new economic model, whether capitalism reformed or an alternative, is an issue which now has a powerful economic as well as ethical underpinning.

The Kingdom at Work Project is not in a position to pursue the economic debate which the explosion of the inequality of wealth, national and global, has kick-started. However, it can pin-point the ethical principles and values on which any economic model for the future needs to be founded. As noted above, the project believes that these are rooted in the communal theology set out in Stage 2, and are reflected in the Catholic concept of 'the common good' outlined at the end of that stage.

The common good and the business world

In their reflections on *The Common Good* (1996), the bishops of England and Wales seek to take a balanced view of the contribution of capitalism to the well-being of humankind. They state:

> No other system has so far shown itself superior in encouraging wealth creation and hence in advancing the prosperity of the community, and enabling poverty and hardship to be more generously relieved (para. 78).

The mechanisms of the market offer secure advantages: they help to utilize resources better, they promote the exchange of products, above all they give central place to the person's desires and preferences, which, in a contract, meet the desires and preferences of another person... Can it be said, after the failure of Communism, that capitalism is the victorious social system, and that capitalism should be the goal of the countries now making efforts to rebuild their economy and society? If by capitalism is meant an economic system which recognizes the fundamental and positive value of business, the market, private property and the resulting responsibility for the means of production, as well as free human creativity in the economic sector, then the answer is certainly in the affirmative... But if by capitalism is meant a system in which the economic sector is not circumscribed within a strong juridical framework, which does not place it at the service of human freedom in its totality, and which fails to see it as a particular aspect of that freedom, the core of which is ethical and religious, then the reply is certainly negative (Appendix 1, paras. 40 and 42).

The distinction has always to be kept in mind between a technical economic method and a total ideology or world view (para.79).

Catholic Social Teaching stresses that the danger for humankind lies not so much in this or that feature of capitalism, but in 'the concrete risk of an "idolatry" of the market' (*Compendium*, para. 349). It is a danger embodied in the frequent personification of the market, as when the media reports that the market (an anonymous yet apparently all-powerful persona) 'likes' or 'dislikes', 'gains' or 'loses confidence' in, is 'happy' or 'unhappy' with current economic developments. The personification, and at times deification of the market is made all the more destructive by the myths that such idolatry produces.

This is not to claim that the principles on which Catholic Social Teaching is based are self-evident truths or acceptable to all. In 1996, the Bishops of England Wales believed that 'the loss of confidence in the concept of the common good is one of the primary factors behind the national mood of pessimism' (*The Common Good*, para. 116). However, they also asserted that 'the political arena has to be reclaimed in the name of the common good.... (and that) the common good must be made to prevail, even against strong economic forces that would deny it' (para. 119).

More recently, an important report on the *Vocation of the Business Leader,* summarizing the findings of a consultation on that theme held at the Pontifical Council for Justice and Peace in the USA in 2011, has focused on the economic characteristics of the common good cashed out in terms of business as 'a community of persons'. The document states (para. 57):

> While the phrase 'community of persons' is not common in business literature today, it actually best expresses the full realization of what a company or corporation can be. The etymology of the words 'company' and 'companions' - *cum* (with), and *panis* (bread) suggests 'breaking bread together'. The etymology of the word 'corporation' - the Latin *corpus* (body) suggests a group of people united in one body.

The report continues (para. 58):

> Businesses are… essential to the common good of every society and to the whole global order (para. 35)… The purpose of business… is not simply to make a profit, but is found in its very existence as a *community of persons*… When we consider a business organization as a community of persons, it becomes clear that the bonds which hold us in common are not merely legal contracts or mutual self-interest, but commitments to real good, shared with others to serve the world.

Whilst Catholic Social Teaching recognizes that 'the demands of the common good are dependent on the social conditions of each historical period' (*Compendium*, para. 166), it maintains that the concept of the common good is reliant on a number of key principles. *Vocation of the Business Leader* (in the Foreword) sums up these principles as follows:

> Business leaders are called to engage the contemporary economic and financial world in the light of the principles of *human dignity* and *the common good*. This reflection offers business leaders, members of their institutions, and various stakeholders a set of practical principles that can guide them in their service of the common good. Among these principles, we recall the principle of meeting the needs of the world with goods which are truly good and which truly serve in a spirit of solidarity, the needs of the poor and the vulnerable; the principle of organising

work within enterprises in a manner which is respectful of human dignity; the principle of subsidiarity, which fosters a spirit of initiative and increases the competence of the employees - considered "co-entrepreneurs"; and, finally, the principle of sustainable creation of wealth and its just distribution among the various stakeholders.

Below, we explore how these principles inform the *economic* contribution of each of the gifts of the kingdom community to society. However, first we need to note a number of other principles of relevance to the nature of a communal economy, drawing both on material from Catholic Social Teaching and elsewhere.

Key principles informing a communal economy

The gift relationship

'If human relations are structured in a way that reflects the character of God's own giving, they should be marked by unconditional giving (over against)… the alternative principle of conditional giving that covers barter, commodity exchange, and debtor-creditor relations of all sorts', writes Kathryn Tanner (2005, p. 63). In short, a communal economy, which reflects the nature of the kingdom community, derives its meaning and nature from a gift relationship: the gifts or creation (life), of salvation (liberation), of incorporation (love) and of revelation (learning). Such an economy is based on the assumption that if 'the way God's giving is to be realized by us… is communal or common' (p. 74), then abundance not scarcity will be its hall-mark.

Inclusivity and universality

An important principle undergirding 'an economy of grace' (Tanner, 2005) is what Catholic Social Teaching calls 'the universal destination of goods' (*Compendium*, paras. 171-184). The latter's foundation is the conviction that 'God gave the earth to the whole human race for the sustenance of its members without excluding or favouring anyone' (para. 171). It is not surprising, therefore, that 'the unconditionality of God's giving implies the absolute inclusiveness of God's giving: God gives without restrictions to everyone and everything, for the benefit of all' (Tanner, p. 72). Consequently, 'In an increasingly globalized society, the common good and the effort to obtain it cannot fail to assume the dimension of the whole human family, that is to say, the community of peoples and nations' (*Caritas in Veritate*, p. 16). As Pope

Francis puts it: 'We… have to say "thou shalt not" to an economy of exclusion and inequality. Such an economy kills' (*The Joy of the Gospel*, 2013, para. 53). Indeed, 'the present scenarios of profound transformation of human work call even more urgently for an authentically global development in solidarity that is capable of involving every region of the world including those less advantaged' (*Compendium*, para. 321).

'Structures of sin'

Nevertheless, there are major obstacles which the model of a communal economy faces, termed by Catholic Social Teaching 'structures of sin'. One such 'structure' is what John Hughes describes as 'the idolatrous cult of work as the measure of all value' (p. 23). He argues that work has assumed this domination because of the triumph of what he calls 'utility', 'mere functionality, reducing humans to animals or machines, opposed to anything vital or transcendent' (p. 218). Over against work as utility, Hughes places work as art, interpreted 'as the gratuitous, intellectual, responsible, delightful creation of things that are beautiful, because they are useful *and* good, rather than merely useful' (p. 222). He believes that the artist is one of the best analogues we have for the divine labour of creation - gratuitous - loving - delightful - a form of play - integral to the inner Trinitarian life (Hughes pp. 225-226). From this perspective, a communal economy takes on the transcendent character of creativity not of utility.

The bishops of England and Wales see the structures of sin threatening society as 'the growing priority of technology over ethics…, the growing primacy of things over persons, and… the growing superiority of matter over spirit' (*The Common Good*, para. 118). They describe what they deem to be the necessary response as follows (para. 119):

> For these threats to be resisted, the political arena has to be reclaimed in the name of the common good. Public life needs rescuing from utilitarian expediency and the pursuit of self-interest. Society must not turn its back on poor people nor on the stranger at the gate. The twin principles of solidarity and subsidiarity need to be applied systematically to the reform of the institutions of public life. The protection of human rights must be reinforced, the mechanisms of democracy repaired, the integrity of the environment defended. The common good

must be made to prevail, even against strong economic forces that would deny it.

The gifts of the kingdom community

We next turn to explore ways in which Catholic Social Teaching, together with the writings of a number of other commentators, more specifically reflects and informs the nature of an economy based on the kingdom community's gifts of life, liberation, love and learning.

The gift of life

'The kingdom inaugurated by Christ perfects the original goodness of the created order and of human activity, which were compromised by sin,' quotes the *Compendium* (para. 325). Or, as we have argued [Stage 2], the kingdom community's gift of life transforms and transcends humanity's search for a sense of material and physical security. To further this process of transformation, God calls humankind 'to cultivate and care for creation' (para. 256). 'Work represents a fundamental dimension of human existence not only in the act of creation but also in that of redemption' (para. 263).

This does not mean that a sense of physical and material security is unimportant. 'Workers have rights which Catholic teaching has consistently maintained are superior to the rights of capital. These include the right to decent work, to just wages, to security of employment, to adequate rest and holidays, to limitation of hours of work, to health and safety protection, to non-discrimination, to form and join trade unions, and, as a last resort, to go on strike' (*The Common Good*, Appendix 1, para. 91). We return to some of these rights later.

Catholic Social Teaching sees work as having an objective (task) and subjective (relationship) dimension. The former is the 'contingent aspect of human activity, which varies in its expressions according to the changing technological, cultural, social and political conditions' (*Compendium*, para. 270). The latter is work's 'stable dimension... it does not depend on what people produce or on the type of activity they undertake, but only and exclusively on their dignity as human beings' (para. 270). 'The subjective dimension of work must take precedence over the objective dimension... (or) work loses its truest and most profound meaning... (and) work activity and the very technology employed... are transformed into enemies of (the worker's) dignity' (para. 271). In short, 'work is for man and not man for work' (para.

272). However, John Hughes argues that there is a danger of thinking 'that inhuman work need only be transformed subjectively' (p. 23) whereas the 'structures of sin' also need addressing at an objective (for example, managerial and social, global as well as local) level.

Consequently, life is about the good before it is about goods. 'The life of man… must not be reduced to its materialistic dimension, even if material goods are extremely necessary both for mere survival and for improving the quality of life (*Compendium*, para. 375). 'The common good embraces and supports all the goods needed to allow each human being and all human beings to develop, individually and communally' (*Vocation of the Business Leader*, para. 34).

The gift of life is likewise about needs before it is about wants. 'Needs (refer to)…the requirement of life or the good life… Wants (refer to)…a psychological phenomenon: they are "in the mind" of the wanter', write the Skildeskys (2012, p. 89). The problem is that 'having discarded the concept of the good life, modern economics can make no sense of the distinction between needs and wants' (p. 89). (If people become) slaves of 'possession and of immediate gratification… (they further) the so-called civilization of "consumption" or "consumerism"' (*Compendium*, para. 334). This makes humankind victims of what Pope John Paul II has termed 'inadmissable superdevelopment' which focuses attention upon the 'excessive availability of every kind of material goods for the benefit of a small segment of society globally' (*Best Kept Secret*, p. 30). 'Endless growth… is senseless' (Skildeskys, p. 7) and 'the unending pursuit of wealth is madness' (p. 8).

Catholic Social Teaching argues that fullness of life embraces the right to private property. However 'the right to private property is subordinated to the principle of the universal destination of goods' (para. 282) and to 'the right to common use, to the fact that goods are meant for everyone' (para. 177). At the same time 'the issue of ownership and use of new technologies and knowledge - which in our day constitute a particular form of property that is no less important than ownership of land or capital… must be placed in the context of legal norms and social rules that guarantee that they will be used according to the criteria of justice, equity and respect for human rights' (para. 283). Catholic Social Teaching adds that 'those people and societies that go so far as to absolutize the role of property end up experiencing the bitterest type of slavery' (para. 181).

On the issue of workplace wealth creation, 'the (Catholic) Church acknowledges the legitimate role of profit as an indicator that a business is functioning well' (*Vocation of Business* Leaders, para. 51). However, it warns that 'profit is a good servant, but it is a poor master' (para. 53). 'Accumulation by itself, even were it for the common good, is not a sufficient condition for bringing about authentic human happiness' (para. 334). 'It is essential that within a business the legitimate pursuit of profit should be in harmony with the irrenounceable protection of the dignity of the people who work at different levels in the same company' (para. 340). 'Any business that does not enhance its workers and serve the common good is a moral failure no matter how healthy its financial bottom line appears' (*Best Kept Secret*, p. 22). 'Once profit becomes an exclusive goal, if it is produced by improper means and without the common good as its ultimate end, it risks destroying wealth and creating poverty' (*Caritas in Veritate*, p. 39).

Finally, concerning the natural environment, Catholic Social Teaching states, '(Man) must not make arbitrary use of the earth, subjecting it without restraint to his will, as though it did not have its own requisites and a prior God-given purpose, which man can indeed develop but must not betray (*Compendium*, para. 460). 'Care for the environment represents a challenge for all of humanity. It is a matter of common and universal duty, that of respecting a common good' (para. 466). 'Responsibility for the environment... is (one) that present generations have towards those of the future' (para. 467). 'A correct understanding of the environment prevents the utilitarian reduction of nature to a mere object to be manipulated and exploited. At the same time, it must not absolutize nature and place it above the dignity of the human person' (para. 463).

The gift of liberation

Though the world of work has been offered the kingdom community's gift of life, it has often exploited, misused and neglected it. As a consequence, argues John Hughes (2007, p. 229), 'Our work, and indeed our entire economy, stand under judgment. Everyone at every level, is responsible for these things, and cannot evade accountability for them: workers, employers, managers, traders, consumers, share-holders, legislators; however much the structures of our particular society may lead us to feel bereft of this responsibility in the face of implacable systems and 'necessary' courses of action'.

Catholic Social Teaching believes that one of the major casualties of this situation is the destruction of human dignity. 'The dignity of each human person and the pursuit of the common good are concerns which ought to shape all economic policies,' states Pope Francis (*The Joy of the Gospel*, 2013, para. 203). 'The economy exists for the human person, not the other way round' (*The Common Good*, para. 111). However, 'if the whole structure and organization of an economic system is such as to compromise human dignity, to lessen a man's sense of responsibility or rob him of opportunity for exercising personal initiative, then such a system… is altogether unjust' (*Vocation of the Business Leader*, para. 46). 'Labour… is not a mere commodity. On the contrary, the worker's human dignity in it must be recognised. It therefore cannot be bought and sold as a commodity' (*The Common Good*, Appendix 1 para. 83). The gift of liberation is about enabling people, individually and collectively, to reclaim and express their God-given dignity.

Personal liberation

'The proper exercise of personal freedom requires specific conditions of an economic, social, juridic, political and cultural order that are too often disregarded or violated… Removing injustices promotes human freedom and dignity', states the *Compensium* (para. 137). One such injustice is unemployment. 'The obligation to earn one's bread by the sweat of one's brow also presumes the right to do so. A society in which this right is systematically denied, in which economic policies do not allow workers to reach satisfactory levels of employment, cannot be justified from an ethical point of view' (*The Common Good*, Appendix 1, para. 43). There is need for liberation not only from 'the many pockets of non-work, concealed work, child labour, underpaid work, exploitation of workers… but also (from)… over-working, (from) work-as-a-career that often takes on more importance than other human and necessary aspects, (from) excessive demands of work that makes family life unstable and sometimes impossible, (from) a modular structure to work that entails the risk of serious repercussions on the unitary perception of one's own existence and the stability of family relationships' (Compendium, para. 280). As one means of liberation, Catholic Social Teaching urges the need for a minimum wage (*The Common Good*, para. 97), though there is currently growing pressure for the payment of a *living* wage.

'When people work, they do not simply make more, they become more' (*Vocation of the Business* Leader, para. 45). Liberation lays on people the responsibility to use their freedom to further the common good. 'By his work and industriousness, man... summons the social and community energies that increase the common good, above all to the benefit of those who are neediest' (*Compendium*, para. 266).

Collective liberation

'Economic freedom is only one element of human freedom. When it becomes autonomous, when man is seen more as a producer or consumer of goods than as a subject who produces and consumes in order to live, then economic freedom loses its necessary relationship to the human person and ends up by alienating and oppressing him' (para. 350). One of the consequences is that 'unlimited free markets tend to produce what is in effect an "option against the poor" ' (*The Common Good*, para. 85). However, 'in and of itself, the market is not and must not become, the place where the strong subdue the weak' (*Caritas in Veritate*, p. 71). Pope Francis stresses the option *for* the poor with equal conviction (*The Joy of the Gospel*, 2013, para. 202):

> As long as the problems of the poor are not radically resolved by rejecting the absolute autonomy of markets and financial speculation and by attacking the structural causes of inequality, no solution will be found for the world's problems or, for that matter, to any problems. Inequality is the root of social ills.

When market forces take on an oppressive character, they may well lead to protests and strikes. 'The Church's social doctrine recognizes the legitimacy of striking... (but only) when every other method for the resolution of disputes has been ineffectual' (*Compendium*, para. 304). However, its teaching also states that 'it is unfair for those taking part in an industrial dispute to use the inflicting of hardship or serious inconvenience on... third parties as deliberate tactics' (*The Common Good*, para. 96). Protests and strikes are seen as 'morally unacceptable when accompanied by violence, or when objectives are included that are not directly linked to working conditions or are contrary to the common good' (para. 304).

Collective liberation is seen as bringing to the fore the requirement that organizations and institutions within the world of work put justice, reconciliation and peace, locally and globally, at the top of their agendas. 'Businesses that produce goods which are truly good and services which truly serve contribute to the common good' (*Vocation of the Business Leader*, p. 17)

The gift of love

'Helpless alone and gifted in relationship: this is where we start addressing the world of economics from a Christian standpoint,' states Rowan Williams (2012, p. 229). 'An inherent characteristic of work is that it first and foremost unites people. Therein lies its social power; the power to build community. This understanding helps avoid the spiritual poverty which often arises in market economies from lack of human relationships within and around a business' (*Vocation of the Business Leader*, para. 58). At the heart of those relationships is the gift of love which 'must be present and permeate every social relationship' (*Compendium*, para. 591). Thus 'a business enterprise must be a community of solidarity, that is not closed within its own company interests' (para. 340). On the wider scale, 'the challenge… is to ensure a globalization in solidarity, a globalization without marginalization' (para. 363).

A communal economy embracing the gift of love embraces a range of virtues. Catholic Social Teaching identifies a number of these as follows:

> 'In commercial relationships the principle of gratuitiousness and the logic of gift as an expression of fraternity can and must find their place within normal economic activity' (*Caritas in Veritate*, p. 73). 'Without gratuitiousness, there can be no social justice' (p. 76).

> 'The economic well-being of a country is not measured exclusively by the quantity of goods it produces but also by… the level of equity in distribution' (*Compendium*, para. 303). 'Looking after the common good means making use of the new opportunities for the redistribution of wealth among the different areas of the planet, to the benefit of the underprivileged that until now have been excluded or cast to the sidelines of social and economic progress' (*Compendium*, para. 363).

> 'Without internal forms of solidarity and mutual trust, the market cannot completely fulfil its proper economic function' (p. 70).

The gift of love necessitates there being an 'increasing awareness of the need for greater social responsibility on the part of business' (*Caritas in Veritate*, p. 79). Once again, the plight of the most vulnerable comes to the fore. 'When we consider a business organization as a community of persons, it becomes clear that the bonds which hold us in common are not merely legal contracts or mutual self-interests, but commitments to real goods, shared with others to serve the world' (*Vocation of the Business Leader*, para.58). Thus, '(we need) businesses (that) maintain solidarity with the poor by being alert for opportunities to serve otherwise deprived and underserved populations and people in need' (p. 17).

As an expression of the gift of love, Catholic Social Teaching frequently stresses the importance of co-operation and partnership. 'The right ordering of economic life cannot be left to a free competition of forces... Free competition, while justified and certainly useful provided it is kept within limits, clearly cannot direct economic life...' (*The Common Good*, Appendix 1, para. 88). 'The common good... involves all members of society, no one is exempt from co-operating, according to each one's possibilities, in attaining it and developing it' (*Compendium* para. 167). Finally: 'The Church's social doctrine teaches that relations within the world of work must be marked by cooperation: hatred and attempts to eliminate the other are completely unacceptable' (para. 306).

The gift of learning

Catholic Social Teaching recognizes that we are moving into an age in which knowledge is a key economic variable. 'Whereas at one time the decisive factor of production was the land, and later capital - understood as a total complex of the instruments of production - today the decisive factor is increasingly man himself, that is his knowledge, especially his scientific knowledge, his capacity for interrelated and compact organization, as well as his ability to perceive the needs others and to satisfy them,' states *Vocation of the Business Leader* (para. 44).

In Catholic Social Teaching the concept of 'development' is one closely associated with learning, both individual and collective. *Choosing the Common Good* (p. 9) states:

> The fulfilment which the common good seeks to serve is the flourishing of humanity, expressed in the phrase 'integral human development'... Such development requires... the opportunities for education. Development must always include... spiritual growth, with openness to God... Every person is called to develop and fulfil themselves, for life itself is

a vocation, a summons which finds its fulfilment only in the mystery of God.

Caritas in Veritate adds that 'the development of individuals and peoples...requires new eyes and a new heart, capable of rising above a materialistic vision of human events, capable of glimpsing in development the "beyond" that technology cannot give. By following this path it is possible to pursue (the kind of) integral human development that takes its direction from the driving force of charity in truth' (p. 152).

On a collective level, *Caritas in Veritate* argues that 'economically developed or emerging countries export (a) reductive vision of the person, and his destiny to poor countries. This is the damage that "super-development" causes to authentic development when it is accompanied by "moral underdevelopment" ' (p. 57). What is required for authentic human development is a synthesis of the 'social, cultural and spiritual' and an end to 'the excessive segmentation of knowledge' (p. 60). Such 'development must include not just material but also spiritual growth, since the human person is a "unity of body and soul" ' (p. 150).

The *Vocation of the Business Leader* is particularly concerned with the development of the business community as such. It states that 'to live out their vocation as faithful stewards to their calling, business people need to be formed in a religious culture which shows them the possibilities and promise of the good they can do and which they ought to do - the good which is distinctively theirs' (para. 83). It believes that (para. 85):

> An education in business... does not merely constitute training in specific skills and theories. Faithful to its own tradition, Catholic higher education cannot fail to be a formation in the moral teaching and social principles of the Church and the dimensions of prudence and justice proper to business. A proper business education includes all appropriate theoretical material, training in every relevant skill and a thorough treatment of the moral teaching and social principles of the Church which must animate professional practice. Exaggerated emphasis in one of these areas cannot compensate for the neglect in another.

That report concludes that Catholic business education must seek 'a unity of knowledge and a rich dialogue between faith and reason, which provides the resources to meet the modern challenges found in business and the wider culture' (para. 84).

People without work

To give some clear boundaries to the Kingdom at Work Project we have defined work as paid employment [Introduction]. However, we are only too well aware, not least in the present economic recession, that an increasing number of people, in particular the young, are not able to find employment of any kind. We have touched on unemployment above in the section on the gift of liberation. Here we want to emphasize that Catholic Social Teaching is quite clear (*Compendium*. para. 287).

> Work is a fundamental right and a good for mankind, a useful good worthy of man because it is an appropriate way for him to give expression to and enhance his human dignity. The Church teaches the value of work not only because it is always something that belongs to the person but also because of its nature it is something necessary.... The Church cannot fail to indicate unemployment as a real social disaster, above all with regard to the younger generation.

Other Christian commentators on the economic scene affirm this view, one with which the Kingdom at Work Project fully concurs. Matthew Fox (1994) writes: 'Unemployment is not natural to the universe; it contradicts cosmic laws... The results of lack of work are spiritually devastating. When people lack work they lack pride; they lack an opportunity to return their unique gift to the community... When people lack work, they also lack hope. The resulting despair eats into a community like an evil spirit...' (pp. 59 and 9-10). Shipley Brayshaw in *Quaker Faith and Practice* (2005) writes in a similar vein: 'Unemployment is in truth an astonishing evil and calm acquiescence therein is discreditable... Poverty caused by enforced idleness, and in the presence of plenty, is so glaring an injustice that no man should accept it tamely' (23.69).

In 1997, the Council of Churches for Britain and Ireland, published an inquiry into *Unemployment and the Future of Work*. The introduction to that report states (p. 3):

Christians go back to the biblical description of men and women as 'made in the image of God'. This points to humanity's being endowed with a sacred and indestructible dignity and with stewardship of a world that God himself saw 'was good'. All humans have the potential for creativity, responsibility and love; none may ever be treated as disposable, menial or unwanted. This is to say, among other things, that the economy is there to serve human beings, not human beings to serve the economy'.

In 2011, the Work Foundation issued a report on *Good Work and Our Times*. In it redundancy was described as 'on the level of bereavement' and 'a cause of personal and social malaise' (pp. 71-72).

This is not to say that access to the gifts of the kingdom community are unavailable to those out of work or engaged in unpaid work, such as homemakers or carers. There are numerous communities of character of which people can become members other than those which constitute the world of work. However, for many the workplace remains that context within which they gain their strongest sense of purpose, fulfilment, dignity and colleagueship (Bunting, 2005, pp. 112-115). Indeed, Melissa Gregg (2011) argues that for some people work appears to have become more important than even their family (pp. 130-134).

Though the determination to be rid of unemployment may not always appear to be to the fore within society at large, many Christian writers argue that work is an essential aspect of what makes us human. Any response to unemployment needs to be at both a theological and practical level. From a theological perspective, Kathryn Tanner (2005) argues that if Christian faith is to challenge a market dominated philosophy which brings massive injustice in terms of wealth and poverty, it needs to espouse 'an economy of grace' which is not determined by an assumption that resources are scarce and need to be hoarded, but that they are in fact abundant and can sustain the whole of humankind if fairly shared. As already noted, she sees the latter approach to economics as reflecting the grace of a God whose giving is unconditional (pp. 63ff), universal (pp. 72ff) and non-competitive (pp. 75ff).

Tanner believes that unemployment in practice denies men and women the universal human right to access the gracious generosity of the Trinity, which we identify in this project as the kingdom community's gifts of life, liberation, love and learning. As Catholic Social Teaching puts it: 'The high level of unemployment... (is) a huge obstacle on the road to human and professional fulfilment... Those who are unemployed or underemployed suffer the profound negative consequences that such a situation creates in a personality and they run the risk of being marginalized within a society, of becoming victims of social exclusion' (*Compendium*, para. 289). We would contend that unemployment not only obstructs the natural way in which people can experience, participate in and share God's life-giving generosity on an economic level (one aspect of the gift of life), but makes it extremely difficult for them to retain a sense of significance and fulfilment (the gift of liberation), be members of a caring and supportive group (the gift of love) and engage with their fellows in the all-important journey of spiritual discovery (the gift of learning).

Stage 5

A communal model of institutions - Christian and secular

A communal theology, spirituality and economy cannot exist as separate or disembodied entities. They need communal forms and structures to give them meaning, purpose and relevance. In Stage 5 of the project, therefore, we look at the way in which the key components of a communal theology, spirituality and economy discussed in Stages 2, 3 and 4 form the foundations for the emergence of a communal model of institutions - Christian *and* secular - which embody the gifts of the kingdom community.

A diaconal church

What form of church, and thus of ecclesiology is required to further the Kingdom at Work Project's purpose of enabling Christians to create workplaces transformed by the gifts of the kingdom community? The ecclesiology we are looking for will be one which enables the church to further that end in two ways. First, it will be an ecclesiology which offers *a model* for any institution, sacred *or* secular, which seeks to give expression to the gifts of the kingdom community. This is because the ultimate purpose of *all* institutions is to become communities of character [Stage 1]. Secondly, it will be an ecclesiology which enables and equips the church to become *a medium of transformation*, not least within the world of work.

The church as servant of the kingdom community

This project is based on the belief that any church seeking to build a world transformed by the gifts of the kingdom community must, first and foremost, be a servant or *'diaconal'* church[1]. Hendrik Kraemer (2005), a lay Dutch Reformed theologian, believes that 'theologians, ministers and laity... need to place their task and vocation under the

---

[1] I have written at length elsewhere about the nature of the diaconal church (Clark 2005, 2008 and 2010). See also Hendrik Kraemer on the diaconal church (2005, pp. 127-188). For some key features of the diaconal church see Appendix 1 at the end of this stage of the project.

light of that profound, revolutionary word; *diakonia*, which is not a merely ethical, humanitarian category but rather the deepest religious category, which lies at the bottom of the Gospel' (p. 187).

Here it is necessary to distinguish between two closely related but different understandings of 'servanthood': servanthood as 'service'; and servanthood as what it means to be a 'servant'. Service is an essential aspect of servanthood. Compassion and care for others are an integral part of a servant ministry and the life of the servant church. Service embodies love for God and love for neighbour in a way that can be seen and responded to by a world that challenges the credibility of any church which does not practice what it preaches. However, the concept of service does not get to the heart of the meaning of servanthood and of the nature of the church as a diaconal church.

Service is primarily action-focused. Being a servant is primarily relationship-centred. The meaning of being a servant is derived from who is served. *The hall-mark of the diaconal church is that it is the servant of the kingdom community and of the Trinitarian God who is sovereign over that kingdom*. The diaconal church is a servant of God as Creator, a servant of Christ as Liberator and a servant of the Spirit as Unifier: in short, a servant of One God in three Persons. However, it is also a servant of the world, and thus of the world of work, which God has created and loves.

Jim Wallis writes (2013, pp. 22 and 24):

> The Christian mission is to proclaim and live the kingdom of God... Christians are not committed to the kingdom of any culture, class, or racial group, or to the kingdom of America or any other nation-state, or even to the kingdom of any church, but rather to the kingdom of God. That kingdom turns all other kingdoms on their head, brings forth the unexpected, and breaks open the unpredictable. We are called to show people how to love God and their neighbours and thereby bring new hope to lives, neighbourhoods, nations and the world.

Being a servant of the kingdom community is no light responsibility. At its most demanding its nature is seen in the image of the suffering servant in Isaiah (40-55) and expressed in the life and death of Christ. In *The Politics of Discipleship*, Graham Ward (2009, p. 291) states that 'the cross is the scepter and the sword of (the) newly established kingdom'.

At the same time, the servant church is endowed with the power of the Trinity to fulfil its calling. This is not a coercive form of power. It is the power of redemptive love. As John Collins (2002, p. 39) puts it, all the sayings of Jesus on the matter of the first and the last, the great and the lowly, are teaching his followers that 'the kingdom of God establishes itself in a community of relationships' undistorted by the misuse of power. Rowan Williams (2012) affirms this viewpoint (pp. 305-306):

> The Church is… the trustee of a vision that is radical and universal, the vision of a social order that is without fear, oppression, the violence of exclusion and the search for scapegoats because it is one where each recognizes their dependence on all and each is seen as having an irreplaceable gift for all. The Church cannot begin to claim that it consistently lives by this; its failure is all too visible, century-by-century. But its credibility does not hang on its unbroken success; only on its continued willingness to be judged by what it announces and points to, the non-competitive, non-violent order of God's realm, centred upon Jesus and accessible through commitment to him.

The diaconal church - a monastic model

'The Church did not enter the world as an institution, but as a community expecting the Kingdom of God', writes Kraemer (2005, p. 126). It is not surprising, therefore, that the diaconal church, as the servant of the kingdom community, reflects the shape of a monastic rather than a Christendom model of church (Clark, 2005 and 2008). It is the monastic model which is to the fore in the case of Celtic Christianity, the Society of Jesus, the early Methodists and the Quakers, all of whose spirituality adds depth to the hall-marks of the kingdom community [Stage 3].

The life of the Celtic monasteries centred round prayer, study and manual labour. They saw worship, learning and work as integral parts of a larger whole. The monasteries also had a key role as springboards for mission, with monks and lay brothers going out in twos and threes to establish what Columba called 'colonies of heaven' (Bradley, 1993, p. 74), or, as we would put it, 'colonies of the kingdom community'. Many of these features still resonate with the ecclesiology of the diaconal church and with its mission of communal transformation.

Though monasteries in the Celtic era varied enormously in size and composition, many were a focus for informal networks of interdependent and interconnected Christian groups beyond their boundaries. As such, the monastery was 'a place of endless coming and going' (de Waal, p. 144), offering meeting points and a resource base for the plethora of scattered 'congregations' which they served. Many monastic centres, such as Iona and Lindisfarne, became influential symbolic places and their leaders, like Columba and Cuthbert, symbolic figures, enhancing a sense of community for those associated with them however dispersed.

Ecclesiological forms

I have argued elsewhere that those forms of the diaconal church most likely to be expressive of the gifts of the kingdom community are the communal group, the network, the hearing, symbolic places, events and people, the communal institution and partnerships (Clark, 2005, pp. 85-101). Here the focus is on three of these, the communal group, the network and partnerships, as of particular importance for the life of the diaconal church and the communal transformation of the world of work.

The communal group

The communal group has been a vital expression of the life and work of the church since its inception. Not only was it foundational in the mission and ministry of the early church, but has been the mainspring for innumerable revivals of the Christian faith throughout history. It is no surprise, therefore, that the communal group has been particularly noteworthy in Celtic Christianity, in the later development of religious orders, in the early days of Quakerism and in the origins of Methodism.

However, it must be stressed that not every group is a communal group. If we had time to explore church history, we would find many instances of groups that were exclusive and closed, distorted the church's understanding of its call to be the servant of the kingdom community and skewed attempts at Christian renewal.

It is the group as a *communal* group which forms the collective foundation of the diaconal church. Within the latter, every group has the hall-marks of 'a kingdom community group'. It is a small but powerful community of character through which the kingdom community's gifts of life, liberation, and love are made manifest. It is also a mini learning community pursuing a journey of spiritual discovery and in that undertaking is always open to learning from others.

The communal group is a key resource for furthering the mission of the diaconal church within *and* beyond the local neighbourhood (Clark, 2010, pp. 198-199). However, the communal group is neither confined to a particular place, such as the parish, nor to a particular organization, such as the institutional church. Its communal potential lies in the fact that it is ubiquitous, able to draw Christians and others together wherever they live or work, and whatever their interests.

The network

The network is also an important structural component of the life and mission of the diaconal church. Like the communal group, the network (though not known by that name) has been seminal in the history of the church. Travelling evangelists and preachers established and sustained communal networks from the days of the early church onwards. Celtic Christianity, the religious orders, as well as the early years of the Society of Friends and of Methodism, from which we can learn so much about a communal spirituality [Stage 3], were notable for the deployment of itinerant evangelists, preachers and ministers who created and serviced those networks.

The diaconal church embraces the network as pre-eminently a means of linking communities of character of diverse kinds and sizes. It is also a means of connecting Christians as individuals. This is particularly important where the mission of the laity as the church dispersed throughout society is concerned, not least within the world of work. The network enables lay people to share their experiences, insights and skills and makes resources available that would not otherwise be accessible to them.

With the development of information technology, the network has come to the fore as an extremely potent means of communication. Networking now has the potential to provide lay people within the world of work with a 'virtual' faith community when they might otherwise find themselves in isolated and lonely situations. In a political context Paul Mason (2011) comments: 'The more people who use the network, the more useful it becomes to each user' (p. 74). It is clear that this burgeoning networking phenomenon will play an increasingly significant role in enabling lay people at work to link up, learn from one another and promote intervention for change.

Partnerships

Strategies and structures to foster partnerships and collaboration are central to the life and work of the diaconal church. As the servant of the kingdom community, the diaconal church is founded on and shaped by an ecumenical imperative. At the same time, the diaconal church sees mission in the workplace as a partnership not only of Christians but involving all those who have similar concerns, even if espousing other faiths and convictions. Mission within the world of work thus becomes an undertaking which engages Christian and non-Christian in a 'mutual embrace', one in which the skills and resources of every individual or collective are valued and employed for the communal transformation of the workplace.

The liberation of the laity

Whose responsibility is the transformational task of the servant church within the world of work? 'The ministry of the people of God in the world is both the primary and the normative ministry of the Church', states the Methodist document *Called to Love and Praise* (1999, 4.5.4). This is also the credo of the diaconal church.

It is a viewpoint taken many decades ago by Yves Congar in his seminal book of 1957 on the place of the laity in the Roman Catholic Church. In *Lumen Gentium*, Vatican II's Dogmatic Constitution on the Church, it is the laity not the hierarchy who are given primacy of place in the mission of the church (Larive, 2004, p. 66). The same viewpoint is argued with some passion by Hendrik Kraemer in his influential book, *A Theology of the Laity*, published in 1958. Kraemer writes (2005): 'The responsible participation of the laity in the discharge of the Church's divine calling is not primarily a matter of idealism and enthusiasm or organizational efficiency, but a new grasp of and commitment to the meaning of God's redemptive purpose with man and with the world' (p. 91). Trevor Beeson (2013, p. 209), reflecting on the ministry of the Church of England over recent decades, writes:

> It must remain the case that the overwhelming responsibility for Christian prophecy in society lies with those of the laity who are involved daily in making decisions that affect, for better or for

worse, the quality of personal and community life. The need for such prophetic ministries cannot be open to doubt.

Nevertheless, since the post-war era little has changed to weaken the hold of clericalism and the way in which it undermines the role of the laity in mission, in particular within the world of work (Clark, 2005, pp. 80-81). Clericalism is defined by Paul Stevens (1999) as 'the domination of the "ordinary" people by those ordained, trained and invested with privilege and power' (p. 52). It creates a 'division between clergy and laity (that) undervalues the lay lifestyle, lay talent, lay leadership, lay experience and lay spirituality' (Lakeland, 2003, p. 195). Margaret Whipp writes: 'As clergy themselves become more totally absorbed in the "ecclesiastical show", they slowly veer towards a *skewed ecclesiology* which forgets to recognize the importance of the church in its daily dispersion. When the operative ecclesiology becomes Sunday-centred, the church is only seriously legitimated in its gathered form where Christians come together for worship and study, prayer and fellowship' (2008, p. 180). If the world of work is to be transformed by the gifts of the kingdom community, the laity must be liberated from the domination of clericalism and the assumption that the church in its gathered form is all-important.

Nevertheless, the Kingdom at Work Project contends that, once free of clericalism, the ordained ministry has a key part to play in equipping lay people to engage more effectively in the communal transformation of the workplace. Hendrik Kraemer (2005) argues that 'the main part of the ministry of the clergy should be to enable the laity to fulfil their peculiar, inalienable ministry' (p. 167). Fulfilling this enabling and educational role is important for ministers of local congregations, as well as for chaplains and ministers in secular employment. I return to the role of the ordained ministry within the diaconal church when considering the meaning of servant leadership at the end of this stage and in Stages 9 to 11.

The church gathered and dispersed

Two forms of the diaconal model of church are essential for the fulfilment of its life and work: being *a gathered church* and being *a dispersed church*. By the gathered church is meant the people of God as servants of the kingdom community gathered to worship, learn, care for one another and enjoy each other's company. By the dispersed church, is meant the people of God dispersed throughout society to serve the kingdom community by building communities that manifest its gifts, wherever they live, work or play.

One of the most crippling weaknesses of the Christendom model of church is that church leaders are poorly equipped to serve the laity as the people of God in the world, particularly in the world of work. This is an all-pervasive deficit and one that I believe has led in large part to the church's marginalization in this day and age. Within the diaconal church, one cohort of church leaders would be concerned with equipping the gathered Christian community to give expression to the gifts of the kingdom community. Another cohort would be designated and trained to help equip the laity dispersed for mission in the wider world. In addition, the diaconal church would encompass a form of leadership which undertook an intermediary role enabling leaders of the church gathered and the church dispersed to complement, learn from and resource one another (Clark, 2005, pp. 110-123). Within the diaconal church, leaders undertaking these roles would be both women and men.

The church and the world of work - 'two cultures'

The diaconal church is not yet a reality. Thus it is little wonder that the mission and ministry of Christians is made particularly difficult by the fact that the still tenacious culture of a Christendom model of church and the culture of the workplace remain, literally, 'worlds apart'. Lois Green, at the time of writing working as a lecturer in information technology, highlights this dissonance in a paper entitled 'The Two Cultures' (1997, pp. 66-67). She states:

> At work I am called upon to be innovative, creative and
>   participative; at church to be passive, conforming and controlled.
> At work I am required to identify my strengths and seek
>   recognition; at church to confess my weakness and claim
>   forgiveness.
> At work there is often conflict, if not always of the aggressive kind;
>   at church conflict is denied or suppressed.
> At work the role of the professional is being severely questioned; at
>   church professionals are imbued with almost mystical powers.
> Work demands intense periods of intellectual and/or physical
>   activity; church places emphasis on being rather than doing, on
>   silence, contemplation and reflection.

Work puts a value on logical thought convincingly articulated; the spiritual life has a point at which logic must cease and words are shown to be the dangerous things they are.

Work demands 'performance measures' and is concerned with 'outcomes'; church puts emphasis on doing one's best and leaving the outcome to God.

Of course there are jobs which require quiet reflection, some bureaucratic work environments, and some enterprising churches. But my main point is that the culture of the church and the culture of working life are so different as to create a barrier which few are motivated to remove.

Such 'cultural dissonance' presents lay people with the very difficult task of retaining a faithful Christian identity and pursuing an effective Christian ministry within the workplace (Whipp, 2008, pp. 35-51). Margaret Whipp (p. 39) suggests four ways in which this form of ministry has been approached, as set out in *Diagram 5*.

Diagram 5

Forms of engagement

COMPARTMENTALIZED	AGONISTIC
WORK and **CHURCH** culture and identity are expressed in mutual exclusion	**CHURCH** culture and identity resists expression of **WORK** culture and identity
ASSIMILATED	INTEGRATED
WORK culture and identity resists expression of **CHURCH** culture and identity	**CHURCH** and **WORK** culture and identity are expressed in mutual embrace

Whipp (p. 39) comments:

I have named... as a sin of broken relationship and failed communion the 'compartmentalized' position which refuses to build a bridge between the worlds of work and worship. I also maintain that it is equally inadequate for Christians to resist the integration of identities-in-tension through practical strategies which are either 'agonistic' (where the significance of working identity is disrespected or denied) or 'assimilated' (where the significance of worshipping identity is disrespected or denied).

She concludes: 'A constructive Christian response to the challenge and discomfort of plural roles and cultural identities cannot lie in exclusion and denial but in integration and embrace' (pp. 38-39).

Theological commitment to 'a mutual embrace', Whipp's 'integrated' form of engagement, is imperative. The communal theology for the world of work described in Stage 2 sets the stage for a true encounter between Christians and their colleagues. Christians in the workplace should be engaged in taking a stance which validates both sacred *and* secular territories. At the same time, John Hull urges the need to discover 'holy ground' (Clark, 2005, p. 88), a meeting place where genuine engagement and dialogue can flourish [Stage 8(3)].

The diaconal church - a model for all institutions

God calls not only his church but also his world to manifest the gifts of the kingdom community. *Because the diaconal church acknowledges that it is the servant of the kingdom community, it has the potential and the responsibility to become a model for every institution, sacred or secular.* This includes all organizations engaged in the world of work. Becoming such a model is the diaconal church's great privilege, as well as daunting responsibility (see Clark 2005, pp. 128-129; 2008a, pp. 199-211).[1]

Consequently, the stance, collective forms, mode of communication, membership and leadership of all institutions needed to create a world that manifests the gifts of the kingdom community will reflect the stance, collective forms, mode of communication, membership and leadership of the diaconal model of church set out above. Only when this transformation happens will we be able to say that we are living in a diaconal world; a global community of character whose understanding of community is informed and enriched by the Christian images of the Trinity and the kingdom whose expression is God's inclusive and universal gifts of life, liberation, love and learning.

---

[1] For key features of Christian or secular diaconal institutions see Appendix 2 at the end of this stage of the project.

In a diaconal world, all institutions, sacred and secular, would embrace the stance of servants of humankind, if not explicitly of servants of the kingdom community. The diaconal institution would create and sustain communal groups, networks, partnerships and forms of leadership of the sort discussed above. Its mode of communication would be dialogical [Stage 8(3)]. Membership (employees) of the institution, at all levels, would be regarded as the latter's key asset, their experience, insights and skills seen as an indispensable human resource. All would be encouraged to become community builders within the life and work of their organizations, institutions and wider society.

Within the diaconal institution, leadership roles would be similar to the leadership roles within the diaconal church. That of servant leader would be pre-eminent.[1] So important is this manifestation of the gifts of the kingdom community that special attention is given below to the nature of such leadership.

Servant leadership

A theology and spirituality of community lead to all institutions being diaconal in nature and servants of the kingdom community. Their leaders must likewise be servants of that community. Servant leadership in church *or* world consists of six complementary roles each embodying one or more of the gifts of the kingdom community. These roles are depicted in *Diagram 6*.

---

[1] How Roman Catholic Social Teaching elucidates the role of servant leader within the business world is discussed in Appendix 3 to this stage of the project. We leave until Stages 9 to 11 of the project consideration of more practical ways in which church leaders can equip lay people for their ministry in the world of work.

Diagram 6

The servant leader

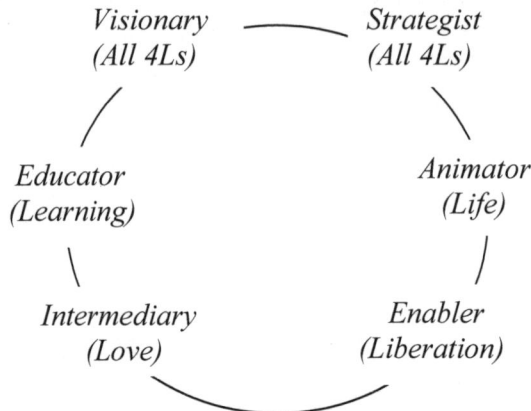

Visionary ——— Strategist
(All 4Ls)   (All 4Ls)

Educator   Animator
(Learning)   (Life)

Intermediary   Enabler
(Love)   (Liberation)

Visionary (All 4Ls)

The servant leader is a visionary who seeks to offer insights into the nature and form of a church *and* world transformed by the kingdom community's gifts of *life, liberation, love and learning*. He or she has the ability to communicate that vision to and inspire others, by example and word. At the same time, the servant leader as visionary seeks to foster others' visions of a church and world transformed, encourages them to share these visions and to reflect on their practical significance.

Strategist (All 4Ls)

The servant leader is a strategist who has the competence to turn visions of a church *and* world transformed by any or *all of the 4Ls* into reality. The role of strategist has much in common with that of 'the designer', a role identified by Peter Senge as essential for the creation of learning organizations (1990, pp. 341-345). The strategist can be described as an 'organizational architect' (p. 343), a person who has the ability to enable visions, values and purposes to inform and shape every aspect of the life and work of the institution concerned, not least in how it can engage effectively with the wider world. Strategists have the ability to discern when the time is right to intervene. They have a clear overview of how social collectives operate and of how change might be brought about. They know where resources, human and otherwise, are to be found and how these might be best employed. The strategist does not raise false hopes or lead people up blind alleys.

114

Animator *(Life)*

The servant leader is an animator who seeks to create a church *and* world that manifest the kingdom community's *gift of life*. The role of animator is, literally, one which animates - it brings the church and secular institutions to life. It is a role which encourages innovation, creativity and risk-taking. The leader as animator inspires people to bring energy and commitment to their task. The animator generates a culture of enthusiasm and enjoyment. He or she fosters respect for the natural environment and concern for the preservation of the planet.

Enabler *(Liberation)*

The servant leader is an enabler who endeavours to bring into being a church *and* world that manifest the kingdom community's *gift of liberation*. The enabler is an attentive listener. He or she looks for the best in their colleagues, as fellow workers and as people. Enablers are concerned with helping people free themselves *from* over dependence on others, not least those who are enablers. They seek to bring release to those held captive by fear, failure and guilt. They strive to free people *for* communal transformation by helping them to employ their insights, skills, and abilities for the redemption and renewal of every social collective. The servant leader as enabler has the ability to stand aside once the person or collective with which they are engaged is able 'to go it alone'.

Intermediary *(Love)*

The servant leader is an intermediary whose task is to create a church *and* world that manifest the kingdom community's *gift of love*. The intermediary builds new and creative connections between person and person, collective and collective. He or she is actively concerned with how experiences, insights and resources can be enhanced and enriched through formal and informal exchanges and sharing. The intermediary plays an active part in resolving conflicts and disagreements, where necessary exercising the skills of reconciler, mediator or negotiator. The leader as intermediary has the ability to draw people together into creative and supportive communities of character and of practice (Wenger, 1998 and 2002).

Educator *(Learning)*

The servant leader is an educator who strives to create a church *and* world that manifest the kingdom community's *gift of learning* (Senge,

1990, pp. 353-357). 'Any monastery that fails to become a learning organization will soon fade away', state Kit Dollard and others, the authors of *Doing business with Benedict* (2002, p. 63). So it is with diaconal institutions. The educator encourages the questioning of evidence, the challenging of values and the testing out of received wisdom. It is a role which fosters new ideas, experimentation and the development of fresh paradigms. Servant leaders as educators sometimes operate as coaches (Fox, 2011) or mentors [Stage 9]. They help others to see and embrace learning as a journey of discovery.

Complementarity and collectivity

Though each of the above roles has an affinity with a particular gift of the kingdom community, all draw inspiration and insights from one or more of the other gifts. It is only when all roles and the gifts on which they draw are recognised as complementary that servant leadership as a whole reveals its deepest meaning.

No one person has the ability, skills and resilience to fulfil all the roles which go to make up servant leadership. Thus servant leadership within church *and* world is invariably a collective phenomenon. This means that within the workplace the concept of the leadership *team* needs to be very much to the fore though, as the Benedictines acknowledge, 'the challenge is (always) to change the team into a community' (Dollard, 2002, p. 114).

No single diaconal institution can go it alone. Neither the church nor any other institution can become fully diaconal until a fully diaconal world has come into being. The Kingdom at Work Project seeks to make a modest contribution to the coming into being of such a diaconal world by furthering the communal character of the world of work.

Appendix 1
Eighteen theses for the diaconal church

1. In the millennium ahead, our world faces a *choice between chaos and community*.

2. If it is to survive, human civilization has *to choose to become a global community of character*, ranging from micro communities (the family) to macro communities (major institutions and nation states).

3. *The Christian vision of 'the kingdom community'* is the supreme exemplification of all such communities, and thus a model for world and church.

4. *The gifts of the kingdom community are life, liberation, love and learning.* They are gifts manifest within the nature of the Trinity and in Christ's teaching about the kingdom of God. They are *universal gifts* offered to all.

5. The *mission* of the church is to model and to build communities of character that are transformed by and manifest the gifts of the kingdom community. *The credibility* and *viability* of the church depends on how faithfully it fulfils this mission.

6. Such a mission can only be fulfilled if the church becomes *a 'diaconal' (servant) church*. The diaconal church is *the servant of the kingdom community* and *of humankind*. As such it *models* for both church and world what it means to be *a community of character*.

7. The diaconal church *respects the autonomy of a secular culture* but *rejects the domination of sacralism or secularism*.

8. *The social collectives that make up the diaconal church* – hearings, groups, networks, the institution as an entity and partnerships – are all *communal* collectives.

9. *Dialogue* is fundamental to the means by which the diaconal church communicates its message.

10. The diaconal church *liberates its laity* to build learning communities that are transformed by the gifts of the kingdom community.

11. The diaconal church has *two main forms*:
   - as the Christian community *gathered* for worship, learning and caring;

- as the Christian community *dispersed* to fulfil its mission in the world.

12. To equip the laity to be the servants of the kingdom community *new forms of church leadership* are needed. These are embodied in the roles of *'servant leader'*. The latter necessitates leaders being trained to equip lay people to become community builders within church and world.

13. *Leaders* of the diaconal church are *women and men*.

14. The leadership of the diaconal church is exercised through three particular roles:
- that of *'presbyter'* - whose task is to equip the gathered church to model the kingdom community in its life and work;
- that of *'deacon'* - whose task is to equip the dispersed church to build learning communities that manifest the gifts of the kingdom community in the world;
- that of *'bishop'* - whose task is to be an intermediary who supports and resources presbyters and deacons and, through them, the laity.

15. The diaconal church embraces *a collective form of church leadership*.

16. Within the diaconal church all work *collaboratively*.

17. The diaconal church is a *democratic* and *self-governing* church, based on the principle of *subsidiarity*.

18. For the diaconal church to fulfil its mission, *the mould of Christendom must be broken*.

Appendix 2
Eighteen theses for the Christian or secular diaconal institution

These theses can be applied to any institution operating within the world of work.

1. In the millennium ahead, our world faces a *choice between chaos and community*.

2. If it is to survive, human civilization has *to choose to become a global community of character*, ranging from micro communities (the family) to macro communities (major institutions and nation states).

3. *The Christian vision of 'the kingdom community'* is the supreme exemplification of all such communities, and thus a model for world and church.

4. *The gifts of the kingdom community are life, liberation, love and learning.* They are gifts manifest within the nature of the Trinity and in Christ's teaching about the kingdom of God. They are *universal gifts* offered to all.

5. Alongside the primary task for which it was established, the *mission* of each institution is to model and build communities that are transformed by and manifest the gifts of the kingdom community. *The viability* of each institution depends on how faithfully it fulfils its primary task *and* communal mission.

6. Its communal mission can only be fulfilled if the institution becomes a *'diaconal' (servant) institution*. A diaconal institution is *the servant of the kingdom community* and *of humankind*. As such it *models* what it means to be *a community of character*.

7. The diaconal institution *respects the autonomy of a secular culture* but *rejects a culture dominated by sacralism* or *secularism*.

8. *The social collectives that make up a diaconal institution* – hearings, groups, networks, the institution as an entity and partnerships – are all *communal* collectives.

9. *Dialogue* is fundamental to the means by which a diaconal institution communicates.

10. A diaconal institution *liberates its members* to build communities that are transformed by the gifts of the kingdom community.

11. A diaconal institution has *two main forms* –

- as a *gathered* community, fulfilling its primary task and communal mission through its own life and work;

- as a *dispersed* community, fulfilling its primary task and communal mission in the world.

12. To equip the members of a diaconal institution to be the servants of the kingdom community *new forms of institutional leadership are needed.* These are embodied in the roles of *'servant leader'*. The latter necessitates leaders being trained to equip the members of their institution to become community builders within that institution and within the world.

13. *Leaders* of a diaconal institution are *women and men*.

14. The leadership of a diaconal institution is exercised through three particular tasks:

- that of *equipping the gathered institution* to model the kingdom community as it engages in the primary task for which the institution was established;

- that of *equipping the dispersed institution* to build communities that manifest the gifts of the kingdom community as it engages in the primary task for which the institution was established;

- that of acting as an *intermediary* which supports and resources the two roles described above and, through them, the members of the institution.

15. The diaconal institution embraces *a collective form of leadership*.

16. Within the diaconal institution all work *collaboratively*.

17. A diaconal institution is a *democratic* and *self-governing* institution, based on the principle of *subsidiarity*.

18. For diaconal institutions to fulfil their communal mission, *the mould of sacred and secular Christendoms must be broken*.

Appendix 3
Catholic Social Teaching on
the role of the Christian as servant leader

In Stage 4 of the Kingdom at Work Project we explored the light that Catholic Social Teaching could throw on the matter of a communal economy. Here we look at its contribution to an understanding of the role of the Christian as servant leader. The material quoted draws almost entirely on a seminal paper on *The Vocation of the Business Leader* (2012), a report on a seminar, set up in February 2011 at the Centre of Catholic Studies at the University of St. Thomas in Minnesota, entitled *Caritas Veritate: The Logic of Gift and the Meaning of Business*.

Servant leadership

The call to servant leadership is very clear within Catholic Social Teaching. The report referred to states: 'Entrepreneurs, managers, and all who work in business, should be encouraged to recognize their work as a true vocation and to respond to God's call in the spirit of true disciples. In so doing they engage in the noble task of serving their brothers and sisters and of building up the Kingdom of God' (para. 86). 'Well-integrated business leaders can respond to the rigorous demands placed upon them with a servant attitude, recalling Jesus who washed the feet of his disciples' (para. 13). 'Faith-based "servant leadership" provides business leaders with a larger perspective and helps balance the demands of the business world with those of ethical social principles' (p. 2). Furthermore, 'Business leaders who do not see themselves serving others and God in their working lives will fill the void with a less worthy substitute' (para. 10).

The servant leader

The six hall-marks of the servant leader are clearly reflected in the Catholic Social Teaching articulated within this report.

Visionary

The Christian business leader is called to make 'good business decisions (based on) a vision of a business as a community of persons' (p. 3). 'Christian business leaders must be able to "see" this world in a way which allows them to make judgements about it, to build up its goodness and truth, to promote the common good, and to confront evil

121

and falsehood' (para. 16). At the same time, 'Faith enables Christian business leaders to see a much larger world, a world in which God is at work, and where their individual business interests and desires are not the sole driving force' (para. 61). 'For Christian business leaders, this is a time that calls for the witness of faith, the confidence of hope and the practice of love' (para. 1).

Strategist

'Building a productive organization is a primary way in which business people can share in the unfolding of the work of creation' (para. 8.). In the report, Christian business leaders are encouraged to ask, 'Am I making sure that the company provides safe working conditions, living wages, training, and the opportunity for employees to organise themselves?' (p. 27). 'The best business leaders use resources effectively and maintain reasonable levels of revenue margin, market share, productivity, and efficiency, in order to ensure the viability of the organization' (para. 52).

Animator

Christian business leaders should ask: 'How does receptivity to God's love animate the relationships of the various stakeholders of a business?' (para. 71) and 'Do I promote a culture of life through my work? (p. 26). They are called to recognize 'the human dignity of employees and their right and duty to flourish in their work' (p. 3). 'Christian business leaders are men and women of action who demonstrate an authentic entrepreneurial spirit, one which recognizes the God-given responsibility to accept generously and faithfully the vocation of business' (para. 61).

Enabler

The leading questions posed here are: 'Do I provide working conditions which allow my employees appropriate autonomy at each level?' and 'Are jobs and responsibilities in my company designed to draw upon the full talents and skills of those doing the jobs?' (p. 26). Christian business leaders need to operate 'with love, so that their work is not merely an exercise in self-interest, but a cultivation of relationships, building communities of people' (para. 82). There is reference here to 'the principle of subsidiarity, which fosters a spirit of initiative and increases the competence of employees - considered "co-entrepreneurs" ' (p. 1). 'When they integrate the gifts of the spiritual life, the virtues and ethical social principles into their life and work, they (Christian business leaders) may overcome the divided life, and receive the grace to foster the integral development of all business stakeholders' (p. 3).

Intermediary

Over against destructive competition, (Christian business leaders should use their influence) 'individually and collectively, to promote human dignity and the common good and not merely the narrow interest of any particular stakeholder' (para. 73). (They need to see) 'their actions not just in terms of the impact on the bottom line, but in the larger context of the impact of those actions, in collaboration with others, on themselves and the world, in the light of God's ongoing creation' (para. 82). 'Businesses (should) promote healthy interdependence among the people of different nations by promoting interaction between them in a way that is mutually beneficial' (para. 3).

Educator

The report states that 'the first act of the Christian business leader, as of all Christians, is to receive; more specifically to receive what God has done for him or her... As a group, business leaders tend to be more active than receptive... The temptation for some is to regard themselves as determining and creating their own principles, not as receiving them' (para. 66). Four leading questions are posed: 'What kind of business policies and practices will foster the integral development of people?' (para. 71); 'Am I promoting the integral development of the person in my workplace?' (p. 27); 'Have employees been selected and trained to be able to meet fully their responsibilities? (p. 27); and 'In anticipation of economic difficulties, is my company taking care that employees remain employable through appropriate training and variety in their work experience?' (p. 27). Finally, the report recognizes that 'Catholic business education has achieved a lot, but has ever new challenges to address' (para. 84).

Transition

Stage 6

Transition

The power of the human scale

The global scale

The purpose of the Kingdom at Work Project is to transform the world of work through a discernment and intervention process founded on a communal theology of the kingdom. Any transformation of this kind faces a global as well as a local challenge.

We have already indicated there are many potentially terminal issues facing humankind if it is to survive a new millennium [Introduction and Stage 2]. We have also noted a number of serious concerns relating more specifically to the world of work. One of these is the growing uncertainty relating to the integrity and viability of the market model underpinning the world's economy, a concern which has been most clearly manifest in the banking collapse of 2008 with financial malpractices still coming to light [Stage 4].

Behind the current economic turmoil there are further causes for concern. One of these is what Al Gore (2013, p. 14) describes as 'the financialization of the economy' which perpetuates the all-pervasive myth that monetary value is the measure of 'reality' (Graham Ward, 2009, p. 94). Real goods and real people are increasingly at the mercy of a monetary system which thrives on the massive, instantaneous and short-term transfer of virtual wealth from one quick source of profit to another, all producing what Joseph Stilgitz calls a 'fake liquidity' (quoted in Gore, p. 15).

Another concern in this context is the consequences of economic globalization. There are many potentially positive outcomes which global integration delivers. However, one of its destructive outcomes has been the inexorable rise of corporations which 'rule the world' (Korten, 1996). Gore notes (p. 113) that in 2012 'twenty-five U.S. - based multinational corporations have revenues larger than many of the world's nation-states' and that 'more than half (53%) of the 100 largest economies on earth are now corporations'. As a result the power to challenge the universal domination of a market-led economic system in which well-run and humane businesses are absorbed into remote and impersonal ones is slipping away not only from nation-states but from those organizations which claim to represent the world political order. The case of Cadbury's the chocolate business based in Birmingham is but one example. Deborah Cadbury (2011) graphically describes how a firm deeply rooted in Quaker principles, and which took 186 years to build up its global position alongside its exemplary care for the welfare of its employees, was in six short months, from August 2009 to January 2010, swallowed up by Kraft Foods, the world's second largest food company. Despite remonstrations by employees, trades unions and government, the wider world appeared seemingly powerless to intervene.

We have also noted that there is a growing awareness that capitalism as an economic model has an inherent propensity to skew economic and social equality in a way that makes it virtually impossible for earned income to challenge accumulated wealth. Whilst capitalism remains unfettered, therefore, there is little chance of redressing the economic imbalance within and between societies that is fast becoming evident on a global level [Stage 4]. As Thomas Picketty (2014) argues, the inequality that results is unsustainable socially *and* economically.

A world economy with these inbred features would seem to make nonsense of any attempt by Christians to transform the world of work. What can often isolated individuals achieve in the context of workplaces whose life and culture are apparently at the mercy of economic forces way beyond their control? What use is it to set out a theology, spirituality, communal economic principles and a servant role for institutions in the world of work which can be simply obliterated by global forces way stronger than even historic and humane businesses? For the remaining stages of this project to have any meaning, such questions need to be acknowledged and addressed.

The kingdom community - an alternative reality

The project's key image when discussing a communal theology for the world of work was that of the kingdom community with its gifts of life, liberation, love and learning [Stage 2]. We argued that the kingdom community and its gifts ultimately derive their meaning and their power from a communal Trinity - three distinct Persons yet in the most profound of relationships. As Alistair McFadyen puts it (1990, p. 27): 'The Father, Son and Spirit are neither simply modes of relation nor absolutely discrcte and independent individuals, but Persons in relation and Persons only through relation'.

Over against the 'reality' of the principalities and powers of this world and, more specifically of the might of unfettered financial markets and global corporations, the Christian sets the reality of the non-coercive power of the kingdom community. Christ taught that the kingdom community, and the nature of the relationships it embodies, is 'not of this world' (Jn 18: 36). That remains true. However, he also stated that the kingdom is very much 'amongst' us (Lk 17: 21). Its presence brings a radically new understanding of what it means for men and women, collectively and individually, to reflect the image of God within their life and work. It challenges the view that 'there is no alternative' to today's principalities and powers, within the world of work as elsewhere.

The significance of the discernment and intervention stages of this project rests on the project's conviction that it is the affirmation or neglect of the gifts of the kingdom community that needs to become the measure of whether or not the economic forces evident in our world and its places of work are ultimately creative or destructive. The might of unrestrained financial markets and of global corporations may seem to be overwhelming but, in thc long-term, those forces cannot sustain the world of work, and a human civilization which depends upon it, unless they are transformed by the gifts of the kingdom community. Therefore, the task of the Christian at work, together with others of like mind, is to begin to build alternative and sustainable economic and social models which however modest to begin with offer hope for the future.

The kingdom community and the human scale

The gifts of the kingdom community manifest themselves primarily though relationships, especially through the multitude of human scale encounters and events of daily life. As Alistair McFadyen states, 'The basic paradigm of humanity is one-to-one relationships' (p. 257). He adds that such relationships 'are indispensable to personal identity and being, that the humanity of relations may only be retained where one-to-one interaction is possible, where the conditions for dialogue and intimacy are met... Proximate and small-scale relationships are therefore of fundamental importance' (p. 258).

Christ too recognized that what is small scale, not least in the life of the kingdom, is often the precursor of what in time can become a great deal more significant. He noted that the kingdom was like the tiny mustard seed which ultimately grew into 'the greatest of all shrubs' (Mk 4: 30-32), and like the inconspicuous leaven which eventually transforms the whole loaf (Mt 13: 33). Paul took such insights even further when he wrote that 'the word of cross is folly to those who are perishing, but to us who are being saved it is the power of God' (1 Cor 1: 18). In fact 'God chose what is foolish in the world to shame the wise, God chose what is weak in the world to shame the strong, God chose what is low and despised in the world, even things that are not, to bring to nothing things that are' (27-29).

The way in which the gifts of the kingdom community are manifest will often be small scale, non-coercive and gradual in their influence. Nevertheless, it is such manifestations which ultimately hold the key to the survival and flourishing of the world of work and of the form of economy which underpins it. Thus the later exploration of how everyday 'signs' and 'critical incidents' might offer pointers to the presence of the kingdom community is not dealing with events and happenings of minor importance, irrelevant or hopelessly trivial in the context of the global economic forces impinging on the workplace [Stage 7]. It is concerned with triggers for communal transformation which have a vital and enduring significance for working organizations of all shapes and sizes.

Ernst Schumacher

The importance of human scale initiatives surfaced in a notable way in 1973. That year Ernst Schumacher published *Small Is Beautiful*, a critique of Western economics during the energy crisis of that era and a riposte to the gathering momentum of globalization. Schumacher's work was also set in the context of a growing awareness of the depletion of the planet's resources and the urgency of building a sustainable world for humankind.

His conviction was not that small was beautiful in simply an aesthetic sense but that small was essential if the destructive influences of global capitalism and of an impersonal, large-scale and complex technology were to be checked (1980). The latter was 'a technology for the few at the expense of the masses, a technology of exploitation, a technology that is class-orientated, undemocratic, inhuman, and also unecological and nonconservationist' (p. 40).

Schumacher believed that the way forward was for humankind to adopt a technology on an 'intermediate' scale and operate in groups of a human and humane size. He states (p. 57):

> Experience shows that whenever you can achieve smallness, simplicity, capital cheapness, and nonviolence, or, indeed any one of these objectives, new possibilities are created for people, singly or collectively, to help themselves, and that the patterns that result from such technologies are more humane, more ecological, less dependent on fossil fuels, and closer to real human needs than the patterns (or life-styles) created by technologies that go for giantism, complexity, capital intensity, and violence.

The Schumacher Society, established to promote his ideas after his death in 1977, has continued to champion human scale economic and social initiatives within the life of society. Each year a Schumacher Award is presented to a grassroots organization making a particularly significant contribution to human scale economic or social development. They state that the award 'symbolizes countless other unsung heroines and heroes who are working to transform society, often with little or no support' (www.schumacher.org.uk).

The Human City Institute

In 1998 and 1999, the Human City Institute in Birmingham, of which I was then Director, was twice shortlisted for the Schumacher Award because of its innovative 'human city sites programme' (Clark, 2012, pp. 35-41). This programme is mentioned here because it demonstrates how the affirmation of human scale initiatives - and the facilitation of their networking - can make a vital contribution to city-wide communal regeneration, including that of the world of work. Leonie Sandercock (1998, pp. 129ff), an Australian expert in urban and regional planning and advisor to many cities concerning urban renewal, has written about the dynamism of human scale initiatives, especially where these develop into what she calls 'a thousand tiny empowerments'.

The Human City Institute was set up in 1997. It came out of the Human City Initiative, a venture initiated in Birmingham two years earlier and founded on a communal theology similar to that underpinning this project (Clark, 2012, pp. 1-9). The Institute's purpose was to promote an understanding of what a major city, increasingly dominated and shaped by a global market economy, might look like if, instead, its life and work were founded on 'the humanizing power of community' (pp. 1-4).

The Institute's human city sites programme began in 1998. Some thirty small community initiatives across the city were invited to commit themselves for one year to an agenda of their own choosing which would contribute in however modest a way to the creation of 'a human city'. The groups concerned were termed 'human city sites'. Over the course of a year, the sites were supported by visits from members of the Institute's staff. Stories about their work were published in the Institute's *Bulletin*, which went out to over 3000 people across Birmingham. Though, for staffing reasons, the original sites' programme was not repeated after the first year, its importance was reflected in its adoption by the Institute's Human Neighbourhood Project (pp. 42-51) which ran for several more years in Birmingham, Bradford and Swindon. In that project, some 40 'human neighbourhood sites' were involved.

The Institute's human sites programme was largely concerned with the voluntary sector. However, it touched the world of work more specifically through agendas chosen and offered by groups associated with two other Institute initiatives: a Human Face of Policing Project (pp. 55-57) and a Human School Project (pp. 52-55). An evaluation of the sites programme in these very different contexts came to the conclusion that its focus on the human scale was 'of profound significance for the future of urban renewal' (p. 41), a conclusion which has direct relevance to the communal potential of human scale initiatives in relation to the world of work. It should be noted that the importance of the human group for the success of businesses has also been stressed by Etienne Wenger (1998, 2002) in his advocacy of what he calls 'communities of practice'.

In 2002, the Human City Institute published a short paper entitled 'twelve signs of a human city' (pp. 31-34). One interesting feature of the document was that all the signs concerned were just as applicable to 'the human business' as to 'the human city'. One hall-mark of both was the human group. Thus, when applied to the human business, one of the twelve signs reads: 'a human business is dependent on a multitude of human groups contributing in their own ways and situations to the creation of such a business. It is a business where "small is beautiful". It values the human scale and the human touch. It is a business with a human face' (see the Appendix 1 to Stage 7(Introduction)).

'Signs' and 'critical incidents'

The next stage of this project explores how 'signs' and 'critical incidents' can enable the Christian at work to discern the presence of the gifts of the kingdom community within the workplace Many of the signs and incidents suggested relate to human scale phenomena. This is because the project is founded on the conviction that addressing the human scale can often reveal the condition, for good or ill, of the workplace as a whole and that intervening to bring about change at the human level has the potential to trigger important and long-lasting communal transformation. Thus the discernment and intervention process which follows affirms the power of the human-scale as an important focus for the Christian in his or her mission at work.

The value-added consequences of networking

Human scale initiatives are of value in their own right. However, their power and influence for communal change can often be greatly increased when those involved in similar initiatives share their experiences, insights, skills and resources. Here the importance of dialogue comes to the fore, a form of communication explored at greater depth in Stage 8(3). Alistair McFadyen (1990) sees dialogue as lying at the heart of all creative networking. He believes dialogue gains its authenticity and significance from 'God's intention of (treating) humankind as dialogue-partners and of (the essence of) human being itself as an extended dialogue' (p. 269). He continues: 'The Christian language of community and of redemption can only achieve its full meaning in the kingdom - the community where the true meaning of communal and personal life will be perfected and lived out in structures of intersubjectivity and formally reciprocal co-intention' (p. 270).

In our day and age, 'structures of intersubjectivity' and 'reciprocal co-intention' have been given new meaning and impetus by the emergence of the worldwide web. Al Gore (2013) speaks about this development as the coming into being of 'the global mind' (pp. 44-89). He recognizes a number of the dangers which the Internet poses. However, he regards it as having huge potential for 'building vibrant and open "public spaces"... for the discussion of the best solutions to emerging challenges and the best strategies for seizing opportunities' (p. 369). Amongst the latter were the democratizing potential of such happenings as the Arab Spring (Mason, 2012) and the Occupy Movement (Gore, p. 57), even if both failed to realize this potential.

The communal transformation of the world of work could be another significant outcome.

The Human City Institute

The communal energy created by linking up human scale initiatives is demonstrated by the endeavours of the Birmingham Human City Institute. The potential for urban regeneration of the human city sites which was developed by the Institute (described above) was greatly enhanced by sites being able to learn about other sites with similar concerns and to share experiences and insights with them. Networking was facilitated not only by the Institute's *Bulletin* but by meetings of representatives of the sites, by a public market-place where they put on displays of their work (Clark, 2012, p. 39) and by a regular human city sites *News-sheet* reporting stories of what sites were doing (p. 38).

Each human neighbourhood site in the three cities involved (Birmingham, Bradford and Swindon) was invited to have a page on the Institute's web site in order to make their endeavours public and to facilitate exchanges with other human neighbourhood sites (p. 47). Seminal links were also made by site members visiting similar initiatives taking place in the three UK cities involved in the project, as well as in Chicago under the auspices of the *Imagine Chicago* project.

Educational 'butterflies'

At the same time as the Human City Institute was developing its human sites programme, another initiative within the world of work was taking place in Birmingham, this time related to education. Tim Brighouse, then the inspirational Director of Education for Birmingham, produced what he called a booklet of *School Improvement Butterflies* (1995). In his Introduction to the booklet, he defined 'butterflies' as 'very small initiatives taken by schools which have a disproportionate effect as a catalyst for improvement'. He wrote: 'Butterfly theory… is based on the hypothesis that if sufficient butterflies flap their wings in somewhere like the Amazonian forests eventually there will be a climate change such as a thunderbolt many miles away!' The booklet contained a diverse range of human scale initiatives that Birmingham schools were taking to boost the life of their schools as learning communities. By documenting and sharing such initiatives teachers were helped to understand the importance of human scale innovations, as well as the great potential for communal change created when those involved in these ventures shared insights and resources.

Christian networks and movements for transformation

These examples point to the fact that, though individual initiatives on a human scale can be highly significant triggers of change, their potential can be greatly enhanced if those involved network together. Further value is added if the network begins to take on the shape and characteristics of a movement for communal change. The transition from being a network to becoming a movement, as in the case of the monastic movement and early Methodism, have typified the most successful attempts to renew the church down the centuries. The same has been true on the secular scene. Jim Wallis (2013) notes that 'it takes the power of movements to change politics' (p. 195), even if such change at times seems painfully slow and can take many destructive turns, as has been the case with the Arab Spring.

The world of work

The Christian at work and Christian agencies engaged in this field of mission will greatly strengthen their impact on the world of work by linking up with those pursuing a similar transformational agenda, be they Christian or not, within or beyond the same workplace. These connections may well facilitate the emergence of networks that have the potential to lead to a sustainable movement of individuals, groups and agencies committed to the transformation of the world of work. The trades union movement of the nineteenth and early twentieth century was a case in point.

Evangelical groups and networks

At present there is a limited number of networks and no movements of this kind in evidence in the UK. Most noteworthy are the evangelical networks of Christians engaged in the world of work (Clark, 2005, pp. 254-264). In this context, the three most active facilitating agencies are the long established Christians at Work, the London Institute for Contemporary Christianity and the more recently established Transform Work UK. These agencies have worked hard to create groups of Christians meeting within the same workplace or networks associate with similar occupations.

Such groups and networks can be of considerable value when they are genuinely open to discerning the signs of the kingdom community at work, seeking to support their members in intervention in response of such discernment and pro-active in care and prayer for all members of their workplace. However, if the ultimate purpose of such groups is to convert their fellow workers to Christianity they will not be operating on the basis of the communal theology underpinning this project. Their message that being a Christian at work is primarily about the salvation of individuals and not the communal transformation of the workplace can then create major difficulties for those Christians at work attempting to engage in the kind of mission underpinned by a theology of the kingdom community as set out in this project.

Kingdom community oriented networks

In the UK there are a number of agencies and associations with a theology which reflects that of this project. Amongst these would be the Industrial Christian Fellowship, the Young Christian Workers and the Quakers and Business Group. The last of these perhaps reflects most fully the kingdom theology and principles on which this project is based. The group interacts, especially via the Internet, as a network of Quaker practitioners actively involved in business. It holds an annual conference, occasional seminars and produces informative material, notably publications such as *Good Business Ethics at Work* (2000) which sets out to relate Quaker principles to good business practice.

One factor limiting the scope of such networks, however, is that they remain largely restricted to a single denomination. A second is that there is a tendency to focus attention mainly on middle and top management. A third is that a number of these groups are less concerned with connecting and supporting Christian lay people at work than workplace chaplains, as in the case of the Industrial Mission Association, or ministers in secular employment, like CHRISM.

Part 2
Discernment and intervention

theological underpinnings

this is where the kingdom community can inform a process where we engage with the Work world.

is a journey both in + out

Discernment itself focuses on the journey in + its focus is our lives
SD - 1-4. not where we have agency
But we tend to focus on the journey in - contemplative prayer, retreat!

see. judge - act

but with a outward component, → embracing the gifts of the kingdom that means - connecting with the Will of the kingdom → discerning what

We think also of discerning where we shd do but the stage before is just why noticing

we can discern the 4 Ls mapped onto "Good Work" initiatives eg DW, SDGs + we can notice signs (to do with tasks, contexts, relationships)

Discernment is part of a process, of enduring.

Intervention	Individual	Collective
implicit	Being there	being together
explicit	Saying/doing something	discerning + implementing collective action

138

Stage 7

Discernment

Introduction

Stages 2 to 5 of the Kingdom at Work Project set out the theological, spirituality, economic and structural foundations that inform and guide its approach to mission in the world of work: the task of discernment and of intervention. Stage 6 has described how the project seeks to link principles and practice by focusing on human scale initiatives. The next consideration is how to build on these foundations in order to decide what form of intervention is needed to enable the workplace to manifest more fully the gifts of the kingdom community.

Discernment as an art

John Hughes (2007) writes: 'Production, exchange and consumption cannot simply pretend innocently to follow the slavish whims of popular desire, but must be subjected to an endless discernment based not upon the question 'what can I get out of this?', but 'is this truly good and useful?', 'is it serving its true end?, 'is this in accordance with the divine will?' '(p. 232). Discernment concerns the spiritually reflective process of identifying the gifts of the kingdom community: life, liberation, love and learning.

In the context of this project, discernment is grounded on the communal theology set out in Stage 2 and in the communal spirituality described in Stage 3. As noted when discussing the latter, discernment is an art not a science and one which needs a life-time of practice. It is an art which needs to be undertaken with humility and the readiness to acknowledge mistakes. It must be open to the new and the unexpected ('critical incidents' as they are called in Stage 7(2)). Observations and insights need to be checked out against those of other Christians within the same workplace or beyond, an undertaking in which the guidance of a mentor is vital [Stage 9].

Discernment is a prerequisite for the task of deciding where and when the Christian at work should intervene in the workplace.[1] It is the

---

[1] It is worth noting that the process of discernment and intervention resonates with the 'see', 'judge' and 'act' approach to lay ministry at

springboard for deciding the form of intervention required to enable the workplace to manifest the gifts of the kingdom more fully.

In Stage 3 a number of methods to assist the process of discernment were described ('the practice of the presence of God', the Examen and theological auditing). Here two other approaches to discernment designed specifically for this project are explored - discerning the gifts of the kingdom community through what are called **'signs'** [Stage 7(1)] and/or through what are termed **'critical incidents'** [Stage 7(2)]. As far is known neither of these approaches to mission in the world of work has been tried elsewhere. Ways in which signs and critical incidents might inform how far **leadership** within the workplace manifests the gifts of the kingdom community are also considered.

Signs

The project's first approach to the task of discernment is by means of signs. Signs are defined as:

ongoing or recurrent features of the workplace which reveal the gifts of the kingdom community.

To the discerning Christian signs can range from what appears clear evidence to brief glimpses of the kingdom community at work. What distinguishes signs from critical incidents is that the former are ongoing features of workplace life. They are not unscheduled or unexpected happenings.

Signs are an important aspect of the discernment process because they:

o   are associated with features typical of the workplace and its culture

o   can be evident within *any* workplace.

---

work adopted by the Roman Catholic Church's Young Christian Workers, an approach based on the insights of Cardinal Cardijn its founder. That approach to ministry is commended in the report on *The Vocation of the Business Leader* seminar (2012, para. 87), held in 2011 at the Centre of Catholic Studies at the University of St. Thomas in Minnesota quoted at some length in Stage 5. The 'see, judge and act' methodology is discussed more fully in Stage 9 when education and mentoring are under consideration.

Critical incidents

Critical incidents have been defined elsewhere in a number of ways according to the working context concerned. The term has most often been used in connection with sectors such as health or law and order and/or related to events that create some kind of crisis. Here critical incidents are identified in a way relevant to the nature of this project. Critical incidents are defined as:

> *unscheduled or unexpected happenings which reveal the gifts of the kingdom community*.

Signs and critical incidents as pointers not indices

The signs and critical incidents suggested in this stage of the project are at best pointers but often more like glimpses or intimations of the gifts of the kingdom community at work. They are never infallible or precise indicators. Signs and critical incidents are in many respects similar to the parables of the kingdom which, grounded in everyday life, are usually metaphors and similes offering an insight into the gifts of the kingdom community, dynamic and compelling yet never fully definitive or complete.

Nevertheless, if it is true that 'the world glints and winks and shines everywhere with the possibility of it (the kingdom)', as Francis Spufford comments (2012, p. 125), it would be a denial of our responsibilities as Christians if we failed to pursue the communal transformation of the workplace because discerning the signs of the kingdom community at work was too difficult or dangerous an undertaking. In the context of this project, the hope of transformation depends on Christians choosing a mission task on the basis of what they have discerned of the kingdom community at work, through signs or critical incidents, yet remaining open to a change of direction in the light of new experiences and insights.

Because the task of discerning the gifts of the kingdom community through signs or critical incidents is never a quick fix, Christians at work need all the resources available to them for that task. In what follows, some resources on hand to help discern signs of the kingdom community are considered first. Then the task of discernment through critical incidents is explored. This order for engaging in discernment is important because it is often easier to discern evidence of the kingdom community revealed by unscheduled or unexpected happenings at work (critical incidents) if we have first become aware of those revealed by ongoing features of the workplace (signs).

Resources for the discernment of signs

Resources for the discernment of signs of the kingdom community may come from a number of quarters. They are offered to those prepared to study the nature of a communal theology, spirituality, economy and the structure of communal institutions. This source of resources has been discussed in Stages 1 to 6 of this project.

Resources for discernment are also offered through the day-to-day experiences and insights of those at work, whether holding Christian convictions or not. This source of resources can be tapped into through studying the attempts of the secular world to foster communal workplaces and, *implicitly if not explicitly*, to access the gifts of the kingdom community in that task.

Signs of the communal workplace within the secular world of work

Pointers to key features of the communal workplace emerge from the endeavours of those in business and related sectors, past and present, who have regarded their vocation as not only the profitable provision of goods and services, but as contributing to the well-being of their workers and the wider world, even though their endeavours may not have been explicitly motivated by Christian convictions. Below are given a number of examples of such endeavours, inspired by Christian convictions or otherwise, and the communal features associated with them.

The Victorian era and the family firm

Concern for the communal quality of the workplace is no recent phenomenon. From the early days of the industrial revolution there were entrepreneurs who had more than making a profit at heart. One of the earliest pioneers to insist on the social responsibility of business was Robert Owen. In the early 1800s he began to develop his cotton mill at New Lanark on principles which treated the welfare and education of his workers as of paramount importance. Throughout the nineteenth century many entrepreneurs followed Owen's example. Prominent amongst these philanthropic 'mercantile princes', as James Munson calls them (1991, p. 14), were 'the Nonconformists',

Congregationalists, Baptists, Wesleyan and Primitive Methodists, Quakers and Unitarians (p. 3), through whom 'the Victorian economic miracle was to a considerable degree made possible (p. 34)'.

For instance, Jeremiah Coleman (raised a Baptist but later becoming a Congregationalist), the so-called 'mustard king', entered the family's mustard firm in Norwich in 1851 and provided 'numerous benefits for his workers' (p. 24). In 1853, Titus Salt (Congregationalist) opened his alpaca wool factory a few miles north of Bradford. Alongside it he built Saltaire, a model village for his employees. This included wash-houses with tap water, bath-houses, a hospital and an institute for recreation and education, with a library, a reading room, a concert hall, billiard room, science laboratory and a gymnasium. The village also had a school for the children of his workers, almshouses, allotments, a park and a boathouse.

Richard Tangye (Quaker) started his tool-making firm in Birmingham in 1855. He 'established half-day holidays on Saturdays and provided a dining hall, educational classes, concerts and lectures for his workers' (p. 22). George and Richard Cadbury (Quakers) moved their business to healthy surroundings on the outskirts of Birmingham and, in 1879, began to build there a model village called Bournville, the first so-called 'garden suburb' (p. 27), to house their workers. They also provided a wide range of educational and recreational facilities for them. William Hartley (Primitive Methodist) established his jam making factory in Aintree in 1886 with 'model housing nearby' for his workers (p. 26). He offered 'a system of profit-sharing... free medical care and... a non-contributory pension scheme for his employees' (p. 20).

In 1887, William Lever (Congregationalist) built Port Sunlight 'a model housing estate for his workers' (p. 15) near his soap-making business on the Wirral Peninsula. Lever's aim was 'to socialize and Christianize business relations and get back to that close family brotherhood that existed in the good old days of hand labour' (Hesketh, 2007). His garden village had allotments, a cottage hospital, schools, a concert hall, open air swimming pool, church and a temperance hotel. Lever introduced welfare schemes, and provided for the education and entertainment of his workforce, encouraging recreation and organizations which promoted art, literature, science or music. In 1904, Joseph Rowntree (Quaker) began building New Earswick near his chocolate factory in York in an attempt to create a balanced village community for his employees and their families. Rents were kept low and social and educational facilities provided.

The decline of the family firm

During the twentieth century many factors contributed to the ending of an era of benevolent paternalism exemplified by those Victorian entrepreneurs who had championed the communal workplace. Family firms were always at the mercy of the failure of founding fathers to produce heirs committed to or capable of following in their foot-steps. Two world wars and the severe economic depression of the 1930s also threatened the future of many nineteenth century businesses which, to survive, had to become far more innovative, flexible and expansive. Soon after, the exponential growth of central government, the coming of the Welfare State and the National Health Service, together with a massive expansion of educational provision, removed the need for such firms to provide housing, social and health benefits and learning opportunities for their workers.

From the 'sixties onwards, society came increasingly to question the paternalistic style of the management of all institutions, including those associated with the world of work, the new titles of 'managing director' and 'chief executive' encapsulating a more professional yet bureaucratic approach to leadership. The growing globalization of trade and commerce and the consequent emergence of massive multi-national companies lead to many enterprises originally grounded on Victorian values, such as those founded by the Rowntree and Cadbury families (Deborah Cadbury, 2010), being absorbed into global corporations. Any residual familial concern for their workers was consigned to history.

The growth of a communal business culture in the twentieth and twenty-first centuries

Nevertheless, the twentieth century saw a communal culture gradually re-surfacing and becoming more explicit, codified and acknowledged as important within much of the business world. In this development a number of organizations, large and small, acted as noteworthy catalysts for change and sowed the seeds for the wider emergence of the concept of the communal workplace.

The Chartered Institute of Personnel and Development (CIPD)

In the first decade of the twentieth century, Taylorism with its introduction of 'time and motion' working, and Fordism with its creation of assembly line production deskilled many male workers, a factor leading to more and more women and young people entering the workforce (www.cipd.co.uk - CIPD's *Centenary Timeline*). In part as a response to the needs of younger people, and through the advocacy of the philanthropist Seebohm Rowntree, a Welfare Workers' Association was set up in 1913. Over the following decades, alongside the expansion of industry and mass production, a 'human relations movement' gathered momentum, a number of firms appointing staff given specific responsibility for the health and welfare of their employees. In 1946, after numerous changes of title before that date, the Welfare Workers' Association became the Institute of Personnel Management. Over subsequent years this human relations movement grew apace leading, in 1994, to the Institute of Personnel and Development (IPD) picking up the baton. It took on chartered status as the CIPD in 2000. By 2013, it had 135,000 members worldwide.

In January 2011, the CIPD produced an influential report on a project entitled *Shaping the Future - Sustainable Organization Performance. What really makes the difference?* The report's 'Executive Summary' states that 'the importance of sustaining the organization's people, financial, environmental and societal contribution… needs to be a top priority for HR and business leaders' (p. 1). The project offers four 'toolkits' to help practitioners to achieve this goal, embracing many features of the communal workplace. The second of these toolkits, *Achieving alignment, shared purpose and agility* sets out a range of 'aspects' for checking the strength of a firm's 'alignment' (the 'consistency, fit, links or integration between the values, behaviours or objectives of different groups of stakeholders').

The Work Foundation

The First World War saw an increasing number of women and young people working in very poor conditions in munitions plants across the country. As a result an initiative was taken which led to the emergence of two organizations which for the next century sought to promote the concept of business as a communal enterprise. In 1918, the Reverend Robert Hyde, then a civil servant in the Ministry of Munitions, founded the Boys' Welfare Association for young men working in the munitions industry. In 1919 this changed its name to the Industrial Welfare Society. In 1965, it became the Industrial Society and, in 2002, changed its name to the Work Foundation. From its inception the organization sought to improve the communal quality of working life across the business world and to promote positive relations within industry. In 2010, financial problems led to the organization needing to enter into an alliance with Lancaster University though it still continues its work in a more limited form.

For example, in 2011, a Good Work Commission set up by the Work Foundation produced an important report entitled *Good Work and our Times*. Its Foreword states: 'In the last 20 years it seems that the primacy of financial capital has overshadowed the contribution and investment potential of the people working within and for an organization. If we can take any true positives out of the credit crunch, one of them is an overdue rebalancing of this view' (p. 2). The report explores the nature of 'good work' at some depth and offers many pointers to what this project interprets as the signs of the kingdom community within the workplace.

The International Organization for Standardization (ISO)

The International Organization for Standardization is the world's largest developer of voluntary international standards. It was founded in 1947 when delegates from 25 countries decided to create a new body 'to facilitate the international co-ordination and unification of industrial standards' (www.iso.org). The organization now has members in 164 countries and a Secretariat in Geneva. The standards offered cover many aspects of working life from health to the environment, the latter being first addressed in 1971. The standards it sets are regarded as normative by many companies and institutions. ISO itself does not oppose the certification of companies which meet its standards but leaves the task of certification as such to independent bodies.

In November 2010, 'following five years of negotiations between many different stakeholders across the world', ISO launched an International Standard providing guidelines for Social Responsibility. It was named *ISO 26000*. It was to provide 'guidance on how businesses and organizations can operate in a socially responsible way. This means acting in an ethical and transparent way that contributes to the health and welfare of society'. In March 2011, *ISO Focus*, the magazine of ISO, took Social Responsibility as its sole theme. It sets out what it terms that theme's seven 'core subjects: accountability, transparency, ethical behaviour, respect for stakeholder interests, respect for the rule of law, respect for international norms of behaviour and respect for human rights' (pp. 22-23). Although these are broad 'subjects' they point in the direction of empirical signs of the communal workplace.

It is of interest to note that, in 2010, the organization explicitly stated that ISO 26000 'is not a management system standard. It is not intended or appropriate for certification purposes or regulatory or contractual use. Any offer to certify, or claims to be certified, to ISO 26000 would be a misrepresentation of the intent and purpose and a misuse of the International Standard'. It also added that 'there will be no accredited certification to ISO 26000 as this is contrary to the intent and spirit of the standard' (www.iso.org).

The Corporate Social Responsibility movement (CSRM)

The Corporate Social Responsibility movement (CSRM) forms a much more diffuse movement encompassing organizations already mentioned and many others. Nevertheless it needs to be included here as it has contributed a good deal towards a business culture increasingly prepared to take on board responsibility for the well-being of all its stakeholders and of the planet. The roots of corporate social responsibility go back to the pioneering initiatives of the nineteenth century identified above. However, as an identifiable movement, the origins of the CSRM lie in the 1960s when the terms 'social auditing' and 'the responsible company' were first mooted. Influential in the movement's development was a growing concern for the conservation of the planet's resources which surfaced about this time. The 1970s saw the movement fostering a global partnership concerned with 'sustainable development', given impetus by such formative events as the 'Earth Summit' in Rio de Janeiro in 1992 and Agenda 21 which sought to turn the Summit's concerns into action.

A growing number of businesses have taken the CSRM to heart. These include Ben and Jerry's (ice cream) in the States and the Body Shop (cosmetics) in the UK which both shaped their working culture accordingly. Despite criticisms that CSR is a vague, diffuse and unenforceable concept, the movement has continued as a catalytic force promoting work-related agencies concerned with the common good and the communal workplace. It has also furthered the creation of ethical codes of conduct by many organizations, from self-generated initiatives to the UN's Global Contract, launched in 1999, with its ten principles focusing on human rights, labour relations and the environment.

In 2001 the FTSE4Good Index was launched by FTSE, the leading global index providers. This aimed to set 'an objective global standard for socially responsible investment' (www.ftse.co.uk/Indices/FTSE4Good_Index_Series). The criteria for the selection of companies cover three main areas: environmental sustainability, positive relationships with stakeholders and upholding universal human rights. Despite criticisms that some of the companies included in the list do not uphold these principles, FTSE4Good Index has made its reputation as the only official focused benchmark tracking individual company shares in the ethical sector.

Business in the Community (BITC)

Business in the Community was set up in 1982 (www.bitc.org.uk). In its early days it was given considerable impetus by the CSRM. It is one of the Prince's Charities, a group of not-for-profit organizations of which the Prince of Wales is President. BITC seeks to encourage the positive impact of businesses within the workplace, within the local community and on the environment. In 1997 BICT set up its Awards for Excellence programme, now known as the Responsible Business Awards. In 2002 it launched its first Corporate Social Responsibility Index 'to help companies systematically measure, manage and integrate responsible business practice'. In 2013, it stated that 'Responsible Business has never been higher on the political and public agenda'. BITC now has a network of some 11,000 businesses engaged in its various programmes and campaigns.

The Institute of Business Ethics (IBE)

The Institute of Business Ethics originally operated as part of the Christian Association of Business Ethics (CABE). The latter was established in 1938 by a group of Roman Catholic laymen who held senior positions in industry and commerce in order to promote the study and application of Christian principles to the conduct of business. CABE was initially known as the Catholic Industrialists' Conference.

IBE as such was launched in 1986, the day after the 'Big Bang', to seek to maintain an ethical business culture rooted in the principle that 'my word is my bond'. In 2000, IBE became a registered charity committed 'to advance public education in business ethics and related subjects with particular reference to the study and application of ethical standards in the management and conduct of industry and business generally in the United Kingdom and elsewhere' (www.ibe.org.uk). In

2003, IBE launched a major initiative to encourage businesses to develop their own code of business ethics and offered illustrative content for a code based on a stakeholder model, updated in 2008. Amongst other concerns, IBE suggests that any code of business ethics must cover employees, customer relations, shareholders or other providers of money, suppliers and society or the wider community (*Developing a Code of Business Ethics,* 2003, p. 32ff.).

The learning organization

The term 'the learning organization' does not refer to any particular body or agency but to a form and process of openness and transformation which enables organizations to develop, change and flourish. Its principle exponent is Peter Senge, in particular his book entitled *The Fifth Discipline* (1990). In that book he describes learning organizations as 'organizations where people continually expand their capacity to create the results they truly desire, where new and expansive patterns of thinking are nurtured, where collective aspiration is set free, and where people are continually learning how to learn together' (p. 3). In his book he proposes five disciplines which are needed in order to create a learning organization: systems thinking (patterns of interrelationships), personal mastery (people working on their own goals), mental models (an appropriate organizational culture), shared vision and team learning. Since Senge's initial work on the concept, the idea of the learning organization has become embedded in numerous courses and consultancies addressing how businesses might remain open to ongoing change and cultural transformation, so that they can thrive in a highly competitive market. The development of the movement has been shaped by a large literature and an international journal of the same title.

Investors in People

This organization was launched in 1991 to offer a voluntary framework to enable businesses 'to get the best from their people'. Investors in People states that it sees 'people as the engine of success for responsible, sustainable and profitable business. These are people who take the initiative, develop ideas, motivate colleagues and delight customers' (www.investorsinpeople.co.uk). The framework contains a 'Standard', a set of requirements needed for a business to be recognized as an 'Investor in People' and be allowed to display the latter's logo. Additional requirements enable companies to be recognized as attaining this Standard at bronze, silver or gold level. In 2010, after some criticisms of the body's operations and assessment procedures, its administration was taken over by the UK Commission for Employment and Skills supported by the Department for Business, Innovation and Skills.

Great Place to Work

Great Place to Work originated in New York in 1981 through the endeavours of Robert Levering and Milton Moskowitz. They came to believe that 'the key to creating a great workplace was not a prescriptive set of employee benefits, programmes and practices, but the building of high-quality relationships in the workplace... characterized by trust, pride, and camaraderie'. They established an Institute to further that conviction. In 1997, *FORTUNE* (in the USA) and *Examine* (Brazil) partnered with the Institute's research arm to produce the world's first *100 Best Companies to Work For* workplace rankings. The organization has continued to grow apace since then (Michael Burchell and Jennifer Robin, 2011). Great Place to Work now operates in more than 45 countries on six continents. Based on results of surveys representing over 10 million employees around the globe, these best companies' competitions form the basis of 'the world's largest... set of studies of workplace excellence, management and the role of trust in workplace culture'.

Great Place to Work came to the UK in 2000. Its mission is 'to build a better society by helping companies to transform their workplaces' (www.greatplacetowork.co.uk). In 2001, Great Place to Work UK produced the first of its annual lists of 'great places to work for' which was published by the *Sunday Times*. Since then the *Financial Times* and *Guardian* have taken over that task (see *Great Workplaces* 2011, 2012, 2013, 2014). Great Place to Work UK offers to provide participating companies with a Trust Index based on a survey of employee's responses to a detailed questionnaire and a Culture Audit. If companies score enough points they appear on one of the organizations numerous lists relating to key features of 'the good or great workplace', though Great Place to Work UK maintains that it 'is not in the business of helping organizations get on lists' but there 'to help any organization learn from the best and improve their workplace'.

Best Companies

This organization, with a purpose very similar to Great Place to Work, was set up in the UK in the first decade of the twenty-first century (www.b.co.uk). In 2006, it produced its *Best Companies Guide* which lists the businesses which have been accredited by it, these being rated as very good (one star), outstanding (two stars) or extraordinary (three stars). A company not so accredited is named 'one to watch'. Companies are rated largely on the basis of their employees' comments. Best Companies publishes a list of its top 100 companies annually in conjunction with *The Sunday Times*.

Engage for Success

In 2009, David MacLeod and Nita Clarke produced a major report for the Department of Business entitled *Engaging for Success - enhancing performance through employee engagement.* There are numerous definitions of 'engagement' in circulation but Engage for Success describes it as 'a workplace approach designed to ensure that employees are committed to their organization's goals and values, motivated to contribute to organizational success, and are at the same time enabled to enhance their own sense of well-being' (www.engageforsucess.org). Following up this report in March 2011, the Prime Minister launched Engage for Success. The latter is an independent body which consists of a large Task Force, Core Team and Project and Community Sub-groups drawn from all sectors. The Engage for Success website went live in November 2012 when *Employee Engagement - the evidence*, a report setting out 'the evidence for the effectiveness of employee engagement in raising performance and productivity across the UK economy' was published. It describes its 'four enablers of engagement' as: a strong strategic narrative, engaging managers, employee voice and organizational integrity. It is now one of the leading bodies in the UK promoting the increasingly ubiquitous concept of 'engagement'.

Economy for the Common Good Association

This movement began in October 2010 in Austria (www.gemeinwohl-oekonomie.org). It advocates an alternative economic model founded on the principle of 'the common good' and co-operation instead of on profit and competition. The catalyst in the creation of this movement was Christian Felber, an Austrian university economics professor and his book *Die Gemeinwohl-Ökonomie (The Common Good Economy)*. The association makes no reference to Catholic Social Teaching in its website literature and states openly that it tries not to be 'ideological'.

By the end of 2013 the association had over 1400 companies signed up as supporters of the movement, most on the European mainland. The association is mentioned here because of its unique approach to the creation of the communal workplace. It is gradually becoming known on the UK scene.

The association offers a Common Good Balance Sheet covering issues such as the 'Just income distribution', 'Corporate democracy and transparency', 'Ethical customer relations', 'Reduction of environmental impact' and 'Contribution to the local community'. Companies, usually in partnership with other companies similarly involved, draw up their own Common Good Report in the light of the items on the Balance Sheet. This report is peer evaluated and, from 2014, must also be checked by an external auditor. The company then receives an audit report and certificate. It is honour bound to make its Common Good Report available to the public. There is a strong emphasis on mutual learning throughout the whole process.

Historical triggers of the communal workplace movement during the twentieth and twenty-first centuries - an overview

The first half of the twentieth century, given impetus by two world wars, the growth of mass production and the increasing involvement of women and young people in industry, gave rise to growing concern for the welfare of employees. This development was exemplified by the forerunners of the Chartered Institute of Personnel and Development and, in due course, by the appointment of professionals to address human relations concerns within the world of work.

From the middle of the twentieth century onwards, growing concern about the pollution of the planet through carbon emissions and limits to economic growth, exacerbated by the exploitation of natural resources, came to the fore. Here the Corporate Social Responsibility movement with its commitment to sustainable development played an important role, supported by many other bodies such as the International Organizations for Standardization and, much later, the FTSE4Good Index list of companies. These organizations, along with such agencies as Business in the Community, also stressed the social responsibility of business to it local community and wider society.

For much of the twentieth century the Trade Unions movement pressed for the right of employees to a fair wage and decent working conditions to be honoured. The movement began to decline from the 1980s onwards, leaving the way open for a free market culture to dominate the economic scene. However, there was a growing conviction across the world of work that the well-being of employees was of fundamental importance if businesses were to thrive, values related to this conviction being promoted by bodies such as the Work Foundation and Investors in People.

Over recent decades, the rise of globalization and of multi-national companies, many becoming wealthier than nation states, has raised the question of who takes responsibility for the well-being of *all* stakeholders and not just of investors. The Institute for Business Ethics was set up to address this kind of issue and, in partnership with the GoodCorporation (www.goodcorporation.com), a body established in 2000 to monitor good corporate behaviour, drew up and helped to promote 'The GoodCorporation' Standard. Seeking to uphold the responsibility of companies to serve a wider constituency than their workforce were also bodies such as Business in the Community and Good Place to Work.

More recently the business world has been addressing the issue of how closely the sustainability and productivity of companies are correlated with the degree to which their workforce is 'engaged' with the company for which they work. Engage for Success was established explicitly to promote this concept. It has already produced research which claims that it has confirmed this correlation beyond reasonable doubt.

Nevertheless, approaches to the creation of the communal workplace which do not take the free market model of the economy as a given are as yet barely on the horizon. Economy for the Common Good is one such organization, as are 'the Schumacher Circle', the latter including bodies such as the Schumacher Society (www.schumacher.org) and the New Economics Foundation (www.neweconomics.org).

Other sources of signs of the kingdom

The communal workplace movement

To ignore what the world of work can teach us about noteworthy features which create and sustain the communal workplace is to turn our backs on a significant source of research and empirical insights. It is also to reject the fact that the kingdom community is already alive and active, recognized explicitly or not, within the world of work. Therefore, in seeking to discern the signs of the kingdom community at work, it is important that note is taken of those features of the communal workplace to which secular bodies, such as those described above, bear witness. These features may be identified through what they state are indices of the communal workplace even though the latter may be described in terms like 'the socially responsible company', 'the learning organization' or 'the good or great workplace'. Communal features may also be revealed in how those bodies operate in practice.

Public sector and voluntary sources for the discernment of signs

Attempts to identify features of the communal workplace are also evident beyond the business sector as such. Two examples are mentioned here.

The school as a communal workplace

In 1996, I published a book entitled *Schools as learning communities - transforming education*. This drew together insights from my fifteen years of teaching post-graduate students in the field of community education. My thesis was that the school, along with all other educational institutions, needed to have the hall-marks of the communal workplace built into its system if it were going to fulfil its purpose as a genuine learning organization. I argued that there could be no education without community - and no community without education.

One chapter of the book (pp. 62-80) sets out 38 'communal guidelines' under headings such as 'the environment', 'interaction' and 'relationships' which, on the basis of considerable research, appear to be notable indicators of the strength or weakness of the school as a community. Another chapter (pp. 81-98) sets out another series of guidelines to help assess how fully the school espouses education in its most 'open-to-learning' form [see Stage 8(3) for more on the concept of 'open-to-learning']. Both sets of guidelines provide important insights into signs of the kingdom community at work, the theological nature of which, even in a book written for a professional readership, is stated at the outset (pp. 53-55).

The human city

Whilst Director of the Human City Institute based in Birmingham, I gathered a list of signs of 'the human city' which could offer a value-based profile of such a city. In 2002, the Institute published a document entitled 'twelve signs of a human city' (Clark, 2012, pp. 31-34). Most of the signs were applicable not only to the city as a whole but to each sphere of life within it, including the business world. Consequently the Institute also published a further paper entitled 'Twelve signs of a human business' (pp. 57-59). Because this list offers some important insights into the nature of the communal workplace it is reproduced in Appendix 1 at the end of this stage of the project.

Resources for the discernment of signs offered by Christian collectives

Pointers to possible signs of the kingdom community at work are not confined to secular organization or agencies. In recent years, a few religious bodies have sought to set out guidelines for the creation of the communal workplace as illustrated below.

The Quakers and Business Group

The Quakers and Business Group would not call itself an explicitly Christian body. However, when discussing a communal spirituality for the world of work [Stage 3], it draws on the inspiration of 'the Light' in discerning the hall-marks of the 'good business'.

The group's publication *Good Business Ethics at Work* (2000) seeks to relate Quaker principles to good business practice. It does this by using a distinctively Quaker method of discernment. This begins by stating an 'Advice' indicating a principle of Quaker practice. This is followed by a 'Question' which prompts the reader to examine whether he or she has honoured this principle in practice. The booklet covers topics such as 'honesty and integrity', 'business and profit', 'obligations to shareholders and investors', 'ethical trade', 'environmental responsibility' 'health, safety and security', 'advertising and promotion', 'taxes', 'gifts and donations', 'trade unions' and 'whistle blowing'. The booklet is a rich and thoughtful source of insights into what are described in this project as the gifts of the kingdom community at work and has been drawn on freely in suggesting the signs listed later.

The Christian Association of Business Executives

In 2006, the Christian Association of Business Executives (CABE) published thirty-one 'Principles for those in business' (www.cabe-online.org). These were inspired by John McLean Fox, a former chairman of CABE and a tertiary Franciscan. The principles are meant to be prompters for individual reflection and practice, one for each day of the month, by Christian executives involved in business. CABE believes that the principles 'provide a sound and robust framework within which business can be conducted honourably and responsibly… (as well as helping) to develop personal values and standards'. The principles cover concerns such as 'priority aims', 'corporate values' and 'responsibilities to stakeholders'. They also include 'personal qualities' like 'creativity, joyfulness, forgiveness, courage, openness and honesty, prayerfulness, maintaining personal integrity' and so on. CABE's principles are intended to be more a rule of life for the Christian business executive than a means of discerning particular signs of the kingdom community within workplace. However, they offer useful insights into the nature of those signs.

'Stealing the churches' clothes'

All that has been said above indicates that the Christian seeking to discern the signs of the kingdom community at work is not lacking in possible pointers or guidelines from both Christian and secular sources. Many of the family firms of the nineteenth century offer important insights from the hard won experience of founding and sustaining caring businesses. In the ensuing decades others, like CIPD and the Work Foundation, have responded to the early commitment of family firms to promoting the human dimension of the business world. Some initiatives, such as the Corporate Social Responsibility movement and those committed to the concept of the learning organization, have taken on board changing ethical and educational perspectives within society at large. More recently, a growing number of agencies has researched the experience of employees and managers to ascertain and promote those features which they believe identify a 'good' or 'great' workplace.

Can Christian faith add anything to features of the communal workplace already identified by those mainly secular initiatives reviewed above? Here we agree with Gillian Stamp that for too long Christians have allowed the secular business world when 'in search of a soul', as she describes that communal quest, to 'steal the churches' clothes' (1992). She writes:

> I spend most of my professional life working with employers and voluntary groups as they seek to design organizations that will use their staff to the full and remain viable in the face of unprecedented economic and social uncertainties. These organizations range from huge multinationals like British Petroleum to women's co-operatives in the newly independent nation of Namibia. On the basis of what I have learnt from them I would like to suggest that, in much that they do to strengthen their organizations, they are in effect 'stealing the churches clothes'.

This project takes the 'clothes' referred to by Gillian Stamp as the principles and priorities embraced by the communal theology and other communal foundations set out in Stages 1 to 6. These principles and priorities form the distinctive features of what this project means by the concept of the communal workplace. These principles and priorities need claiming and proclaiming by the church as that which makes the contribution of Christian faith to the communal transformation of the workplace unique. Though Christian faith always needs to be open to how those features of the communal workplace embraced by the businesses and other agencies described above complement, confirm and inform Christian principles and priorities, this project contends that the latter offer an essential resource for all those seeking the creation of workplaces that manifest the gifts of the kingdom community. These principles and priorities are identified below and consideration given as to how they take further, as well as often call into question the understanding of the communal workplace espoused by the contemporary working world.

Principles and priorities for the task of discernment

The primacy of community

The Trinity and the kingdom are two pivotal images which point to the primacy of community in the divine purposes for creation. This project contends that these images when taken together exemplify the nature of community at its zenith [Stage 2]. It has been argued that unless our world becomes a community of communities, and the world of work plays a pivotal role in that task, it may well not survive let alone flourish in the millennium ahead.

In contrast, for the world of work as it stands, it is wealth creation and profit which are the ultimate concerns. Community building, internal and external to the workplace, is of growing importance. However, it is a task which remains secondary and often subservient to the so-called 'bottom line'.

The gifts of the kingdom community are prerequisites for the transformation of the world of work

The gifts of the kingdom community are life, liberation, love and learning. These 4Ls are inclusive and universal gifts. Because they embody the power of Trinity and kingdom, they are prerequisites for the communal transformation of the workplace and essential resources for those committed to that task. The signs of the kingdom community manifest within the workplace elucidate and express in practice the meaning of the 4Ls [Stage 7(1)].

In a secular context, indices of what is often referred to as 'the good workplace' (rather than 'the communal workplace') are largely shaped by so-called business ethics. A major problem here is that such ethics are often captive to the norms of a market-driven economy. For example, in its publication *Developing a Code of Business Ethics* (Webley, 2003), the Institute of Business Ethics refers to no religious principles which might inform or challenge that code. Thus *The GoodCorporation Standard* (2010), which the Institute designed in partnership with the GoodCorporation agency, is simply stated as being 'based on a core set of principles that define a framework for responsible management in any type of organization'. There is no indication where this framework originates and questioning of how the values of a market-led economy might be dominating the models of management offered.

Some forms of accreditation for 'the good workplace' set by monitoring agencies - such as bronze, silver and gold by Investors in People and the one to three stars awarded by Best Companies - are rewards for achievement within the context of the current economic culture and not evidence of an intention or ability to pursue the common good in any new or radical way. Even the now fashionable concept of 'engagement', the commitment of the employee to his or her organization as the hall-mark of a good business, though obviously of communal importance to the latter, is too inward-looking to strengthen a commitment to co-operation and partnership beyond the workplace concerned (*Employee Engagement - the evidence*, 2012).

A denial of inclusive and universal communal principles is also apparent in the approach of a number of bodies seeking to 'sell' the idea of the good workplace, notably Business in the Community, Investors in People and, in particular, Great Place to Work and Best Companies. One problem is exemplified by the way in which the last two bodies deliberately promote competition between participating businesses by ranking the latter according to their scores taken from the good workplace questionnaire provided, and then publish the resulting 'league tables' in the national press. This means that the outcome for all those participating is inevitably a win-lose situation.

A related problem is that the agencies supposedly promoting best business practice are themselves competing with one another to get the custom of the business world and the fees that come from clients. Instead of openly publishing their indices of the good workplace with a view to encouraging the development of the communal workplace *throughout* the world of work, they only reveal these indices to those paying to participate. Even in this context, therefore, market forces are creating a good workplace industry.

More in accord with the principles of openness and partnership are organizations, such as the Chartered Institute for Personnel and Development, the International Organization for Standardization and the Institute for Business Ethics, which offer their guidelines for the creation of the communal workplace to *any* company interested. This provides an opportunity for such companies to check out the extent to which signs of the good workplace are evident in their own practice as a process of self-development and not in competition with others. Noteworthy in taking an approach to furthering the communal workplace which is rooted in partnership is Economy for the Common Good which insists on participants producing their own Common Good Report, this being peer and consultancy audited and eventually being made public for all to learn from.

A communal spirituality offers the means of accessing the power revealed by the signs of the kingdom community

Christians at work might well be inhibited by the enormity of the task of transforming a world of work dominated by the profit motive and the practice of unregulated competition currently so integral to it.

However, they have the privilege of being able to draw on resources unrecognized or untapped by the secular world of work. Primacy of place amongst these resources is those associated with a communal spirituality [Stage 3]. The latter offers to Christians at work the means of tapping into the power of life to enhance innovation and creativity, the power of liberation to open up the channels of forgiveness, reconciliation and renewal, the power of love to enhance caring and sharing, and the power of learning to deepen an understanding of what it means is to be fully human individually and collectively.

A communal spirituality offers openness to and awareness of what is revealed by the Giver of the 4Ls. It also fosters prayerful reflection and the support and guidance of fellow Christians. The Quakers and Business Group see such reflection as waiting on 'the Light' and the Christian Association of Business Executives as one informed by the prayer life of its members.

The Christian at work's recognition of the need for the resources of a communal spirituality is not shared by many working collectives even when pursuing ideals of corporate social responsibility, the good workplace and the common good. Such collectives not infrequently assume that drawing up mission statements will of itself bring about transformational change. However, the medium often denies the message. We only need to turn to the recent banking crisis to see the fallibility of human endeavour, a failure which reflects the naive assumption that individual self-interest will ultimately promote the common good. Archbishop Vincent Nichols, speaking at St Paul's Institute (April 2013), reflects on the banking crisis as follows (www.stpaulsinstitute.org.uk):

> In recent times narratives about what makes for a good society have been viewed with suspicion. It is the hard won individual freedom to pursue my own good in my way within the law that is celebrated. This mentality has legitimated the pursuit of narrow self-interest, sometimes with a tendentious claim that benefits will eventually yield better outcomes for everyone. It has made possible the atrophying of common values at the heart of good business, and undermined institutions that stand between the market and the state, from the family to all kinds of

community forms through which our relationships are enriched and extended.

Signs of the kingdom community are revealed in and through the life and teaching of Christ

Lesslie Newbigin argues (1980, pp. 15 and 20) that the kingdom community 'is not the propounding of an ideology or a philosophy or a religious doctrine. It is in the strictest sense an announcement of an event, of a happening'. Nor is it 'merely a theological phrase... (It now has) a name and a human face', that of Jesus Christ.

Because the image of the kingdom was so much to the fore in the life and teaching of Christ, it is the gospels in particular that reveal the nature of the gifts of life, liberation, love and learning. First and foremost in this context are *the events* of the life of Christ: for example, the healing of the man paralyzed for 38 years (life) (Jn 5: 1-15); the stilling of the storm (Jn 6: 16-24) and Christ's eating and drinking with all and sundry (liberation) (Mk 4: 35-41); washing the disciples' feet (love) (Jn 13: 1-17); and Martha and Mary (learning) (Lk 10: 38-42).

The way of the cross also offers radically new pointers to the nature of the kingdom community. It shows that its coming is costly. If the Christian is faithful to the gospel message, there are likely to be times when seeking the communal transformation of the workplace can be a very demanding undertaking particularly in situations when such intervention leads to confrontation and conflict.

In *his teaching*, Christ drew on his experience of everyday life and real people to identify the hall-marks of the kingdom community. What the signs of those gifts might look like was illustrated by stories relating to the daily and often commonplace experiences of life. In this context, such parables as that of the sower and his seed (life) (Mk 4: 2-20); the lost sheep (liberation) (Lk 15: 3-7); the good Samaritan (love) Lk 10: 25-37; and the wise builder (learning) (Mt 7: 24-27), offer signs of the kingdom community of considerable human depth.

Nearly all the signs we later suggest as pointers to the communal workplace are closely related to features of the kingdom exemplified within the life and teaching of Christ. Though the biblical passages may not always fit neatly with the culture of today's workplace, Christ was after all drawing his illustrations from a predominantly rural society, they add a human and dynamic dimension to these signs.

161

A problem with many indices of 'the good workplace' offered by secular bodies committed to developing the latter's potential for enhancing good business practice is that they lack the humanity of the biblical narrative. Because such indices are usually decoupled from stories or case-studies that would give them some depth, they come over as lists of abstract markers rather than signs of the workplace as a dynamic community. Even the so-called 'Common Good Balance Sheet' (www.gemeinwohl-oekonomie.org) offered by Economy for the Common Good, a very enlightened body in this connection, is laden with long and complex indices described in bureaucratic terminology.

The primacy of community means that it is workplace relationships which should be the main focus of mission

It is important for the Christian at work to be well informed about how Christian faith interprets the nature and meaning of work. However, in the context of mission, this project contends that it is even more important how the gifts of the kingdom community are manifest within and beyond *the workplace*. It must be remembered that this project defines the latter as that network of relationships which links those involved in a shared occupational endeavour usually focused on or emanating from some identifiable location. For Christians therefore, evaluating the strength of workplace *relationships* takes precedence over, though in no way removes from consideration, evaluating communally the nature of the work being undertaken.

It is to the credit of the organizations considered at the outset, from the family businesses of the nineteenth century to the communally aware bodies of past decades, that they have recognized the qualities of the good workplace to be primarily dependent on the quality of relationships found therein. This concern has witnessed the exponential growth of the human relations industry, exemplified by the steady growth in membership of such bodies as the Chartered Institute of Personnel and Development. In 2013, this association had over 130,000 members internationally working in HR, learning and development, people management and consulting. Unfortunately human resources departments have over recent decades become increasingly embroiled with the bureaucracy of employment and other legislation and the human face of the profession has been obscured.

Those on the margins of society should be of special concern to the communal workplace

The kingdom community gives precedence to the needs of those on the margins of society - the poor, homeless, suffering and marginalized [Stage 2]. This agenda is exemplified by the nature of the birth, the ministry and the death of Jesus Christ. Through his origins, life and work he became one with all people but expressed particular concern for the least and lowest (Lk 4: 18-19; Mt 11: 2-6; Phil 2: 5-11). In his ministry of healing and of teaching about the kingdom he constantly sought the redemption and well-being of those on the edge of society. Thus the hall-marks of the communal workplace need to show that it is in some way seeking to meet the needs of the marginalized.

In the world of work, as witnessed by the Corporate Social Responsibility movement, those on the margins of society are a cause for concern. Many working organizations seek to reach out to the less fortunate, locally and globally, through the activities of employees or through the donation of money or goods to good causes. However, it is the interests of their own employees, shareholders, suppliers and stakeholders which continue to take precedence over all others.

The gift of learning is particularly important in the task of transforming the workplace

The life and teaching of Christ and the experience of Christian communities of character down the ages [Stage 1] have interpreted the quest for community as a vital life-changing journey of discovery in search of the fullest expression of what it means to be human: in mind, body *and* spirit [Stage 2]. Learning in this sense is not only a human endeavour but a response to that which is revealed by the Giver of that gift. It is particularly in the context of learning as a gift of the kingdom community that revelation and the human quest for meaning and purpose come together.

The world of work, for example as witnessed by interest in the concept of the learning organization, has half grasped the importance of the gift of learning. However, despite the insights of such pioneers as Peter Senge (1990), learning in the world of work has tended to be restricted to instruction and training, with a corresponding emphasis on knowledge and skills. Thus many workplaces lack a commitment to learning as an open-ended quest for a deeper understanding of the nature of human relationships and how the latter can enable them to develop as communities of character [Stage 1].

Groups, networks and partnerships are organizational structures which frequently manifest signs of the kingdom community

Signs of the kingdom community are manifest not only in the life and teaching of Christ but in the forms of social collective which his ministry brought into being [Stage 5]. Thus the life of the disciples and of the development of the early church offer many signs of what we have called communities of character, social collectives which manifest the gifts of life, liberation, love and learning. Likewise, Celtic culture, the experience of the monastic and religious orders, such as the Jesuits, the heritage of the Society of Friends and Methodism bear witness to the dynamism of communal groups and networks [Stage 3].

It has been argued that collectives such as these can be especially influential in furthering the communal transformation of the world of work [Stage 5]. Thus it is encouraging that the role of groups (often as teams), networks and partnerships loom large in the literature concerned with the good workplace. Etienne Wenger (1998, 2002) has written convincingly of the foundational importance of small 'communities of practice' for a flourishing world of work. A wide range of case-studies which stress the communal significance of groups, networks and partnerships are documented by David MacLeod and Nita Clarke (2009) in *Engaging for success: enhancing performance through employee engagement,* in *Good Work and Our Times* (July 2011) from the Work Foundation, and by Michael Burchell and Jennifer Robin (2011) in *The Great Workplace.*

Signs of the kingdom community are frequently discernible in human-scale incidents and events

We have argued in Stage 6 that the signs of the kingdom community are often present in happenings which may appear mundane or insignificant. Christ's teaching about the kingdom as being like a mustard seed (Mk 4: 30-32) or his comments on the generosity of the widow who threw two coins of minimal value into the temple treasury (Mk 12: 41-44) are but two biblical stories which exemplify this reality.

Thus in seeking to discern the signs of the kingdom community within the workplace, every incident, however minor, needs to be kept under review. The power of human-scale signs lies in the fact that energizing and resourcing them are the gifts of a mighty and eternal kingdom community.

Signs of the kind of leadership able to foster the communal workplace are most in evidence where servant leadership is the norm

In Stage 5 of the project we identified servant leadership as that form of leadership best fitted to create and sustain the communal workplace. The signs of the kingdom community are most likely to be discerned through words and deeds which typify the six main roles of servant leadership, that of visionary, strategist, animator, enabler, intermediary and educator, each of which is associated with one or more of the gifts of the kingdom community.

Characteristics of effective leadership identified within secular management studies often touch on these roles. However, they are rarely aware of their value-added *communal* importance when enriched and empowered by one or more of the 4Ls.

Appendix 1

Twelve signs of a human business

(Clark, 2012, pp. 57-59)

1. A human business is committed to being a new kind of business.

o A human business is a place alive with the energy of hope, enables imagination and creativity to flourish and looks for the revitalization of every aspect of its corporate life.

o It is a business which is a dynamic community of communities that offers a powerful sense of security, significance and solidarity to all its members.

o It is '*a rainbow business*' which delights in diversity and difference in pursuit of the common good.

o It is a business which creates a new culture and a new language to embody and communicate what it means to be human.

o 'A human business enables those who share a vision of the human business to work together with others to make that vision a reality.'

2. A human business is committed to those who work there, service it and all whom it serves.

o A human business is about 'value for people' before value for money.

o It is a business where '*all matter and each counts*'.

o It is a business where people acknowledge and respect one another, where they care and where they share.

3. A human business is committed to affirming the whole of human experience.

o A human business treasures the human achievements of its past and celebrates the human endeavours of the present.

o It is a business committed to human wealth creation.

o It is about the fulfilment of all that it means to be human; in body, mind and spirit.

o It is a business with a heart and a soul.

o It is a compassionate and 'faith-full' business.

o It is a place of fun and laughter.

4. A human business is committed to a life-enhancing environment.

o   A human business gives life to those who work there, service it and all whom it serves.
o   It is provides a safe, clean and healthy environment.
o   It is a business within which people can move about easily and comfortably.
o   It offers an environment of natural beauty and architectural grace.
o   It harnesses and uses all its resources in ways that sustain the planet.

5. A human business is committed to social justice.

o   A human business recognizes, repents and confronts the suffering that inhumanity causes.
o   It places the concerns of the poor and the marginalized high on its agenda.
o   It is committed to the vision of a just, peaceful and inclusive business world, revitalized by forgiveness and reconciliation.
o   It upholds human rights and human responsibilities.

6. A human business is committed to truth and integrity in business practice.

o   A human business fosters a culture of trust founded on mutual respect and honesty.
o   It is about open, informative and straight communication within all spheres and at all levels of business life.

7. A human business is committed to the transforming power of the human group.

o   A human business is dependent on a multitude of human groups contributing in their own ways and situations to the creation of the human business.
o   It is a business where 'small is beautiful'.
o   It values the human scale and the human touch.
o   It is a business with a human face.

8. A human business is committed to being a place of lively and creative encounters.

- A human business provides spaces and places where people can meet and talk openly and freely.
- It encourages all who work there and service it to come together to share their experiences, stories and concerns.
- It provides forums for vigorous discussion and debate about the meaning and nature of the human business.
- It fosters many forms of networking that can link and connect those striving to build the human business.

9. A human business is committed to genuine partnership.

- A human business recognizes that the humanity of the part and the humanity of the whole are inextricably linked.
- It is a business which relates to other sectors (public, private and voluntary), neighbourhoods, cultures, faiths and generations in innovative and creative ways.
- It is a business which demonstrates the commitment, empathy, tolerance and tenacity which all true partnerships require.
- It is a business which works with any other business that shares its vision.

10. A human business is committed to democratic leadership and participation.

- A human business gives a voice to all who work there and service it, and hears what they say.
- It enables those who work there and service it to participate in those decisions that affect them.
- It is a business which believes in the mutual accountability of those who work there, service it and those whom it serves.
- It is a business where those who lead use their power to empower others.

11. A human business is committed to learning for living.

- A human business is a learning business.
- It is a business involved in an ongoing quest to discover what it means to be human.
- It is a business which creates a multitude of opportunities for attentive listening, innovative exchanges, open dialogue, ongoing reflection and the birth of new understandings.

o   It is a business which helps to provide an education for life.

12. A human business is committed to ongoing change.

o   A human business is about fundamental and continuing change because its concern is the transformation of the inhuman into the human.

o   It is a business which never ceases to challenge and redeem those things which would destroy its humanity.

Stage 7

Discernment

1 Signs

The nature of signs

There may be those who react negatively to the Kingdom at Work Project's attempt to suggest a list of signs which purport to identify the presence of the gifts of the kingdom community within the workplace. It is true that there is some ambivalence in the Gospels concerning the nature and status of signs. Christ was forthright in his condemnation of those who sought signs wrought by him, usually of a miraculous nature, to prove his credentials (Mk 8: 12; Mt 12: 38-39; John 2: 18; Jn 4: 48). He warned against false prophets and false signs (Mt 24: 24). He stated that signs would only become clear to those attuned to the inner meaning of his message (Mt 11: 25) and who had 'ears to hear' (Mk 4: 9) and eyes to see.

However, the Gospels are also an account of those who were able to discern the true signs of the kingdom, embedded in many aspects of the life and teaching of Christ, and as a result responded to the call to follow him. Thus the Gospels are not a negation of signs. Indeed John states that there were many other signs not recorded therein (Jn 20: 30). The Gospels embody a narrative which invites the hearers, and later their readers, to sort the wheat from the chaff, the genuine from the false signs of the kingdom. Therefore what matters in the context of this project is that all that has been said before about a communal theology, spirituality, economy and communal structures [Stages 2 - 5] is brought to bear on the task of discernment.

The discernment of signs at work

In the context of this project, signs are defined as *ongoing or recurrent features of the workplace discerned as revealing one or more of the gifts of the kingdom community at work*. The discerning of these signs has been undertaken by the author of the project through research and reflection informed by all the previous stages of the project as well as in conversation with a number of those engaged in spiritual direction and business consultancy. The signs offered are not in any way a definitive or complete list of possibilities. They are meant to be a range of suggestions of what the four gifts of the kingdom community might look like in practice. However, only the Christian in a particular workplace can decided whether or not they are applicable to or helpful in their situation. There may well be other signs, not suggested here, which the Christian discerns to be present and important in their place of work. How these signs can be added or used is described below.

Grouping signs at work

The signs offered are grouped under four headings according to which of the four gifts of the kingdom community - *life, liberation, love* and *learning* (the 4Ls) - they are judged to reflect most clearly. Some could appear under other or more headings. The four groupings taken together form what is called here 'a signs chart'.

Within these four groupings, the signs suggested are placed under sub-headings identifying the main sociological components of the workplace. These sub-headings are:

- *Task* - the nature of the work in which workers are engaged. This may be:

  internal - relating to the nature of the work as such and how it is undertaken,

  or -

  external - relating to the work's impact on the wider world

- *Context* - the physical, material and environmental aspects of the workplace

- *Relationships* - the interpersonal features of the workplace. These may be:

  internal - embracing employees and/or stake holders, or -

  external - concerning how the workplace as a whole relates to the wider world.

A further sub-heading entitled model is added at the end of each grouping. A model is a collation of typical features or characteristics which, taken together, offer a holistic representation, picture or image of the phenomenon concerned, in this case the communal workplace. For any workplace to be regarded as a model of the kingdom community, it needs to manifest signs relating to all 4Ls.

The use of the signs chart

Definitions of terms used in the chart

Workplace - That network of relationships which links people involved in a shared occupational endeavour usually focused on or emanating from some identifiable location

People or workers - Those actively engaged as employees within the workplace concerned

Users - Those who use the goods or services offered by the workplace - customers, clients, patients, pupils, etc.

Social collective - Any identifiable and ongoing group or larger body usually located within the world of work

Organization - Any larger social collective of which the workplace is a part

For whom is the chart intended?

Those using the signs chart will normally be Christians at work, wherever possible in the company of other Christians from the same or a different workplace and with the guidance of a mentor. However, where possible, it could be useful if some of those employed in the same workplace, not necessarily identifying themselves as Christians, were willing to fill in the chart. Likewise it could be valuable if those who were users of the goods or services of the workplace concerned, but not necessarily Christians, were also prepared to fill in the chart.

Does the chart represent a 'subjective' or 'objective' form of evaluation?

Any evaluation of the strength of the signs of the kingdom community will be subjective. This means that any evaluation is in the hands of the Christian employed in that workplace, where possible assisted by Christian colleagues and a mentor. It should be noted that most secular organizations engaged in the task of evaluating whether businesses are 'good workplaces' rely heavily on the subjective assessment of employees [Stage 7(Introduction)].

What has guided the choice of biblical references?

These have been taken in large part from the Gospels, especially where some reference is made, directly or indirectly, to the kingdom. They are simply illustrations of how the biblical material can speak to the characteristics and happenings of the world of work today. Other biblical references of note could be added and it is hoped that Christians at work will pursue their own search. A comprehensive web site and series of reference books relating to the whole bible and its concern with the world of work is currently in the process of development and production by the Theology of Work Project in the USA (www.theologyofwork.org).

Is the Christian at work meant to apply the chart to the whole of their workplace?

No. The project invites the Christian at work to choose a social collective which is part of their workplace of which they have personal experience and which is of importance to them. This collective could be an office, school class, hospital ward, work team or section, shop, department, etc. It should be one within which they spend a good deal of their time and have a clear role. However, if desired the Christian at work could apply the chart to their workplace as a whole provided that the latter is not too large and complex a collective.

Is the evaluation meant to be of the situation as it is or the situation as it might be?

The evaluation is meant to relate to the nature and features of the workplace as it is at the point in time when the assessment is made. It is a snap-shot of the current situation. The project assumes that such a snapshot will give the Christian at work useful guidance as to the nature of the intervention required to enable their workplace to manifest the gifts of the kingdom community more fully, provided of course that such intervention does not take place too long after the evaluation has been made.

Are the signs offered in the chart too general to evaluate?

Because the signs offered are meant to be ongoing or recurrent features of all workplaces they are inevitably of a general nature. However, every workplace is unique. It is therefore up to the Christian at work to decide the extent to which specific aspects of happenings within their workplace offer evidence or otherwise of the signs suggested.

For example, in relation to the workplace as *a life-giving community*, the Christian at work might decide that where an organization holds a so-called 'planet earth hour' or 'earth day' it affirms sign 12 (the goods produced and services offered contribute, directly or indirectly, towards the preservation of the planet and the conservation of its resources);

that clean toilets help to affirm sign 16 (the working environment is healthy); that an attractive eating area illustrates sign 19 (the working environment is life-enhancing); that the provision of a prayer space fulfils sign 23 (places are provided where people can be quiet and reflective); and that inter-departmental sporting events or dramatic productions contribute to sign 29 (there is fun and laughter).

In relation to the workplace as *a liberating community*, the Christian at work might decide that their organization's 'vision days' contribute towards sign 3 (people are inspired by the organization's vision for the future); that a show-case to display employees' non-work interests and skills reflects sign 18 (people are valued as human beings); and that trade shows to display to the public the organization's goods or services help to enhance sign 20 (people take a pride in their work).

Reflecting the workplace as *a loving community*, the Christian at work might conclude that the employment of numerous teams or clusters underpins sign 6 (the importance of small groups for task-achievement shapes organizational practice); that some form of profit-sharing contributes to sign 11 (people share a common purpose); that support for employees who have been bereaved illustrates sign 32 (there is interest in and support for the families of workers); and that an organization's strong links with Business in the Community furthers sign 33 (opportunities are offered for workers to engage in voluntary projects outside their place of work).

In the context of the workplace as *a learning community*, the Christian at work might see the quality and variety of the training programmes as contributing to sign 1 (work is seen as a journey of discovery); suggestion boxes and questionnaires asking for new ideas as enhancing sign 7 (people are expected to offer ideas for the improvement of the goods produced or services offered); new employees being given a tour of the local neighbourhood as reflecting sign 12 (people are expected to become familiar with the economic and social needs of the area in which the workplace is located); and a fair hearing being given to whistle-blowers as exemplifying sign 16 (people are encouraged to challenge 'received wisdom').

Could there be other signs discerned by the Christian at work not mentioned here?

Yes. The Christian in a particular workplace might discern what they believe to be important signs of the kingdom community not mentioned in the chart. Space is offered at the end of the chart for such signs to be added.

Why try and evaluate the strength of the signs by assigning them a score?

The invitation to the Christian at work to evaluate the strength of each sign is simply to get an overview of where intervention to give fuller expression to the gifts of the kingdom community could be of most value in furthering the communal transformation of the workplace.

Are too many signs suggested?

The list of signs has been made as comprehensive as possible in order to ensure that most aspects of the workplace relevant to the 4Ls are covered. However, the overall purpose of the chart is to help point the Christian at work towards *one sign* which they believe to be currently the most important in guiding their mission of enabling their workplace to manifest more fully the gifts of the kingdom community. As Stage 8 of the project spells out at some length, their task is then to find specific and practical ways in which their chosen mission task can be most effectively addressed. Only the Christian at work, though as always wherever possible in discussion with fellow Christians and a mentor, can decide what practical form intervention should take in their particular situation.

Self-guided discernment

Though the signs chart is offered as a resource for all who might wish to use it, those wanting to align themselves with this project are at liberty to choose a self-guided approach to discernment. In this case they will put the compendium of signs suggested here on one side and seek to discern the gifts of the kingdom community in their workplace in their own way. Provided that this unstructured form of discernment remains grounded in the communal theology set out earlier and leads to some form of intervention to enhance their workplace communally, such an approach comes within the scope of this project. However a self-guided approach to discernment may make it particularly difficult to obtain an overview of their workplace as a model of the kingdom community in action. It should also be stressed that a self-guided approach can be greatly enhanced by being undertaken with the support of a group of Christians engaged in a similar undertaking and/or with the support of a mentor.

Discernment in the workplace using the signs chart

Signs are *ongoing or recurrent features of the workplace which reveal the gifts of the kingdom community at work*. Below are set out a series of steps to assist in the discernment of how fully the gifts of the kingdom community are manifest within your workplace.

1. *Choose a social collective* within your workplace of which you have personal experience and which matters to you.

The term 'social collective' refers to any identifiable and ongoing group or larger body within your place of work. For example, this collective could be an office, school class, hospital ward, work team or section, shop, department, etc., or your workplace as a whole if this is not too large and complex a collective. The collective should be one within which you spend a good deal of your time and have an identifiable role.

2. *Read and reflect on the signs listed below* and use them to offer prompts or pointers to the gifts of the kingdom community present within your workplace.

As stated earlier, it is not assumed that the compendium of signs offered here is infallible or exhaustive. If necessary the project invites you to discern and employ other signs which you believe reveal the gifts of the kingdom community within your place of work.

3. *Choose one of the 4Ls* (life, liberation, love or learning) on which you wish to focus your attention.

If it is difficult to find time to check out all the signs offered here, it is suggested that you focus your attention on one of the 4Ls which you think may have particular relevance to the life of your workplace as a community. However, if you wish to obtain an overview of the extent to which your workplace as a whole may offer a model of the kingdom community at work, you will need to consider all the signs suggested.

4. *Work carefully through the list of signs set out below*.

Place a tick in one of the boxes to indicate how fully you consider the sign concerned to be in evidence within your workplace (4 = very strongly in evidence - to 1 = not very much in evidence).

If you think a particular sign is not relevant or you feel unable to evaluate it, tick the grey column.

If necessary, at the end of the exercise add any other sign(s) not mentioned which you believe to be present. Rate it (them) in the same way. This step gives you the opportunity to discern signs other than those suggested which you think may reveal the communal strength or weakness of the collective chosen.

Note - Rating these signs is not meant to be an objective or exact science. The intention is to give you some guidelines to help in deciding your mission task [Stage 8].

5. *Reflect on the implications of what you have discerned* for any action you might take to enable your workplace to manifest the gifts of the kingdom community more fully.

6. *Move on to intervention* [Stage 8]

This step reminds us that discernment is not an end in itself but a means of making mission a reality.

Note - *To help in this discernment process, try to obtain the involvement of fellow Christians at work and/or the assistance of a mentor.*

Your task of discernment can be greatly enriched and earthed by being undertaken with the help and encouragement of a group of fellow Christians who are also committed to mission in the world of work. Obtaining the support of a mentor, for yourself and/or the group, is also very important.

A signs chart

The workplace as a life-giving community[1]

Task *(Internal)*	4 High	3	2	1 Low	
1. People are committed to their work[2]	✓				
2. Work is life-enhancing[3]		✓			
3. Work is enjoyable		✓			
4. Work is creative[4]		✓			
5. People have time to do their work well[5]			✓		
6. People manage their time productively[6]			✓		
7. There are adequate rest breaks during the working day				✓	
8. People are offered social and recreational opportunities and facilities				✓	
9. There are adequate periods of leave[7]		✓			

---

[1] Jn 1: 1-4 (the source of life); Jn 6: 47 (life eternal); Jn 7: 68 (words of eternal life); Jn 10: 10 (life in all its fullness); Jn 11: 25-26 (the resurrection and the life); Jn 14: 6 (Christ as the life)

[2] Lk 9: 15-62 (no looking back)

[3] Jn 14: 6 (Christ as the life); Jn 15; 1-8 (Christ as the vine); Jn 10: 10 (life in all its fullness); Jn 6: 47 (life eternal)

[4] Gen 1: 1-27 (the Creation); Lk 19: 11-27 (the use of money lent)

[5] Mk 4: 30-2 (the mustard seed); Mt 13 :33 (the leaven)

[6] Mt 25: 14-30 (the story of the talents)

[7] Mt 14: 23; Lk 5: 6 (Christ retires to pray)

Task *(External)*	4 High	3	2	1 Low	
10. The goods produced and services offered are of lasting quality[1]	✓				
11. The goods produced and services offered contribute, directly or indirectly, towards the well-being of society and world	✓				
12. The goods produced and services offered contribute, directly or indirectly, towards the preservation of the planet and the conservation of its resources[2]	✓				
13. The goods produced and services offered contribute, directly or indirectly, towards the alleviation of poverty, hunger, homelessness or disease[3]	✓				
14. The goods produced and services offered contribute, directly or indirectly, towards a fair distribution of the earth's resources[4]	✓				
15. The goods produced and services offered contribute, directly or indirectly, towards the well-being of future generations[5]	✓				

[1] Jn 6: 27 (that which endures); Mt 7: 16-21 (good fruit)
[2] Mt 6: 28-29 (the lilies of the field)
[3] Mt 25: 31-46 (the last judgment); Mk 10: 17-25 (the rich young man); Lk 12: 13-21 (the rich fool)
[4] Lk 1: 53 (the rich sent away empty)
[5] Mk 9: 3; Mk. 10: 13-16; (valuing the young)

Context	4 High	3	2	1 Low	
16. The working environment is healthy					
17. The working environment is safe[1]					
18. The nature and volume of noise is appropriate for the kind of work involved[2]					
19. The working environment is life-enhancing[3]					
20. People are able to move about freely and easily					
21. There are places where people can meet informally[4]					
22. Places are provided where people can be quiet and reflective [5]					
23. There are appropriate facilities for the less physically able					
24. The approaches and entrance to the workplace are physically attractive					
25. The approaches and entrance to the workplace are user-friendly					
26. The resources provided are adequate for the task[6]					

---

[1] Mt 7: 24-25 (the house built upon rock)
[2] 1 Kings 19: 9-13 ('the still small voice')
[3] Lk 12: 27 (consider the lilies)
[4] Lk 7: 36 (the meal in the Pharisee's house); Lk 10: 38 (at Martha's house); Mk 14: 12-16 (the upper room)
[5] Mt 6: 6 (praying in private)
[6] Mt 6: 11 (our daily bread)

Relationships *(Internal)*	4 High	3	2	1 Low	
27. People's well-being is a priority[1]					
28. The workplace fosters a culture of generosity[2]					
29. There is fun and laughter[3]					
30. People celebrate special personal and family occasions together[4]					

Relationships *(External)*	4 High	3	2	1 Low	
31. The workplace is not a nuisance or hazard to those living nearby					
32. The advertising of goods or services does not exploit the vulnerable[5]					
33. There is a commitment to enabling other social collectives to become life-giving communities[6]					
34. There is co-operation with other social collectives seeking to build a life-giving society and world[7]					

---

[1] Jn 6: 35 (Christ the bread of life); Jn 15: 1-8 (the vine and the branches); Mt 5: 45 (sun and rain fall on all)

[2] Mk 12: 41-44 (the widow's gift); Lk 7: 36-50 ('wasting' what is precious)

[3] Lk 7: 33-35 (Christ eating and drinking with all and sundry)

[4] Lk 5: 29 (Levi's feast); Lk 15: 22 (the prodigal son)

[5] Mk 9: 42 (do not cause 'little ones' to sin)

[6] Lk 9: 1-9 (the sending out of the twelve)

[7] Mt 8: 11-12 (outsiders in); Mk 9: 40 (for us if not against us); Jn 10: 16 (an inclusive kingdom)

Model	4 High	3	2	1 Low	
35. The workplace offers a model of what it means to be a life-giving community					

The workplace as a liberating community[1]

Task *(Internal)*	4 High	3	2	1 Low	
1. Care is given to welcoming, inducting and mentoring new workers[2]					
2. What is expected of people is clear and agreed[3]					
3. People are inspired by the organization's vision for its own life and work[4]					
4. People are able to give full expression to their gifts, skills and experience[5]					
5. The division of labour affirms people's different gifts, skills and experience[6]					
6. Initiative and risk-taking are encouraged[7]					
7. Work done well is openly commended[8]					

---

[1] Romans 8: 21 (glorious liberty)
[2] Mk 1: 16-29 (call of the first disciples); Lk 9: 57-62 (the nature of discipleship)
[3] Lk 11: 9-13 (God is true to his promises)
[4] Lk 1: 46-55 (the Magnificat); Lk 2: 28-32 (Simeon meets Christ); Mk 1: 7-8 (the message of John the Baptist)
[5] Mt 25: 14-30 (the story of the talents)
[6] Ephesians 4: 11-14 (many gifts needed)
[7] Mk 2: 23-28 and Mk 3: 1-6 (breaking the Sabbath laws); Lk 16: 1-9 (the shrewd steward)
[8] Mt. 25: 21, 23 (good work commended)

8. People receive honest and creative feed-back on their work[1]					
9. People receive a fair wage in relation to the nature of the work in which they are engaged[2]					
10. There is no excessive gap between the financial rewards offered to those at the top and those at the bottom of the organization[3]					
11. People are able to negotiate flexible working hours					
12. Ample opportunities for career development are offered					
13. People are willing to go the extra mile when necessary[4]					
14. The organization does its utmost to offer job security					

Task (External)	4 High	3	2	1 Low	
15. Opportunities are offered for work experience beyond the workplace[5]					

---

[1] Lk 10: 7 (the worker gets what he deserves)
[2] Mt 20: 1-16 (the labourers in the vineyard); Lk: 3:14 (being content with one's wages)
[3] Mt 6: 19-21 (do not seek after wealth)
[4] Mt 5: 41 (go the extra mile)
[5] Mt 28: 18 (make disciples of all nations)

16. The goods produced and services offered contribute, directly or indirectly, towards the liberation of those in society or world who experience persecution or oppression[1]					
17. The goods produced and services offered contribute, directly or indirectly, towards justice and peace[2]					

Relationships (Internal)	4 High	3	2	1 Low	
18. People are valued as human beings[3]					
19. People find a sense of significance in and through their work[4]					
20. People take a pride in their work[5] work[5]					
21. People are free from anxiety and fear[6]					
22. People are not isolated or lonely[7]					

---

[1] Mt 5: 6, 11 (suffering for what is right); Lk 3: 5 (the crooked made straight); Lk 1: 79 (light to those in darkness); Mk 10: 32-34 (Christ is determined to go to Jerusalem)

[2] Mt 5: 9 (the peacemakers); Mk 11: 15-17 (cleansing the temple); Lk 1:79 (the way of peace); Jn 14: 27 (genuine peace)

[3] Mt 10: 29-31 (more value than sparrows; hairs of our head); Jn 10: 3 (the sheep known by name)

[4] Ibid

[5] Mt 5: 14-16 (let your light shine)

[6] Mt 8: 23-27 (stilling of the storm); Mk 6: 45-52 (walking on the water); Lk 12: 22-31 (do not be anxious); Lk 1: 73 (service without fear); Jn 20: 11-18 (Mary in the garden)

[7] Jn 15: 14 (friends of Christ)

23. Greed and avarice are not part of the workplace culture[1]					
24. People do not boast or brag about their achievements[2]					
25. People openly acknowledge their mistakes and failures[3]					
26. Forgiveness for acknowledged mistakes or failures is an integral aspect of workplace culture[4]					
27. People do not retaliate or seek retribution[5]					
28. There are effective means available for resolving conflict in a fair and supportive way[6]					
29. The resolution of conflict is used to enhance relationships[7]					

---

[1] Mt 6: 19-21 (treasure in heaven); Mk 10: 17-24 (the rich young ruler); Mk 11: 15-19 (cleansing of the temple); Lk 12: 13-21 (the rich fool)

[2] Mt 5: 5 (blessed are the meek); Mt 6: 5-8 (praying in public); Mk 10: 43-45 (servanthood); Mk 9: 33-37 (true greatness); Mk 10: 31 (the last will be first); Lk 1: 51-52 (the proud scattered); Lk 14: 7-14 (the humbled exalted); Lk 18: 9-14 (the Pharisee and the publican)

[3] Lk 15: 3-7 (the lost sheep); Lk 15: 18, 21 (the prodigal son); Lk 18: 9-14 (the Pharisee and the publican); Lk 19: 1-10 (Zacchaeus); Jn 8: 3-11 (the woman taken in adultery)

[4] Mt 6: 12, 14-15 (forgiving and being forgiven); Lk 6: 37 and Mt 7: 1-5 (do not judge); Mt 18: 21-22 (keep on forgiving); Lk 15: 24 (the prodigal son - death to life, lost and found); Lk 7: 36-50 (the forgiveness of sinners); Jn 8: 1-11 (casting the first stone); Mt 18: 23-35 (the king who forgave)

[5] Mt 5: 38-42 (absorbing and deflecting violence); Lk 6: 27-36 (loving one's enemies - turning the other cheek - giving your coat away - do not resist those who take your goods - the golden rule); Lk 6: 37-42 (do not judge)

[6] Mt 5: 23-24 and Mt 5: 38-42 (forgiveness and reconciliation)

[7] Mt 5: 23-24 (if you have a grievance be reconciled to your brother)

30. Grievance procedures are fair and transparent					
31. The workplace is one where diverse competences and skills are seen as an asset[1]					
32. People are self-reliant[2]					
33. People have the courage of their convictions[3]					
34. People are encouraged to express their opinions openly and constructively[4]					
35. People are actively involved in discussing and implementing changes which will affect them					
36. Problem-solving and decision-making are a collective responsibility					
37. People relate to those in authority with appropriate respect[5]					
38. People's out-of-work interests and skills are recognized and affirmed					

---

[1] 1 Cor 12: 1-27 (varieties of gifts enrich the whole)
[2] Mt 7: 7-8 (ask and seek)
[3] Lk 11: 5-10 (persistence rewarded)
[4] Mt 5: 13-16 (salt and light)
[5] Mk 12: 13-17 (render to God and to Caesar what belongs to each); Mk 11: 27-33 (the nature of true authority); Mk 12: 1-12 (the tenants who reject the true heir)

Relationships *(External)*	4 High	3	2	1 Low	
39. There is a commitment to enable other social collectives to become liberating communities[1]					
40. There is collaboration with other social collectives seeking to build a liberating society and world[2]					

Model	4 High	3	2	1 Low	
41. The workplace offers a model of what it means to be a liberating community					

---

[1] Lk 4: 18-30 (the sermon at Nazareth); Lk 9: 1-9 (the sending out of the twelve)

[2] Mt 8: 11-12 (the outsiders are in); Mk 9: 40 (for us if not against us); Jn 10: 16 (an inclusive kingdom)

The workplace as a loving community[1]

Task (Internal)	4 High	3	2	1 Low	
1. People communicate in ways that are clear					
2. People communicate in ways that are open and transparent[2]					
3. People communicate in good time					
4. People communicate in ways that are helpful and informative[3]					
5. The volume of communication is manageable					
6. The importance of small groups for task-achievement shapes organizational practice[4]					
7. There is creative work-focused networking[5]					
8. People are proud of their organization[6]					

---

[1] Lk 10: 27 (the great commandment); Jn 13: 34 and Jn 15: 12-13 (love one another)

[2] Mt 24: 11 and 24 (rejecting false prophets) Jn 8: 31,36 (the truth makes us free); Ephesians 4: 15 (speaking the truth in love);

[3] Christ the story teller

[4] Mt 10: 1-4 (Christ works through twelve disciples)

[5] Mt 11: 2-6 (disciples tell of Christ to John); Jn 4: 28-29 (the woman of Samaria tells others)

[6] Mt 10: 32-33 (acknowledging Christ); John 6: 68 (Christ is the only one to follow); Jn 13: 36-38 (Peter offers his life in the service of Christ)

Task *(External)*	4 High	3	2	1 Low	
9. The goods produced and services offered contribute, directly or indirectly, towards a compassionate society and world					

Relationships *(Internal)*	4 High	3	2	1 Low	
10. The human scale and 'the human touch' are part of the workplace culture[1]					
11. People share a common purpose[2]					
12. People experience a sense of solidarity in and through their workplace[3]					
13. Accountability is mutual across all grades and statuses[4]					
14. There are ample opportunities for informal encounters and conversations[5]					
15. Social networking via the Internet which does not interfere with the task is seen as valuable for enhancing morale					

---

[1] Jn 15: 14-15 (friends not servants)
[2] Mt 6: 24 (the problem of serving two masters); Mk 3: 23-30 (a house divided)
[3] Jn 17: 20-28 (being one); Ephesians 4: 11-16 (many gifts but one body)
[4] Mt 13: 24-30 (weeds and wheat); Mt 13: 47-50 (fish discarded); Mt 21: 28-31 (the two sons)
[5] Lk 10: 38-42 (Martha and Mary); Jn 4: 27 (the woman of Samaria)

16. People care for one another[1]					
17. People are nurtured at times of stress and anxiety[2]					
18. People share their material resources[3]					
19. The workplace has a culture of collaboration[4]					
20. The culture of the workplace is one of honesty and integrity[5]					
21. People respect one another[6]					
22. People trust one another[7]					
23. Women and men are accorded equal rights and responsibilities[8]					
24. There is no discrimination on racial grounds[9]					
25. There is no discrimination on grounds of sexual orientation					

---

[1] Jn 13: 34 and Jn 15: 12-13 (love one another); Mt. 5: 43-48 (loving those who hate us); Mt 25: 31-40 (caring for those in need); Lk 10: 25-37 (the good Samaritan)

[2] Jn 10: 11-16 (Christ the good shepherd): Mt 11: 28-30 (help for the heavy-laden)

[3] Mk 6: 30-44; Mk 8: 1-10 (feeding of the five and four thousand)

[4] 1 Cor 12: 14-26 (all parts of the body count)

[5] Mt 7: 16-21 (false prophets and their fruits); Mt. 24: 11 and 24 (false prophets)

[6] Lk 7: 9 (the centurion's faith)

[7] Mt 8: 5-13 (the centurion's servant); Mk 13: 13 (enduring to the end); Jn 20: 24-29 (Thomas believes)

[8] Jn 4: 9 (Christ talks with a Samaritan woman)

[9] Ibid

26. People work hard to overcome social and cultural divisions[1]					
27. Workplace rituals and symbols help to bond people together[2]					
28. Those who find it difficult to handle change are offered empathy and support[3]					
29. Visitors always receive a welcome[4]					

Relationships (External)	4 High	3	2	1 Low	
30. Dispersed members of the workforce are brought together regularly to further a sense of common purpose and commitment					
31. The organization's mission statement includes a commitment to social responsibility[5]					
32. There is interest in and support for the families of workers					

---

[1] Mk 2: 15 (mixing with all kinds of people); Lk 10: 25-37 (the good Samaritan); Lk 14: 21 (the great banquet)

[2] Mk 8: 34 (the cross); Mk 14: 22-25 (the last supper); Jn 13: 1-17 (the washing of feet)

[3] Mt 5: 6, 10 (those who suffer for the truth will be rewarded); Mt 19: 21 (give to the poor and receive treasure in heaven); Mk 10: 29 - 30 (those who deny themselves for Christ will receive ample reward in heaven)

[4] Mt 25: 35 (the stranger welcomed)

[5] Mt 5: 7, 9, 10 (the Beatitudes)

33. Opportunities are offered for workers to engage in voluntary projects outside their place of work[1]				
34. People show respect for and courtesy towards users of their goods or services				
35. Relationships with suppliers are straight and open				
36. Stakeholders play an active and creative role in the life of the organization				
37. There are good relations with trades unions				
38. There is an openness to enter into partnership with social collectives beyond the workplace committed to building a compassionate society and world[2]				

Model	4 High	3	2	1 Low	
39. The workplace offers a model of what it means to be a loving community					

---

[1] Mt. 5: 41 (the extra mile); Mt 6: 1-4 (giving to charity anonymously)
[2] Mt 8: 11-12 (the outsiders in); Mk 9: 40 (those for us are not against us); Jn 10: 16 (the kingdom is inclusive)

The workplace as a learning community[1]

Task *(Internal)*	4 High	3	2	1 Low	
1. Work is seen as a journey of discovery[2]					
2. There is time and opportunity for reflection[3]					
3. People are ready to question their own assumptions[4]					
4. Learning is seen as a personal responsibility[5]					
5. Learning is seen as a collective responsibility[6]					
6. People are expected to learn from past experiences[7]					
7. People are expected to offer ideas for the improvement of the goods produced or services offered[8]					

---

[1] Mt 23: 8 (Christ as teacher and his learners as brethren); Jn 14: 6 (Christ as the way and the truth); John 8:12 (Christ as the light); Lk 17: 20 (the kingdom of God is here and now)

[2] Mt 6: 33 (seeking the kingdom first); Mt 7: 7-11 (asking and seeking); Mt 13: 44 (the treasure in the field); Mt 13: 44 (the pearl of great price); Lk 2: 46-47 (Christ at twelve); Lk 14: 25-33 (being disciples)

[3] Mk 6: 45 (into the hills to pray)

[4] Mk 10: 17 (rich young man); Lk 10: 26 (eternal life); Lk 10: 29 and 36 (Christ questions his hearers); Jn 5: 6 (the wish to get well)

[5] Mk 4: 9 (ears to hear); Lk 11: 1 (teach us to pray)

[6] Jn 9: 39-41 (spiritual blindness)

[7] Mt 7: 24-27 (the wise builder); Mt 10: 16 (be wise as serpents); Mt 25: 1-13 (the wise maidens)

[8] Lk 10: 29-37 ('Who is my neighbour?'); Mk 8: 27-33 ('Who do men say that I am?')

8. It is expected that learning will lead to innovation and change[1]					
9. There are ample opportunities for people to develop their knowledge and skills					
10. People are enabled to learn skills which make them employable in a diversity of situations					
11. Learning is regarded as a life-long commitment[2]					

Tasks (External)	4 High	3	2	1 Low	
12. People are expected to become familiar with the economic and social needs of the area in which the workplace is located					
13. People are committed to learn from, and share their knowledge, insights and experiences with social collectives beyond the workplace[3]					

Relationships (Internal)	4 High	3	2	1 Low	
14. People listen attentively[4]					
15. People advocate their views whilst remaining open to be questioned on them[5]					

---

[1] Mt 7: 24-27 (hearing and doing); Mk. 8: 34-38 (taking up our cross)
[2] Mk 13: 31 (Christ's words are eternal); Lk 9: 62 (no looking back)
[3] Acts 10: 1-48 (God shows no partiality)
[4] Lk 10: 38-42 (Martha and Mary)
[5] Jn 3: 1-15 (Nicodemus)

16. People are encouraged to challenge 'received wisdom'[1]					
17. There is a culture of openness to learning[2]					
18. There is a culture of dialogue[3]					
19. People are encouraged to grow and develop as whole persons[4]					
20. Experiences and insights are openly shared[5]					

Relationships (External)	4 High	3	2	1 Low	
21. There is a commitment to enable social collectives beyond the workplace to become learning communities					

Model	4 High	3	2	1 Low	
22. The workplace offers a model of what it means to be a learning community					

---

[1] Mt 5: 21-48 (You have heard… but I say…)
[2] Mk 13: 15 (the example of children)
[3] Jn 3: 1-15 (Nicodemus); Jn 4: 7-30 (the woman of Samaria);
[4] Jn 10: 10 (life in all its fullness)
[5] Jn 4: 7-30 (the woman of Samaria); Mt 5: 14-16 (we are to be the light of the world)

Other signs of the kingdom community (own additions)

Signs of the workplace as a life-giving community	4 High	3	2	1 Low	
1.					
2.					
3.					
Signs of the workplace as a liberating community					
4.					
5.					
6.					
Signs of the workplace as a loving community					
7.					
8.					
9.					
Signs of the workplace as a learning community					
10.					
11.					
12.					

Stage 7

Discernment

2 Critical incidents

Discernment in the workplace using critical incidents

Critical incidents are *unscheduled or unexpected happenings within the workplace which reveal the gifts of the kingdom community at work.*

As with signs, the examples of critical incidents offered are placed under categories relating to the four gifts of the kingdom community - *life, liberation, love* and *learning* - which each incident is judged to reflect most clearly. Within these categories, the incidents offered are then grouped under sub-headings describing the main sociological components of the workplace. These are:

- *The task* - the nature of the work in which workers are engaged. This may be:
  - *internal* - relating to the nature of the work itself and how it is undertaken or
  - *external* - relating to the work's impact on the wider world
- *The context* - the physical, material and environmental aspects of the workplace
- *Relationships* - the interpersonal features of the workplace. These may be:
  - *internal* - embracing all employees and stake holders, or
  - *external* - concerning how the workplace as a communal entity relates to the wider world.

Because critical incidents are one-off happenings which rarely reflect all the signs of the kingdom community the category of *Model* is not relevant here.

Below are set out a series of steps to assist you in discerning, through observation of and reflection on critical incidents which occur within your workplace, how fully the gifts of the kingdom community are manifest there.

1. *Choose a social collective* *to observe within your workplace of which you have personal experience and which is important for your working life.*

The term 'social collective' refers to any identifiable and ongoing group or larger body within your place of work. For example, the collective could be an office, school class, hospital ward, work team or section, shop, department, etc., or your workplace as a whole if this is not too large and complex a collective. The collective should be one within which you spend a good deal of your time, where you have an identifiable role and which is of importance to you.

2. *Read and reflect on the examples of critical incidents* *set out below and use them to offer prompts or pointers to critical incidents within your workplace.*

The examples of critical incidents offered here are drawn from real life situations. As set out here, they will not occur in your particular place of work. Nevertheless, the examples are meant to illustrate the sort of incidents for which you need to be looking out. Some may seem minor happenings but all can offer important insights into the communal strength or weakness of the workplace concerned.

3. *Observe* *over a limited period of time, from a day up to a week, any critical incidents which occur within the social collective you have chosen. Make a note of these incidents as soon as possible after they have occurred and, if possible, no later than the end of the same day.*

Note here your important role as a 'reflective practitioner'. It is important that you record the critical incidents observed as soon as possible as important details may otherwise be forgotten.

4. *At the end of your observation period* *choose one of the critical incidents* *which you feel raises particularly important issues about the strength or weakness of your workplace as a community. Such issues could be concerned with work as such (the task), the working environment (the context), or relationships (relationships).*

5. *Set quality time aside to* *discern how fully* *the critical incident chosen reveals the presence of one or more gifts of the kingdom community. Note down what you have discerned.*

The critical incident chosen should be reflected on carefully and prayerfully. The incident concerned may reveal that your workplace is communally strong - in which case the issue is how you develop this quality more fully. On the other hand, the critical incident may reveal your workplace to be communal weak - in which case the issue is how you might address this deficit. This step is an especially important part of the discernment process as it will be the basis on which you decide your mission task.

6. Move on to intervention [Stage 8].

This step reminds us that discernment is not an end in itself but a means of making mission a reality.

Note - To help in this discernment process, try to obtain the involvement of fellow Christians at work and/or the assistance of a mentor.

Your task of discernment can be greatly enriched and earthed by being undertaken with the help and encouragement of a group of fellow Christians who are also committed to mission in the world of work. Obtaining the support of a mentor, for yourself and/or the group, is also very important.

Examples of critical incidents
The workplace as a life-giving community

Life affirmed

Task

Internal

At the beginning of a section's formal meetings, the section leader decided that ten minutes be set aside for people to report briefly on interesting or creative developments that had happened since the last gathering.

Context

A member of staff took the initiative of bringing in flowers and foliage from her garden to decorate the foyer of her work premises.

A garden centre decided to use a wide range of the plants on sale to demonstrate how its products could beautify its own environment.

At a factory where production methods had for a long time produced waste of a dirty and dangerous nature, a new manager decided that debris and waste should be cleared away at the end of each shift and involved the workforce in agreeing a realistic health and safety policy.

Relationships

Internal

The board of a small business did its utmost to offer employees the security of long-term contracts but as the economic situation worsened went further and wrote into company policy that when times were particularly difficult employees would be expected to reduce their hours before anyone was made redundant.

Life denied

Task

Internal

A manufacturing firm secretively produced goods with built-in short-term obsolescence.

External

To avoid tax liabilities within the UK, a large retail company decided to establish its financial base in a country with lower tax rates.

Relationships

Internal

By introducing a rigid piece-work system, the management of a mobile phone assembly department succeeded in setting one worker over against another and undermined any sense of work being an enjoyable collective endeavour.

A call-centre manager deeply concerned about meeting the targets set for her allowed employees no time or space to meet informally or to socialize.

The workplace as a liberating community

Liberation affirmed

Task

Internal

As a result of a critical Ofsted report for his school, an inexperienced head teacher became far more open to his capable governing body which he had previously seen as threatening his authority.

Relationships

Internal

A personal assistant to a chief executive forgot to inform him of an important engagement. Immediately the mistake was realised, she went in apprehensively to inform him. She was thanked for her honesty, assured that 'we all make mistakes' and given a vote of confidence in her skills and conscientiousness.

In a workshop for those with severe physical disabilities one of the employees commented to a visitor about a fellow worker: 'She doesn't speak or hear, but there's nothing wrong with her'.

When a group's vehicle broke down on an adventure expedition organized by a large business, the participants were amazed when a young man who had been ribbed for being hopeless at rock-climbing and caving was discovered to be a first-rate mechanic.

External

A doctors' surgery team decided to sign up a number of its patients' consultative group to support elderly residents in nearby care homes who were nervous about having their annual influenza vaccination.

A retailer in a small town took the initiative of referring customers to other shops if she could not meet their particular needs.

The manager of a large supermarket decided to go over to a 'fair trade' policy to encourage its customers to respond to the needs of overseas workers whose efforts were poorly rewarded.

203

Liberation denied

Task

Internal

At a weekly feed-back meeting of a distribution business, those sales representatives who had failed to reach their target were made to stand on the table at which they were sitting.

Relationships

Internal

'He's a poor old soul so he can wait for a bit' one shop assistant was heard to whisper to another when serving a number of customers vying for her attention.

Employees of a large business came to work one day to find redundancy notices posted on their computer screens.

The workplace as a loving community

Love affirmed

Task

External

A business supplying the construction industry decided to offer its large heap of off-cuts from planks and beams free of charge to anyone interested to take them.

Relationships

Internal

In a school staff meeting two teachers had a major disagreement about a school trip resulting in one of them sending the other a 'flame' email. Instead of sending a 'flame' email back, the recipient sought out his antagonist for a personal conversation in which he acknowledged that he may have misinterpreted and devalued her. She responded in a positive way and the relationship was mended.

A worker's wife died of cancer leaving him three young children to look after. He was sent a letter by his work colleagues containing a long list of services, from shopping to lawn mowing, which they offered to undertake for him at no cost.

External

A solicitor's firm changed its regulations to allow occasional days for its employees to spend time undertaking some form of voluntary work within the city in which it was located.

A supermarket made up several hundred parcels of goods at Christmas to supply food-banks for those suffering from the effects of the economic recession

Love denied

Task

Internal

A worker who was open and friendly to colleagues frequently failed to do work he promised to do.

Relationships

Internal

'A bit of soft porn does nobody any harm.' (A male employee's comment on a calendar he had pinned on the office notice-board.)

A culture of male machismo on a factory floor led to a number of incidents of sexual harassment of women working there.

A supermarket check-out assistant who needed to ask a customer a question could not gain her attention because the latter was on her mobile phone. When she persisted with her question the customer hissed: 'Can't you see - I'm on my phone!' The customer later complained to the management who reprimanded the check-out assistant and offered the customer free shopping coupons for her next visit.

At a school assembly the head of a school with a 'no bullying' policy ranted at pupils for minor acts of misbehaviour.

External

A company justified its use of child labour in the country where its goods were made by arguing that they were operating in 'a highly competitive world market'.

The workplace as a learning community

Learning affirmed

Task

Internal

A multi-national company ruled that all its employees should meet in small groups *across* occupational boundaries once a year to suggest how the running of the company might be improved.

External

A group of community workers linked to a voluntary agency who had spent most of their working lives in the UK was sent to a large city in the USA for a month to study community organizing. They came back inspired and re-energised by their experience.

Relationships

Internal

A local authority invited a number of disadvantaged young people from a diversity of ethnic and social backgrounds, aged between 16 and 19, to share their hopes for the future of their city in a one-to-one conversation with city leaders. The leaders reported that their eyes had been opened by the articulateness and perceptive insights of the young people.

External

As a leadership training exercise, a group of middle managers was taken round deprived areas of a city and given time to chat to residents about how they coped with unemployment, racial discrimination and poverty. They returned very impressed by the resilience of the people to whom they had spoken.

Learning denied

Task

Internal

On an in-service course, the training officer of a large company was so hung up on her desire to produce impressive power-point presentations, accompanied by her repetition of what was being projected, that she allowed trainees little opportunity for personal reflection or group discussion.

Relationships

Internal

At an important staff meeting, a manager who spent a good deal of her time extolling the virtues of 'attentive listening' did most of the talking.

External

A local authority set up a major consultative exercise in which citizens were invited to write onto cards their views as to how city services might be improved. Without further consultation, it then decided on which of many suggestions it would take action.

Stage 7
Discernment
3 Servant leadership
Signs

The six roles which most clearly characterize servant leadership were identified in Stage 5. The task of the Christian at work at this stage in the project is to discern whether *leadership* within the workplace affirms or denies the gifts of the kingdom community.

Other than for the roles of visionary and strategist (which span all 4Ls), the signs for the presence of the gifts of the kingdom community are closely related to those set out in Stage 7(1) of this project. Therefore, in relation to the roles of animator (life), enabler (liberation), intermediary (love) and educator (learning), the discernment process involves the Christian at work *referring back to the signs* relating to those particular gifts and seeking to discern the degree to which they are present *because of the strengths or weaknesses of the leadership being exercised*.

Suggested steps for discernment

1. <u>Choose a social collective</u> to observe within your workplace of which you have personal experience and which is important in your working life.

The term 'social collective' refers to any identifiable and ongoing group or larger body within your place of work. For example, this collective could be an office, school class, hospital ward, work team or section, shop, department, etc., or your workplace as a whole if this is not too large and complex a collective. The collective should be one within which you spend a good deal of our time, where you have an identifiable role and which is of importance to you.

2. Focus attention on <u>one person</u> within your chosen social collective who exercises an important <u>leadership role</u>. (This could be you!)

3. Read and reflect on <u>the signs</u> relating to <u>leadership</u> listed below and use them to offer prompts or pointers to the gifts of the kingdom community present within your own workplace.

4. *Choose one leadership role* related to the leader already identified (visionary, strategist, animator, enabler, intermediary or educator) on which to focus your attention.

5. *Work carefully through the list of signs suggested below* (or those set out in Stage 7(1))

Place a tick in one of the boxes to indicate how fully you consider the sign to be in evidence *in relation to the leadership style of the person you have chosen* (4 = very strongly in evidence - to 1 = not very much in evidence).

If you think a particular sign is not relevant or you feel unable to evaluate it, tick the grey column.

6. *If necessary, add any other sign(s)* related to that leadership role not suggested here but which you believe to be in evidence.

Score your own sign(s) in a similar way a similar scale.

7. *Move on to intervention*. [Stage 8]

This step reminds us that discernment is not an end in itself but a means of making mission a reality.

Note - *To help in this discernment process, try to obtain the involvement of fellow Christians at work and/or the assistance of a mentor*.

Your task of discernment can be greatly enriched and earthed by being undertaken with the help and encouragement of a group of fellow Christians who are also committed to mission in the world of work. Obtaining the support of a mentor, for yourself and/or the group, is also very important.

A signs chart for servant leadership
The leader as visionary
(All 4Ls)

Task *(Internal)*	4 High	3	2	1 Low	
1. The leader is passionate about the worth of the product or services offered[1]					
2. The leader has a clear sense of purpose and direction[2]					
3. The leader is able to see 'the big picture'[3]					
4. The leader is able to take a long-term view[4]					
5. The leader is creative[5]					
6. The leader engages in lateral thinking[6]					
7. The leader is concerned with tapping into people's imagination before exploring the feasibility of new ideas					

[1] Jn 14: 6 (Christ the way, truth and life)
[2] Mt 16: 13-23 (Caesarea Philippi – the prediction of the passion); Mk 9: 2-8 (the transfiguration); Lk 2: 41-52 (Christ at twelve); Lk 4: 16-30 (the sermon at Nazareth); The passion narrative
[3] Mt 4: 1-11 (the temptations)
[4] Mt 28: 16-20 (the great commission)
[5] Mk 14: 24 and 1 Cor 11: 25 (a new covenant); Jn 13: 34 (a new commandment)
[6] Mt 9: 16-17 (new garments and fresh wineskins needed); Mk 2: 27 (the Sabbath made for man); Many parables of the kingdom

	4	3	2	1	
8. The leader sees problems as opportunities not obstacles[1]					
9. The leader has energy and enthusiasm[2]					
10. The leader gives impetus to the task[3]					
11. The leader ensures that visions are shared[4]					

Relationships (Internal)	4 High	3	2	1 Low	
12. The leader inspires others[5]					
13. The leader offers hope[6]					
14. The leader commands authority[7] authority[7]					
15. The leader is an attentive listener[8]					

---

[1] Mk 9: 23 and 10: 27 (all things possible)

[2] Mk 11: 15-17 (the cleansing of the temple); Lk 9: 53 (Christ's is determined to go to Jerusalem)

[3] Mk 6: 7-13 (the sending out of the twelve); Lk 10: 1-16 (the sending out of the seventy)

[4] Mt 28: 16-20 (the great commission)

[5] Jn 8: 12 (Christ as the light); Mt 9: 27-28 (blind men healed); Mk 5: 24-34 (a woman's faith); Jn 4: 39-42 (Samaritans believe); Jn 20: 26-29 (Thomas convinced)

[6] Mt 10: 31 (we are valued by God); Jn 14: 1-3 and 27 (be not troubled); Jn 14: 18 (we are not left desolate)

[7] Mk 1: 22 (teaching with authority); Jn 14: 6 (Christ the way, the truth and the life)

[8] Jn 8: 3-11 (the woman accused of adultery)

	4	3	2	1	
16. The leader 'walks the talk'[1]					
17. The leader encourages people to use their imagination					

Relationships (External)	4 High	3	2	1 Low	
18. The leader is committed to using the organization's goods and services for the well-being of society					
19. The leader is committed to using the organization's goods and services to help the alleviation of poverty, hunger, homelessness or disease[2]					
20. The leader is committed to using the organization's goods and services for the preservation of the planet and the conservation of its resources					
21. The leader is committed to using the goods produced and services offered for the well-being of future generations[3]					

---

[1] Mt 16: 21 (Christ predicts his passion); Jn 1: 14 (the Word became flesh); Jn 10: 12 and 15 (the good shepherd lays down his life for the sheep); Jn 13: 1-17 (the washing of feet)
[2] Lk 4: 16-19 (the sermon at Nazareth)
[3] Mk 9: 42 (do not betray the next generation)

Model	4 High	3	2	1 Low	
22. The leader offers a model of visionary servant leadership[1]					

---

[1] Jn 13: 1-17 (the washing of feet)

The leader as strategist
(All 4Ls)

Task *(Internal)*	4 High	3	2	1 Low	
1. The leader is able to use visions and values to give direction and impetus to relevant action[1]					
2. The leader has a clear overview of how the workplace as a whole operates[2]					
3. The leader has the competence and experience to plan strategically[3]					
4. The leader is aware of the spectrum of material and physical resources available[4]					
5. The leader has the ability to access material and physical resources to achieve effective the task[5]					
6. The leader is aware of the need for limited achievements at the outset to boost commitment[6]					

---

[1] Lk 10: 1-12 (the sending out of the seventy); Mt 16: 21 (Christ's reveals his destiny to his disciples); Mt 28: 18-30 (the great commission)
[2] Mt 4: 4-11 (the temptations); Mt 16: 21(Christ indicates the way ahead); Jn 14: 1-3 (Christ's understanding of heaven)
[3] Mt 7: 24-25 (the wise man who built his house upon rock); Mt 25: 1-13 (the wise maidens)
[4] Mt 6: 11 (praying for daily bread); Mt 6:31 (God knows our material needs)
[5] Mk 6: 30-44 (the feeding of the five thousand)
[6] Mk 12: 41-44 (the widow's small offering)

7. The leader is skilled in managing change[1]					
8. The leader is flexible as to how outcomes are achieved[2]					
9. The leader is able to adapt or set aside received wisdom or traditional practices[3]					
10. The leader recognizes when to engage in short-term and when to engage in long-term interventions[4]					
11. The leader is aware of the difference between risks worth taking and risks which need to be avoided[5]					

Relationships (Internal)	4 High	3	2	1 Low	
12. The leader talks of 'we' and 'us' rather than of 'you' or 'they'[6]					
13. The leader is skilled in facilitating the potential of small groups[7]					
14. The leader is skilled in facilitating the potential of networks					

---

[1] The world changing ministry of Christ
[2] Lk 15: 11-32 (the father allows the prodigal son his head)
[3] Mt 5: 43-48 (love your enemies); Jn 5: 18 (breaking the Sabbath)
[4] Mk 14: 36 (Christ prays that not his will but God's be done)
[5] Lk 19: 12-27 (the use of the talents)
[6] Jn 15: 12-15 (Christ's followers as friends not servants)
[7] Mk 3: 13-14 (the calling of the disciples); Mk 6: 7 (the sending out of the twelve)

15. The leader is aware of the workplace's diverse human resources[1]					
16. The leader is able to achieve the effective integration of the workforce's diverse skills and abilities[2]					
17. The leader does not raise false expectations[3]					

Relationships (External)	4 High	3	2	1 Low	
18. The leader knows how to access human resources from beyond the workplace					
19. The leader engages with those beyond the workplace who have the potential to become valuable partners[4]					
20. The leader works to ensure that the products or services of the workplace assist those in need in society and world[5]					

---

[1] Mk 2: 13-17 (Christ associates with tax collectors and sinners); Lk 16: 14-24 (all comers at the marriage feast)
[2] Ephesians 4: 11-16 (Christ's diverse gifts make up one body)
[3] Mt 8: 18-20 (to follow Christ is to be homeless); Mk. 8: 34-38 (taking up our cross)
[4] Mk 9: 40 (if not against us then for us)
[5] Mt 25: 34-40 (serving those on the margins)

Model	4 High	3	2	1 Low	
21. The leader offers a model of strategic leadership[1]					

---

[1] The world-changing ministry of Christ

The leader as animator

(Life)

The leader enhances the signs of the gift of life set out in Stage 7(1)

The leader as enabler

(Liberation)

The leader enhances the signs of the gift of liberation set out in Stage 7(1)

The leader as intermediary

(Love)

The leader enhances the signs of the gift of love set out in Stage 7(1)

The leader as educator

(Learning)

The leader enhances the signs of the gift of learning set out in Stage 7(1)

Critical incidents

The six roles which most clearly characterize servant leadership in institutions, sacred and secular, were identified in Stage 5 of the project. The task of the Christian at work discussed here is to discern whether *leadership* within the workplace is affirming or denying the gifts of the kingdom community.

Here we offer some examples of critical incidents which might point to the presence of the gifts of the kingdom community - life, liberation, love and learning - in relation to these six leadership roles.

Suggested steps for discernment

The following steps are meant as a guide for the Christian seeking to employ critical incidents to discern how fully the gifts of the kingdom community are present within the workplace *because of the strengths or weaknesses of the leadership being exercised.*

1. Choose a social collective to observe within your workplace of which you have personal experience and which is important in your working life.

The term 'social collective' refers to any identifiable and ongoing group or larger body within your place of work. For example, this collective could be an office, school class, hospital ward, work team or section, shop, department, etc., or your workplace as a whole if this is not too large and complex a collective. The collective should be one within which you spend a good deal of our time, where you have an identifiable role and which is of importance to you.

2. Focus attention on one person within your chosen social collective who exercises an important leadership role. (This could be you!)

3. Read and reflect on the examples of critical incidents set out below and use them to offer prompts or pointers to critical incidents relating to leadership within your workplace.

The examples of critical incidents offered here are drawn from real life situations. As set out here, they will not occur in your particular place of work. Nevertheless, the examples are meant to illustrate the sort of incidents for which you need to be looking out. Some may seem minor happenings but all can offer important insights into the communal strength or weakness of the workplace concerned.

4. Observe over a limited period of time, from a day up to a week, any critical incidents relating to the nature of that person's leadership which occur within the social collective you have chosen to observe. Make a note of these incidents as soon as possible after they have occurred and, if possible, no later than the end of the same day.

Note here your important role as a 'reflective practitioner'. It is important that you record the critical incidents observed as soon as possible as important details may otherwise be forgotten.

5. At the end of your observation period choose one of the critical incidents which you feel raises important issues about the strengths or weaknesses of leadership within your workplace. Such issues could be concerned with leadership in relation to work as such (the task), the working environment (the context), or relationships (relationships).

6. Set quality time aside to discern how fully the critical incident chosen reveals the presence of one or more gifts of the kingdom community. Note down what you have discerned.

This incident may reveal that some form of intervention to change the nature or style of leadership is needed if the gifts of the kingdom community are to be affirmed and expressed more fully.

7. Move on to intervention. [Stage 8]

This step reminds us that discernment is not an end in itself but a means of making mission a reality.

Note - To help in this discernment process, try to obtain the involvement of fellow Christians at work and/or the assistance of a mentor.

Your task of discernment can be greatly enriched and earthed by being undertaken with the help and encouragement of a group of fellow Christians who are also committed to mission in the world of work. Obtaining the support of a mentor, for yourself and/or the group, is also very important.

The leader as visionary

(All 4Ls)

Task

Internal

The manager of the research department of a large engineering company commissioned the setting up of a data base on which the know-how, expertise and skills of employees were noted for all to access and use as and when appropriate. (Liberation and learning affirmed)

Relationships

Internal and external

The chief executive of a city council arranged a two day consultation at which those from every sector of city life were brought together to share their vision for the city for the next ten years. (All 4Ls affirmed)

The leader as strategist

(All 4Ls)

Task

Internal

A businesswoman in a small rural town networked all the local traders to get their commitment and co-operation in setting up a new and imaginative Christmas market week-end which boosted the local economy. (Life, liberation and love affirmed)

Relationship

Internal

The principal of a college of higher education suffering a serious decline in recruitment failed to employ the personal skills and resources of his staff and to make good use of these to aid recruitment. (Liberation, love and learning denied)

The leader as animator

(Life)

Task

Internal

An office manager brought all his staff together to help him draw up and implement long-term plans for their workplace to make it lighter, more attractively decorated, and in all other ways, more user friendly. (Life affirmed)

Relationships

Internal

The head of a college department training community and youth workers instigated an induction programme for students entailing a number of 'ice-breaking' events, one of which was an afternoon cruise on the local river. (Life affirmed)

The leader as enabler

(Liberation)

Task

Internal

The manager of a large store adopted a policy of 'three mistakes and you're out' for his check-out staff. (Liberation denied)

Relationships

Internal

A new secondary school head teacher was very committed to her pupils but saw her governing body as a threat and related to the more articulate parents of her school children with some apprehension. (Liberation denied)

The leader as intermediary

(Love)

Task

Internal

A new chief executive of a hospital spent a good part of her first week 'walking the talk' and linking up members of her staff whom she felt had experience, insights and skills which could be disseminated more widely through innovative connections. (Love affirmed)

Relationships

Internal

A director of education within a large city invited a secondary school pupil to work-shadow him as part of her work experience. He treated her with great courtesy, during official meetings sought to bring her into the conversation whenever possible and invited her to sit alongside him as he travelled or ate lunch. (Love affirmed)

The leader as educator

(Learning)

Task

Internal

The manager of a human resources department was insistent that his staff undertook a recently devised in-service training course but failed to check out with them how they were applying what they had learned to their daily work. (Learning denied)

Relationships

Internal and external

A newly appointed chief constable spent the first six months in her post listening attentively to her colleagues of all ranks and to the public before setting out proposals for a radical redirection of her force's endeavours. (Learning affirmed)

Stage 8

Intervention

Introduction

The rights and responsibilities of Christian intervention

The initiator

Throughout the Kingdom at Work Project it is assumed that those involved in the tasks of discernment and intervention are Christians actively involved in the workplace. In relation to Stage 8, that of intervention, we shall sometimes refer to such Christians as the *initiators*. Initiators are those who intervene in the task, context or relationships dimensions of the workplace with a mission task of enabling it to manifest more fully the gifts of the kingdom community.

Initiators may or may not have formal leadership roles. However, because the latter are of great importance in enabling work and the workplace to manifest the gifts of life, liberation, love and learning, some examples given in Stage 8(2) focus on the leader as an initiator.

The right to intervene

We have argued that the stance of the Christian initiator towards all those they encounter needs to be that of servant [Stage 5]. As Margaret Whipp (2008) puts it, the relationship of Christians to their colleagues can never be a matter of 'power-over', but should be of 'power-with' or 'power-for' those with whom they work (p. 138).

It is important to be clear what right the Christian as such has to intervene in the workplace, implicitly or explicitly, individually or collectively, in ways which might be challenging or discomforting. Here, two issues need to be addressed: 'By what authority does the Christian engage in mission at work?' and, closely related to that question, 'What kind of agreement with those involved does intervention require'? We consider these issues more fully when exploring the first two phases of the intervention cycle, 'Authority' and 'Agreement', set out below (*Diagram 7*).

The responsibility to intervene

For the committed Christian, intervention to enable the workplace to manifest the gifts of the kingdom community is not an optional extra. Like every other sphere of life, the world of work reflects what Francis Spufford (2012) calls 'the crack in everything' (pp. 24-53) or, as he expresses it rather more emphatically, 'the human propensity to fuck things up' (p. 27). The workplace has the potential to be a rich and diverse community of character [Stage 1]. However, it can also be a social collective of a highly dysfunctional kind. Work can be hard and tedious; working conditions can be dangerous, dirty and depressing; workers can be treated as less than human, objects to be exploited in order to boost productivity; mistrust, disloyalty, manipulation and dishonesty can permeate and corrupt the workplace culture; the potential workers have to learn and develop their skills and experience can be neglected.

Such forces destroy the communal potential of the workplace and make it all the more important that Christians offer the workplace a new vision, promise, commission and resource. The vision is that of a world and workplaces which, as communities of character, manifest the gifts of life, liberation, love and learning. The promise is that the world of work can be transformed from one which denies or negates those gifts into one where they are acknowledged and utilized for the common good, for the benefit of those within and the wider world.

Thus Christians at work have a commission. They are called to initiate (by discernment and intervention) this transformation with commitment and passion. They are not in the world of work to condone 'the crack' but to help heal it and to enable the workplace to reach its full human potential. In that task, they have a massive resource. They are offered the inspiration of a communal theology, the power of a communal spirituality, the principles of a communal economy, and the model and support of a diaconal church [Stages 5 and 10].

The mission task

We define the focus of intervention as *'the mission task'*. The *overall* mission task of the Kingdom at Work Project is that of enabling Christians to create workplaces transformed by the gifts of the kingdom community: life, liberation, love and learning. The *specific* mission task is to enable a particular workplace to be transformed by those same gifts. Unless otherwise stated when used below, the term 'mission task' refers to the *specific* mission task.

Entry points

Signs

One approach to choosing the mission task is to choose *a sign* which is deemed to have the potential to enhance the presence of one or more of the gifts of the kingdom community [see the signs suggested in Stage 7(1)]. The sign chosen may point to a gift which has been rated high (very strongly in evidence) or low (very little in evidence). In the former case, affirming the endeavours of all those responsible and intervention to enhance that gift even further could be an important mission task. In the latter case, the mission task is to find ways of redeeming the situation

Alternatively, the Christian initiator might decide to focus on a sign of their own choosing, not listed in Stage 7(1), which they believe to be particularly important.

Critical incidents

Another way of choosing the mission task is to focus on *a critical incident* identified through the discernment process set out in Stage 7(2). This should be an incident which seems to be of particular significance in highlighting how the workplace might more fully manifest one or more gifts of the kingdom community.

If the critical incident chosen reveals that a gift of the kingdom community is clearly present within the workplace, then the mission task will be to find ways in which that gift can be further enhanced. In this case, intervention should include some form of affirmation or celebration of what has already been achieved. It is always important that the initiator offers recognition of the communal qualities of the workplace where in evidence.

However, if the critical incident chosen reveals how a gift of the kingdom community is being denied or ignored within the workplace, the mission task will again be to find some means of redeeming that situation.

A critical incident which generates strong feelings, affirmative *or* negative, is often the most likely to point to some form of intervention which has the greatest potential to bring about transformation of the workplace task, working environment or working relationships.

Outcomes

Before the Christian initiator decides on their mission task, it is important that hoped for outcomes are specified. It is also important that the initiator is clear how they will know whether or not the mission task has been accomplished. It can be helpful if the mission task and the outcomes hoped for are recorded. It has been stressed many times already that wherever possible the proposed task should be discussed, and if necessary revised, in the light of conversations with Christian colleagues and/or a mentor.

Implicit and explicit intervention

Intervention can take the form of an initiative which does not make any reference to Christian concepts, when it is ***implicit***, or that which includes some *verbal* attempt to make the Christian motivation for the intervention known, when it is ***explicit***.

Implicit intervention

'Implicit' and 'explicit' intervention in the workplace are discussed at some depth by Margaret Whipp (2008, pp. 96-117). In her thesis, the 'implicit' model of intervention is defined as 'incarnational presence', a presence which does not employ any use of overt Christian language or symbols (p. 96). Whipp describes four types of Christian she identifies as involved in implicit intervention (p. 101). These are:

- 'the silent servant' (epitomized by the worker-priest movement in France, post second world war);

- 'hidden, holy people';

- 'transformers' who are change agents who actively seek out 'partnerships for the common good' (in many ways akin to those we term 'servant leaders');

- and 'closet Christians', described as the silent majority who are hard put to hold on to a faith perspective in workplaces which they often describe as 'a spiritual desert: arid, hostile, unrewarding'.

In this project, *implicit* intervention is seen as actions, individual *or* collective, which are undertaken to transform the workplace but based on the conviction that the medium embodies the message. Such forms of intervention should never become subtle means of proselytization. They should be seen as endeavours whose communal worth is self-evident to Christian and non-Christian alike. However, if questions about the motivation behind implicit intervention are raised, the Christian initiator may need to be ready to engage in explicit intervention, for example through some form of dialogue as described in Stage 8(3).

Explicit intervention

In her own discussion of intervention at work, Margaret Whipp interprets 'explicit' intervention as a pro-active and overt attempt to make disciples. She identifies four types of 'Christian' involved in such endeavours (pp. 106-115). These are:

- 'Evangelists… (who) never miss an opportunity for (speaking) the gospel' (p. 114);

- 'Subtle signallers' who communicate the Christian message through 'car stickers and fish badges, screen savers and crosses…, lanyards and wrist bands (which) beam out a silent message inviting interest and response' (pp. 109-110);

- 'Secret agents' who wait in the shadows for opportunities to introduce the more vulnerable to the gospel message;

- 'Crusaders' who take a more confrontational approach to the 'secularization' of the workplace.

We empathize with Margaret Whipp's evident concern that explicit intervention can often be of a proselytizing nature. In the context of this project's purpose of creating workplaces transformed by the gifts of the kingdom community, such forms of intervention would also be dysfunctional. Nevertheless, we recognize that implicit intervention may sometimes be inadequate, not least in failing to offer workplace colleagues some understanding of the gifts of the kingdom community, as well of the Giver of those gifts. Consequently we believe that *explicit intervention* has its proper place within the world of work.

In relation to this project, we define intervention as *explicit* if it involves the use of concepts, language or symbols which are derived from and informed by a communal theology, spirituality, economy and diaconal structures [Stages 2 to 5]. The Christian at work here has the important task of using language and symbols which not only have a clear association with Christian faith but carry meaning for and can impact on the workplace culture. Explicit intervention comes to the fore when the Christian openly seeks to communicate something about the nature of the gifts of the kingdom community through dialogue [Stage 8(3)], intervenes by means of Christian symbols or overt messages [Stage 8(4)], or when engaged in prayer and worship [Stage 8(5)].

Individual and collective intervention

Intervention can be either individual or collective. *Individual intervention* is defined as the initiator's action for change which does not necessitate involving others as active partners in that undertaking. Such action is often of a spontaneous nature and short-term.

Collective intervention is defined as action for change which is undertaken in partnership with others. Such an approach to intervention is usually planned ahead and will be of some duration.

The intervention cycle

Management studies indicate that intervention for organizational change has a number of phases. All need to be addressed if intervention (in our case the mission task) is to be successful. Here the project offers a tool - 'the intervention cycle' (*Diagram 7*) - for identifying and understanding these phases. The fact that each phase of the cycle begins with the letter 'A' is simply an aide-memoire.[1] Although the eleven phases of the cycle are drawn from management theory, all are seen as having some clear affinity with one or more of the kingdom community's gifts of life, liberation, love and learning. These affinities (in brackets) are noted against the heading for each phase.

The phases of the intervention cycle are addressed in a clockwise direction. The discernment phase is identified by the term 'Audit'. The Audit phase of the cycle always comes first as it is essential for discerning the presence of the gifts of the kingdom community in the workplace and thus for identifying the initiator's mission task.

---

[1] This cycle, in a slightly different form, is also described in *Schools as Learning Communities – Transforming Education* (Clark, 1996, pp. 106-12).

The second and third phases of the intervention cycle, Authority and Agreement, are important for both individual *and* collective intervention. However, because individual intervention is likely to be more spontaneous, shorter-term and less complex than collective intervention, the remaining phases are usually of more relevance to collective intervention. Thus in the examples of intervention we offer later, the remaining phases of the cycle are largely considered in relation to collective intervention [Stage 8(2)].

Diagram 7
The intervention cycle
The 'eleven As'

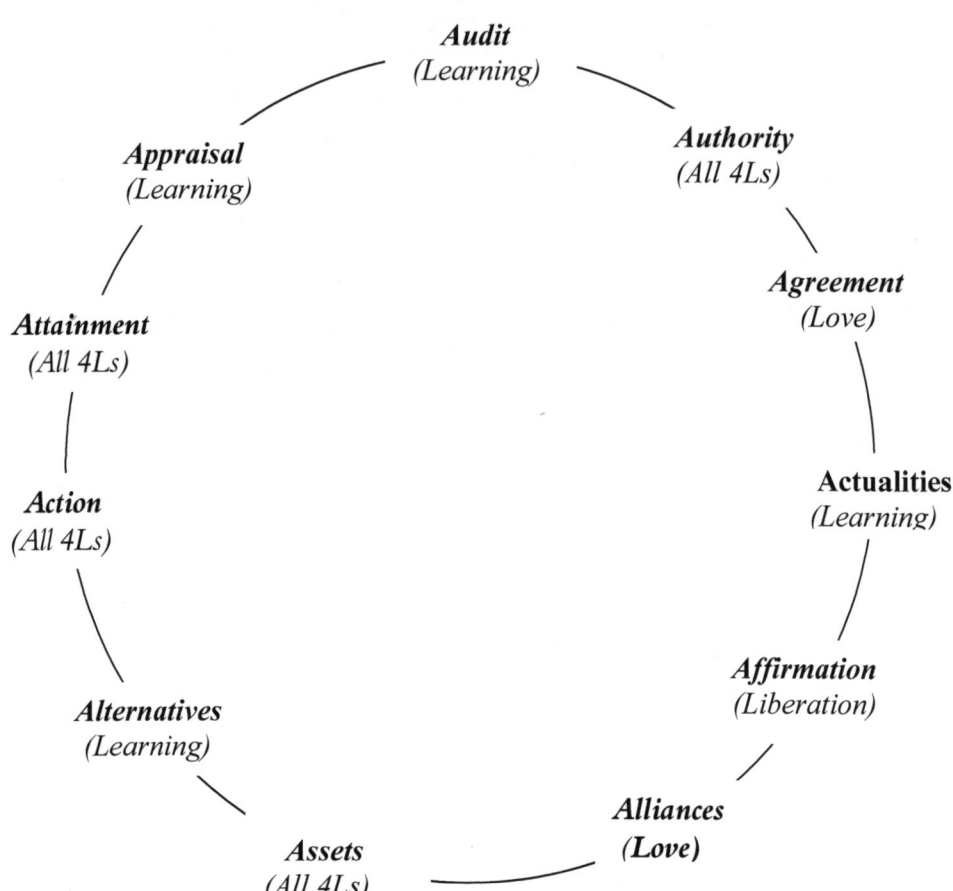

Audit
(Learning)

Appraisal
(Learning)

Authority
(All 4Ls)

Agreement
(Love)

Attainment
(All 4Ls)

Actualities
(Learning)

Action
(All 4Ls)

Affirmation
(Liberation)

Alternatives
(Learning)

Assets
(All 4Ls)

Alliances
(Love)

The collective intervention cycle
The 'eleven A's'

Audit (Learning)

This phase of the intervention cycle refers to the art of discerning the gifts of the kingdom community at work [Stage 7]. It prepares the way for identifying the mission task and the outcomes which the Christian initiator at work hopes to achieve.

Authority (All 4Ls)

From the perspective of the project's theology of community, the initiator's authority for intervening to transform the workplace derives, first and foremost, from their call to model the communal life of the Trinity: God as Creator, Christ as Liberator and the Holy Spirit as Unifier. Graham Ward believes that the character of such intervention must have 'a double axis: absolute submission to God, on the one hand, and equality with respect to all neighbours, on the other' (2009, p. 298).

Secondly, the initiator's authority to intervene within the workplace derives from their membership of a diaconal church whose calling is to be the servant of the kingdom community and a model for every social collective, sacred or secular [Stage 5]. It is on this authority that the diaconal church assumes the right to commission the people of God at work to undertake their ministry as servants of the kingdom community. Unfortunately, because the church currently focuses so much time and energy on the local congregation and its ministry to the immediate neighbourhood, the mission of the laity as the church dispersed in order to transform the world of work rarely features on its agenda. The same kind of marginalization holds true for many ordained ministers engaged as chaplains or 'ministers in secular employment' (*Church Times*, 8/4/2011, p. 23).

In the third place, the authority of the Christian to intervene within the workplace comes from the world of work itself. Here the initiator's authority may take a number of forms: associational, ascribed and attained. *Associational* authority is that given because, socially and culturally, the lay person happens by birth and upbringing to have social attributes in common with their fellow workers: race, class, age, accent and so forth (Younge, pp. 111-140). However, associational authority is a dubious form of legitimization for intervention in a world where such social and cultural norms are often seen as potentially exclusive. Thus, the other two forms of authority, ascribed and achieved, which legitimize the Christian's intervention, are from a communal perspective far more authentic.

Ascribed authority is that which is bestowed on any worker who occupies some formally recognised position of leadership. Intervention is clearly easier when it is given legitimization by the official status of the initiator. However, *achieved* authority carries the greater weight. This refers to the influence the initiator has because of their experience, knowledge or skills, on the one hand, and/or because of their personal standing with their fellows through such attributes as integrity, trustworthiness, empathy and caring, on the other. Achieved authority is of special importance in giving the initiator the right to engage in the communal transformation of the workplace. It is worth recalling here that the kingdom community was inaugurated by One whose authority was achieved not simply ascribed (Mk. 1: 22).

The authority of the Christian as initiator to engage in the communal transformation of the workplace is at its strongest when all sources of legitimization, Trinitarian, diaconal and authority - the last associational and ascribed, but especially achieved - reinforce one another. Before the mission task commences, the initiator needs to consider whether or not they have sufficient authority for such an undertaking and, if not, what they can do about it (for example, through some form of partnership as indicated in the Agreement phase below).

Agreement *(Love)*

Intervention undertaken by the initiator must never be of a coercive kind. Where intervention requires the help or co-operation of work colleagues or other social collectives, some form of agreement, be it formal or informal, is essential. For such an agreement to carry weight, all of those directly involved need to have understood and accepted the aims and objectives of the intervention, the means suggested for achieving them and the hoped-for outcomes.

Whenever possible the initiator should try to obtain a form of agreement that is 'covenantal' rather than only 'contractual' in nature. Contractual agreements are dominantly task-focused, functional and formal. Covenantal agreements are first and foremost relationship-based. A covenantal agreement more fully mirrors the gifts of the kingdom community. It involves mutual respect and trust and is more likely than a contractual agreement to pave the way for the creation of genuine partnership. Reaching covenantal agreement is greatly facilitated by the process of dialogue explored in Stage 8(3).

Actualities (Learning)

This phase of the cycle focuses on the need for the initiator to be aware of the realities of the workplace situation. Actualities may include physical aspects of the working environment, time factors, working practices, the working culture of the organization, existing relationships between participants (employees, customers and clients, and suppliers), the nature and interests of stake holders and the impact of the wider economic climate on the workplace. Openness to take on board such actualities is necessary if it is hoped to access the kingdom community's gift of learning. An enquiring and reflective approach to intervention enhances the Christian initiator's credibility and builds a culture of trust (Alliances). This, in turn, engenders a culture of consent (Agreement) and greater receptivity to the mission task.

Affirmation (Liberation)

This phase of the cycle refers to the importance of the initiator validating the experience, skills and insights of all those who might be involved in the intervention process. Affirmation also requires that the initiator remains open to being surprised by the contribution of those whose abilities and ideas may initially have been overlooked or undervalued. Affirmation embodies the kingdom community's gift of liberation because it recognises and employs the often hidden qualities and abilities colleagues possess.

Alliances (Love)

Collective intervention is a team effort. In engaging in intervention, the initiator needs to seek out individuals, groups or other collectives which recognize the mission task as important and are willing to be involved in achieving it (even though its Christian significance may remain implicit). Such alliances may be made up of those willing to be engaged in the task itself and/or of those not actively engaged but ready to offer resources or support (Assets). Alliances are an essential means of harnessing the kingdom community's gift of love.

Assets (All 4Ls)

Along with looking for allies, the initiator needs to ensure that adequate resources are available for the task chosen, know where they are located and how they can be accessed. Such resources will include relevant information, plant and equipment, transport, useful experience and skills (Alliances), as well as any necessary training and financial support. These resources will often give expression to the generosity (grace) of one or more of the four Trinitarian gifts.

Alternatives (Learning)

This phase of the intervention cycle should prompt the initiator to consider different ways of approaching the mission task. Being flexible about the means by which that task could be pursued facilitates the ability to respond quickly and effectively to unforeseen problems and challenges. Readiness to explore alternative methods of intervention, especially where imagination is given full rein, is an important means of embracing the kingdom community's gift of learning.

Action (All 4Ls)

The Action phase is synonymous with accomplishing the mission task. That the action phase comes late in the intervention cycle is no accident. It is because unless all the phases preceding Action have informed and shaped the preparation and planning, it is less likely intervention will bring about any significant change. Action may be informed and guided by a diversity of intervention strategies which lack of space prevents being explored here.

Attainment (All 4Ls)

This phase of intervention concerns assessing whether or not the mission task has been achieved. For the Christian initiator, Attainment will be at two levels. One consideration is whether or not the specific mission task has been accomplished; the other, whether or not this has helped to further the communal transformation of the workplace through the fuller expression of one or more of the 4Ls.

Appraisal (Learning)

This phase of the cycle comes into play once intervention, successful or otherwise, has ended. If intervention has not achieved the mission task, the Christian initiator will need to explore the reasons for this. In this case, it is important to revisit earlier phases of the intervention cycle as some of these might not have been fulfilled as adequately as required. In this connection, it is especially important to revisit that phase of the intervention cycle concerned with Alternatives. One aspect of this phase is for all concerned to ensure that what has been learnt during the course of the intervention cycle is used to prepare the way for more effective intervention in the future. This phase of the cycle will be enriched by drawing on the kingdom community's gift of learning.

Stage 8

Intervention

Implicit

1 Individual

The intervention process

The nature of individual intervention

The first ***implicit*** means of intervention to be considered is that undertaken by the Christian as an individual initiator. Such intervention is often spontaneous, informal and of short-term duration. Thus, expecting individual intervention to have any chance of becoming a means of significant transformation in the workplace might seem at first sight to be naïve. However, as argued in Stage 6, human scale initiatives can be important triggers for significant communal change.

Whatever the nature of individual implicit intervention, it remains crucial that the Christian at work is *personally* seeking to exemplify the meaning of life, liberation, love and learning through their own actions and behaviour. As Robert Banks puts it: 'One role-model is worth a hundred instructions' (1987, p. 97).

Tim Wright stresses that the stance of the individual Christian initiator towards others also needs to be open, affirmative and creative. Using the biblical metaphors of salt and light, he writes (2009, p. 12):

> When we act as salt and light in the workplace, we have the potential either to inspire others to new and different ways of being and doing, or of being dysfunctional. As salt we can be like salt in a wound, reminding people of their weaknesses and shortcomings and making them feel bad about it. Or we can be like the salt in cooking that is unobtrusive, but brings out the best flavour in the meal.
>
> When we are trying to be light for the world, we become more conscious of the darkness around us. We may be tempted to put our energy into condemning the darkness rather than illuminating a different and better alternative. We can be like the

blinding light of the interrogator who shines the light in the prisoner's eyes to remind them of their weakness. Or we can be like the gentle light of the dawn that dispels the darkness and reveals the beauty that was hidden by the darkness.

Examples of the individual intervention process

Below are offered some examples of how the gifts of the kingdom community, discerned through signs or critical incidents, might be made manifest by the *implicit individual intervention* of the Christian at work. The examples are taken from the list of signs and critical incidents set out in Stages 7(1) and 7(2) respectively.

The nature of the individual implicit intervention *process* outlined below is similar whatever sign or critical incident has been identified as a springboard for intervention, and whatever mission task and hoped for outcome are associated with the action taken. This process consists of:

o identification of *the mission task*, here of an *implicit* kind, and a commitment to address the affirmation or denial of a particular gift or gifts of the kingdom community which that task reveals;

o spontaneous or reflective intervention of *an individual nature* which will further the mission task through the initiator's own endeavours or their encouragement of others to engage in similar initiatives.

The examples below are set out in a form which illustrates these two aspects of implicit individual intervention.

Life-giving

Sign (Task)

There are adequate rest breaks during the working day

Implicit mission task

To use all scheduled breaks to further refreshment and rejuvenation for those concerned

Possible related interventions

I will knock off immediately the break begins and try to put my working concerns and commitments on one side during that time.

At break times, I will listen to others concerns at least as often as I talk about my own.

I will encourage others to engage in similar initiatives.

Critical incident (Life affirmed - Context)

A member of staff took the initiative of bringing in flowers and foliage from her garden to decorate the foyer of her work premises.

Implicit mission task

To make our working environment as life-enhancing as possible

Possible related interventions

I will display fresh flowers, foliage and beautiful pictures or artefacts in my individual work space.

I will display in my work space postcards of interesting and attractive places sent to me by colleagues when on holiday.

I will encourage others to engage in similar initiatives.

Liberating

Sign (Relationships)

Forgiveness for acknowledged mistakes or failures is an integral aspect of the workplace culture.

Implicit mission task

To put the human worth and dignity of colleagues before any incident or happening that might threaten to disrupt working relationships

Possible related interventions

I will make clear that I recognise that I also make mistakes.

I will be fully open to the acceptance of genuine apologies and honest regrets.

I will ensure that I do not harbour grudges or entertain lasting resentments.

I will encourage others to engage in similar initiatives.

Critical incident (Liberation denied - Relationships)

'He's a poor old soul so he can wait for a bit' one shop assistant was heard to whisper to another when serving a number of customers vying for her attention.

Implicit mission task

To make sure we value all customers equally and treat them fairly.

Possible related interventions

I will affirm each person due to be served whoever they may be.

I will not devalue customers because of their personal appearance or circumstances.

I will pay particular attention to those who have difficulty in asserting their legitimate rights as customers.

I will encourage others to engage in similar initiatives.

Loving

Sign (Relationships)

Visitors always receive a welcome.

Implicit mission task

To acknowledge and welcome all visitors whoever they are.

Possible related interventions

I will look out for and help visitors who may seem a bit lost in strange surroundings.

I will ensure that visitors have a comfortable environment in which to wait.

I will welcome any visitors I encounter with a positive word or gesture.

I will encourage others to engage in similar initiatives.

Critical incident (Love affirmed - Relationships)

A solicitor's firm changed its regulations to allow occasional days for its employees to spend time undertaking some form of voluntary work within the city in which it was located.

Implicit mission task

To make the most of any time given us to serve those outside our workplace

Possible related interventions

I will regard 'time-out' to serve the wider community as a positive contribution by our business to this city.

I will give of my best to the organization or agency where I am placed.

I will try to take a personal interest in the agency concerned outside my normal working hours.

I will encourage others to engage in similar initiatives.

Learning

Sign (Relationships)

There is a commitment to enabling social collectives beyond the workplace to become learning communities.

Implicit mission task

To engage with accessible social collectives to explore how they might develop more fully as learning communities

Possible related interventions

I will access and read literature about what it means to be a learning community (or, as in some cases described, 'a learning organization').

I will visit and learn from other collectives which are seeking to operate as learning communities.

I will share with other collectives what my workplace is doing to try and become a learning community.

I will share with others, through web site, Internet or other personal communication, my understanding of and commitment to what it means to be a learning community.

I will encourage others to engage in similar initiatives.

Critical incident (Learning affirmed – Task)

A group of community workers linked to a voluntary agency who had spent most of their working lives in the UK was sent to a large city in the USA for a month to study community organizing. They came back inspired and re-energised by their experience.

Implicit mission task

To channel our new insights and enthusiasm for community organizing into our daily work

Possible individual interventions

I will learn more about community organizing as it is undertaken in this country.

I will use my insights to enable residents in the neighbourhood in which I work to develop their leadership skills more effectively.

I will post pictures and descriptions of community organizing in the States on our agency's website.

I will pursue ways of bringing community organizers from the States to the UK to speak about their approach to community development.

I will encourage those who went with me to the States to engage in similar initiatives.

Servant leadership

The situations set out below are offered as examples of how a sign or critical incident might prompt the Christian at work *in a leadership position* to use his or her role to enhance the gifts of the kingdom community through implicit individual intervention.

Visionary

(All 4Ls)

Sign (Task)

The leader sees problems as opportunities not obstacles.

Implicit mission task

To approach all problems in the belief that they often open rather than close doors

Possible individual interventions

I will not respond immediately and negatively to problems which come my way.

I will get the facts as to why any problem is a problem.

I will question assumptions that appear to indicate that there is only one way in which I can respond to a problem.

I will work on the assumption that a glass is half full rather than half empty.

Critical incident (All 4Ls affirmed – Relationships)

The chief executive of a city council set up a two day consultation at which those from every sector of city life were brought together to share their vision for the city for the next ten years.

Implicit mission task

To recognise the importance of ensuring that each constituency and collective within the life of this city has an opportunity to share their vision for the future of our city

Possible individual interventions

I will not devalue or ignore any collective's vision for the future of our city.

I will listen especially attentively to the visions of those collectives with which I rarely engage.

I will give time to working out and sharing with other collectives my own vision for the future of our city.

I will explore new ways in which I can work together with others to help make visions a reality.

Strategist

(All 4Ls)

Sign (Relationships)

The leader does not raise false expectations

Implicit mission task

To help people to live with the realities of the situation whilst retaining their morale

Possible individual interventions

I will affirm the importance of visions and hopes.

I will affirm what people are already doing as always being something from which lessons can be learnt and on which new initiatives can be built.

I will listen attentively to people's hopes without colluding in any premature assumptions that these will become a reality.

I will present the facts of the situation as clearly and objectively as possible.

I will attempt to test out expectations which may initially seem to me unattainable.

I will make clear that ambitious plans are usually long-term and need a number of more modest short-term achievements en route to attaining them.

Critical incident (Life, liberation and love affirmed – Task)

A businesswoman in a small rural town networked all the local traders to get their commitment and co-operation in setting up a new and imaginative Christmas market week-end which boosted the local economy.

Implicit mission task

To draw together a fragmented business sector to boost trade and raise morale

Possible individual interventions

I will seek to make it clear that I am not out to boost my own standing in the town.

I will affirm and use each trader's distinctive contributions to the Christmas market.

I will work hard to promote the event so that its success can be a springboard for future initiatives.

I will strive to help new friendships and partnerships to emerge as a result of our working together.

Animator

(Life)

Sign (Task)

The leader manages his or her time productively

Implicit mission task

To treat the use of time as a both a resource and a matter of good stewardship

Possible individual interventions

I will arrive at work on time.

I will ensure that I am on time for appointments.

I will not encroach on the time I allocate to one task or person at the expense of another person.

I will regard the time I give to those accountable to me as important as that which I give to those to whom I am myself accountable.

When the situation necessitates it, I will be flexible about my scheduled time-table.

Critical incident (Life affirmed - Task)

An office manager brought all his staff together to help him draw up and implement long-term plans for their workplace to make it lighter, more attractively decorated, and in all other ways, more user-friendly.

Implicit mission task

To explore how I can make our working environment life-enhancing for everyone using it.

Possible individual interventions

I will discover how different groups of users respond to this working environment.

I will observe and communicate to my staff what other collectives have done to enhance their working environment.

I will discuss with the workforce how we might make our working environment more life-enhancing for them and other users.

I will ensure that my own part of the work space is life-enhancing for myself and others.

Enabler

(Liberation)

Sign (Relationships)

The leader encourages other social collectives to become liberating communities.

Implicit mission task

To bring together social collectives who do not normally meet or communicate with one another in order to spark new ideas and insights

Possible individual interventions

I will ensure I am well acquainted with the experience and abilities of social collectives which might have something to offer to the task in hand.

I will look out for ways of breaking the mould by creating new networks, alliances and partnerships.

Critical incident (Liberation denied – Relationships)

A new secondary school head teacher was very committed to her pupils but saw her governing body as a threat and related to the more articulate parents of her school children with some apprehension.

Implicit mission task

To regard the school's governing body and its parents as a resource not a problem

Possible individual interventions

I will seek to get to know personally the members of my governing body and as many as possible of the parents of the children at my school.

I will listen attentively and respectfully to their views and opinions.

I will keep them well informed.

I will make time and space to consult them on matters of mutual concern.

I will seek to use the skills and experience of governors for the benefit of the school.

Intermediary

(Love)

Sign (Relationships)

The leader is able to empathize with and support those who find it difficult to handle change.

Implicit mission task

I will respect and consider carefully the views and feelings of all staff affected by change

Possible individual interventions

I will make clear that I honour whatever contribution my staff have in the past made to the organization.

I will try to understand the reasons why certain of my staff are blocking change.

I will make clear that I am keeping to the task in hand whilst dealing with more personal problems in other ways.

I will find ways to enhance my negotiating skills.

I will enter into a genuine dialogue with all who oppose the changes concerned.

Critical incident (Love affirmed – Task)

A new chief executive of a hospital spent a good part of her first week 'walking the talk' and linking up members of her staff whom she felt had experience, insights and skills which could be disseminated more widely through such innovative connections.

Implicit mission task

To recognize the importance of linking up people who have an innovative contribution to make to the well-being of the whole

Possible individual interventions

I will show that I value everyone's experience.

I will show that I value professional, practical and individual skills.

I will affirm and use new and imaginative insights.

I will listen to the experience and suggestions of service users.

I will network those whose ideas and skills might be enhanced by being more closely connected.

Educator

(Learning)

Sign (Relationships)

The leader is an attentive listener

Implicit mission task

To develop the art of being a good listener

Possible individual interventions

I will go out of my way to acquire the skills of an attentive listener.

I will practice the art of being open to learning from all staff.

I will consult staff as to whether they feel that I have really heard what they have on their minds.

Critical incident (Learning denied – Task)

On an in-service course, the training event, the training officer of a large company was so hung up on her desire to produce impressive power-point presentations, accompanied by comments repetitive of what was being projected, that she allowed trainees little opportunity for personal reflection or group discussion.

Implicit mission task

To ensure that learning is undertaken as a person-centred endeavour and a partnership between trainer and learner

Possible related interventions

I will discover the needs, concerns and questions of those I teach before I embark on my own agenda.

I will ensure that teaching aids further learning.

I will use the experience of learners as an essential resource.

I will ensure that learners have time to share their experiences, concerns and questions with one another.

I will be open to learning from those I train or teach.

I will encourage others to engage in similar initiatives.

Stage 8

Intervention

Implicit

2 Collective

The second implicit means of intervention open to the Christian initiator is what is termed here 'collective intervention'. This form of intervention concerns initiatives taken in partnership with others. Such intervention is normally planned, of some duration and involves more than one other person. Collective intervention can range from human-scale initiatives to large-scale projects (for example, producing a mission statement for the organization).

Suggested steps for implicit collective intervention

1. Following on from the discernment process [Stage 7], choose one sign or critical incident which you consider to be of particular importance in indicating what needs to change in order that your workplace might be transformed by the gifts of the kingdom community.

2. In the light of this sign or critical incident decide on a mission task [Stage 8 (Introduction)] which you believe would further such change.

3. Consider all phases of the intervention cycle [Stage 8 (Introduction)]. For example:

> *Decide with whom you will try to build alliances in order to achieve your mission task.*

> *Decide together how you will take action to implement your mission task*

> *Determine how you will know when to terminate the task and how this will be done.*

4. Implement the mission task.

5. Terminate the mission task

6. Review with other participants how successfully the mission task has been accomplished. For example:

What have been the achievements?

What have been the problems?

What has been learnt in the process?

7. Decide together on <u>any next steps</u>.

Note - To help in this collective intervention process, try to obtain the involvement of fellow Christians at work and/or the assistance of a mentor.

Examples of the collective implicit intervention process

This section offers a number of practical examples of how the planning and implementation of collective implicit intervention derived from the discernment process might be given direction and shape by using the intervention cycle described in Stage 8 (Introduction). Two examples (one of them concerning *leadership*) are concerned with mission tasks informed by the signs of the kingdom community set out in Stage 7(1) and 7(3). Two other examples (one of them concerning *leadership*) are related to mission tasks taken from the critical incidents set out in Stage 7(2) and 7(3).

Signs

Liberation

(Task)

Sign (scoring low)

The goods produced and services offered contribute, directly or indirectly, towards a world of justice and peace

Situation of Christian initiator

A library assistant in a local branch library

Implicit mission task

To promote justice and peace issues through the services of my local library

-----

Audit (Learning)

The discernment process [Stage 7] will have identified the mission task set out above.

Authority (All 4Ls)

In trying to widen the promotional work of the branch to include justice and peace issues, do I have the support of the librarian in charge?

In trying to widen the promotional work of the branch to include justice and peace issues, do I have the support and trust of my work colleagues?

Agreement (Love)

What would be the contract to enable the librarian in charge and my colleagues to support this initiative? How might I set this up?

How can I get the interest and support of library users for such an initiative?

Actualities (Learning)

How interested are library users in justice and peace issues?

What opportunities are there for promotional moves in this direction?

With what other related promotional initiatives might I be competing?

What sort of material would attract library users' attention?

What sort of material would attract wider public interest?

Affirmation (Liberation)

How can I assure all library colleagues that their own endeavours are valued?

Alliances (Love)

How can I undertake this initiative in partnership with my colleagues, with other bodies engaging in justice and peace issues and with library users?

Assets (Life)

What resources have we to support such an initiative and for how long?

What resources might we get from local government?

What resources might our partners offer?

Are there human resources available which could make this a lively and dynamic initiative?

Alternatives (Learning)

What diversity of approaches are open to us in planning to set up this promotion?

Which will appeal most strongly to work colleagues, library users and the general public?

Action (All 4Ls)

Here the initiator and partners would seek to set in process a course of action to further the mission task, where possible guided by relevant models of engagement. This process would take into consideration the answers to questions such as those suggested above.

Attainment (All 4Ls)

Has the promotion been successful or not?

Appraisal (Learning)

What are the reasons for the attainment of the mission task?

In pursuing this task, have one or more gifts of the kingdom community been enhanced?

In what ways?

or

For what reasons has the attainment of the mission task failed or been limited?

In the light of the answers to the questions suggested above, what now might be the plans for accomplishing the mission task?

The servant leader
- as educator

Learning

(Relationships)

Sign (scoring high)

People advocate their views whilst remaining open to be challenged on them

Situation of Christian initiator

The headmistress of a large urban comprehensive school seeking to enhance further a school culture already open to dialogue and creative discussion

Implicit mission task

To encourage pupils to exchange their opinions openly on a variety of issues and ensure that the outcomes enhance the life and work of pupils and the school

-----

Audit (Learning)

The discernment process [Stage 7] will have identified the mission task set out above.

Authority (All 4Ls)

In developing dialogue and discussion further how can I gain the support of my staff, governors, pupils and parents?

Agreement (Love)

What would be the contract with these groups for taking a culture of open expressions and discussions of opinion further? How might this be set up?

What might be the ground rules for such a development?

Actualities (Learning)

Which pupils do not contribute easily to an open exchange of opinions? How might they be encouraged to share their views more fully?

Which important topics remain taboo?

What time is already given to such discussions and is this adequate?

How are these discussions being mentored and monitored? Could this be improved?

Which staff are not involved? How could their participation be encouraged?

How might the outcomes of these discussions influence the life and work of the school?

Affirmation (Liberation)

How could the importance of the views of pupils be more fully affirmed amongst themselves, by staff, by governors and by parents?

Alliances (Love)

How can governors and parents be actively involved in this initiative?

Assets (Life)

What resources of time and staff are available to sustain this initiative?

What resources might governors and parents offer?

Alternatives (Learning)

What ways are open to us for developing dialogue and discussion amongst pupils?

What options might be available for enabling the outcomes to influence the life and work of the school?

Action (All 4Ls)

Here the initiator and partners would seek to set in process a course of action to further the mission task, where possible guided by relevant models of engagement. This process would take into consideration the response to such questions as those suggested above.

Attainment (All 4Ls)

Has the development of dialogue and discussion, and their outcomes, enhanced the skills and experience of the pupils?

Has the life and work of school been enhanced?

Appraisal (Learning)

What are the reasons for the attainment of the mission task?

In pursuing this task, have one or more gifts of the kingdom community been enhanced?

In what ways?

or

For what reasons has the attainment of the mission task failed or been limited?

In the light of the answers to the questions suggested above, what now might be the plans for accomplishing the mission task?

Critical Incidents

Life denied

(Relationships)

Critical incident

By introducing a rigid piece-work basis, the management of a mobile phone assembly department succeeded in setting one worker over against another and undermined any sense of work being an enjoyable collective endeavour.

Situation of Christian initiator

A worker in a computer assembly department facing similar problems

Implicit mission task

To enable my colleagues within the assembly department to enjoy their work as a collective endeavour

-----

Audit (Learning)

The discernment process [Stage 7] will have identified the mission task set out above.

Authority (All 4Ls)

Do I have the support and confidence of my work colleagues to question the existing production arrangements? If not, how might I gain this?

Do I have the support and confidence of management to question the existing production arrangements? If not, how might I gain this?

Agreement (Love)

On what terms would my work colleagues support the exploration of production arrangements that would make work more of a collective and enjoyable endeavour?

How can I set up an agreement to achieve this change?

On what terms would management support the exploration of production arrangements that would make work more of a collective and enjoyable endeavour?

How can I set up an agreement to achieve this change?

Actualities (Learning)

What evidence is there that piece-work helps or hinders production?

What factors help or hinder production during the day and/or on an ongoing basis?

What changes might my work colleagues and/or management suggest in order to ensure that work is an enjoyable collective endeavour?

How could this be done whilst maintaining existing production targets?

What would be the response of management and my work colleagues if the sense of collective endeavour increased but production declined?

Affirmation (Liberation)

How might management enable my work colleagues to feel that their concerns are recognised and addressed?

How might management enable my work colleagues to feel that they are valued as people?

How might management enable my work colleagues to feel that their skills and experience are valued?

Alliances (Love)

How might the problem of a rigid piece-work system undermining any sense of work as an enjoyable collective endeavour be addressed as a partnership between management and the work force?

Who else might be involved to help improve this situation?

Assets (Life)

What resources related to time, lay-out of the plant, equipment and training, etc. might be needed to improve the sense of work as an enjoyable collective endeavour?

What human resources might be drawn on to improve the sense of work as an enjoyable collective endeavour?

Alternatives (Learning)

Is there a choice of approaches by which a sense of work as an enjoyable collective endeavour could be improved? If so, what might these be?

Action (All 4Ls)

Here the Christian initiator and partners would seek to set in process a course of action to further the mission task, where possible guided by relevant models of engagement. This process would take into consideration the response to questions such as those suggested above.

Attainment (All 4Ls)

To what extent has the sense of work as a more collective and enjoyable endeavour been achieved?

To want extent has this resulted in the enhancement of one or more of the gifts of the kingdom community?

Appraisal (Learning)

What are the reasons for the attainment of the mission task?

In pursuing this task, have one or more gifts of the kingdom community been enhanced?

    In what ways?

or

For what reasons has the attainment of the mission task failed or been limited?

In the light of the answers to the questions suggested above, what might be the plans for accomplishing the mission task in the future?

The servant leader
- as educator

Learning affirmed

(Relationships)

A newly appointed chief constable spent the first six months in her post listening attentively to her colleagues of all ranks and to the public before setting out proposals for a radical redirection of her force's endeavours.

Situation of Christian initiator

A recently appointed superintendent of police wanting to take new policing initiatives.

(She is deputy head of a county operational support department with 500 staff involved in a wide diversity of policing duties)

Implicit mission task

To listen attentively to all those in the operational support department of which I am deputy head, and to the general public, to ensure that any new initiatives in policing we take reflect their insights and concerns

-----

Audit (Learning)

The discernment process [Stage 7] will have identified the mission task set out above.

Authority (All 4Ls)

Do I have the support of the head of our operational support department to explore new initiatives in the way we undertake policing in this county?

Do I have the support and trust of the staff in our department when it comes to taking new initiatives in policing?

Agreement (Love)

What would be the agreement on the basis of which my head of department and the workforce would actively support new initiatives for policing this county more effectively?

Actualities (Learning)

To what extent have we taken on board new developments in policing and where do we lag behind?

What are the deployment and the responsibilities of the police staff in this county?

Where are we adequately staffed, or where under strength?

To what extent are we being helped or hindered by government policy?

To what extent are the public with us or to what extent are they critical of our endeavours?

Affirmation (Liberation)

How can I assure staff that their current endeavours are valued?

How can I ensure that my head of department knows I am taking his views seriously?

How can I arrange my time so that I can get out and about to listen to the view and concerns of police staff?

How can I assure all staff that their voice is being heard?

How can I get the honest views and learn the concerns of the whole force?

How can I ensure that the public knows that we are taking their concerns seriously?

Alliances (Love)

How can we build partnership with other bodies serving the public, and with the public themselves, to support any new initiatives in policing we take?

Assets (Life)

What resources of our own, material and human, might we redeploy to support new initiatives?

What resources do we have from government for new initiatives?

What resources might our partners offer?

Alternatives (Learning)

Is a choice of initiatives possible? If so, what might these be?

Which will appeal most strongly to all concerned?

Which stand most chance of making policing in this county most effective?

Action (All4Ls)

Here the initiator and partners would seek to set in process a course of action to further the mission task, where possible guided by relevant models of engagement. This process would take into consideration the responses to questions such as those suggested above.

Attainment (All 4Ls)

Has our plan to listen to the views and concerns of all been successful?

Has this consultation process carried the head of department, the staff and the public with us?

Appraisal (Learning)

What are the reasons for the attainment of the mission task?

In pursuing this task, have one or more gifts of the kingdom community been enhanced?

In what ways?

or

For what reasons has the attainment of the mission task failed or been limited?

In the light of the answers to the questions such as those suggested above, what now might be the plans for accomplishing the mission task?

Stage 8
Intervention
Implicit or explicit
3 Dialogue

So far throughout Stage 8, the Kingdom at Work Project has been concerned with intervention in the life of the workplace, individual or collective, which is *implicit*, that is where Christian commitment which gives impetus to the mission task is not made public. In section 3 of Stage 8, a form of intervention is explored which, from a Christian perspective, may be either *implicit* or *explicit*: ***mission as dialogue*** (Walcot, 1997, pp. 81-85). At the end of her thorough investigation of how Christians might most effectively bear witness to their faith at work, Margaret Whipp (2008) writes: 'The central finding from all my explorations into religious expression in the workplace is that the most authentically Christian model for witness at work is the… liberative and transformative potential of dialogue' (p. 155).

The dialogical nature of the kingdom community

The meaning of dialogue

'Dialogue comes from the Greek word *dialogos* and means "through the word". The implication being that through the word we arrive at meaning. In essence dialogue is a flow of meaning - a living experience of inquiry within and between people, a conversation in which people think together in relationship' (Howard and Welbourn, 2004, pp. 67-68). Dialogue is a conversation in which participants share their concerns in a spirit of mutual inquiry and reflective response. As Alistair McFayden (1990) puts it: 'In dialogue one not only gives oneself to the other, but receives oneself back from the other too' (p. 125).

'Contrast this (dialogue) with the word "discussion" which has the same root as "percussion" and "concussion" ', writes David Bohm (1996, p. 7). The latter words describe forms of hard hitting interaction. Thus 'discussion is almost like a ping-pong game, where people are batting the ideas back and forth and the object of the game is to win or to get points for yourself... In a dialogue... nobody is trying to win. Everybody wins if anybody wins' (p. 7).

However, to engage in dialogue does not mean to dumb down one's own concerns or convictions. 'In fact', writes Thomas Thangaraj (1999), 'where people have no convictions to share, there can be no dialogue' (p. 99). Dialogue is a vital means of communication because, unlike many other forms of verbal exchange, it not only encourages the expression of strongly held convictions and sentiments but is able to handle them in a way which uses their dynamism for creative ends. In the context of the communal theology and spirituality on which this project is based, these convictions are about the centrality and manifestation of the gifts of the kingdom community.

Dialogue is the very opposite of monologue. Alistair McFayden (1990, pp. 123-124) writes:

> In monological communication a person is in relation only in and for her or himself. The other is intended as an object whose existence in the relation coincides with one's own purposes, desires, needs and intentions which have been self-constituted and validated. The communication is oriented towards the success of self-constituted and validated goals, and not towards a genuine mutuality of understanding in which the validity of these goals, and of the intention and understanding one has of and for the other and the relation, are open to question and negotiation.

From a Christian perspective, dialogue gains its validity and its power from reflecting the relational energy of the Trinity. 'In my opinion, the personal identity of communicating persons is the most beautiful mirror of the Trinity', states Francis Jacques (quoted in Whipp, p. 85). Margaret Whipp comments: 'The vocation for the Christian life is not simply to adore the love of God-in-Trinity but to participate in God's conversational embrace of the world' (p. 86). 'Because God's communication takes dialogical form, it should be conceived in terms of grace... (which enables) human beings (to be) addressed as God's dialogue-partners', writes McFayden (p. 19). 'This discovery of the openness and creativity of language as a locus for revelation reflects on the dynamic nature of the Trinity as a relational and open community,' states Whipp (quoting Chopp, pp. 165-166).

The importance of dialogue as a means of enabling the gifts of the kingdom community to transform social collectives is well summed up by McFayden: 'The Christian vision of God's kingdom is of a *society* under the rule of Christ, who orders and structures identities and relations in a dialogical manner, and in the power of the Spirit, who is the organisational energy of openness' (p. 268). He continues: 'Christian faith is ultimately concerned with the conditions of perfect community and dialogue: the kingdom of God' (p. 269).

The gifts of the kingdom community expressed in and through dialogue

Mission as dialogue embodies the four hall-marks of the kingdom community: life, liberation, love and learning. *The gift of life* is made manifest in the way in which dialogue facilitates the giving and receiving of life. Because 'dialogue may be considered as a process of self-transcendence (movement towards the other) and return (receiving oneself back from the other)', as McFayden argues, its essence is what Rosemary Haughton calls 'an exchange of life' (1982, pp. 18-47). This life-enhancing relationship, first and foremost with God as our 'dialogue-partner', is then expressed in and through the Christian's life-enhancing relationships with all other dialogue-partners.

Mission as dialogue is also an expression of *the gift of liberation.* Whipp (p. 158) writes:

> Liberative conversation and the transition from monologue to dialogue is experienced by Christians first and foremost as a gift - since it is only by means of God's self-communication to us, of the Word becoming flesh and dwelling among us, thereby taking up the word of this world into his eternal Word, that the Trinitarian possibility of true communication exists in the first place.

Mission as dialogue is impossible unless conversation is permeated throughout by the kingdom community's *gift of love.* 'Those who come to it must come... with humility, love, faith and hope... Freire said "love is at the same time the foundation of dialogue and dialogue itself" ', state Sue Howard and David Welbourn (2004, p. 70).

Mission as dialogue is an essential medium for discovering and appropriating *the gift of learning.* Closed ideologies destroy the educational potential of dialogue. As Benedict XVI (2009) states: 'Secularism and fundamentalism exclude the possibility of fruitful dialogue and effective cooperation between reason and religious faith' (p. 117). As will be seen, dialogue has much in common with what has been previously described as double-loop and triple-loop learning [Stage 2]. However, McFayden writes: 'Communication orientated towards genuine mutuality of understanding, or conformity to Christ, is a diachronic spiral of understanding in dialogue, rather than a loop or circle indicating the exchange between static identities' (p. 133). Through the giving and reflecting back which it facilitates, mission as dialogue offers a new understanding of the gifts of the kingdom community which can open up redemptive and transformational possibilities for ourselves, our workplace and the wider world.

The middle ground as holy ground

The time and space for reflection which often occur in genuine dialogue make it easier for a third entity, the Trinity, to be recognized as present within the conversation and facilitate the manifestation of the gifts of the kingdom community. 'It is now fifty years', wrote Alan Ecclestone in 1975, 'since Martin Buber spoke clearly of the significance of the I-Thou relationship, insisting upon the need to recognize the sphere of the "between" or inter-human, *pleading for the rebirth of dialogue* (our italics), patiently explaining the meaning of the crisis of communication and urging men to look for the new theophany in the night of their desperation' (p. 118).

Nobody illustrates the importance of this holy space or 'middle-ground' better than John Hull (1993). In the context of inter-faith dialogue, he writes:

> There is a Christianity that says, 'I am holy and you are holy but the ground between us is not holy. If we meet on that ground, if we touch, we shall be contaminated.' There is another Christianity that says, 'I am not holy; I am on the way; my spirituality and that of the tradition I represent is incomplete. But I have an affinity with you, my Muslim brother, my Jewish friend, my Hindu colleague, if you are prepared to say, 'I am not holy; I am on the way; the tradition I represent is not complete'. Then we will both say, 'but the ground where we meet is holy ground because this is the place where we claim our complete humanity'.

The art of mission as dialogue

Kit Dollard and colleagues (2002) in their book entitled *Doing business with Benedict* argue that 'the most common cause of breakdown in business relationships between people is (poor) communication' (p. 111). Dialogue offers a tried and tested means of responding creatively to the many difficult conversations that occur within the workplace. This does not mean that to engage in dialogue is an easy option. As will be indicated more fully below, dialogue requires a clear understanding of the principles and practices on which such conversations are founded. It also necessitates the ability to give practical expression to that understanding through an open-to-learning stance towards other participants involved in the dialogue and an ability to choose and employ appropriate forms of words.

Mission as dialogue is particularly difficult for the Christian who is seeking to give expression to their faith through the conversations they have within the world of work, be such conversations implicitly or explicitly Christian in character. What has been called 'the "the hidden curriculum" of the workplace' (Casey, 1995, p. 80), all too often leads to what Margaret Whipp describes as 'the management of motivation' in a dominantly market based culture, 'the flattening of dissent' where fear of conflict means that the overt expression of a faith perspective is suppressed, and 'the inculcation of instrumentalism' which is associated with 'discursive practices which constrict and control the prevailing language and thought forms in ways which lead to a shriveling of spirituality and an impoverishment of creative potential' (p. 80). For the Christian at work, there is also the challenge of what was identified in Stage 5 as 'the two cultures', the divide between the ethos and language of the church and that of the world of work.

Thus 'in the goal-oriented climate of the workplace, the freedom of authentic conversation is not something what may be naturally or effortlessly attained... It has to be earned through the skills and commitments of habitual listening' (Whipp, p. 158). Nevertheless, Whipp believes that 'however partial and provisional our discernment of the presence and activity of the eternal Word in our work, we can participate through dialogue in a new discovery of spiritual freedom and joy' (p. 158). At the same time, if Christians are to engage in an effective form of dialogical witness at work, they need to become 'bi-lingual: nurtured, on the one hand, in the identity-forming symbols of their own worship and witness (religious language), whilst, on the other

269

hand, becoming fully fluent and confident in the grammar and dialect that belongs to the powers-that-be (secular language)' (p. 117).

Implicit and explicit aspects of mission as dialogue

In conversations where the Christian believes it best if his or her faith-related reasons for intervention remain *implicit* in nature, as is often the case with the kind of intervention described in Stage 8(1) and especially 8(2), then any accompanying dialogue will exclude the use of Christian language. However, if and when it is agreed, formally or informally, by those involved in any conversation that it is appropriate for the Christian to be open about his or her faith-related commitment, then the ensuing dialogue is defined as *explicit* in nature. Whether implicit or explicit, as noted above, such intervention is termed 'mission as dialogue' (Walcot, 1997, pp. 81-85).

Mission as implicit dialogue

When mission as dialogue is *implicit*, the Christian at work engages in conversation in ways that reflect his or her hope, though not overtly expressed, that others involved might gain greater awareness and experience of the gifts of the kingdom community, whether or not the origins of those gifts are acknowledged or employed for the transformation of the workplace. Thomas Thangaraj (1999, p. 98) describes the nature of implicit dialogue, in the context of world mission, as follows:

> Dialogue is witness even without an evangelistic agenda. Seeing dialogue as a preparation for the announcement of the good news is misguided. In dialogue one lives out the good news that God accepts all as God's own children and engages with continuous dialogue with God's own creation. In expressing our responsibility, solidarity, and mutuality with others in ... various types of dialogue... we are, in fact, making the good news present in the midst of our dialogue. It is a witness that simply expresses itself through 'being there' with others in conversation, exchange and action.

Kevin Walcot (1997, p. 83) adds an ecclesiological reflection on 'mission as (implicit) dialogue':

> For some... this might mean the church militant becoming the church hesitant, and perhaps not before time... But... the church hesitant may yet become as sweet a sound as the church

militant and triumphant used to be to our ears. It need not mean the church somnolent. It might do much to reverse the trend towards the church irrelevant, and... it might set the church on a course which could prevent it from becoming... the church insolvent!

He concludes (pp. 84-85):

> Some will always feel that they have not been missionary if they have not 'proclaimed' Christ. But we must surely err in thinking that this has to be a monologue, when it could be witnessing to our faith by our life and above all by our loving relationships with others. Witness is martyrdom, *martyrion*, a new kind of self-imposed martyrdom, to our own preconceptions, to our deeply felt need to be needed, to the discipline of letting go, to risk and vulnerability.

As already noted, mission as implicit dialogue has strong affinity with what was described in Stage 2 as double-loop learning. That is, it is a form of conversation in which all involved are open to questioning their assumptions and sharing their concerns within what is agreed as a mutually helpful frame of reference, even if the conversation does not employ language of a distinctively Christian character.

Mission as explicit dialogue

In this form of dialogue it is accepted as legitimate by *all* involved that the Christian participant be able to share his or her faith convictions through the use of concepts, language or symbols derived from and informed by the kind of communal theology, spirituality, economic principles and diaconal structures discussed in Stages 2 to 5 and/or of the signs of the kingdom community set out in Stage 7(1). Dialogue which is *explicit* has a good deal of affinity with what was defined in Stage 2 as triple-loop learning. Openings for mission as explicit dialogue often occur during spontaneous or informal conversations.

The relation between mission as implicit and mission as explicit dialogue

Mission as dialogue needs to be motivated by and expressed in forms of words which, implicitly or explicitly, seek to communicate the relevance of the kingdom community and its gifts to the workplace. The model set out below (*Diagram 8*) represents key aspects of mission as implicit or explicit dialogue. It should be noted that the conversational ground rules, process and forms of words are similar for both implicit *and* explicit dialogue. Explicit dialogue does not form an approach to mission detached from implicit dialogue. Instead, it builds on the principles and ground rules undergirding the implicit approach but, in addition, offers to the Christian participant a means of openly expressing how these principles are rooted in and help our understanding of Christian faith and, in particular, of the gifts of the kingdom community.

Key components of implicit and explicit dialogue

In describing the nature of dialogue, the focus here is on an innovative approach and methodology offered by Sue Clark and Mel Myers in their book *Managing Difficult Conversations at Work* (2007). In effectively managing such conversations, the authors stress the importance of the participants engaging in what they call 'open-to-learning' dialogue. From the perspective of the Kingdom at Work Project, their work is seen as very helpful in informing and elucidating the meaning of mission as implicit and explicit dialogue.

Over against an open-to-learning approach to conversation, which they believe characterizes true dialogue, Clark and Myers set a 'closed-to learning' conversational stance which makes genuine dialogue impossible. Unfortunately, research (Argyris and Schön, 1974, 1978; Clark and Myers, 2007, pp. 41-43) shows the closed-to-learning stance to conversation to be very much the norm within the workplace. Clark and Myers believe this makes it hard to handle effectively the many difficult conversations which occur daily within the world of work.

Clark and Myers' open-to-learning approach (p. 35) reflects what was earlier defined as 'double-loop learning' [Stage 2]. What they describe as a closed-to-learning stance (p. 34) leads to what was earlier called 'single-loop learning' [Stage 2]. In *Diagram 8* the key components of mission as dialogue are set out. These are derived very largely from the open-to-learning approach to conversation described by Clark and Myers.

Diagram 8
Mission as dialogue
An open-to-learning model

Mission task	Implicit (the 4Ls implicit) [Double loop]		Explicit (the 4Ls explicit) [Triple loop]	
	Stance	Dialogue	Stance	Dialogue
Discernment – to discern the mission task as the focus of implicit or explicit dialogue	Readiness of speaker to **question their assumptions** and to engage in dialogue as a **partnership**	**Advocacy** – excluding Christian concepts *in conjunction with –* **Inquiry** – inviting a response to advocacy which excludes Christian concepts	Readiness of speaker to **question assumptions** and to engage in dialogue as a **partnership**	**Advocacy** – including Christian concepts – *Tools:* Stories Interpretation Proclamation *in conjunction with –* **Inquiry** – a response to advocacy which includes Christian concepts

Mission as implicit or explicit dialogue

Mission task

This is placed in the left-hand column of *Diagram 8* and applies to both implicit and explicit dialogue. How the mission task for the Christian at work is identified has been discussed in Stage 8(Introduction). It is a task derived from a process of discernment by means of which the Christian at work has identified where they believe the gifts of the kingdom community to be in evidence within the workplace but where they need to be given fuller expression. The mission task guides and shapes every intervention to make manifest the gifts of the kingdom community in the workplace, including implicit and explicit dialogue.

Stance

Stance (columns two and four in *Diagram 8*) refers to the approach and attitude taken by any Christian seeking to intervene through dialogue, implicit or explicit, within their workplace. Here two features of the Christian participant's stance are of special importance. First is their ability to question any assumptions they carry with them into the conversation. Second is a commitment to engage in conversation as a partnership.

Questioning assumptions

Clark and Myers (2007) define an assumption as 'any idea, interpretation, inference or belief that, for the purposes of discussion, planning and action, a person takes to be true' (p. 253). They write: 'The aspect of our thinking that is the most critical for the management of difficult conversations concerns the assumptions we make... (Assumptions) reflect our personal views about how things are, and thus the sense we make of our own and other people's behaviour' (pp. 33, 33-34). When we adopt a stance of being 'open-to-learning', we are in a position to question our assumptions and, as and when necessary, break clear of 'old patterns of thought (which) limit what we are to think, hear or say' (p. 35).

These old patterns of thought might include our assumptions about how others involved in the dialogue will react to what we say (for example, they are bound to be cynical or angry), about the impossibility of challenging the 'received wisdom' of the workplace culture (for example, that to admit a mistake is an indication of weakness), or even about the absolute truth of our own faith convictions (including those on which our mission task is based).

Readiness to question our assumptions has a vital part to play in facilitating dialogue. It enables us to affirm all those involved in the conversation as of equal worth, and not perpetuate any temptation to stereotype or scapegoat others. It enables us to hear and understand what others have to say and evaluate their contribution as objectively as possible. It gives us the opportunity to gain new insights that might otherwise pass us by. In particular, such a stance accords with being open to the kingdom community's gifts of life, liberation, love, and especially learning. If such openness is not demonstrated by the Christian who is participating in the conversation, there will be little chance of facilitating the openness of others involved.

Dialogue as partnership

Dialogue is not dialogue if it is not a conversational partnership. Clark and Myers define partnership as 'a way of addressing a difficulty that sees the conversation as an opportunity for finding jointly acceptable ways forward rather than as something to be managed alone' (p. 255). Partnership only becomes possible when we are prepared and able to question our assumptions. If our stance towards others involved in the conversation is one of being open-to-learning, differences and disagreements become discussable in a way that offers by far the best chance of resolving them. This open stance lies at the heart of the Agreement phase of the intervention cycle discussed in Stage 8(Introduction) and is one means of accessing and employing the kingdom's community's gift of love. An open stance to conversation also has much in common with the Affirmation phase of the intervention cycle (associated with the gift of liberation) which is founded on empathy and a readiness to validate the experience and views of others. Affirmation also embodies the kingdom community's gift of liberation because it recognises the hidden qualities and abilities of the other person.

Where mission as dialogue is concerned, it is important that any conversational partnership is grounded on a culture of trust, be it formal or informal, is open about the purpose of the conversation and about the outcomes hoped for. Wherever possible, any partnership should possess the features of a person-centred covenant, as described in Stage 8(Introduction), rather than just a task-focused contract.

Dialogue as 'advocacy and inquiry'

Readiness to question our assumptions and to engage in conversation as a partnership is a stance that needs to be present and practised throughout the whole of any dialogue at work. However, Clark and Myers (pp. 37-40) argue that for any conversation to be a dialogue, two forms of verbal exchange, set out in columns three and five of *Diagram 8*, must also be present: 'advocacy' and 'inquiry'.

Clark and Myers define *advocacy* as 'statements a person makes that convey the way they see things, their concerns, wishes, views, reasoning, or feelings' (p. 253). They state that advocacy needs to be 'transparent, in the sense that the listener has (or is given) all the information needed to evaluate the truth, relevance and significance of our statements' (pp. 39 and 137).

They also argue that *advocacy always needs to be accompanied by inquiry*. *Inquiry* 'refers to questions we ask in order to discover the other person's wishes, views, reasoning, feeling or problems' (p. 39). Inquiry also enables us to discover whether the listener has fully understood our comments (our advocacy), and if and where he or she has any need for further elucidation or explanation. When we inquire, we need to give our reasons (a form of advocacy) for asking the questions we pose to prevent the latter being felt as some kind of intrusion into the listener's private affairs.

Advocacy without inquiry results in dialogue becoming a monologue. Inquiry without advocacy risks the conversation becoming a threat. Both prevent the conversation becoming a partnership and thereby a dialogue.

Whether mission as dialogue is implicit or explicit, there is no reason why advocacy, *provided it is accompanied by inquiry*, cannot give expression to convictions which the Christian participant holds very strongly. Advocacy may implicitly as well as explicitly bear witness to the kingdom community's *gift of life*, and bring animation and energy to the dialogue. At the same time, because inquiry offers the listener(s) a genuine choice in the way in which they respond, it becomes a means, whether recognized or not, of enabling them to gain a glimpse of the nature of the kingdom community, in particular *the gifts of liberation* and *learning*. And because advocacy with inquiry, and inquiry with advocacy enhance partnership, these forms of verbal exchange can offer participants a chance to experience *the gift of love*.

There is no space here to go into detail concerning how Clark and Myers describe the way in which it is possible to move away from a conversation which is a monologue (closed-to-learning) to one which has the attributes of dialogue (open-to-learning). However, one helpful technique, termed 'alert' and 'cue', which they offer for this purpose (p. 150) is noted below:

> Being aware of our negative feelings (such as embarrassment, fearfulness, anger, frustration, resentment, guilt or confusion…) when they arise (before or within a conversation) can 'alert' us to the fact that we are running into difficulties. By becoming alert in this way, we prevent ourselves from being driven, unthinkingly, into automatic, closed thinking. We can thus use this awareness as a 'cue' to remember the principles and forms of words that make up the open model of conversation.

How a real-life conversation might demonstrate many of the features mentioned above is contained in the example given in Appendix 1.

Mission as explicit dialogue

All that has been said so far concerning dialogue is essential for mission as implicit *or* explicit dialogue. However, because mission as explicit dialogue involves the Christian at work seeking openly to identify and interpret the gifts of the kingdom community in language which can be understood by the other person(s) involved in the conversation, it is important to explore ways in which explicit dialogue can become a reality. Margaret Whipp (p. 164) believes that, in this context, the Christian at work is fulfilling the role of 'a theologian-in-residence'.

The transition from implicit to explicit dialogue

It is almost always the case that mission as explicit dialogue will emerge out of the Christian's engagement in mission as implicit dialogue. For example, it is possible that the other person(s) involved in the conversation may ask the Christian participant to offer their reasons for the point of view they are advocating. Such an opening is most likely to occur where the workplace as a whole embodies a culture of trust and when the Christian at work has gained an authority which is achieved rather than associational or ascribed [Stage 8(Introduction)].

On the other hand, the transition from implicit to explicit mission as dialogue may take place because the Christian at work feels that the

277

moment is opportune for them to put their faith into words and explain why they believe the workplace needs to manifest the gifts of the kingdom community. Here advocacy becomes not just an expression of the way in which (Christians) express 'their concerns, wishes, views, reasoning, or feelings' (Clark and Myers, p. 253), but also their beliefs and values.

Nevertheless, it is essential that such conversations remain a partnership. Thus the Christian will need to negotiate their use of explicitly religious language by employing the skill of inquiry, 'questions we ask in order to discover the other person's wishes, views, reasoning, feeling or problems' (Clark and Myers, p. 39). This may involve the Christian engaged in the conversation posing such questions as:

> As a Christian, do you mind if I tell you why I am convinced about this?

> Would it be OK to say where my faith comes into the picture?

> Can I explain how I believe that being a Christian has something to offer to this discussion?

> I am taking this position because of my Christian convictions. Could I explain what those are?

Even if permission for a transition to the use of Christian concepts has been openly negotiated, it is important that the Christian at work continues to complement any expression of explicit Christian views or comments (advocacy) with questions checking out the listener's understanding and response (inquiry).

Language

'The cultural dissonance' between the world of the church and the world of work has already been noted [Stage 5]. It is a dissonance which may well come to the fore when the Christian at work attempts to make his or her motivation for any form of intervention explicit. Whipp speaks of the 'concealed ruthlessness' with which market-dominated managerial discourse seeks to control the language of the workplace for its own profit-oriented ends. She believes that, along with workplace 'culture, myths, norms, rituals, customs and symbolic practices' (p. 80), the work organization ensures that language is employed predominantly for 'the management of motivation', 'the flattening of dissent', 'the inculcation of instrumentalism', 'the valorization of management' (the portrayal of managers as gurus)', 'the promotion of the product' and 'the bonding of the customer/client' (pp. 79 -81). Thus 'the in-breaking of religious language into a working discourse strait-jacketed by oppressive managerialism may require some considerable daring as well as discursive fluency' (p. 162). Whipp describes this task as moving 'from Babel to Pentecost' in search of 'the dream of a common language' (pp. 82-84). Nevertheless, she believes that (p. 84):

> For the church which faithfully receives the Spirit's gifts (in this project, we identify these as the gifts of the kingdom community), a new and gracious kind of eloquence is discovered in the enactment of a contextually adequate and appropriate interdiscursive witness - not for the claiming of domination and control but for the offering of fresh meaning and life - in communion.

Below is suggested a number of opportunities and tools for engaging in mission as explicit dialogue available to the Christian at work.

Opportunities

In a section on 'respecting privacy' within the workplace, Whipp points out that it is often 'within and amongst (the) "private" interstices in the working day that sensitive questions appropriate to faith-talk arise' (p. 143). Such 'interstices' may include 'where women share confidence in the ladies' toilet, and men exchange titbits of gossip in the corridor' (pp. 142-142). They may also occur 'when colleagues go off to the pub together after work, or enjoy a relaxing conversation in the course of a weekend business trip' (p. 142).

On the other hand, it may be that the opportunity for mission as explicit dialogue arises when decisions having a significant ethical dimension relating to work or the workplace are being made. A number of such situations were identified in Stage 7(2) as critical incidents. Such decisions may have consequences concerning pay and conditions of employment, health and safety, prompt payment of suppliers, the integrity of advertising, the use of cheap labour abroad, or redundancy and so forth, all offering the opportunity for ethical reflection from a Christian perspective (Messer, 2006).

The challenge of spontaneity

From what has been said so far, it might be thought that the project assumes that the Christian will always have the opportunity and time to stand back and reflect on how and when to conduct workplace conversations. However, it is fully acknowledged that life in the workplace is rarely like that! The likelihood is that many of the workplace conversations in which the Christian is involved will necessitate their having to respond quickly, even instantaneously to what has been said. This is why engaging in mission as dialogue requires insights and skills that have to be practiced so often that they become second nature.

In the cut and thrust of workplace relationships, the Christian at work remains as human as anyone else! There will be occasions when the Christian's initial intervention in a difficult conversation may be a response to strong personal feelings which lead them to adopt a closed-to-learning stance to things that have been said. However, such a stance prevents any conversation becoming a dialogue and, consequently, for mission as dialogue to be possible. The only way this situation can be redeemed is for the Christian participant to become aware of and openly acknowledge the closed-to-learning stance they originally adopted and, from then on, to endeavour to assume an open-to-learning approach to the conversation. How a closed-to-learning stance might be transformed into one that is open-to-learning is illustrated in Appendix 1.

Tools

Tools for engaging in mission as explicit dialogue are always associated with the processes of advocacy *and* inquiry (column five of *Diagram 8*). A good deal can be learnt here from the way in which Christ went about his own ministry of teaching (Walcot, 1997, p. 84). Tools of particular note here are story-telling, interpretation and proclamation.

Story-telling

One important form of advocacy through which Christ as teacher sought to discover 'the dream of a common language' (Whipp, p. 84) which might integrate faith and daily life, including daily work, was through *the telling of stories* many of which illustrate what have been identified earlier as signs of the kingdom community [Stage 7(1)].

Numerous openings for story telling were offered to Christ because those in conversation with him asked questions which possessed an explicitly faith dimension, some carefully considered, many more spontaneous. For example:

> Why do John's disciples and the disciples of the Pharisees fast, but your disciples do not fast? (Mk 2: 18-22); Why are you doing what it is not lawful to do on the Sabbath? (Lk 6: 2); Are you he who is to come, or shall we look for another? (Lk 7: 19); Where did this man get this wisdom and these mighty works? (Mt 13: 54); Who is my neighbour? (Lk 10: 29); Which commandment is the first of all? (Mk 12: 28); Lord, will those who are saved be few? (Lk 13: 23); Good Teacher, what must I do to inherit eternal life? (Mk 10: 17); Lord, how often shall my brother sin against me, and I forgive him? (Mt 18: 21); Is it lawful to pay taxes to Caesar or not? (Mk 12: 14); By what authority are you doing these things, or who gave you this authority to do them? (Mk 11: 28).

The Christian's involvement in explicit dialogue at work may likewise be triggered by questions or queries, often spontaneous and informal, though these will be within an historical and cultural context very different from the time of Christ. One response to such questions, and to a number of other situations when an opening to engage in mission as explicit dialogue occurs, is for the Christian participant to employ the use of story. This is not a matter of relating anecdotes in an attempt to keep the listener interested or of recounting personal experiences in order to impress them. It is about recounting in narrative form carefully chosen experiences or incidents, sometimes akin to critical incidents, which illustrate the consequences of affirming or denying the gifts of the kingdom community; life, liberation, love or learning.

Charles Elliott in *Praying the Kingdom* (1985) employs a number of such stories which he terms 'myths' to explore the nature of the kingdom (p. 40). He sees these as having three essential features: they raise awareness of the presence of the kingdom, they 'ring true', and they indicate a moral direction which listeners are invited to take (p. 37). The important thing 'is not about the literal truth of the story, but about the underlying vision of reality reflected in the myth' (p. 38). Such stories cannot prove what is true or morally right. Nevertheless, they can challenge those involved in the dialogue to take 'a leap of faith' and commit themselves, individually or collectively, to a deeper reality which they may have glimpsed.

Elliott warns that 'selecting our myths… is no easy or random task' (p. 38). However, he suggests three sources for such stories which are likely to be most authentic. The first is the Christian's personal experience. If the Christian at work is open to the gifts of the kingdom community, over time he or she will have built up a store of incidents, encounters, happenings and events which can be drawn on to illustrate those gifts in action. A second source to which Elliott refers is 'stories of people we know and respect' (p. 39). Christians need to remember and share experiences of life, liberation, love and learning exemplified by the lives of those, where possible within in the world of work, who have earned public respect and regard. A third source of kingdom stories to which Elliott draws attention, though 'in every way the least satisfactory' (p. 39), are those from the media. Despite issues of veracity or sensationalism, these will often connect more easily with the experience of those engaged in the world of work.

As with the teaching ministry of Christ in his reference to phenomena such as sparrows, the hairs of our head, salt and light, lilies and expensive pearls, stories may take the form of metaphor: 'The kingdom community and its gifts are like this…'. Margaret Whipp argues that the missionary challenge within the workplace requires 'a fresh recognition of the transformative power of metaphor' (p. 84). Metaphor has the potential to draw the worlds of the secular and the sacred, and thus their two frameworks of meaning together. Metaphor offers the Christian at work the 'power for resistance and for re-envisioning' (p. 84) rather than assuming the politically correct 'bottom line' profit-before-all-else approach to every workplace issue.

It is interesting that on numerous occasions Christ used questions (inquiry) to check out that he was dealing with issues which touched his listeners' everyday lives and encouraged them to think for themselves:

> Which of these three, do you think, proved neighbour to the man who fell among the robbers? (Lk 10: 36); Do you not understand this parable (of the sower)? (Mk 4: 13); With what can we compare the kingdom of God, or what parable shall we use for it? (Mk 4: 30); If salt has lost its taste, how shall its saltness be restored? (Mt 5: 13); Which of you by being anxious

can add a cubit to his span of life? (Lk 12: 25; What will the owner of the vineyard do to them? (Lk 20: 15); Whose likeness and inscription is this? (Mk 12: 16).

The Christian at work might consider whether asking questions, even though these will need to be shaped by the culture of the workplace, might be a useful means of helping to clarify the message embodied within any story told. However, because all involved in genuine dialogue are partners in the search for truth, the asking of any questions should be done in a spirit of mutual exploration and not with the assumption that there is any 'right' answer.

An example of the practice of mission as explicit advocacy and inquiry

Beyond the workplace, but closely related to it, it is interesting to note that the Society of Friends, which of all bodies with a strongly Christian ethos is perhaps closest to being a learning community (Jenner, 2008 and Stage 3), open their commentary on Quaker Faith and Practice (2005, 1.01-1.07) with a series of 'advices' (advocacy) in response to 'queries' (inquiry). They believe that this dialogical approach will help to 'lead us into truth, unity and love' (1.01).

As noted in Stage 7(Introduction), the Quakers and Business Group in their booklet *Good Business - Ethics at Work* (2000) follows suit by approaching the task of auditing faithful practice at work through a range of 'advices' and 'queries' covering such concerns as 'honesty and integrity', 'business and profit', 'obligations to shareholders and investors', 'environmental responsibility', 'taxes', 'gifts and donations', 'trade unions' and 'whistle blowing'.

Interpretation

Within the workplace, there may be times when, because of the listener's lack of comprehension of a faith perspective, the Christian senses the need to discern and *interpret* what is happening in the light of the gifts of the kingdom community. However, it is important to stress that interpretation is always owned and accompanied by inquiry: 'I see it this way…', 'My own view is…' or 'There is another way of looking at this issue…'; followed by such questions as 'Does that make sense?' or 'How do you see it?'.

Proclamation

Another important tool when the Christian at work is engaged in mission as explicit dialogue is that of *proclamation*. In the ministry of

Christ as teacher, proclamation had two main foci. One was setting out guidelines for a kingdom-based way of life. Pride of place here lies with the beatitudes (Mt 5: 13). Also typical were Christ's words about not giving priority to earthly treasure (Mt 6: 19-21); not trying to serve God and money (Lk 16: 13); not judging our fellows (Mt. 7: 1-5) and so on. The other focus of proclamation was Christ's more definitive directions. Examples of the latter are his instructions to repent and believe (Mk 1: 15), 'the great commandment' (Mk 12: 28-34) and the commandment to love our enemies (Mt 5: 43-48).

In the case of the Christian in the workplace, proclamation within a dialogical context may well be most appropriate when important ethical issues are at stake. In such situations, the Christian at work may feel compelled to take the stance of 'Here I stand... I can do no other'. Even so, he or she should employ proclamation in the spirit of humility and empathy with colleagues and, as ever with genuine dialogue, always invite a response.

Margaret Whipp writes: The hope is that the Christian at work 'out of the creative friction between her religious and secular experience... learns to voice new images and interpretations in vivid symbols and stories' (p. 85). Whether responding to questions, telling stories, offering 'faith-full' interpretation or engaging in proclamation, mission as dialogue remains an art which has to be learnt and developed over many years and in many different workplace contexts.

Appendix 1

Mission as dialogue during a difficult conversation at work

Examples of a *closed* response (1), an *open* and *implicitly* Christian response (2), an *open* and *explicitly* Christian response (3) and their likely outcomes based on the format set out by Sue Clark and Mel Myers in *Managing Difficult Conversations at Work* (2007).

The situation [based on a critical incident from Stage 7(2)]

During a school staff meeting two teachers had a major disagreement. A (male), a Christian, took B (female) to task for not being prepared to take part in a school trip because he assumed she did not want to give up any of her own time. After the meeting, B sent A a 'flame' email accusing him of putting her down in public.

1. A's *closed* response to B's email

A's first thoughts on receipt of B's email	Commentary
This makes me so angry. How dare she accuse me of putting her down in front of the whole staff! And by email too… she can't even face me.	
After all it was quite obvious to all of us…	Unquestioned assumption (1)
…that the real reason she was against taking the children on a field trip was because she wasn't prepared to give up her own time and … I was the only one with the bottle to call her bluff.	Unquestioned assumption (2)

I'll send her a short sharp email return. Two can play at that game!	Intention to pursue own agenda unilaterally rather than making the conversation a partnership

A's return email

I strongly object to your emailing me like this. I only said <u>what everyone was thinking</u>, that <u>once again you were putting your own interests before those of the children.</u>	Advocacy based on two untested assumptions (as noted above)
You need to get your priorities sorted!	Absence of inquiry/invitation to dialogue

Outcomes

For A: He may feel some short-term satisfaction in his curt response to B.'s email. However, B.'s accusation that A 'put her down' may leave A with an underlying feeling of discomfort.

For the A/B relationship: The episode does not bode at all well for the future working relationship between A and B which is now likely to be characterised by disrespect and mistrust.

For the school: The school community will have to live with unresolved tension between two of its staff. This may well have an impact on the long term effectiveness of the organisation.

2. A's *open* and *implicitly* Christian response

A's first thoughts (as for closed response)	Commentary
This makes me so angry. How dare she accuse me of putting her down in front of the whole staff! And by email too… she can't even face me. After all it was quite obvious to all of us that the real reason she was against taking the children on a field trip was so that she wouldn't have to give up her own time… and I was the only one with the bottle to call her bluff. I'll send her a short sharp email return. Two can play at that game!	as for closed – unquestioned assumptions

…reflection…

…. but hold on… I'm in danger of reacting in the same way as she's just done. <u>I'm supposed to be a Christian and that means being respectful and loving, setting an example to others</u>…	Recognition of need to respond in a manner consistent with Christian beliefs
… <u>treating her as I would want to be treated</u>	Recognition of the other person as equally a child of God and therefore deserving of respect
… and as <u>a fellow human being in sorting this matter out.</u>	Intention to engage in dialogue as a partnership
<u>I need to look at my own position here.</u>	Readiness to question own assumptions

I *was* rather assuming that I was right in thinking that she wasn't prepared to give up any of her own time.	Recognition of a specific unquestioned assumption
And perhaps the point she was making about the trip being too ambitious was a valid one... maybe I got a bit carried away.	Questioning that assumption
I need to find out a bit more about her reasons for saying what she said. I'll go and have a chat with her.	Intention to lay assumption open to being tested through engaging in dialogue as a partnership

Implicit dialogue

Between A and B	Commentary
	Advocacy - statements that give A's reasons for asking B to engage in dialogue:
A to B .... I've just picked up your email. I can see that you're angry with me and I feel bad about that.	- respectful acknowledgement of B's anger, and open information about A's own feelings
I want to say that I'm sorry if I spoke too quickly.	- acknowledgement and apology for own role in the dispute
I've been thinking that maybe I've misunderstood your reasons for being against the trip.	- communication of A's questioning of own previous assumption

<u>I'd like to try again to get this matter sorted out.</u>	- statement of wish to begin again
	Inquiry - A's attempt to find out B's reasons for saying what she said and to be able to engage in dialogue
If I try to listen a bit more open-mindedly this time …<u>would you be willing to explain your thinking to me again</u>?	
B to A… Alright … but I'm still feeling pretty upset. The point I was trying to make was …	

Outcomes

For A: A can feel that in opening up the opportunity for further discussion with B and by indicating a new willingness to listen open-mindedly to her point of view, he has behaved in a professional manner. At the same time he has acted in accordance with his Christian beliefs and offered an important example to others of what these mean in practice.

For the A/B relationship: A is now likely to come over to B as open-minded rather than dismissive. This is likely to foster a more productive working relationship.

For the school: The school is likely to benefit from the results of a better working relationship between A and B.

3. A's *open* and *explicitly* Christian response

Explicit dialogue (based on the same thoughts as 2. above)

Dialogue	Commentary
	Advocacy - statements that give A's reasons for asking B to engage in dialogue:
A to B... I've just picked up your email. I can see that <u>you're angry with me</u> and <u>I feel bad</u> about that.	- respectful acknowledgement of B's anger, and open information about A's own feeling
I want to say that <u>I'm sorry</u> if <u>I spoke too quickly</u>.	- acknowledgement and apology for own role in the dispute
-----	-----
<u>I call myself a Christian but I don't think I acted as I should have done.</u>	*The first explicit reference to how A's Christian faith has influenced his change of heart*
<u>Would you mind if I shared with you where I'm coming from?</u>	**Inquiry** - invitation to partnership. Requesting B's willingness to listen to *how* A's Christian beliefs have prompted his change of heart.
B to A... If you want to. But I don't need a sermon!	

A to B… All I wanted to say was that <u>as Christians</u> we're supposed to help build bridges not destroy them – to try and bring people together through respect and friendship, not push them apart.

Advocacy - statements that explicitly communicate the Christian convictions which prompted A's change of heart.
- explicit reference to Christian concepts.

At the meeting I'm afraid I got carried away and wasn't true to my own convictions. <u>I jumped to conclusions</u> which stopped me really listening to the points you were trying to make. That wasn't fair.

- information about A's perceived mis-match between his beliefs and previous behaviour, including communicating A's questioning of his own previous assumption.

<u>Does this help you to understand why I'd like to get things sorted out and for us to be on good terms again?</u>

Inquiry - checking that B. understands the origin of A's change of heart and therefore is willing to remain a partner in the dialogue.

B to A… I appreciate where you're coming from. But so what?

A to B… <u>I'd like the chance to listen</u> more carefully to your position…

Advocacy - statement of A's current wish for dialogue

<u>Would you be willing to explain your concerns about the school trip again?</u>

Inquiry - A checking with B her willingness to engage in further dialogue in partnership with A

Outcomes (in addition to those for 'implicit' dialogue)

For A: A can feel that he has been able to be open about the fact that his change of heart was influenced by his Christian faith and that this has brought its relevance to the workplace to B's attention.

For the A/B relationship: B's expectations of future encounters with A are likely to be informed by B's knowledge that A is trying to put his Christian faith into practice. At the same time, B's own view of Christian faith may have been positively influenced by A's reference to what has led him to want to repair their relationship.

For the school: A's attempt to act explicitly according to his Christian faith may, in time, help to strengthen relationships within the school.

Stage 8

Intervention

Explicit

4 Christian symbols and messages

A not uncommon form of explicit intervention by the Christian at work is the deployment of Christian symbols and messages, worn by the person concerned or displayed within their work territory. Symbols, such as a cross, which might be worn simply as a piece of jewellery by those who would never think of calling themselves Christians are not our concern here.

During the past decade there has been the growth of public opposition to Christian symbols from an increasingly secular society which claims that they may intrude on the convictions of others, detract from the corporate image of a company or business or are an impediment to performance at work. Recently the European Court of Human Rights has ruled that 'where there is no evidence of any real encroachment on the interests of others', the wearing of a symbol, such as a cross, is perfectly legitimate (*Church Times*, 18/1/13, p. 3). However, it should be noted that the court did not regard religious convictions as adequate to allow the wearing of religious symbols if this contravened health and safety regulations.

The use of Christian symbols and messages as a form of intervention has been described by Margaret Whipp as 'subtle signalling' (2008, pp. 109-111 and p. 114). She writes (pp. 109-110):

> Aware of the risks of overt discussion of taboo topics, *subtle signallers* resort to a range of more indirect verbal or non-verbal signifiers to identify their personal commitment. Car stickers and fish badges, screen savers and crosses, WWJD (What would Jesus do?) lanyards and wrist bands beam out a silent message inviting interest and response.

'Subtle signals' of this kind take two main forms. Some carry an implicit Christian message (fish badges, crosses, etc.). Others use explicitly Christian language as all or part of their message (screen savers, car stickers, wall texts, Christmas cards, etc.). Though not yet in evidence, it is possible that certain symbols and messages could be employed explicitly by the Christian at work to raise awareness of one or more the gifts of the kingdom community: life, liberation, love and learning.

The power of symbols should never be underestimated. In *The Symbolic Construction of Community* (1985), Anthony Cohen describes how community is given form, strength and impetus by cultural and social symbols which, in particular, offer a sense of significance (liberation) and solidarity (love) [Stage 2]. Thus by using Christian symbols and messages, the Christian at work may be engaged in much more than peripheral intervention. The fact that legal action has in recent years been taken against those wearing Christian symbols in the workplace simply underlines this fact. How the individual Christian, as well as the wider Christian community should respond to such opposition is a matter which needs to be informed by the points made in this project concerning appropriate forms of intervention.

Supporting some aspects of the deployment of Christian symbols and messages, Whipp comments: 'A net increase in symbolic signalling - even if restricted to those of shared faith - still effectively raises the profile of Christian presence in a workplace, creating the preconditions for a more fully adequate and locally appropriate witness to develop (p. 111).' Even if it is true that 'the coded message emitted is picked up predominantly by fellow-believers' (p. 110), this can be an important means of mutual affirmation and encouragement and facilitate communal networking for those who, from a mission perspective, often find themselves in the position of a lone ranger.

However, Christian symbols and messages may also have, at best, neutral or, at worst, negative connotations. Though they may help Christians to identify and support one another, they may be quite unintelligible to those who have little familiarity with the symbolic forms of a Christian culture. At the same time, if the deployment of Christian symbols and messages is in reality an attempt at subliminal evangelization, then it is likely that sooner or later such intervention will be perceived as intrusive and even manipulative. As Whipp comments (p. 116):

> Whilst the importance of relationships of trust and friendship and disinterested service are frequently asserted, there are deep contradictions in an agenda which makes the quality of those

relationships subservient to their potential as a platform for the explicit promotion of a decontextualized Christian message.

Consequently, she states that 'it would be simplistic to imagine that an unspoken message is inevitably less threatening than one which dares to speak its name' (p. 110).

Overall, therefore, the most creative deployment of Christian symbols and messages as a form of explicit intervention is as a means of encouraging the kind of dialogue explored in Stage 8(3). Symbols and messages might foster conversations, at an appropriate time and in an appropriate place, between Christians from the same workplace. However, much more importantly, they might lead to honest and open discussions between the Christian at work and any colleagues stimulated to discover more about what motivates them to deploy Christian symbols and messages. Symbols and messages at their best become doors into dialogue not magnets pressurizing people to take on a pre-determined Christian identity.

Stage 8

Intervention

Explicit

5 Prayer and worship

The final form of explicit Christian intervention covered by the Kingdom at Work Project relates to prayer and worship. Prayer and worship are here defined as an *explicit* intervention because they usually take the form of a conscious initiative to further the manifestation of the gifts of the kingdom community within the working world.

Prayer has potency. 'Our future as mankind,' writes Alan Ecclestone (1975), 'will be decided by our prayer' (p. 33). Graham Ward (2009) states that 'what I mean by praying (is) that deep inhabitation of the world, its flesh and its spirit, that stirs a contemplation and a reading of the signs of the times that is more profound than we can ever apprehend or appreciate... We live and act as transistors for the transformation of the world through Christ' (pp. 283-284).

In 'praying for the kingdom... one is adding one's own soul-force to the cosmic struggle of the love of God against the powers of darkness on behalf of their victims,' writes Charles Elliott (1985, pp. 30-31). Thus 'prayer seeks to see where the mortice and tenon, the dovetailing of eternal and temporal things, has come awry, and how re-engagement in penitence and hope may be made' (Ecclestone, p. 105). In the context of this project, prayer is an act of becoming a channel through which the grace of God can flow into the world of work and permeate its undertakings and relationships. It is a life-giving, liberating, love-enhancing and awareness raising process which opens the way for the gifts of the kingdom community to be made manifest, enhancing what is good and challenging what is evil within the workplace.

Prayer and worship are rooted in and spring out of the practice of the presence of God. What is written here takes as given that which was said earlier about the importance of a communal spirituality for guiding and empowering mission in the world of work [Stage 3]. The task in this stage of the project is to look in more detail at the language and forms in which prayer for the coming of the kingdom community within the world of work can be expressed in both a personal and collective context. We then comment on the relevance of the Sabbath and of the Eucharist in informing and energizing mission in the world of work.

Occasionally prayer and worship are initiated from within the workplace. Such is the case, when a workforce comes together for a carol service at Christmas, though in an increasingly multi-cultural society these sorts of event are becoming less common. A Sea Sunday, which includes the blessing of the fleet, is held each year in Guernsey. In Bakewell, Derbyshire, an ecumenical act of worship for farmers and farming, is held annually in the auction market of the Bakewell Agricultural Centre.

Nevertheless, explicit intervention involving prayer or worship is usually undertaken from beyond the workplace. This may be through prayer undertaken at a ***personal*** level. Or it may be a ***collective*** form of intervention, usually undertaken by a gathered Christian community, ranging from a small prayer group to a congregation gathered for worship.

Existing collections of prayers for the world of work

It is perhaps indicative of the uneasy relationship between the church and the world of work that the resources to facilitate the task of praying explicitly for the life of the latter, whether from a personal or collective perspective, are extremely limited. Though there is a small number of books of prayers and web pages offering prayers related specifically to daily work (that is, within the UK - there are many more in the USA), the majority of anthologies of prayers, hymn books and liturgies have few explicit references to the working world as such.

Those anthologies or web sites which do focus on work-related prayers embrace a variety of approaches in the way they set out the prayers on offer. For the *individual* Christian at work, some will include sections focusing on personal concerns or 'dispositions' (Copeland, 2001; Greene, 2004b; Ogden at www.cavhmc.org.uk). A number fit prayers for the Christian at work into a daily or weekly format (de Waal, 2001; Greene, 2004a). Others provide a miscellany from which he or she can pick-and-mix (Adam, 1992; Thompson, 2006; www.catholic.org/prayers).

Collections of prayers for the working world to be used *collectively*, including prayers that can be used in worship, also have diverse foci. Some concentrate on particular occupations or professions (Greene,

2004a; www.aftersunday.org.uk; Ogden at www.cavhmc.org.uk). Others focus on major issues facing the working world, such as unemployment (Greene, 2004a; www.aftersunday.org.uk). A few collections offer prayers for those in positions of leadership (Copeland, 2001; www.icf-online.org). There are also a number of publications which include liturgies or litanies for the world of work (Butland, 1985; *Worship Resources*, 2005).

Prayers for the workplace which reflect the gifts of the kingdom community

One of the weaknesses of the collections of prayers mentioned above is that they are not overtly related to any explicit theology or spirituality relating to mission in the world of work or, in the case of collective prayers, even to the basic components of worship. In a paper on *A Liturgy for Public Life* (CIPL, 1992), Norwyn Denny identifies these components as 'adoration, praise, confession, forgiveness, hearing the word, meditation, offertory, dedication, concerns and intercessions, thanksgiving and commitment'. Only the Industrial Christian Fellowship suggests that prayer, focused on the individual Christian worker, might be linked to major aspects of worship - in their case: 'Thanksgiving and Affirmation, Confession and Challenge, and Intercession' (www.icf-online.org).

In the Kingdom at Work Project, the concern is to find ways in which personal and collective prayers for the world of work might bring to the fore the gifts of the kingdom community whilst, at the same time, enriching the basic components of worship. *Diagram 9* indicates the way in which the project interprets this alignment.

Diagram 9

Worship and the gifts of the kingdom community

Key components of worship	Related gifts of the kingdom community	Personal and collective prayers
Adoration, praise and thanksgiving	The gift of life	See prayers in the text
Confession and forgiveness	The gift of liberation	
Concerns and intercession	The gift of love	
Hearing the word and reflection	The gift of learning	
Offertory, commitment and dedication	Commitment to bearing witness to all 4Ls	

Personal prayers

Presence and discernment

Preparation for intervention in the workplace begins with discerning the signs of the kingdom community therein [Stage 7(1)]. Thus personal prayers need, first and foremost, to be about awareness of the presence of God and his kingdom in every experience of life, not least the workplace. Below are a number of the prayers which point towards such an awareness.

> O Lord,
> You have set before us the great hope
> that your kingdom shall come on earth,
> And have taught us to pray for its coming;
> Give us grace to discern the signs of its dawning,
> And to work for the perfect day when your will
> shall be done on earth as it is in heaven;
> Through Jesus Christ our Lord.

(Percy Dearmer)

In the rush and noise of life, as you have intervals, step within yourself and be still. Wait upon God and feel his good presence; this will carry your through your day's business.

(William Penn, *MPH*, 2007-2008, p. 61)

Lord Jesus Christ,
alive and at large in the world,
help me to follow and find you there today,
in the place where I work,
    meet people,
    spend money,
    and make plans.
Take me as a disciple of your kingdom,
to see through your eyes,
    and hear the questions you are asking,
to welcome all others with your trust and truth,
    and to change the things that contradict God's love,
by the power of the cross,
and the freedom of your Spirit.

(John Taylor, Pawley, 1991, p. 27)

Blessed Lord,
By your life at Nazareth you made holy the ordinary work of the
    day,
And by your teaching revealed your compassion for those who
    labour and are overburdened:
Grant that in the midst of our work we may find rest and peace in
    your presence
And joy in knowing that we are serving you,
Who are our refuge and strength,
And our exceeding great reward.

(Downside Abbey Prayer)

God of the morning,
    as we look to the day ahead of us,
    renew our trust in you.
In the daily news we hear about a world in turmoil,
    and yet we know that this is your world
    and that the agents of your kingdom are at work in it.
As we look at what we plan to do today,
    help us to see each task we undertake

as playing its part in fulfilling your purpose.
In every person we meet, and in every place we visit,
    may we look for signs of your grace.
Help us always to respond to others
    with the love that comes from you,
    through Jesus Christ our Lord. Amen

(Pauline Webb, *MPH,* 2001-2002, p. 25)

However, discerning the presence of God in the workplace is no easy task not least because the world of work and the world of faith at times seem, literally, worlds apart, an experience evident in the following prayer.

Gracious God, sometimes I see the chasm between the way I speak
    my faith and the experiences of my everyday work.
In my devotion to you, I speak of love and hope, of calling and using
    my gifts and everything is held perfectly in your plan.
In daily labour, I wrestle with work targets, difficult personalities,
moral dilemmas and waste of resources,
and faith seems to belong to a parallel universe.
Help me to see that daily work
is the very crucible in which I discover what faith in you means.
Hold in your presence my place of work today:
an unchartered new frontier,
where you kingdom touches earth. Amen.

(Jenny Ellis, *MPH*, 2012-2013, p. 9)

The gift of life (adoration, praise and thanksgiving)

That the Christian at work looks to access the gift of life is reflected in many prayers from the Celtic tradition, albeit in a rural context. Below is part of one quoted by Esther de Waal (1996, pp. 167-168):

Glorious Lord, I give you greeting! ...
Let life everlasting praise you,
Let the birds and the honeybees praise you ...
Let the books and the letters praise you,
Let the fish in the swift stream praise you,
Let the thought and action praise you,
Let the sand-grains and the earth-close praise you,
Let all the good that's performed praise you.
And I shall praise you. Lord of Glory:

Glorious Lord, I give you greeting!

A Sanskrit prayer also portrays the blessings of the gift of life (quoted in *Bakewell Methodist Church at Work*, 2006):

> Listen to the exhortation of the dawn:
> Look well to this day! For it is life;
>> The very life of life.
> In its brief course lie all the verities
> And realities of your existence;
>> The bliss of growth,
>> The glory of action,
>> The splendour of beauty;
> For yesterday is but a dream,
> And tomorrow is just a vision;
>> But today well lived
> Makes every yesterday a dream of happiness,
> And every tomorrow a vision of hope.
>> Look well, therefore, to this day!
>> Such is the salutation of the dawn.

The gift of liberation (confession and forgiveness)

In the 1990s, John Hammersley, at that time chaplain to the Metro Centre in Gateshead, wrote a series of *Psalms of Life* several of which are prayers in poetic form to support the Christian in the workplace. Below, are quoted extracts from three of these to illustrate the gift of liberation offered to the Christian at work.

> My world's turned upside down and I'm in a muddle
>> I'm afraid to do anything, terrified of people!
> It's a comfort to get back to the office:
>> but my work is suffering, I can't do what I want.
>
> ... You have said that I needn't be afraid:
>> I trust in you to help, remove my terror -
> you are my salvation, my lasting joy:
>> I trust you to remove my fear and be my strength. (p. 34)
>
> -----
>
> ... Help me, God, to recognise my faults:
>> when I fail in my expectations to be strong enough to cope,
> to be prepared to give another the credit for being right:
>> more ready to lose face myself

than to lie myself out of trouble.
Teach me to change what needs to be changed:
    give me courage to accept what cannot be altered,
but grant me wisdom to know the difference:
    and always to give the glory to you. (p. 30)

Now, God, I have completed it:
    a sense of achievement is your gift to me today.
It may be just to have survived:
    or to have finally finished what I had set myself to do,
in some very small thing ended:
    or by the achievement of a mighty work.
Thank you for the sense of completion:
    into your hands I commit my life,
for now it has been accomplished:
    the day you have given me is done.   (*CIPL*, R9, 1993)

The gift of love (concerns and intercession)

Personal prayers referring explicitly to the gift of love are in short supply in anthologies of prayers and liturgies for the working day. It seems as if the secularization of the language of the workplace has led to the assumption that the concept of love is too 'soft' or sentimental to be relevant to a competitive market-place culture. However, the gift of love remains essential if communities of work are to be transformed into communities of character [Stage 1]. Three short prayers which refer to this gift are quoted below.

> Work is your gift to us, a call to reach new heights for the good of all. Guide us as we work and teach us to live in the spirit that has made us your sons and daughters, in the love that has made us brothers and sisters. Amen

> (William Byron, SJ, quoted in William Thompson, 2006, p. 6)

Lord Christ, we often forget that your ministry was shaped not only by prayer and quiet reflection but by many years spent at a carpenter's bench. It was on the shop floor, through the hectic world of trade and commerce, that you learnt the art of living and loving. May we be aware that you are one of us and alongside us in our daily work. Through every experience of our working lives, teach us how to live as fully and to love as deeply as you did. Through us, and all who respond to your presence, may the world

of work be transformed into your kingdom on earth as it is in heaven.
Amen

(David Clark in *MPH*, 2011-2012, p. 31)

The love of God
   be 'twixt me and each caller;
The welcome of Christ
   in me and my listening;
The Spirit's wisdom
   in me and my words;
The blessing of God
   on each one who hears me.

I will answer the phone this day
in the name of the sacred Three.

(Ann Lewin in Braley, 1996, p. 24)

The gift of learning (hearing the word and reflection)

The gift of learning is also one that is somewhat neglected in personal prayers for the Christian at work. However, a number of hymns and prayers stress the need for us to be open to and learn from the signs of the kingdom community, including the following:

Teach me, O Lord, thy holy way,
   And give me an obedient mind,
   That in Thy service I may find
My soul's delight from day to day.

(William Matson, *Hymns and Psalms*, No. 748)

Today Lord, open my eyes
   that I might see your image in everyone I meet;
Today Lord, open my ears
   that I might hear your word in the words others speak;
Today Lord, open my mouth
   that I may speak your gracious word of love
   to those whose path I cross;
Today Lord, open my heart, my mind and my whole being;
   that I might be filled with your Spirit and so serve you,
   more truly your disciple, in this, your world.
For Jesus' sake. Amen

(James Booth in *MPH*, 2008-2009, p. 53)

Every day, Lord, I join the race of life, through life, towards life.
As I seek to follow and serve you,
    sometimes, I can't keep up with those around me:
     those who seem so much more gifted,
      or more able to keep running, come what may.
Grant me the confidence and serenity to be myself, just as you made
     me.
    Sometimes, I'm frustrated;
     too many people are lagging behind where I think they should be.
Grant me a willingness and generosity of spirit to allow them to be
     themselves.
Sometimes, I'm confused, uncertain, fearful, even lost:
    I'm not sure what, where, how or when.
Grant me an openness to the prompting of your Spirit
    that I may hear you speaking to me,
    through others, through your Word, through your World.
Then, as I reach the finishing line of the day's comings and goings,
      may I rest in peace with you, those close to me, my neighbours
      and myself.

Amen
(Ward Jones in MPH, 2011-2012)

Commitment and dedication

A number of personal prayers embody the commitment and dedication of the Christian to a ministry in the workplace:

> O Giver of Time, renewed each day with the rising of the sun, I ask for wisdom in how I use the minutes and hours granted to me. May I be generous in using time for acts of compassion and mercy. May I find a rhythm of work, rest, leisure and Sabbath that reflects your will for my life. Daily may my life reflect to others your peace and joy. O Giver of Time, I dedicate my time today to your service. Amen

(From Worship and Daily Life, Thompson, 2006, p. 75)

Gracious God, I lay before you today's chaos. You know all that needs to get done; you know the pressures on me. I bring to you the things that worry me, the things that seem beyond me. I commit to you the hours of this day and ask you to make sense of things that seem disjointed or confusing. Help me to see beyond the day's string of demands to your larger purpose and, most especially, help me to stay rooted in my connection to you. Thank you that you hold me, my day, my job, my co-workers, my workplace, my community - all of us on this chaotic, wonderful planet - in your loving hands. Amen

(William Thompson, 2006, p. 89)

Lord,
In union with your love,
Unite my work with your great work,
And perfect it.
As a drop of water poured into a river is taken up into the activities
    of the river,
So may my labour become part of your work.
Thus may those among whom I live and work be drawn to your
    love.

(Gertrude the Great of Thuringen)

Forth in thy name, O Lord, I go,
 My daily labour to pursue,
Thee, only Thee, resolved to know
 In all I think, or speak, or do.

(Charles Wesley, *Hymns and Psalms*, 1983, No. 381)

Collective prayers

By collective prayers is meant those prayers concerned with the well-being of the world of work as a whole and/or the collective witness of the people of God within that world. They are an especially important resource for worship within the gathered church.

For transformation

Guide us by your Spirit, O God, that we may seek peace and pursue it and follow in the way of righteousness. Increase within us knowledge of the one true light that we may seek the well-being of all, until the kingdoms of this world become the kingdom of Christ, for ever and ever. Amen

(George Fox, MPH, 2012-2013, p. 66)

Presence and discernment

Two of the relatively few traditional hymns which have immediate relevance to the world of work remind Christians at work of the importance of being aware of the divine presence within the workplace and of seeking from the outset to discern the signs of the kingdom community within it.

> Where the many toil together, there am I among my own;
> Where the tired workman sleepeth, there am I with him alone.
> I, the Peace that passeth knowledge, dwell amid the daily strife;
> I, the Bread of heaven, am broken in the sacrament of life.

(Henry Van Dyke, The Methodist Hymn Book, 1954, No. 601)

> Teach me, my God and King,
> in all things thee to see,
> and what I do in anything,
> to do it as for thee.
>
> … A servant with this clause
> makes drudgery divine;
> who sweeps a room, as for thy laws,
> makes that and the action fine.

(George Herbert, Singing the Faith, 2011, No. 668)

A modern hymn with a similar theme is as follows:

> God of offices and kitchens
> Lecture halls and factory floor,
> God of internet, computers,
> T.V. screens and so much more.
> You are always here around us
> Even when we do not know.
> Help us realise your presence
> That our Spirit life may grow.
>
> Ploughing, seeding, patient waiting
> For the harvest of the soil;
> Typing, phoning and collating
> You are with us in our toil.
> In the workshop, store and office,
> Classroom, kitchen, garden, too,
> Help us see your gift and glory,
> Serve you well in all we do.
>
> Scattered in our congregations
> Yet one body called to be;
> Reaching out to fellow Christians,
> Serving the community.
> Thanks to you for love that binds us;
> For the strength to do your will.
> Father keep us true and faithful;
> May we love and serve you still.

(Australian hymn modified by Colin Wood, source unknown)

The gift of life (adoration, praise and thanksgiving)

There are a number of collective prayers for the world of work which demonstrate a deep awareness of the gift of life. These include:

> ... The whole created universe shares in praise and gratitude:
>   for you have made all that is, whether seen or unseen -
> ... The workman labours with the sweat of his brow:
>   he shares in your redemptive work;
> the secretary and teacher work for you;
>   those who use their mind and imagination -
> the executive making important decisions:
>   those who care for others and serve our needs.

… Those whom society rejects are in your special care:
 and those who have no place in a world of work;
without them your creation would be incomplete:
 your plan includes our work and our unemployment…

(John Hammersley, Psalms of Life, p. 35)

A short prayer and a modern hymn reflect the same theme:

May God bless your work
may your labours not be in vain;
may you rejoice to find today
your creator working with you;
and see your work in heaven,
restored to glory in the new creation.

(John Lovatt, Greene, 2004a, p. 1)

God of concrete, God of steel,
God of piston and of wheel,
God of pylon, God of steam,
God of girder and of beam,
God of atom, God of mine,
All the world of power is thine.

Lord of cable, Lord of rail,
Lord of motorway and mail,
Lord of rocket, Lord of flight,
Lord of soaring satellite,
Lord of lightning's livid line,
All the world of speed is thine.

Lord of science, Lord of art,
God of map and graph and chart,
Lord of physics and research,
Word of Bible, faith of Church,
Lord of sequence and design,
All the world of truth is thine.

God whose glory fills the earth,
Gave the universe its birth,
Loosed the Christ with Easter's might,
Saves the world from evil's blight
Claims us all by grace divine,
All the world of love is thine.

(Richard Jones, various publications)

The gift of liberation (confession and forgiveness)

Collective prayers for the gift of liberation compel us to recognize those things which would destroy or ignore the signs of the kingdom community in the workplace. Ann Lewin has a number of poems which take us to the heart of the reasons why workplaces often fail to become communities of character [Stage 1]. One poem is called 'Power Games':

> When we play God
> We throw our weight around,
> Treat people like chess pieces,
> Play our game regardless of their
> Needs, without appreciation of their
> Gifts. Their value lies in
> Cost effectiveness, not in
> Intrinsic worth. And if we
> Lose, we simply change the rules
> And use them to our own advantage.
>
> Lord, it must sometimes
> Break your heart, to see how
> We mismanage your creation,
> Misuse freedom. Are you sometimes
> Tempted to break our teeth,
> Hurl thunderbolts, cry
> Halt?
>
> It must be most
> Frustrating
> Being
> God.

(Ann Lewin, *Between the lines*, 1988, p. 52)

John Ogden in his collection of prayers posted on the worldwide web for the world of work (www.cavhmc.org.uk) also recognises the challenges of working life:

> We pray for people who are suffering from stress or bullying, and for their families whose peace and well-being are damaged as a result. We remember especially any whose lives and careers have been destroyed by oppressive or uncaring management policies.

Surround them, we pray, with your love. May they know your peace. Some are resolved to resist such abuse; for them we ask courage and calm dignity as they pursue their cause. Others seek a way out of the impossible situation; by your spirit grant them peace and patience as they search, and the wisdom to see clearly and make a good decision.

One classic prayer shows how our liberation for the well-being of others rests in the hands of Christ the worker:

O Christ, the Master Carpenter, who at the last, through wood and nails, purchased our whole salvation, wield well your tools in the workshop of your world, so that we who come rough-hewn to your bench may here be fashioned to a truer beauty of your hand. We ask it for your own name's sake. Amen

(Original attributed to Arthur Gray Butler; adapted by the Iona Community)

Albert Bayley has written a hymn which reflects the theme of liberation:

Lord, your kingdom bring triumphant,
give this world your liberty,
may your Spirit's strong compulsion
rule our tides of energy:

where the vessel cleaves the ocean,
or the pilot flies the plane,
where the miner toils in darkness,
and the farmer sows the grain…

by the living voice of preacher
by the skill of surgeon's hand,
by the far borne broadcast tidings,
speaking peace from land to land:

Lord, your kingdom bring triumphant
visit us this living hour,
let your toiling, sinning children
see your kingdom come in power.

(Albert Bayley, in Braley, 1996, p. 16)

The gift of love (concerns and intercession)

The gift of love points us in the direction of compassion, caring, reconciliation and partnership. The following prayers ask God's blessing on those who employ their skills for the benefit of others:

A prayer for those who harvest the resources of the earth

Loving God, in the resources of the earth you have given us riches for all humanity. We pray for all who are involved in harvesting those resources, in agriculture and horticulture, forestry, mining and fisheries. Their work is often dangerous and, for some, beset with uncertainty through weather, pest and disease. We pray for those whose livelihoods have been ruined by disease, by falling prices, and by the shortcomings of disaster management. Help us to enable them to reflect on their future and chart their course with confidence. May they be set free from bitterness and anger. May they know that the community they have sought to serve stands alongside them in their need. Amen.

(www.aftersunday.org.uk)

A prayer for those in designing, engineering and building

Lord God, architect and builder of the universe, we
pray for all involved in building construction:
architects, surveyors, services management and the
finishing trades. May the buildings they create
inspire those who work in them and walk by them.
Help those who strive for better use of modern
technology to reduce energy consumption and
enhance security.
We pray for people involved in civil engineering, who
design and build roads, bridges, power stations,
dams, flood controls and pipelines. Help them to
find the right balance between safety and cost,
both for their own workers and for the wider public.

(www.cavhmc.org.uk)

A prayer for those working in the fashion and beauty business

O Lord, we thank you that you have provided us with the means to care for our bodies and to feel good about ourselves. We are grateful for the hairdressers, clothes and shoe shops, jewellers and

312

beauticians that work in this town (place named). We ask that all those serving our community in this way may know that they are enhancing our sense of well-being and self-worth, and that for this we are grateful. As they engage in this important undertaking, may they be as concerned with enhancing our inward as well as outward beauty, remembering that all of us, with what you have endowed us, are of infinite value to you.

(David Clark, *Bakewell at Work Prayer Book,* June 2009)

See also the prayer for those in education below.

The gift of learning (hearing the word and meditation)

The gift of learning embraces curiosity, inquiry, attentive listening, discernment, reflection and wisdom amongst other things. Collective prayers for the world of work are not plentiful here. However, a number of prayers, traditional and recent, do seek to access this gift:

Teach us, Good Lord,
To serve thee as thou deservest;
To give and not to count the cost;
To fight and not to heed the wounds;
To labour and not to ask for any reward,
save that of knowing that we do Thy will.
Through Jesus Christ Our Lord. Amen.

(Prayer of Saint Ignatius Loyola)

Where cross the crowded ways of life,
Where sound the cries of race and clan,
Above the noise of selfish strife,
We hear thy voice, O Son of Man

(Frank North, *Hymns and Psalms*, No. 431)

Teach me, my God and King,
  In all things thee to see,
And what I do in anything,
  To do it as for thee.

(George Herbert, *Hymns and Psalms*, No. 803)

Ever-speaking God, we thank you for the many ways in which you have opened your word to us and for the many people whose stories have brought that word to life. Help us always to be open to that

313

word, that by your Spirit we may be challenged and changed by it. Through Christ, your living Word. Amen

(Leo Osborn, MPH, 2010-2011, p. 57)

And for those in education:

> God our Father, we thank you that you want us to learn how to become valued members of your worldwide family… We thank you for the way our schools, nurseries and play groups offer their experience, energy and enthusiasm to enable young people to discover what life is about. Support and encourage all teachers in their important and demanding work. May they have the reward of seeing their pupils grow in understanding, integrity and respect for others. Be with all parents that their homes may offer the nourishment and care which enable young people to feel secure and deeply loved. Amen

(David Clark, Bakewell@Work Newsletter, March 2012)

Servant leadership

The gifts of the kingdom are made available through the intervention of every Christian at work. However, those in positions of leadership have a particular responsibility to support and facilitate the emergence of the kingdom community's gifts. Below is a modern psalm which seeks to make manifest the divine origins of servant leadership:

> God is my gracious manager
>> I know I'll always have a job to do.
> You make certain I take responsibility:
>> you see that I'm kept up to the mark.
> You help me feel confident in my work:
>> when things begin to get difficult you're always on hand to listen,
> when we're successful, you congratulate us:
>> you encourage us all in our common enterprise.
> Into our community you bring your communion:
>> as we work together you give us strength to sustain us.
> Now I have a purpose I can aim for:
>> the final goal may not be clear, but I can see what I have to do next:
> for you give me the target I need:
>> and together with my colleagues we'll achieve what's to be done.

(John Hammersley, CIPL, November 1993)

Commitment and dedication

There are a relatively large number of examples of collective prayers and hymns which are concerned with the commitment and dedication, sometimes in the form of commissioning, of the people of God for ministry and mission in the world of work. Below are a few examples:

Almighty God, bestow upon us the meaning of words, the light of understanding, the nobility of diction, and the faith of the true nature. And grant that what we believe we may also speak. Amen

(Hilary of Poitiers)

Your challenge comes to serve you in the world,
to trace your presence in life's daily round,
hear your clear call to come and follow you
and find in all our work your holy ground.

This world is yours! We meet you everywhere:
we turn a stone and find that you are there,
each step we take is but to follow you,
the work we do is but your work to share.

You call us friends and bid us work with you,
within your world to live with graceful hope;
give us the wit and will to grasp your ways
and glimpse the wonder of your kingdom's scope.

Enlarge our vision, Lord, until we dare
to serve you boldly and create a place
where love is real and raw, love can be touched,
your kingdom comes in all its vibrant grace.

Make us the prophets of your life and hope,
the servant people of a world restored,
send us to live our daily life with joy,
to go in peace to love and serve you, Lord.

(Rosalind Brown, 2008, from www.aftersunday.org.uk)

In industry -
    God be in my hands in in my making.
In the arts -
    God be in my sense and in my creating.
In the home -
    God be in my heart and in my loving.

In commerce -
  God be at my desk and in my trading.
In healing -
  God be in my skill and in my touching.
In government -
  God be in my plans and in my deciding.
In education -
  God be in my mind and in my growing.
In recreation -
  God be in my limbs and in my leisure.

(From Coventry Cathedral, in Braley, 1996, p. 14)

Go forth into the world in peace;
be of good courage;
hold fast that which is good;
strengthen the fainthearted;
support the weak;
help the afflicted;
honour all men;
love and serve the Lord
rejoicing in the power of the Holy Spirit.

(Source unknown)

Now go from this place of prayer, that is God's temple,
back into the place of prayer that is God's world.
Go, rejoicing in his calling, celebrating his kingdom and walking in
his grace. Amen

(Source unknown)

The writing of prayers

Praying and prayers as a form of intervention in the world of work are a
potent and creative force for transformation. Both in a personal and
collective capacity, especially through the worshipping life of the
church [Stage 10], the employment of prayers which can enable the
gifts of the kingdom community to bear fruit in the world of work, are
a dynamic means of action.

Nevertheless, as already noted, the availability of prayers which
come to grips with the often harsh realities of the world of work is very
limited. Many of our hymns were written for a more rural and

parochial age. Unfortunately even modern anthologies of prayers and hymns show little awareness of the concerns and needs of the world of work and the ministry of Christians therein. In this context the church still remains bound by the mores of Christendom (Clark, 2005). However, if we dig deep enough, as has been tried in this section of the Kingdom at Work Project, prayers which can make a vital contribution to our endeavour to transform the world of work can be discovered.

At the same time it should be a cause for celebration that every Christian at work has the opportunity to compose their own prayers, share their experiences, concerns and insights with others, through the Internet and in many other ways, and thereby enable their colleagues to have a means of sustenance and support during the working day. It is worth concluding this section on written prayers by quoting three which illustrate how the Christian at work's personal experience can become a means of accessing and employing the gifts of the kingdom community in particular yet imaginative ways.

> Lord God, bless the labour of our hands,
>   whether in industry or in the kitchen;
>   in farming or in our garden;
>   if an office or on our computer;
>   in a hospital ward, or with an unwell friend
>   in holding a spanner or holding our grandchildren.
> May all we do be done to your glory.
> So, Lord, bless the labour of our hands.

(Brian Hudson, *MPH*, 2006-2007, p. 25

A laundry prayer

> God, you have washed me clean and dried me,
> now turn me upside down and shake me out.
> Discharge the static when I cling to things,
> smooth out the creases, brush away the fluff.
> Pull me, reshape me, turn me right side out,
> iron me and air me, ready to be used.
> Let me not be afraid of dirt and sweat,
> repair me if I split, patch up my wear,
> but please, never leave me on the shelf,
> outdated, out of fashion, past repair. Amen

(Diane Coleman, *MPH*, 2007-2008, p. 57)

A commuter's prayer

I failed to get a seat - again,
too many people on the train.
We're stuck in a tunnel;
everybody's sighing;
we're not moving.
I breathe in -
'Let me know your peace and grace.'
I breathe out -
'And help me share it with the people here.'
Breathe in.
Breathe out.
For the sake of my sanity.
For the sake of your kingdom,

(Sheridan James, Greene 2004a, p. 9)

Praying without words

It is not assumed that in prayer and worship for the world of work words, written or spoken, are always necessary. So-called 'arrow prayers', very short prayers offered to God in silence and on the spur of the moment in response to particular situations, uplifting or challenging, are often seen as forms of intervention in some of the literature on faith at work. Examples are: 'Help me not to make a mess of this interview', 'Please give me a clear head as I tackle this task'; 'Give me the skills to sort out this disagreement'; 'Help me to have patience'; 'Make me a good listener'; and, from a surgeon, 'Lord, please take this knife where it has to go!' (David Hanson in *Confronting the Realities of Work*, 2006, p. 14).

The Society of Friends goes further. It sees prayer within and/or for the workplace, not as a matter of the formulation of words but of being open to the Spirit in the midst of daily life. 'Advices and Queries' (1.02 - 1, 2 and 3) in *Quaker Faith and Practice* (2005) contains the following:

> 'Bring the whole of your life under the ordering of the spirit of Christ... Cherish that of God within you, so that this love may grow in you and guide you. Let your worship and your daily life enrich each other... Remember that Christianity is not a notion but a way... Do you set aside times of quiet for openness to the Holy Spirit? Seek to know an inwards stillness, even amid the activities of daily life. Do you encourage in yourself, and in

others, a habit of dependence on God's guidance for each day? Hold yourself and others in the Light, knowing that all are cherished by God.

The Sabbath

Collective prayer usually takes place in the context of Sunday worship. It is important, therefore, to visit the concept of the Sabbath and explore its implications for the worker, Christian or otherwise. The Sabbath may have become a shadow of its former self in contemporary British society but, at least symbolically, it still challenges the working world to take note of the priceless gifts of the kingdom community as giving meaning and purpose to that sphere of activity. The Sabbath, the seventh day of creation, blessed and hallowed by God, on which he rested after the previous six days of cosmic endeavour, stands as a reminder that 'the Sabbath is not for the sake of weekdays; the weekdays are for the sake of Sabbath. It is not an interlude but the climax of living (Fox, 1994, quoting John Merkle, p. 271)'. What does the Sabbath symbolize?

First and foremost, the hallowing of the Sabbath, described by Jürgen Moltmann as 'the feast of creation, which praises the eternal, inexhaustible God' is meant to point all of us, including those engaged in the world of work, to the 'enduring meaning of human existence' (quoted in Cosden, 2004, p. 141). It places God at the heart of the purpose of society, pointing 'man away from what he wills and might achieve back to what God wills and can do for him' (Hughes, 2007, p. 12, paraphrasing Karl Barth).

The Sabbath enables us to take time to reflect on the fact that it is God as Creator who has bestowed on his world *the gift of life*, and that all that we possess or achieve is to be employed for his creative purposes. Thus what matters most within the workplace is not what is produced but whether it is produced for the glory of God or merely the self-satisfaction of human beings. John Hughes spends most of his book on *The End of Work* seeking to challenge 'the utility of labour' as the dominant view of work under a capitalist system, arguing that the Genesis story declares that God works more as an artist. He writes (p. 226):

> God creates purely for the sake of the thing being created, gratuitously, out of sheer delight. He does not create out of any need or lack in himself, nor instrumentally for any other

purpose. God works for no other reward than his love for the thing made. God creates without loss of exertion, without failure, and with perfect delight in the thing made. He simply says 'Let it be' and it is, and he sees immediately that 'it was good'... God's work cannot be opposed to thinking, as if it were more action than contemplation, for it is both simultaneously, without division. Likewise, God's work cannot be contrasted with rest, for God remains unchanging in his action, and his life which is pure act is also perfect rest. Again God's work cannot be contrasted with play, for its very gratuity and immediate delight is precisely best understood as a form of play.

The references to delight and play in the quotation above remind us that the Sabbath is about *the gift of liberation*. Work reflects God's creative activity when it enables men and women to give full expression to their gifts and skills for the glory of the Giver and the salvation of humankind. The Garden of Eden is a salutary reminder of what goes wrong when men and women live simply to consume and satisfy their own desires.

The gift of liberation lies behind the Hebrews' social and political understanding of the Sabbath. The latter brings home the message that our world, including the world of work, needs forgiveness for its many injustices and the liberating hope of a new beginning. Fox (1994, p. 271) writes:

The Sabbath... has deep *political* and *prophetic* implications. The Sabbath can be called a 'mini-Jubilee: no one works, everyone shares'. The Jubilee, like the Sabbath, is a safety valve for humanity's greed and power, a reminder that justice must be regained at least every seventh year for the community, as it must be regained at least every seventh day for the individual.

'The Sabbath is for people and not people for the Sabbath' states Fox (p. 41), re-iterating the words of Christ (Mk 2: 27). Even on the Sabbath, it is *the gift of love* not holy rules and rituals that takes precedence. John Hughes (p. 228) comments that 'under the New Covenant, the Sabbath is no longer a rest after creation, but it is the day when the sick are healed, looking forward to the new creation, for as Christ says: "my father is working still, and I am still working".' The Sabbath is not a day so holy as to forbid any form of work, good or bad.

It is one in which love of God and neighbour, and the implications of that not least for the world of work, take precedence.

The Sabbath also honours *the gift of learning*. The importance of rest and re-creation, of which it can still remind this day and age when work can become 'the be all and end all' of many people's lives (Melissa Gregg, 2011), is central to the meaning of Sabbath. However, rest and re-creation are not to be interpreted as a passive withdrawal from labour. They are intended to give working women and men space and time to reflect, to converse about more than the day-to-day minutiae of working life, to step back and to gain a wider perspective on the meaning of work, and to grow in mind, body and spirit.

The Eucharist

The Eucharist or Lord's Supper, the central act of Christian worship in all the mainstream Christian denominations, like the Sabbath, stands as a symbol of profound importance for the working world as well as for the church.

'Without our human labour, there is no Eucharist', write David Jensen (2006, p. 80). Bread and wine are the symbols of human work, without which there would be nothing to place on the altar. However, Jensen continues, 'Our work alone… does not secure the place of these holy things.' The bread and wine are the results of God's continuing generosity, not only the seed from which the corn and the vine grow but the 'rains that water the earth, soil that nourishes the seedling, sun that radiates upon the land'. 'When our work attends the rhythms of God's creation, we encounter the mystery of God's incarnational presence in the midst of ordinary days.'

The order of service for the Eucharist has varied greatly over the years and differs from one denomination to another. However, the key components of the service remind us, at one point or another, of the offer of the gifts of the Trinity and of the kingdom community: life, liberation, love and learning (see *Diagram 9*), and their relevance to the world of work.

The gift of life is embodied in the bread, also 'the symbol of work, of everyday commerce', as Charles Elliott states (1985, p. 136). In this context 'bread is *both* common work *and* life itself' (p. 138). Thus when the bread and wine are brought to the altar, the work of humankind is being dedicated to God. 'The Kingdom comes when common work…

(is being) seized and dedicated to the highest calling of the Father' (p. 138). At the same time, the Eucharist points us to God as the provider of the necessities of life, acknowledged in the Lord's Prayer when we ask that he gives us 'this day our daily bread'.

The gift of liberation comes to the fore in the breaking of bread. This act reminds us of three realities. First, that we are a broken people and a broken world. As Francis Spufford (2012, p. 27) puts it in colourful language, the default condition is 'the human propensity to fuck *things* up', a condition as true of the world of work as anywhere else.

> What we're talking about here is not just our tendency to lurch and stumble and screw up by accident, our passive role as agents of entropy. It's our active inclination to break stuff, 'stuff' here including moods, promises, relationships we care about, and our own well-being and other people's, as well as material objects whose high gloss positively seems to invite a big scratch.

Secondly, the act of the breaking of bread points to the profound mystery of redemptive suffering. It is only as Christ accepted the role of a suffering servant, paradoxically the zenith of servant leadership, and was himself prepared to suffer alongside a broken world, that what was in fragments could be offered the gift of wholeness or holiness. It is Christ's total identification with fallen humankind, and with a fallen world of work, which offers the hope of healing, resurrection, reconciliation and liberation.

Thirdly, and reflecting the example of Christ, the breaking of bread points to the need for 'the "breaking" of any earthly system that is not totally interpenetrated with the life of Christ. It is only when it (this earthly system) has… been broken open that it can be shared with the poor, the vulnerable and the excluded' (Elliott, p. 138). The Eucharist points to the necessity of workers and workplaces being liberated from that which fosters selfishness, greed and injustice in order to play their part in the creation of a world which manifests the gifts of the kingdom community.

The gift of love is seen in the Eucharist's witness to a 'God (who) so loved the world that he gave his only Son, that whoever believes in him should not perish but have eternal life' (Jn 3: 16). 'To "feed on Christ" is to be caught up in the quality of love; to be, in other words, a sign of the kingdom' (p. 140). David Jensen (p. 86) reflects on this gift of love in a eucharistic and economic context as follows: 'The gift of the Lord's

Supper inaugurates a communion of ceaseless giving that cannot be reduced to commodity exchange'. He continues (p. 83):

> The eucharistic economy of gift and communion runs counter to understandings of work that stress individualism and competition. In a eucharistic economy, there is no such thing as 'my work'; that I preserve at the expense of another's. In order for my work to succeed, the current mantra stresses, I need to beat out the other guy: my work and myself always take precedence. In a eucharistic economy, however, the good work of one invariably redounds to the work of another... Competitiveness and individualism by themselves prove self-destructive and wasteful, because they leave little room for the common good.

In the Eucharist, *the gift of learning* is focused on the ministry of the Word, the reading of and reflection on the scriptures, the singing of hymns and the sermon (if included). All these offer us an opportunity to relate faith to the signs of the kingdom community evident in every walk of daily life, including the workplace, and to our call to further the coming of that community.

An opportunity to learn about the meaning and nature of community in its fullness, and not least the importance of the communal workplace, is provide by the symbolic significance of the whole of the Eucharist as a community building experience - its rhythms of gathering, preparation, reflection, prayers for others, the peace, the offering, thanksgiving, breaking and sharing and the commissioning of participants to 'serve the Lord'.

Part 3
Facilitation and support

Stage 9
Education and mentoring
Faith and work courses

In the UK there are a number of courses available to help equip Christians for ministry and mission in the world of work, though a good deal more resource material is available from international sites especially in the USA. UK courses/'tool kits' known to be on offer in 2014 are:

Mind the Gap - connecting Faith and Work (1997, but out to print). Higginson, R. Church Pastoral Aid Society publication

Christian Life and Work (2000) London Institute for Contemporary Christianity (www.licc.org.uk/shop/product/christian-life-and-work)

Christians in the Workplace (material undated but introduced about 2003) Diocese of Chelmsford (www.chelmsford.anglican.org/CITW)

Let Your Light Shine (2003) London: The Methodist Church

Alpha in the Workplace (introduced about 2005) (www.alphafriends.rog/workplace)

Being a Disciple at Work (material undated but introduced about 2005) Diocese of Peterborough (www.peterborough-diocese.org.uk/workingdisciple)

Joined up Living - Weekday Faith (Lent course, 2005) Diocese of Coventry (contact phil.aspinall@acrcadis-vectra.com)

God at Work (introduced about 2008) Led by Ken Costa. Holy Trinity, Brompton (www.godatwork.org.uk)

God and Work (introduced about 2008) After Sunday. Other modules planned. (www.afteresunday.org.uk/main-resource/god-and-work).

About Our Father's Business - a Faith and Work Resources Toolkit (2010) Jones, I. and Hayes, B. (www.saltleytrust.org.uk/publications/; (or) www.cigb.org.uk)

Executive Toolbox (2013) Engaging with Work. London Institute for Contemporary Christianity (www.licc.org.uk/engaging-with-work/executive-toolbox)

Other one-off courses on faith and work issues have been run, particularly by regional chaplaincies concerned with the economy such as the Black Country Urban Industrial Mission. However, with few exceptions, these initiatives have experienced a very limited take up. Thus the task of finding a way of equipping lay people with insights and skills that can inspire and prepare them for mission in the workplace remains a challenging one.

The logistical problems of addressing this undertaking are clear. Lay people have little time or energy to give to attending faith and work courses after a full day's work, not least if they are commuting long distances to their place of employment. The demands of family life and the need for relaxation are also prior claims on their week-ends or other time off.

Nevertheless, the overriding reason for the neglect of lay education for mission in the workplace is the fact that it is given a very low priority by the institutional church. The latter's interest in the ministry of lay people in paid employment remains largely in recruiting them to fill church offices where their professional skills can be of value, or getting them to be involved in some other form of ministry based on the life and work of the gathered church. In the Church of England, for example, only a handful of dioceses (Hereford, Peterborough Chelmsford, Durham, Worcester, Lichfield, Coventry and Birmingham) are known to the author as having made any attempt in the past to offer courses and/or resources *specifically* concerned to equip lay people for mission within the workplace. Amongst training institutions of all denominations, only Cliff College offers any course (an MA validated by Manchester University) *explicitly* concerned with mission in the world of work and that has found recruitment very difficult.

A missional appraisal of faith and work courses

If faith and work courses have only limited impact on the church, they have even less on the task of transforming the workplace. As noted in the Introduction, a discipleship rather than kingdom model of mission remains to the fore. Thus many such courses assume that the mission of the Christian at work is to bear individual witness to their faith in the hope that this will somehow attract their fellow workers to become interested in the faith. The idea that mission at work is first and foremost about the creation of *the workplace* transformed by the gifts of the kingdom community is not, as yet, even a vision on the horizon.

Consequently most faith and work courses give little attention to how lay people might first discern what God is already doing in their places of work and then consider how they might share in that endeavour. They are not about how to practice the presence of God therein and allowing that awareness to inform and shape the mission task. Nor is a spirituality which might resource such discernment and intervention on offer. In too many cases the approach to mission is mainly concerned with witnessing to a predetermined faith-focused 'package' within the workplace.

Many faith and work courses have a relatively superficial theological, spiritual and/or economic underpinning. This is in part because they try to cover too much ground in too short a time. For the same reason they are often anecdotal in relation to practical application. They assume that it is up to lay people as individuals to do the best they can to promote the Christian message in their places of work. There is little sense of the mission task being a collective responsibility sometimes involving a partnership with those who have different or no faith commitments.

An educational appraisal of faith and work courses

Numerous faith and work courses adopt a didactic approach. They set out a tightly structured programme ranging over a number of sessions, usually from three to seven. For example, the *Christian Life and Work* course follows a weekly pattern of: Monday - Who are we working for? Tuesday - Why on earth are we working? Wednesday - Ministry at work. Thursday - Relating to the boss. Friday - Handling pressure. Saturday - Spirituality in the fast lane. The five session study programme offered by the Chelmsford Diocese, *Christians in the Workplace*, follows the themes of: Discovering spirituality @ work; Praying @ work; and three sessions on God @ work in our work. Ken Costa's *God at Work* course takes an issue-related approach, the sessions being entitled: Work matters; Ambition; Tough decisions and choices; Stress and work-life balance; Failure, disappointment and hope; Money and mission. After Sunday's *God and Work* programme offers seven modules entitled: Our understanding of work; Christian work; God as worker in Scripture; Creation and redemption; Work, labour and toil; Work and well-being; Shabbat and rest. *Executive Toolbox* offers three 24-hour modules.

Though such a structured approach is logical and developmental, it is not particularly person-centred. It gives little opportunity for Christians at work to address their own agendas and concerns and minimizes the time available for the exchange of participants' personal experiences and insights arising from within their own places of work. This means that participants have little time to explore at any depth the day-to-day difficulties they have in relating their faith to their work. Though a video or CD is sometimes provided to give the course topics more interest, the prescribed material still dominates the direction, timing and content of each session. Thus many courses have the feel of a set curriculum that has to be covered rather than a journey of discovery. They come across as 'closed-to-learning', as was defined in Stage 8(3), and adopt a single-loop approach [Stage 2]. Such an educational process allows little opportunity to question core values shaping the workplace culture and ethos.

Because of their didactic nature, many faith and work courses regard the group leader more as the director of a structured curriculum than as a partner in learning, more as a tutor than a mentor. The director or tutor appears to be there more to teach and instruct than to negotiate with each participant what their learning path might be and how this might shape mission in their particular place of work.

An educational appraisal of the Kingdom at Work Project

The Kingdom at Work Project has been designed as a developmental endeavour which is wholly educational in nature. This gives it a number of important features which embrace learning as education in contrast to learning as socialization (nurture, instruction and training) [Stage 2], and which reflect an open-to-learning not a closed-to-learning approach [Stage 8(3)].

The project is focused on accessing the gifts of the kingdom community as a response to the immediate experiences and insights of the Christian at work and not to any widely assumed needs or issues related to the workplace. It encourages the Christian at work to develop their skills of discernment as an ongoing journey of spiritual discovery and in the light of that journey to intervene to bring about communal transformation (Clark, 1996, pp. 81-84; Clark, 2005, pp. 34-37).

The project does not accept the economic or cultural status quo currently existing throughout the world of work as unchangeable. It encourages the Christian at work to raise questions about the values operative within the world of work and to challenge any economic model and related workplace culture based on the assumption that 'there is no alternative'.

The project regards as essential the building of partnerships and the exchange of ideas and insights between all those, holding Christian or other convictions and looking for the communal transformation of the workplace.

Related initiatives

Currently, only two other British initiatives to enable Christians to connect faith and work appear to operate with the educational and open-to-learning approach espoused by this project. The *Joined up Living - Weekday Faith* Lent course (2005) designed by sector ministers in the diocese of Coventry has five sessions all of which begin with the experience of the Christian at work. Its sessions are entitled: 'What's happening to me?; What's going on in some situations at work?; How can we talk about God in all this?; What about God in our work situations?; So what does it means for what we do?'

The other initiative, more a process of reflection and action than a course as such, is the Roman Catholic Church's Young Christian Workers' *Review of Life*. This is based on Cardinal Cardijn's (its founder's) now well-known 'SEE, JUDGE, ACT' method. The approach is as follows (www.ycwimpact.com):

o The 'SEE' stage of the process encourages each person in turn to talk about a situation, conversation or event in daily life which is: real and factual; made them think a little, feel bad or good, ask questions, get angry or want to help, etc.; happened recently; involved them or someone they know. If more than two 'facts' emerge, the group chooses the two most urgent or relevant ones. The group then help one another to explore the facts/events/situations to gain greater understanding, including the causes and effects of what has happened. A series of questions are suggested to help reflection and understanding.

331

o The 'JUDGE' stage of the process involves the group discussing the rights and wrongs relevant to the experiences and situations shared. A number of questions are suggested to assist this process. The group then reads from Scripture (usually beginning with the Gospels) for inspiration and guidance in their reflection and for encouragement to act, with further questions offered to help this process.

o The 'ACT' stage of the process involves the group discussing possible ways of responding to the situations described during the 'SEE' session. Each person identifies, with the help of the others, some practical action he/she might take. The person who is the focus of the exploration also decides what action he or she will take. Alternatively, the action can be something which the group as a whole decides to undertake or organize and in which every member has a distinctive part to play. Again questions are offered to help this process.

o In the 'REVIEW' stage of the process the group considers the situations discussed at the last meeting and the actions decided. Each person reports on how they acted, the difficulties faced and how obstacles were overcome. The group is charged with being encouraging and affirming no matter how things have worked out. Each member of the group is helped to see the value in what they have done or attempted to do and to reflect further on this. The members try to see the connection between the actions they have sought to take and what it means to be a follower of Christ. More questions help this process.

The Young Christian Workers' process of intervention has been described at some length because many aspects of it have such a close affinity with the Kingdom at Work Project's educational approach. Although with less theological underpinning and more informal in methodology, the 'SEE' and 'JUDGE' stages of *The Review of Life* reflect the Kingdom at Work Project's approach to discernment [Stage 7], the 'ACT' stage reflects its intervention stage [Stage 8] and the 'REVIEW' stage mirrors the project's reflection and review stage [Stage 12]. Furthermore, 'the role of the chaplain' as described throughout *The Review of Life* has many characteristics in common with how the project sees the role of mentor.

The role of mentor

The material embodied in the Kingdom at Work Project is intended to offer what might be called a mission manual for mentors. Because intervention to transform the workplace is a difficult and demanding task it has been stressed many times that Christians at work need access to a mentor with the experience and skill to support and guide them in that undertaking. Below are set out some key features of the mentoring role.

Overview

The role and responsibilities of 'mentor' are very well documented (see, for example, Megginson et. al. (2005); Megginson et. al. (2006), Cutts (2010) pp. 140-157). However, in the context of this project, the mentor's role is seen as having greatest affinity with the servant leader's roles of *enabler* (reflecting the kingdom community's gift of liberation), *educator* (associated with the gift of learning) and, to some extent, with that of *intermediary* (reflecting the gift of love) [Stage 5].

To illustrate, **the mentor's role as enabler** of the mentee (the Christian at work) requires the mentor to set out clear ground rules for his or her relationship with their mentee. It is a role which embraces the abilities and skills of the affirmer, the attentive listener, the encourager and the liberator from dependency. The role involves helping the mentee not only to address a range of choices but to focus on those of most relevance to their own working situation. It is about enabling the mentee to identify and use all relevant resources. The role of enabler encourages the mentee to stick to the mission task despite inevitable difficulties and set-backs.

The mentor's role as educator is about negotiating the way in which the mentee can engage with resources offered by Kingdom at Work Project. It encourages the mentee to be open-to-learning [Stages 2 and 8(3)]. It helps the mentee to make choices based on their questioning of their workplace's values and culture. This role involves keeping the mentee focused on clarifying and implementing their mission task, ensuring that the latter is pursued with professional skill, personal commitment and determination. It is a role which looks for an interchange of experience and the growth of all involved. The mentor as educator encourages reflection and review and offers feed-back as and when necessary.

The role of mentor as intermediary is about the encouragement of partnership building and the sharing of insights, experiences, skills and resources. It assists the mentee in dealing creatively with conflict and disagreements.

The role of mentor in relation to the Kingdom at Work Project

It has been noted above that this project provides a mission manual for mentors. This does not mean that the mentor's task is to ensure that the mentee (the Christian at work) engages with every single stage of the project. Indeed, the mentor's first responsibility is to learn about the working context and ascertain the missional needs of the mentee and to then draw out from the material on offer here that which is most relevant to the mentee's unique situation. Amongst some of the possible approaches that the mentor might take are:

o helping the mentee to decide which stage(s) of the project are most relevant to their ministry in the workplace

o helping the mentee to identify and understand the communal principles and structures informing discernment and intervention [Stages 2 to 5]

o enabling the mentee to become well acquainted with how the discernment and intervention processes can be applied to their situation [Stages 7 and 8]

o assisting the mentee in the choice of a mission task [Stage 8 (Introduction)]

o helping the mentee to identify and acquire the skills and resources needed to implement the mission task

o enabling the mentee to review critically what aspects of the project have helped or hindered their approach to mission in the workplace [Stage 12].

On a broader front mentors could well find themselves in a position to:

o enable the gathered church and its leaders to become more aware of what they can do to further mission in the world of work [Stage 10]

o encourage chaplains and self-supporting ministers, especially so-called ministers in secular employment, to review and adapt their role and responsibilities to further mission and ministry in the world of work [Stage 11]

Mentoring a group

Those Christians at work committed to working through chosen stages of this project could do so on a one-to-one basis with the help of a mentor. However, from the perspective of the diaconal church, mission in the world of work should be a collective and collaborative endeavour [Stage 5]. Thus it is hoped that, whenever possible, Christians at work will engage in the learning process as a group, sharing their insights, experiences, skills and proposed intervention and its consequences with fellow Christians. Because of this, mentors should have not only appropriate mentoring abilities but group work skills.

The equipping and source of mentors

The requirements of the role of mentor set out here mean that those selected for this role will need to be equipped with the appropriate expertise. The task of mentor is a skilled role. If mission in the world of work is to assume the significance that this project is convinced it warrants, the church will also need to draw on the expertise of those already equipped as mentors through secular professional training to assist and guide it.

An important source of mentors could be from amongst chaplains and self-supporting ministers, not least ministers in secular employment [Stage 11]. The distinctive diaconate, particularly as interpreted by Methodism in the UK, is also well suited to provide mentors for Christians at work (Clark, 2005, pp. 273-295). Mentors might also come from the ranks of early retired lay people who have considerable experience of the world of work. Eventually, however, every church leader who has responsibility for the life of a gathered church should be equipped with mentoring skills or at least make sure that certain members of their congregations are trained for this role.

The faith and work deficit in the selection and training of ordinands

Across 2010 and 2011, Hannah Matthews undertook an enquiry on behalf of the Saltley Trust in Birmingham (2013) into how effectively mission and ministry relating to faith in the workplace was being addressed in the selection and training of ordinands in the West Midlands. The research covered training agencies of all denominations though the majority were Anglican. Her conclusions were that this sphere of mission was only superficially touched on in selection and that there was a dearth of agencies explicitly addressing this important aspect of initial training for ordinands. 'The overall picture suggests that questions of work do not figure highly and receive minimal attention and energy', she states (p. 59). The project's particular concern here is that this deficit results in an ordained ministry ill-equipped to act as mentors for mission, especially in relation to mission in the world of work.

In relation to the selection criteria for ordinands, Matthews notes limited attention being given to how candidates link issues raised by their current occupations to their future ministry. At best, she states, any selection criteria concerning how candidates relate faith to work could 'easily become a "hoop" through which initial ministerial training was embarked upon' and the 'strong focus on the congregational milieu could obscure questions of engagement with the workplace' (p. 20).

Initial training courses for ordinands, especially part-time courses where trainees remain in secular employment, more often bring the experiences of daily life to bear on the nature of candidates' future ministry. However, 'opportunities to reflect on faith and work were occasional or optional rather than foundational' (p. 56). Indeed 'there was a risk of "training-out" valuable experiences gained from previous jobs' (p. 35). Where a focus on previous working experience did occur, the application of faith to work was largely concerned with 'contextual theology' in general rather than being specifically related to current issues within the world of work. In relation to the latter, any training that did occur was more anecdotal than analytic (p. 28). *Of particular concern from the vantage point of this project 'there was surprisingly little discussion of the theology of the Kingdom of God and its implications for work and workplaces' (p. 44).*

In the context of the need for mentors to further mission at work, little 'was said about how those training for authorised ministry were helped to enable congregations to make or express their own connections' between faith and work (p. 25). Ordinands receive little help in the use of 'tools for enabling others' to link their faith and their work (p. 56).

Matthews describes a range of factors, many of which have already been referred to in this project, which hinder theological institutions giving explicit attention to mission in the workplace and to the training of mission mentors in that context. These constraints include tutors with limited experience of the current state of the world of work (p. 27), the failure of church leaders actively to support new developments in this field of mission (p. 42), too few placements provided for ordinands in the business, commercial or financial sectors (p. 51), inadequate connections between training agencies which could enable them to share insights and experiences in this sphere of mission (p. 63), and the lack of relevant resources from an online 'hub' with a broader theological stance than many web sites currently focused on this field of mission (p. 54). *Overall, there were no models in evidence of the kind of training needed to enable ordinands to understand the role, responsibilities and importance of mentors for mission at work.*

It would seem, therefore, that if mission in the world of work is to move into the mainstream life of the church, local and national, gathered and dispersed, remedying the deficit in preparing for this challenging endeavour clearly evident in the selection and training of ordinands is imperative. Without this deficit being addressed it is hard to see how mission in this key sector of the life of society can ever be more than individual Christians at work, isolated, unsupported and under-resourced doing their best in a piece-meal and inadequate way.

Stage 10
The gathered church

Stage 10 of the Kingdom at Work Project explores the role and responsibilities of the gathered church in furthering the mission of the church in the world of work. By 'gathered church' is meant any congregation which uses and maintains some form of physical plant, usually employs a number of staff and is identified with a particular locality, even if a significant proportion of its members are gathered from beyond that locality. It is the contention of this project that the gathered church has a major responsibility and considerable potential to equip its members to engage in the communal transformation of their places of work, but that this role remains largely undeveloped. It is also the project's contention that the gathered church has considerable potential to act as a catalyst for the communal transformation of the world of work which is situated on its own door-step, but is failing to address even that task.

The gathered church as a workplace

Before addressing these issues, it is important to recognize that the gathered church is a place of work in its own right. It usually employs a minister or priest, and sometimes other support and administrative staff. If it is to engage in mission within the wider world of work, the gathered church needs to exemplify that model of the workplace as a microcosm of the kingdom community which it is inviting other workplaces to embrace.

This means that for the mission of the gathered church to have credibility in the world of work it needs to become a dynamic and thriving community of character [Stage 1]. In that context, it needs to have espoused a communal theology, spirituality and ecclesiology [Stages 2, 3 and 5], and reflect the principles of a communal economy [Stage 4] in shaping its own life and work, as well as addressing how it gives expression to servant leadership.

Furthermore, as a place of work in its own right, the gathered church has the task of discerning signs or critical incidents [Stage 7] which bear witness to the presence of the four key gifts of the kingdom community within its life. For example, as signs of these gifts [Stage 7(1)], does the environment (plant and surroundings) 'enrich the

338

senses' and do 'people manage their time productively' (the gift of life)? Are 'people able to give full expression to their gifts, skills and experience' and are they 'open about their mistakes and failures' (the gift of liberation)? Do 'people communicate in good time' and is 'the culture of the workplace... one of honesty and integrity' (the gift of love)? Do 'people question assumptions' and is learning seen 'as a collective responsibility' (the gift of learning)? With respect to all these gifts, is the church's life and work in danger of becoming inward looking or does it engage with the needs of the wider world? Finally, does it manifest the qualities of servant leadership?

Where the gathered church discerns it is failing to embody the gifts of the kingdom community as fully as it might, the test of its commitment and integrity lies in whether or not it is prepared to take action to address that deficit [Stage 8]. This means its becoming a genuine learning community and equipping its members and leaders to develop its communal character in the future.

Other Christian agencies and organizations

Christian agencies and organizations of all kinds have a particular responsibility to engage in the discernment and intervention process set out in this project. What is said above about the importance of the communal transformation of the gathered church *as a place of work* also applies to a range of Christian bodies such as church schools, Christian welfare agencies, Christian residential homes and hospices, and so on. As noted in the Introduction, it is believed that the discernment and intervention process could be of particular value to certain organizations, like church schools, which have been seeking for some years, often with mixed results, to identify the Christian hall-marks of such collectives.

Preparing for mission in the world of work

The gathered church not only has the responsibility of exemplifying the gifts of the kingdom community as a place of work and community of character, but of preparing its people to be able to further the communal transformation of their own places of work (Clark, 2008b). Here the task of the gathered church is to place itself at the service of the dispersed church. Now and then such initiatives are mentioned in published material: for example, in Greene, (2002) pp. 21-23, 29-31; MDO (2009) F1 - F5, H1- H3; *Faith, Work and Economic Life*, (2011) pp.

6-7, 10-11; *About our Father's Business* (2010) pp. 23-26. However, such references are very limited in number and scope.

In order to raise the awareness of gathered churches to the sort of endeavours that might be taken to equip their members for mission in the world of work a number of suggestions are offered here. Virtually all of these initiatives have been employed by a gathered church somewhere or other, though they often represent one-off ventures with little follow up or continuity of endeavour. If the gathered church is to become a community of character, it is essential that such initiatives become an integral part of its life.

Raising awareness and networking

Many congregations know relatively little about the kind of paid work in which their members are involved. Such ignorance means that the sharing of experiences is restricted, discernment of the gifts of the kingdom community in the workplace remains undeveloped and action for the communal transformation of workplaces never takes place. Furthermore worship rarely embraces the world of work, prayer for those engaged in workplace ministry is neglected and their pastoral care is inhibited.

The first task, therefore, in furthering the responsibility of the gathered church for mission in the working world is for the congregation to discover more about what their colleagues are doing in their working lives. This should include being in touch with the work of young people at school or college. It could also involve learning about the voluntary work in which church members, not least the retired, are involved. Below are set out some suggestions to help address this awareness-raising task. In the case of some of the initiatives suggested, it should be checked out whether people are prepared for information about their work to be made public.

Suggestions

o Have a regular 'slot' in the church magazine for people to write about their work. Stay up-to-date with their situation by asking people to describe how national or local changes are affecting them in their field of work.

o Invite people to offer job profiles of what work they do, and to identify for what they would appreciate prayers - to go in the church newsletter or on a notice board.

o Give opportunities for people to illustrate in some way (photos or collage, etc.) the nature of their daily work. Provide a table in the church foyer on which work symbols are laid out, and/or make and display a collage of logos, badges, letter-heads, symbols of work, T-shirt 'advert', etc. (MDO, 2009, F3).

o Put together a 'map' of the work undertaken by church members – this could be an 'occupational' map (people grouped by occupations or voluntary work interests), or a geographical map (showing where people work) - and display in a prominent location.

o Produce a 'directory' of church members' names and occupations as a key to the map mentioned above, or to be used separately as a means of mutual awareness, support and prayer (MDO, 2009, F3).

o Distribute a mini-questionnaire to church members asking what they do at work and which of their working concerns are uppermost at the moment - distribute the findings (probably anonymously) as material for discussion and/or prayer groups (see Education below) (Greene, 2001, p. 21).

Worship

Church worship rarely focuses on the contribution of its members to the transformation of the world of work or on the challenges, concerns and problems which impinge on the coming into being there of the kingdom community. However, as illustrated below, worship can be profoundly enriched when it focuses on the potential of the 4Ls within the workplace.

Suggestions

o Use a range of aspects of worship [Stage 8(5)] to affirm and celebrate what people do in their working lives.

o Refer to the work of church members at the blessing of the offering (Greene, 2001, p. 29).

o Refer to the offering and the need for the transformation of daily work (bread and wine) during the service of holy communion (Greene, 2001, p. 29).

o Have an 'open slot' each week where people are invited to shares issue or concerns on any work-related (paid or voluntary) theme - certain of these concerns could later be included in the intercessions (Greene, 2001, p. 29).

o As part of the intercessions, ask people to bring forward an object representing their work, place it on the communion table and offer a short prayer relating to their working lives.

o Use hymns related to the world of work. Unfortunately, there are few of these in church hymn books [Stage 8(5)]. However, a helpful selection of hymns is offered in Bernard Braley's anthology (1996).

o Link peoples' working experience to Christian themes in the church calendar (eg. a midwife to speak about preparing for birth - Advent; a farmer to speak about farming today - Rogation Sunday, etc.).

o Have symbols of work in the church (perhaps the collage mentioned above) which can be referred to during worship to trigger greater awareness of ministry and mission in the world of work.

o Invite people to come to church in their working clothes and to speak or pray about their work during the service.

o Use the distribution of a pinch of salt to each person during worship to symbolize the calling of Christians to be salt in their places of work (Greene, 2001, p. 29 and Stage 8(1)).

o Arrange services on work-related themes and contexts – schools/colleges, hospitals, shops, business, transport, local government, etc.

o Gather together in worship those with similar occupations and listen to and pray for their concerns – health, finance, business, law and order, local government etc.

o Use power-point pictures during the service to remind people of the importance and needs of the world of work.

o Ask people during worship to speak about the opportunities and concerns they face at work. This may best be done by means of interviews. One church successfully invited a number of its unemployed members to share their experience of being made redundant.

o Interview people concerning what they will be doing 'This Time To-morrow' (often called TTT) and how their faith relates to their situation then (Greene, 2001, p. 29).

o Affirm people who are taking up new jobs or moving to new work situations (Greene, 2001, p. 28) - including children moving schools or young people going to college.

o Ask the worship leader to preach a series of sermons on 'taking faith to work' or topical themes related to the world of work (Greene, 2001, p. 27).

o Encourage lay readers or local preachers to draw more illustrations from their experiences in the world of work (see below under Leadership).

o Hold a 'commissioning service' to raise awareness of the responsibility of the whole congregation to strive for the communal transformation of the world of work.

o While the benediction is said, the worship leader asks the congregation to turn towards the exit door to indicate the significance of their ministry in daily life (Greene, 2001, p. 28).

Some examples of orders of service engaging with the world of work can be found in Butland (1985); Braley (1996) pp. 94-95; and MDO (2009) H1, 2 and 3.

Reflection, learning and training

The importance and nature of education for mission in the world of work has been explored in Stage 9 of this project. For this to be both adequate and effective preparation for mission needs to be an integral part of the life of the gathered church. Below are described educational initiatives which the gathered church might take. Some of these are of an awareness raising or supportive nature. At the same time, the more rigorous equipping of lay people with the skills and resources to engage in discernment and intervention for the communal transformation of the workplace remains essential [Stages 7 and 8].

Suggestions

o After a service focused on faith and work, provide coffee and, in small groups, organize a follow up for reflection and action within and beyond the gathered church.

o Draw together church members engaged in related occupations or with similar responsibilities (such as school governors) to reflect on what it means to be a Christian in the working world.

343

o In house groups discuss issues concerned with the working world and pray for church members in their work. Invite people to come and share their experience of being a Christian at work.

o Set up a course to explore the theology, spirituality and/or ethics of work or the workplace.

o Offer school pupils or students the opportunity to reflect from a Christian perspective on any form of work experience in which they have been or are involved.

o Offer parents the opportunity to meet together and discuss how faith relates to their children's schooling and to the curriculum (Greene, 2008, p. 32).

o Offer parents whose children are moving on to higher education the opportunity to meet and discuss how faith relates to their choice of college and course, and their life once there (Greene, 2008, p. 32).

o Set up a 'breakfast/lunch club' for people to exchange and explore ideas about faith at work.

o Hold a day (or longer) church retreat to practice and reflect on the art of communal living Benedictine style: working (indoors and outdoors), eating, studying the scriptures and praying together.

Pastoral care

The pastoral care of those engaged in mission in the world of work is of great importance. All members of the congregation need to be aware that the world of work can bring just as much stress as domestic or health problem. Opportunities for support should be forthcoming through the pastoral ministry of the priest or minister and the normal pastoral care procedures of the gathered church. Peer support is very important in this context. Likewise the prayers, individual and collective [Stage 8(5)], of the congregation for the needs of those at work are important.

Those without work

Under this heading come the needs of those who cannot get work, have been made redundant or are unemployed because of health or related concerns. If the church has a large enough membership there may be an opportunity to draw together those who are unemployed in order to share their experiences and to facilitate peer support.

Mission to the local world of work

Many gathered churches will serve a neighbourhood in which are located a variety of workplaces: shops, small businesses, professional services, voluntary agencies, etc. Some mission initiatives which the gathered church might take in this context are suggested below. Appendix 1 offers a case-study of a gathered church which has undertaken a ministry to its local places of work in a pioneering but replicable way.

Suggestions

o Get to know those who work in the locality and build personal links which affirm and support them in their endeavours.

o Build links with (local) agencies which are assisting those at work (or out of work) and research how the church might support such agencies – job centres, local Chamber of Commerce, Business Link, etc.

o Set up or support a food bank for those out of work.

o Provide a lunchtime venue for people to come and share work concerns together – possibly a 'lead' speaker.

o Invite local work organizations to display their 'services'/'products' in the church with their comments as to how they feel they are contributing to the well-being of the community – body, mind and spirit.

o Invite local shops and businesses to offer examples of their produce or services for display during a Neighbourhood 'Harvest' Celebration (MDO, 2009, F5).

o Hold a prayer walk focusing on and praying for places of work in the locality (*About our Father's Business*, 2010, p. 26)

o Produce a prayer booklet with weekly or monthly prayers for local businesses and professional services to be used during worship and privately (*Bakewell@Work Prayer Booklet*, 2009).

Leadership of the gathered church's mission to the world of work

Leadership of the gathered church as a place of work

The gathered church is itself a place of work. Thus the form of leadership, usually with an ordained minister or priest in the pre-eminent role, should seek to model the kind of servant leadership which exemplifies all communal workplaces. Stage 5 describes the key roles associated with servant leadership as visionary, strategist, animator, enabler, intermediary and educator. For its witness within the world of work to be credible, the leadership of the gathered church needs to emulate these roles.

Engaging the whole of the gathered church in mission in the world of work

In engaging all members of the gathered church in concern for and support of mission in the wider world of work, the leadership roles of strategist, animator and intermediary will be particularly prominent. Whenever worship focuses on mission in the world of work, the roles of visionary, animator and educator have an especially important part to play.

Equipping working members of the gathered church for mission in the workplace

The leadership of the gathered church needs to offer training and support to its members actively involved in furthering the gifts of the kingdom community within their places of work. It may do this in two ways. On the one hand, reflection, learning and training will necessitate the leadership of the gathered church being able to fulfill the roles of enabler and educator. As one aspect of these roles, the leadership of the gathered church should seek to train those who can act as mentors to church members at work [Stage 9]. On the other hand, pastoral care of church members at work is also vital. This will require the roles of enabler and intermediary to come to the fore, with attentive listening being of special importance.

Engaging the gathered church with the world of work on its doorstep

Where the gathered church is located in close proximity to shops, businesses, professional bodies or public services, its leadership has a responsibility to facilitate the missionary involvement of the congregation as a whole. The case-study of Bakewell (Appendix 1) demonstrates how even a relatively small church can become actively involved in this form of mission. In this context, the leadership of the gathered church will need to employ all the roles described under the heading of servant leadership.

A leadership deficit

It will be obvious that the diversity of experience, knowledge and skills required to enable the gathered church to engage in mission in the world of work, within its locality or further afield, are considerable. No one person, be they ordained or not, can be expected to possess all the attributes and skills required. At the same time, the lack of leadership resources available to the gathered church in this field of mission is made all the more acute by the failure of training institutions to equip ordinands with the relevant mentoring skills required [Stage 9].

As noted in that stage of the project, Hannah Matthews in her research entitled *Faith and Work in Theological Education and Training; an Enquiry* (2013) found that though the work experience of theological students prior to training was formally acknowledged as important, it often served simply as 'an "entry requirement" and often failed to be built on in subsequent experiences of ministerial formation' (p. 19). Even where training institutions did pay some attention to enabling ordinands to reflect on the relation between their faith and their work, 'little was said about how to support others in making such connections for themselves' (p. 24).

A team ministry approach

The only realistic way in which such a leadership deficit can be addressed is for the gathered church to embrace a team ministry approach. The minister or priest-in-charge needs to become the leader of a team, including lay people, which has within it the skills to facilitate mission in the workplace.

One potential resource for such teams would be the ministry of deacons, if that became a role which equipped the church dispersed for mission rather than that of an assistant priest. The former role is currently far more developed within British Methodism than within any other UK denomination. Hannah Matthews believes that 'the link between faith and work is... potentially more significant for the diaconal order (than priests or presbyters) and its candidating procedure' (p. 15). Elsewhere, I have argued that a 'renewed diaconate' should take greater responsibility for equipping the people of God for mission in the world of work (Clark, 2005, pp. 273-300; 2008, pp. 194-196). How the role of deacon might be developed along these lines is well illustrated in the Bakewell case-study (Appendix 1).

Chaplains and ministers in secular employment, where closely linked to a gathered church, could well be deployed by a team as mentors to assist in preparing the laity for mission in the world of work. However, this would require that they accept some significant changes in how they interpret their current roles, a matter discussed in Stage 11.

Lay worship leaders (lay readers and local preachers) have potentially an important contribution to make to any team addressing this sphere of mission by ensuring that the services they lead reflect the needs of the working world. Andrew Britton (2002) suggests that lay readers should 'preach on every occasion about the application of the gospel to the contemporary world (with)… illustrations from the world of work in every sermon' (p. 24). It is a sad reflection on much preaching by worship leaders that the world of work, of which some of them are still a part, rarely gets a mention. Only very occasionally does the church show recognition of this deficit, for example in the form of workshops for lay worship leaders focused on how to use their experience of the working world to enrich preaching and intercessions (MDO, 2009, F4).

Last, but by no means least, there may well be lay people within the gathered church with long experience of the world of work, perhaps early retired, who could offer such a team ministry invaluable experience and skills as mentors for mission in the workplace.

It would seem, therefore, that the resources to raise the profile of this sphere of mission within the life of the gathered church are potentially considerable. The real stumbling-block is the institutional church's failure to recognize the importance of mission within the world of work, to raise the awareness of ordinands to its significance and to train church leaders to operate within teams which possess the skills and resources to equip the gathered church for this field of mission.

Appendix 1
Bakewell Methodist Church - a case-study

Since 2004, as a retired Methodist deacon, I have been able to exercise a part-time ministry focused on the relationship between the gathered church and the local working community. This has been a ministry based on Bakewell Methodist Church which is located in the Derbyshire Peak District. Until 2010, I was assisted in this ministry by a fellow Methodist deacon in training employed by the Methodist Peak Circuit.

What follows is a case-study of a programme we developed entitled 'Bakewell Methodist Church@Work' when focused on the gathered church, and 'Bakewell@Work', an ecumenical initiative, when concerned with the working life of Bakewell itself. I believe that the programme shows what can be achieved even when the time and energy of the leadership involved is limited.

Background to the town and its churches

Bakewell is a market town situated in the Peak District National Park. Its economy has been shaped over the years by agriculture and the wool trade, lead mining, quarrying and, most recently, tourism. The town and vicinity are a home to some 200 businesses, mostly small-scale and of a very diverse kind serving a catchment area which reaches as far as the boundaries of Sheffield, Chesterfield, Matlock and Buxton. Each Monday is a market day when the centre of Bakewell is taken over by a multitude of stall-holders. Bakewell has an Agricultural Business Centre of national note, as well as a show ground where the historic annual Bakewell Show is held. The headquarters of the National Peak Park Authority is based in Bakewell. Well over a million people visit the town and its environs every year.

The resident population of Bakewell is some 4,000. This includes a high proportion of retired people. The young people of the town and vicinity are served by a Church of England Infant School, a Methodist Junior School, S. Anselm's, an independent school, and Lady Manners Secondary School. A cottage hospital and medical centre are based in the town.

Bakewell has an historic parish church, a Methodist Church, a Roman Catholic Church, a Quaker Meeting House, an Elim Church and a Gospel Hall. All but the last are members of the Association of Bakewell Christians (ABC). ABC was established in 1966 and, since that time, has been very active in the life of the town.

Bakewell Methodist Church, part of the former Wesleyan Connexion, was built in 1866. The church is in the Peak Circuit of the Sheffield District. Its membership currently stands at around 110. The congregation is largely retired, though many members are still very active. The church has a relatively small number of people of working age but they play a full part in the life of the church. The church receives many visitors each year. The church buildings were renovated in the early 1990s and now comprise of a very attractive church, large hall and a number of ancillary rooms.

Bakewell Methodist Church@Work

Visioning

In the autumn of 2007, Bakewell Methodist Church took the lead role in organizing a series of four 'hearings' on the theme of *Faith in Bakewell*. The sessions were entitled 'Faith in education', 'Faith in health', 'Faith in business' and 'Faith in the environment'. Each hearing was led by two or three keynote speakers, followed by group discussion and an open forum. Over a hundred people from the local churches and the town attended the hearings. The findings, published in an attractive booklet, were set out under the communal headings used in this project - life, liberation, love and learning. Though one or two faith and work initiatives had already been taken by the Methodist Church before this event, the hearings set the scene for many of the subsequent faith and work initiatives described below.

Research and Networking

In October 2006, the Methodist Church launched a faith and work programme involving a number of initiatives. The first of these was an exhibition in the church foyer consisting of a collage of logos, badges, letter heads, T-shirt slogans and photographs illustrating the work (including voluntary work) in which members of the congregation were involved. The exhibition was planned to coincide with a faith and work service in which four members of the congregation were interviewed about how their faith related to the work in which they were involved. For the intercessions, five other church members brought forward symbols of their work, laid them on the communion table and offered a short prayer for the work and workplaces in which they were engaged.

About the same time the first *Bakewell Methodist Church at Work* booklet was published. This listed the names of church members and the paid or voluntary work in which they were engaged. The booklet included an introduction which described its purpose as follows. To help church members:

-to become more aware of the impressive range of services to the community in which those attending our church are actively involved during the week;

-to share experiences and insights about how the gospel can be communicated through these areas of work;

-to reflect through worship, house groups and other gatherings on how our faith can inform our work, and how our work can inform our faith;

-to support one another in these activities through our prayers and pastoral care.

The booklet carried three prayers on the back inside cover for church members to use in their personal devotions when reflecting on faith and work concerns. Further editions of the booklet, with names, occupations and prayers revised were published in 2008 and 2011. (How to set up this kind of display and produce such a booklet is described in MDO, 2009, F3).

Worship

Faith and work services have so far been repeated in August 2007, August 2008 (a united service with the local Society of Friends), May 2010, May 2011 and October 2012. One of these was 'a law and order' service in which three members of the congregation involved in that field of work, together with Bakewell's police community support officer, were interviewed by the worship leader. At a number of these services final commissioning prayers were used. Examples of these are as follows:

Minister
Go forth into the world in peace; be of good courage; hold fast that which is good; render to no one evil for evil; strengthen the faint-

hearted; support the weak; help the afflicted; honour all people; love
and serve the Lord, rejoicing in the power of the Holy Spirit.

Congregation
As members of the Body of Christ, we commit ourselves in our daily
lives:
    to be attentive to the presence of Christ in all we meet;
    to work with Christ to build his kingdom in the world;
    to be channels of forgiveness and reconciliation;
    to bring comfort, hope and joy to those in need;
    to bear witness to the love of God in all we say and do.

Into our daily lives we take with us a mighty strength:
    God's power to guide us,
    God's might to uphold us
    God's eyes to watch over us,
    God ear to hear us,
    God's word to give us speech,
    God's hand to guard us,
    God's way to lead us,
    God's shield to shelter us,
    God's host to protect us. Amen

Reflection, learning and training

The hearings described above also fall into this category. However, the
Bakewell Methodist Church@Work programme has been involved in
several other ventures. A number of house group meetings have been
held to enable those in paid employment to share their concerns and
help them focus on how their faith and work might be more effectively
integrated. Some of these groups have made use of material here
incorporated into the Kingdom at Work Project.

In April 2009, when the recent banking crisis had just come to a
head, an open forum was held at the church on the theme of
'Weathering the economic storm – and taking up the challenge' with
the Vice-President of the Methodist Church, a solicitor, the Chair of
the local Chamber of Trade, and the Mayor of Bakewell as keynote
speakers.

In May 2009, the Methodist Peak Circuit organized a workshop for its local preachers on the topic of how they might bring their working experience to bear on their leadership of worship, in particular into their preaching.

In February 2010, the Methodist Church sponsored an exhibition entitled 'Learning for Life'. The four Bakewell schools were asked to send material to illustrate how they approached this theme. The material was displayed in the church foyer. At the same time, a Sunday morning service was held in the Methodist Church to reflect this theme and in which local schools were also involved.

Pastoral care

Pastoral support has been offered to members of the Methodist congregation at work in the traditional way but, for those in employment, there has been a particular focus on work related issues.

Mission to the local world of work

In September 2007, instead of Bakewell Methodist Church holding its normal harvest festival, Bakewell businesses were invited to contribute an item for display which represented the working life of the town. Some seventy businesses contributed examples of their work. The display filled the church, the church foyer and walls of the main hall. It was open for three days and attended by over 200 visitors. The Sunday morning service took the form of a 'harvest' thanksgiving for the 'produce' of Bakewell as a working community, with members of the latter taking part. (How to set up this kind of 'harvest' celebration is described in MDO, 2009, F5).

Each November an ecumenical farming service attended by well over a hundred people from across the Peak District is held in the large auction room of the Bakewell Agricultural Business Centre.

The Bakewell@Work initiative

In 2007, the Methodist Church was instrumental in setting up the Bakewell@Work initiative, a venture which has sought to build a bridge between the church and the town, in particular with the Bakewell business community. Bakewell@Work has been taken forward mainly by members of the Methodist Church but it operates as an ecumenical initiative under the auspices of the Association of Bakewell Christians.

Newsletter

At Christmas 2007 and 2008, Christmas cards, with greetings from the churches, were delivered to all the businesses in Bakewell. From October, 2009, the first edition of the *Bakewell@Work Newsletter* was produced. This was originally a two-sided A4 sheet carrying comment and prayers intended to connect the churches with Bakewell's working community. However, from March 2012, the *Newsletter* became a four sided publication, the content of the third and fourth pages becoming the responsibility of a newly established Bakewell Traders' Committee, the first two pages remaining the responsibility of the churches.

In March 2012, the *Newsletter* asked the headteachers of the four Bakewell schools to write about their personal vision for education. A prayer written to complement their contributions was included. This focused on the four gifts of the kingdom (the 4Ls have been inserted here):

> God our Father, we thank you that you want us to learn [learning] how to become valued members [liberation and love] of your worldwide family. We are grateful for the schools, nurseries and play groups of Bakewell [learning]. We thank you for the way they offer their experience, energy and enthusiasm [life] to enable young people to discover [learning] what life [life] is about. Support and encourage all teachers [learning] in their important and demanding work. May they have the reward of seeing their pupils grow [liberation] in understanding, integrity and respect [love] for others. Be with all parents that their homes may offer the nourishment and care [love] which enable [liberation] young people to feel secure [life] and deeply loved [love].   Amen

The August, 2012, issue of the *Bakewell@Work Newsletter* focused on visions for a healthy community contributed by local health providers (doctors, the local hospital, dentists, chemists, opticians, the leisure centre and so on).

Some 500 copies of the *Newsletter* are currently distributed throughout the town three times a year. This joint endeavour between the churches and the business community has stimulated many people to take a greater interest in its content. A team of some twenty church distributors has been established to deliver the *Newsletter*. Because members of the team are asked to visit the same dozen or so businesses or services each time, a pastoral relationship has gradually been built between the visitors and those visited.

Prayer booklet

In October 2009, a *Bakewell at Work Prayer Booklet* was published under the auspices of the Association of Bakewell Christians. The booklet contained the names of all the Bakewell businesses and services grouped under twelve monthly headings according to the nature of their work. Prayers relating to each aspect of the life of the town were written and published for each month, with a list of the relevant businesses or services underneath. The booklet is 'prayed through' by the Bakewell churches over the course of the year. An updated edition of the booklet is planned. Below are two examples of prayers from this booklet.

Prayer for the local supermarket and food shops – September

> We give thanks, O God, for those in Bakewell who provide your gift of food to put on our tables. We thank you that, in this town, we not only have enough and more to satisfy our needs, but are blessed by choice. We pray for those who work often unsocial hours to meet our physical well-being and to ensure that we never go without. As they serve us in this important way, may we and they remember the needs of a world where so many live in hunger. As we enjoy your good gifts, may we be generous in what we offer those, near or far, less fortunate than ourselves.

Prayer for all working agencies involved in tourism – October

> For the beauty and heritage of this National Park we give you thanks, O God. We are privileged to live here, to spend holidays here or to visit this place. We thank you for all those who work to maintain and develop this lovely part of your creation, the staff of the Peak District National Park Authority, those in the local tourist information office, and all in and around Bakewell who offer hospitality to visitors. May they serve those whom they meet with thoughtfulness, courtesy, care and patience, and offer them a genuine welcome as for a short time they become part of this community.

The Bakewell Community Project - Building Bridges

The purpose of the Bakewell Community Project (2012 - 2014) is to engage all the organizations in the town in building new or stronger bridges between businesses and customers, agriculture and commerce, professional agencies and patients or clients, school and community, church and community, young and old, 'up-the-hill and down-the-hill', town and tourists, politicians and constituents, the town and the natural environment, Bakewell, and the wider world - and so forth. Its aim, from the perspective of the Kingdom at Work Project, is to give practical expression to the gifts of the kingdom community. Amongst those involved in the project are Bakewell businesses, professional bodies, voluntary organisations, institutions and groups of all types and sizes, and from all sectors, as well as a number of individuals prominent in the life of the town.

The project was set up under the auspices of the Bakewell@Work initiative and formally launched at the Methodist Church during a week-end in October 2012. The launch included an exhibition of photographs, taken by the Mayor of Bakewell, a professional photographer, and entitled 'Bakewell - a human community'. On the Sunday morning, a service was held at the Methodist Church on the theme of 'What is community?'. At this service, the Mayor of Bakewell and three other residents spoke of their vision for the town.

Those bodies opting into the Bakewell Community Project are known as 'Community Sites'. Each site was asked to choose and work at one bridge-building initiative during 2013. Sites receive a certificate to acknowledge their commitment to their pledge. Many of the certificates are displayed in local shops and professional agencies.

In 2013 over a hundred pledges were received and included:

- year twelve students going into a local residential home teaching residents songs and enjoy singing together (secondary school)

- introducing customers to local places to visit and to walks in Derbyshire through a slide show on the counter, a leaflet and a number of web sites (a restaurant);

- collecting goods for a local food bank (Methodist Church)

- organising a major summer event for young people (Parish Church)

- collecting computer cartridges as a fund raising effort for the Macular Disease Society (opticians)

- running a number of free 'taster' sessions to introduce older residents of Bakewell who have no experience of computers to the great benefits to be gained from learning some basic computer skills (a computer shop)

- supporting local businesses by inviting their members to meet for coffee in different Bakewell cafes on the second Tuesday of every month (Bakewell Women's Institute)

- sending a bouquet of flowers to each of the residential homes at Easter (flower shop)

- seconding staff for a training event on better customer relations (deli).

During 2013, the *Bakewell@Work Newsletter* carried news of the pledges and the progress being made in achieving them. The Easter edition included a Christian meditation on 'The man in the middle - a bridge builder'. An ongoing display about the project, including a list of all the pledges made, was set up in the local Midlands Food Co-operative, by invitation of its manager.

Due to the success of the Bakewell Community Project in 2013, it was decided to continue it throughout 2014. Although most Community Sites renewed or offered new pledges, and others came on board, the challenge was how to sustain the impetus of the project. This was done by grouping the pledges under 'Ten visions for Bakewell' according to the focus of each pledge. The ten visions were:

The great workplace! Businesses as community builders.
All matter - each counts! Caring for those 'on the edge'
Getting together! Harnessing the power of gathering
Life begins at 80! Enriching life for those in our residential homes
Learning for living! Pursuing a life-long journey of discovery
Arts for all! Engaging every generation
Going green! Maintaining a sustainable and beautiful planet
Working together! Hands across the town
In the know! Keeping everyone in touch
A just world! Meeting the needs of the poorest.

Throughout 2014 each vision was promoted by drawing public attention to the pledges related to that vision. Promoting the vision of 'The great workplace!' (a subject of direct relevance to the Kingdom at

Work Project) involved drawing attention to the pledges of the businesses seeking to further that vision. In addition some informal market research was undertaken by church members into the views of a cross-section of Bakewell businesses on what they believed made a great workplace. Students on work placements from the local secondary school were also involved in this research. 'Going green!' was furthered by an ambitious 'Green Festival' at the Bakewell Agricultural Centre organized by the Bakewell Society of Friends who had made that undertaking their pledge for the year. The event attracted several thousand people. To further the vision of 'A just world!', the pledges of Community Sites involved in overseas aid and development were made known in the Bakewell@Work Newsletter and by means of a display describing their work in the Bakewell Food Co-operative. If and how the project will be taken forward in 2015 and beyond remains to be decided.

Material related to Bakewell Methodist Church@Work and

to the Bakewell@Work initiative

Bakewell Methodist Church@Work booklet (2006, 2008, 2011) - written up in MDO, 2009, F3

Bakewell at Work 'harvest' celebration (2007) – written up in MDO, 2009, F5

Faith in Bakewell – a report and reflections on four workshops organised by the Association of Bakewell Christians (May 2008)

Bakewell@Work Newsletter (every four months)

Bakewell@Work Prayer Book (2009)

The Bakewell Community Project - Building Bridges (2012-2014) - printed material

See also Bakewell Methodist Church web site - www.bakewellmethodist.org.uk

-----

MDO, 2009, worksheets. Electronic copies can be downloaded from - www.methodist.org.uk/businessworksheets . (This material is also available from David Clark at david@clark58.eclipse.co.uk)

Stage 11
Chaplains and ministers in secular employment

This stage of the Kingdom at Work Project looks at the current situation of chaplains and ministers in secular employment (MSEs) to assess how well placed they are to act as mentors, that is enablers and educators of Christians at work [Stage 9]. This review is necessary because chaplains and MSEs represent the largest *explicit* investment, in ecclesiological and economic terms, that the church has made in relation to ministry within the world of work. This stage of the project first considers the capacity of chaplains, then that of ministers in secular employment to undertake the role of mentor.

Chaplaincy
Categories and Models

It is currently possible to identify four broad categories of chaplaincy and five models of how it operates. These categories and models are set out in *Diagram 10*.

Diagram 10
Categories and models of chaplaincy

Categories

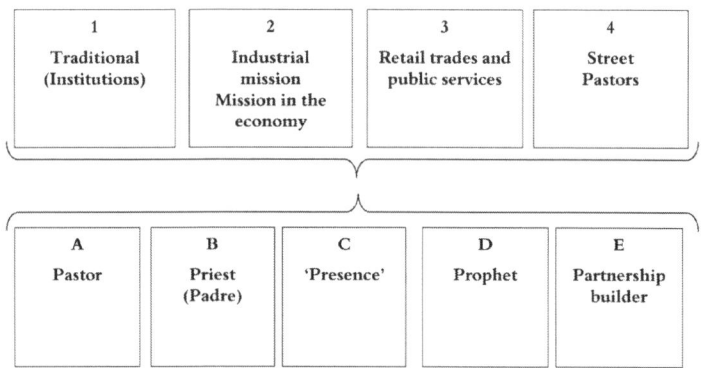

Models of practice (the 5Ps)

Categories

Category 1 consists of traditional forms of chaplaincy associated with institutions such as the National Health Service, universities and public schools, the armed forces and the prison service. *Category 2* relates to chaplains involved in what in some quarters is still called 'industrial mission', now often couched in terms of 'mission to the economy'. It also embraces rural chaplaincies. *Category 3* concerns chaplaincies concerned with the retail trade, supermarkets, ASDA and TESCO being prominent here, together with a diversity of public or emergency services. *Category 4* relates to the burgeoning number of 'street pastors' exercising a ministry to late night clubbers frequenting city pubs, clubs and parties, an initiative which began in 2003 in London. In 2012, there were some 250 such pastors exercising this form of ministry (www.streetpastors.co.uk*)*. Overall, these categories well portray the picture painted by the title of the Industrial Mission Association's national conference in 2012: 'Diverse World - Diverse Chaplaincy'.

A number of factors have brought about major change in the nature of chaplaincy. The first is that chaplaincy is very much an ecumenical undertaking, though in many contexts the Church of England, as the Established Church, retains pride of place. A second factor is that, in numerous situations, chaplaincy has had to respond to the inexorable growth of a multi-faith society. For example, in higher education, Pat Ashworth states that though 'about three-quarters of all chaplaincy staff... are Christian' (*Church Times*, 8/2/08), two thirds of chaplaincies were engaged in 'interfaith activities' and nearly a third took the form of 'interfaith associations'. This development has gone hand in hand with the emergence of 'multi-faith spaces', rooms set aside for reflection, prayer and worship by those associated with a diversity of faith communities or none. It is estimated that there could now be as many as 1,500 of these in various locations across the country (*Church Times*, 13/4/12).

A third factor is the growing number of women chaplains, a far cry from the early days of male led and male dominated industrial mission. A fourth factor is the rise in the proportion of volunteer, part-time chaplains, an increasing number of them being lay people. A *Chaplaincy Feasibility Study* for the Methodist Church carried out in 2009 states that 101 Methodist chaplaincies fall into Category 1 (*Diagram 10*), whilst 378 relate to Categories 2 or 3 (p. 9). However, it is noted that in relation to Categories 2 and 3, 80% of Methodist chaplains are part-time and unpaid. Malcolm Torry comments: 'Most… chaplaincy work is now being done by volunteers' (p. 170), *IMAgenda* (February - April, 2013. p. 3) adding that these are invariably part (often very part) time.

The reality is that today 'chaplaincy (especially in the commercial sector) is in a state of flux and change and… is driven, in the main, by the economic climate today and the churches (in)ability to support ministry in the workplace' (Sue Hutson, p. 5). The 'economic climate' has over recent decades seen a shift from a concentration on heavy industry and large manufacturing concerns to the retail trade, public sector, service sector, financial services and, permeating all sectors, a revolution in information technology. However, even Category 1, the traditional (institutional), has been feeling the heat of the economic recession and a reduction in the number of full-time paid chaplains, as in the case of the National Health Service and higher education, and they remain an ever-present threat where not a reality.

Models of practice

Whatever *category* of chaplaincy is concerned, *models* of practice cut across all of them. It is these models which give the clearest picture as to whether or not chaplains are in a good position to fulfil the role of mentor, a role this project sees as essential in equipping lay people to develop their ministry and mission within the world of work. As seen in *Diagram 10*, five models of chaplaincy (the 5Ps) are identified: A Pastor, B Priest, C 'Presence', D Prophet and E Partnership builder.

Pastor

The model of the chaplain as pastor is now very much the norm and is to the fore in any analysis of job descriptions for chaplains (Threlfall-Holmes, p. 103). Malcolm Torry states that 'most of (chaplaincy) activity is now pastoral in nature' (p. 171). Peter Cope and Mike West comment that 'much IM work (has become) mainly pastoral in character' (p. xiv). However 'there is a wide variety of genres or metaphors within the pastoral-care model' (Threlfall-Holmes, p. 120). For example, Miranda Threlfall-Holmes herself differentiates 'between pastoral care and pastoral counselling' (p. 104).

Priest

The model of the chaplain as priest (in certain contexts, such as that of the military, called 'padre') reflects what Threlfall-Holmes terms 'the historical-parish model' (pp. 121-122). The norm is for all such

361

chaplains to be ordained. It is a model particularly in evidence within Category 1, the traditional (institutional) form of chaplaincy. Here the chaplain acts as a parish priest but within a community of practice rather than one of place. Functions to the fore in this model are the leadership of worship, the celebration of the sacraments and presiding at rites of passage. Chaplaincies reflecting this model, even in categories other than the traditional, will involve chaplains being asked to take baptisms, preside at weddings and officiate at funerals, even if only occasionally. This model often leads to chaplains assuming the role of the church's symbolic figures within the world of work. In that capacity they have routinely come to be regarded by Christian and non-Christian alike as representing 'the church in the workplace'.

'Presence'

To reflect this model of practice, chaplains have simply to 'be there'. Miranda Threlfall-Holmes describes this model as 'open-ended and process - rather than results-driven' (p. 134). Some chaplains believe that their 'being there' enables them to reflect the presence of God within the workplace. Thus the term 'presence' is often used to refer to the chaplain as one who, in an incarnational sense, represents the person of Christ. It is the chaplain's *implicit* rather than explicit witness - being a friendly face, being an attentive listener, offering words of affirmation or comfort, being a trouble-shooter, even contributing to employee training (Threlfall-Holmes, p. 103) and 'being around' in a diversity of other ways - which, in the case of this model, is the heart of the matter.

Prophet

This model of chaplaincy was much more prominent in past decades than today. The early years of industrial mission, for example, took this model very seriously. It expected chaplains, often on behalf of workers over against management, to expose exploitation and challenge injustices in an open and explicit manner. It was a model which also saw chaplains as active advocates for the unemployed and marginalized. However, as the more confrontational nature of industrial relations has diminished, as the full-time and paid nature of industrial chaplaincy has declined and, above all, as the pastoral model has moved centre-stage, the prophetic model has become the exception rather than the rule. Even so chaplains who served in the earlier days of industrial mission still like to add the word 'prophetic' to their description of chaplaincy, though this often reflects a sense of nostalgia rather than current reality (Randell Moll in *IMAgenda*, February - April 2013, pp. 6-9). Recently the term 'critical friend' has come to the fore, in any attempt to try and reinstate the prophetic in a dominantly pastoral context.

In the case of chaplaincies which fall into the traditional category and are usually funded by the institutions concerned - health, the military, higher education, prisons, and so forth - any 'prophetic' kind of pronouncement has always been difficult and likely to be received as inappropriate. In that situation, therefore, chaplains usually go with the cultural flow and focus practice on the priestly and pastoral models.

Partnership builder

This model of practice embraces the roles of negotiator, mediator, reconciler and/or networker. Malcolm Torry sees this model to be of particular importance and thus calls his history of workplace chaplaincy *Bridgebuilders* (2010). It is a model which fits a context such as city-centre chaplaincy, as described by Alison Maddocks in Nottingham (2009), better than some other situations. Maddocks describes this model as involving her with individuals and social collectives. In relation to the former, she writes that 'the importance of this "bridging" role, enabling the individual to take a step which they might struggle to take on their own, should never be underestimated'. In relation to social collectives she states that 'the chaplain often has an overview which enables them to help organizations, departments or teams in conflict to see when they are pursuing common or related aims and to help to bring them together'.

The boundaries of these five models of practice are of course blurred. The work of many chaplains will represent most of these models at some time or other. Nevertheless, the pastoral and (for those ordained) the priestly models are now dominant. The issue which faces us here is the extent to which chaplaincy, embedded in the categories and models of practice set out above, can be a significant resource for such initiatives as the Kingdom at Work Project, in particular in offering personnel able to take up the role of mentor.

Chaplaincy and the Kingdom at Work Project

The problem which the Kingdom at Work Project has in seeking to affirm the considerable experience, insights, skills and resources of the world of chaplaincy is that the theology, spirituality, approach to the economy and ecclesiology espoused by most categories and models of practice start from a place far removed from that of the project. This disjunction is examined below. Then the potential of chaplains as a resource for the creation of workplaces transformed by the gifts of the kingdom community, the purpose of this project, is explored.

A kingdom theology?

Many of those writing about chaplaincy, especially when focusing on the category of industrial mission or mission in the economy and/or on the model of the chaplain as prophet, argue that chaplaincy is inspired and given impetus by a kingdom theology. Margaret Kane, the first woman industrial chaplain, for twelve years consultant on industrial and social affairs to successive Bishops of Durham, believed fervently in 'the centrality of the kingdom' (1986, p. 19). Julian Reindorp (2000) states that 'Kingdom theology has been at the heart of IM (industrial mission)' (p. 62). Malcolm Torry (2010) believes that 'industrial mission has wanted to positively influence society, the economy, and society's institutions, so that they might conform more closely to the Kingdom of God' (p. 185). Peter Cope and Mike West (2011) write that 'the vast majority of IM staff have based their work on a Kingdom Theology' (p. 138).

Nevertheless, it is less evident that a theology of the kingdom lies at the heart of other categories of chaplaincy or models of practice. Such a theology may be implicit within the model of 'presence' and even of partnership building, but it is much less so within the models of pastor and priest. Even industrial mission has over the years offered more evidence of embracing a theology of the kingdom in principle than in practice, the latter becoming increasingly dominated by the model of pastor. Genuine prophets have thus been few and far between. Shigeko Masumoto (in Ballard and Brown, pp. 254-255) in her perceptive critique of industrial mission in 1983, argues that the kingdom values espoused by industrial mission seem 'to have been produced from a particular cultural value system rather than from the Christian tradition' and that within industrial mission there was often a lack of 'radical questioning... on the basis of the criteria of the Kingdom of God' (p. 254). She believes that, as a result, industrial mission's approach to mission has been more about working with the system than transforming it, 'following social values rather than leading them' (p. 255).

That chaplaincy is *in practice* a form of ministry not very clearly identified with or shaped by a theology of the kingdom means that it is not, at least explicitly, based on the same foundations at the Kingdom at Work Project. Consequently it does not manifest in practice an understanding of a communal theology, spirituality, economic principles and an ecclesiology reflecting the foundations on which this project is based. Perhaps the one exception is that industrial mission, or mission in the economy, has continued to encourage active engagement with, as well as offered food for thought on the changing nature of the global economy (Brown and Ballard, 2006), with *IMAgenda* still engaging its readers in reflection on current social and economic issues.

The demise of a kingdom theology as foundational for chaplaincy, leaves the latter espousing a dominantly pastoral model. That model has important attributes. However, it is inadequate for the communal transformation of the workplace, that which this project takes to be at the heart of mission in the world of work. In particular, the prophetic model of chaplaincy is put to one side both in principle and in practice. This leaves the church uncritical of the failure of the workplace to express more fully the gifts of the kingdom community and complicit in the ways in which that failure can be destructive of human well-being and the common good.

Ecclesiology

It is when ecclesiology is considered that the current forms of chaplaincy diverge most obviously from the perspective of the Kingdom Community Project.

Chaplaincy in its current state fails to call into question the still dominant model of the Christendom church. I have dealt at greater length with this issue elsewhere (Clark, 2005 and 2008). The point to be noted here is that forms of chaplaincy, ordained or lay, which remain captive to a Christendom model of church cannot hope to produce prophets or even change agents within the world of work. The Kingdom at Work Project is founded on the conviction that an understanding and affirmation of the model of the diaconal church is essential if any kind of faith-inspired intervention to transform the workplace hopes to succeed. The medium must embody the message.

The most important concern arising from the captivity of chaplaincy to the Christendom model of church is the way in which it distorts the place and status of the laity in the mission of the church within the world of work. In Stage 5, this project aligned itself with a quotation from the Methodist document *Called to Love and Praise* (1999, 4.5.4) which states that: 'The ministry of the people of God in the world is both the primary and the normative ministry of the Church'. It was argued that this was also the credo of the diaconal church, that form of church which it was contended most clearly reflects a theology of the kingdom community.

This is not how the models of chaplaincy currently to the fore within the life of the mainstream denominations construct the role of the laity. Shigeko Masumto puts the point forcefully. She writes (in Ballard and Brown, pp. 255 and 256): 'Clericalism is one of the biggest weaknesses of IM [and, we would add here, of most others categories of chaplaincy and models of practice]... As a result the voice of the laity is hardly heard'. As a consequence, 'Chaplains are not yet freed from the old model of the church... church centredness... (Such a) church inevitably thinks that it can discharge its task (mission within the world of work) by sending (in) chaplains'.

Clericalism leads to exaggerated and misleading claims. John Breadon speaks of chaplaincy as being 'par excellence, the church in the world' (2010, p. 21). Malcolm Torry claims that 'since the Second World War workplace chaplaincy has been the church's most important piece of work' (p. xi). In response to the Diocese of London in 2004 closing down the posts of all paid industrial chaplains, he states that 'the church was... left with no voice in (London's) economy and workplaces' (p. 165). Torry believes that if the church is to re-engage with the world of work, what is needed is 'more workplace chaplains' (p. 185). There are also those still convinced that the way forward for a church in decline is 'chaplaincy for everyone... (p. 160ff; Jonathan Green, 2012, p. 6)... emerging from the heart of every congregation!' (Green, p. 4), even if such chaplains have to be part-time and/or voluntary.

From this perspective, the implicit assumption is that the presence of lay people within the workplace counts for little. The consequence is that in much of the literature on the role of the chaplain there is 'a lay deficit', a deafening silence concerning the nature and significance of the ministry and mission of lay Christians within the workplace. Recent material on chaplaincy by Torry (2010), Threlfall-Holmes (2011) and Cope and West (2011), as well as recent editions of *Crucible* (July-September, 2009, and October-December, 2011) and of the *Epworth*

Review (December 2010), which deals with the role of chaplains, makes virtually no reference to the ministry of lay people in the world of work and to how chaplains should relate to and facilitate that ministry.

In most cases when lay people are referred to in the literature about chaplaincy, the emphasis is on how they can be a resource to chaplains or, as noted below, be drawn into (voluntary) chaplaincy (Torry, p. 185; Jonathan Green, p. 4). Even Ted Wickham, the founder of industrial mission in the UK, albeit inadvertently, encouraged an understanding of lay people as a support group for chaplains. He did manage to set up a network of lay work groups which would identify themselves as committed Christians, worship and study together, plan mission together and 'enjoy fellowship with each other' (Cope and West, p. 35). However, the emphasis was as much on their being a new form of church in the workplace as on a kingdom-centred ministry of their own concerned with the transformation of the world of work. Consequently, as early as 1966, Tom Chapman could write: 'The great failure of industrial mission, as I see it, has been the inability to use the vast potential of lay man (sic) power' (Brown and Ballard, p. 126). In 1988, the Church of England's Board for Social Responsibility, in an appraisal of industrial mission, stated that 'IM has been noticeably unsuccessful in becoming a lay movement' (p. 81).

A good deal of attention has been focused on Category 2 (*Diagram 10*), chaplaincy in the context of industrial mission and mission in the economy. However, all the other categories of chaplaincy and models of practice appear equally oblivious to the primary place of the laity in mission in the world of work. The chaplain is assumed to be *the* representative, even *the* personification of the church in the world of work, whilst the vast cohort of lay people present within the workplace, the church's primary missionary resource therein, is ignored. *The Kingdom at Work Project seeks to turn this situation on its head*. Its aim is to offer a strategy for mission that regards the ordained ministry, as well as the growing body of lay chaplains, as first and foremost the servants of the kingdom community, and thus of the people of God daily concerned with the transformation of those workplaces in which they are involved.

Lay chaplains

There is currently an upsurge in lay chaplaincy, typified by the Methodist Church's strap-line of 'Chaplaincy everywhere' and the title of some recent courses such as 'We are all chaplains now', as in the case of Churches Together in Kent. This development is the result of a number of factors within and beyond the church.

Within the church, the reduction in the number of chaplains paid by the church has in part resulted from a drastic reduction in church finances over recent years. Perhaps more significant than the withdrawal of financial support has been the fact of an underlying suspicion that many chaplains, especially those serving the industrial sector, have too often operated as lone rangers and done little to enrich or sustain congregational life.

Beyond the church, secular institutions have also suffered from the recent financial squeeze. It is no surprise, therefore, that a number of full-time paid chaplains who fit into the traditional category, for example within the National Health Service, have been made redundant. Nonetheless, chaplaincy in the traditional sense has proved reasonably resilient and there is some evidence that institutions are still reluctant to dispense, at least on a part-time basis, with what has been a long-standing feature of a Christendom culture.

Those factors bringing about the decline in the number of paid chaplains have been seen as a golden opportunity for lay people to step into the breach. This has happened to the greatest extent in relation to chaplaincy in the retail trade and in relation to the relatively new category of street pastor. Lay chaplaincy is usually unpaid and undertaken for short and intermittent periods, often for a few hours rather than days per week. Many laity seem to have volunteered for this role because, often as early retirees, they wish to keep in touch with 'the real world' and one with which the gathered church seems to have lost touch.

There is a good deal to commend the concern of lay people to engage as chaplains on a face-to-face level with those beyond the fringes of the church. However, in a mission context, this development presents the same kind of problems as discussed above in relation to full-time ordained models of chaplaincy. In particular, the importance of empowering lay people at work for mission is still ignored and the mentoring skills required to help equip them for this tough assignment remain in abeyance. The wider church salves its conscience that, through the recruitment of lay chaplains, it is fulfilling its ministry within the world of work. However, the communal transformation of the workplace and the manifestation therein of the gifts of the kingdom community are ignored. The workplace as such is left to further or undermine human well-being and the common good as it wills.

Chaplains as mentors

There is an urgent need for chaplains once again to embrace a kingdom theology and resume their calling to become actively involved in the communal transformation of the workplaces they serve. To fulfil that mission, it is as important for chaplains as for lay people at work to use the kind of resources offered by this project, in particular to employ the art of discernment and the skills of intervention. However, as argued above, the mission deficit of the church in the world of work will never be addressed effectively until lay people are educated and enabled to take up their responsibilities as the key resource of the church within the workplace. Such a change of direction in the church's approach to mission at work will require the training of mentors to equip lay people for that task. Chaplains are one potential source of those with the experience and skills to fulfil that role.

The model of chaplaincy which currently comes closest to reflecting that of mentor is most clearly in evidence within the Roman Catholic Church. *Industrial Mission - an Appraisal* (1988, pp. 85-86) states that from the perspective of the Catholic Church -

> The field of economic and industrial affairs is the field of the lay apostolate... the priest 'leaves his people at the factory gates', and the relationship of clergy to industrial and economic mission must be through the enabling, formation and animation of the laity for this work. On that view, the appointment of industrial chaplains as such would represent a retrograde step in the development of the 'new ecclesiology'... (of Vatican 2 about the laity).

At the same time, although most current forms of chaplaincy are based on a theology and an ecclesiology which diverge from that of the Kingdom at Work Project, there are a few instances where chaplains are attempting to fulfil those functions, especially of enabler and educator of the laity, which typify the role of mentor.

Enablers

ChaplaincyPlus, an independent evangelical chaplaincy serving the business community of Birmingham which began in 2003, seeks to offer personal support to the 700 or so Christian contacts it has made, in large part through social media networking. This support includes a counselling service, but also working through small informal groups and short courses. A range of other agencies, such as After Sunday, Christians at Work and Transform Work UK, mostly evangelical in their theology, though not designating themselves as chaplaincies, seek to undertake a similar enabling function relating to both individual Christians and Christian groups in the workplace.

In the 'SEE, JUDGE, ACT' process developed by the Roman Catholic Church's Young Christian Workers, described in Stage 9 of this project, the chaplain plays an important mentoring role. The instructions to the chaplain are included here in full because they offer some important pointers as to what being mentor to a group might entail (www.ycw.impact.com).

In relation to 'SEE', the chaplain's role is described as follows:

o   To prepare with the group leader.
o   To listen carefully.
o   To ask questions which make things clearer.
o   To help the young people to express themselves.
o   To encourage everyone to take part.
o   To take his/her own notes.

Relating to the 'JUDGE' stage, the chaplain's role is:

o   To put the group in discovery mode.
o   To allow them to be touched, challenged and enriched by the Word.
o   To put the passage in context if necessary.
o   To witness to his/her faith in a sensitive way.
o   To help the group to respect each other.

Relating to 'ACT', the role is:

o   To help the group move on to 'ACT'.
o   To prompt them to keep a link with the situations described in the "SEE" section
o   To help them to be realistic.
o   To help them identify others who can help.
o   To support them in living out the action after the meeting.

In the 'REVIEW' stage, the chaplain's role is:

o   To help each one understand the importance of their action and its Christian meaning.
o   To gently prompt those who forgot or did not get round to it.
o   To ask about their situations outside the meeting.

One example of a chaplain acting as mentor within an industrial mission team is that of Peter Challen of the South London Industrial Mission [Stage 3]. Challen developed an enabling process called 'theological auditing' (Challen in Clark, 1997, pp. 115-116). This was a programme whereby individuals or groups (by no means always Christians) were helped to reflect on their working lives in the light of 'themes of faith' such as 'creation', 'jubilee', 'shalom' and 'covenant'. They then explored how these themes might be applied to and expressed through their work.

Educators

Numerous courses have over the years been set up by chaplains themselves, or others, to train chaplains. Notable here have been those offered by the William Temple Foundation in Manchester, South Yorkshire Workplace Chaplaincy and the Greenwich Peninsula Chaplaincy. The Methodist Church has on its web site a course entitle *Chaplaincy Everywhere*, a small group resource which consists of seven carefully designed sessions (www.methodist.org.uk/missiom/chaplaincy). An MTh in Chaplaincy Studies (mainly focused on the traditional model) is currently offered by Cardiff University and St. Michael's College, Llandaff.

The main failing of these courses is that they pay little or no attention to how chaplains, as mentors, might help to educate and equip lay people for their ministry in the workplace. Typical is the chaplaincy section of the Methodist Church's website which identifies seven roles that 'make a good chaplain' but fails to include that of being a mentor of lay Christians in the workplace. The need for chaplains to be active in supporting and resourcing the mission of the lay people within the world of work is only made explicit in the Mission in the World of Work module of the MA in Mission Studies (validated by Manchester University) offered by Cliff College, Derbyshire

Chaplains have now and then set up programmes to equip lay people for mission in the world of work. The lay groups which Ted Wickham and his team established in the early days of industrial

371

mission possessed something of this character. In 1988, *Industrial Mission - an Appraisal* listed seven so-called 'models of lay involvement' (pp. 82-83). Most of these courses were too small-scale or short-term to be taken as genuine educational 'models' and only one or two focused practically on equipping lay people for mission in the workplace. However, one model of lay training was a notable exception - Methodism's Luton Industrial College, set up by William Gowland in 1955. For many years this offered a wide diversity of courses to support lay people in bringing their faith to bear on their working life. Yet, again reflecting the inability of the church to sustain any enduring momentum in this field of mission, the college was closed in 1996.

Courses have on a few occasions been offered to gathered churches by industrial mission teams to try and raise the former's awareness to the importance of mission in the world of work. Active from time to time in this respect have been the Sheffield, South London, Peterborough, Black Country, Northumbria and Liverpool chaplaincy teams (Peter Cope and Mike West, pp. 126-128). However, none of these courses has focused in any clear, consistent and ongoing way on equipping laity with the theological and practical skills to undertake their ministry within the workplace.

Such initiatives offer some hope that chaplains could use their considerable experience and expertise to equip themselves for the role of mentor. However, for that to happen, there needs to be a sea-change in the theology and ecclesiology currently underpinning most models of chaplaincy and, above all, in how chaplains view the role of lay people at work in relation to the church's mission in the workplace

Summary

Categories and models of chaplaincy (*Diagram 10*) have been explored at some length in this stage of the project because it seems to be taken for granted by many people, as well as by many chaplains themselves, that chaplaincy is *the* key to enabling the church to engage with the world of work. It is recognized that, influenced by this point of view, many lay people are taking up the role of chaplain, albeit in a voluntary and part-time capacity, because they feel that it involves them and a marginalized church in 'the real world'.

However, this project remains unconvinced that the recruitment of more chaplains is the answer to the church's failure to engage effectively with the working world. Indeed, it can be argued that where chaplains are taken to be the most important representatives of the church in the world of work, they are, in reality, distorting the mission of the church in the workplace, a task which a diaconal church founded on a kingdom theology takes as being the primary responsibility of lay people.

This is not to devalue the work in which chaplains are at present involved. Their pastoral role is important to many, Christian and non-Christian alike. This is not only true in relation to the more established models of chaplaincy but in the burgeoning field of street pastors. The chaplain's availability, not least in the role of priest, to undertake rites of passage for those who rarely attend church is still appreciated by the public. Chaplains remain a sign that the church cares for the world of work. And, as noted, they sometimes offer the world of work the much needed role of partnership builder or intermediary.

Nevertheless, a Copernican revolution will be required if chaplains are to break free from the mould of a Christendom church, escape the omnipresent danger of clericalism and offer their considerable resources as mentors to equip the church's primary but neglected missionary resource, its laity already engaged within the workplace. To initiate such a revolution, the recommendation of this project is that *all training courses for chaplains, initial or in-service, ordained or lay, should henceforth include the skills of mentoring Christians at work, and those of enabling the gathered church to support the latter, as a core component of their curricula.*

Ministers in secular employment (MSEs)

This section examines the extent to which the role of MSEs is furthering the mission of the church in the world or work and, in particular, what needs to happen to encourage MSEs to take up the role of mentor to lay people at work. Much of what follows could apply to all self-supporting ministries (SSMs) though these are usually entered into more specifically to serve the needs of the gathered church.

In 2010, Teresa Morgan and Graham Lewis undertook a survey of SSMs within the Church of England (www.1pf.co.uk/SSM), a report of which appeared in the *Church Times* (1/4/11 and 8/4/11). The survey indicated that of 3,100 SSMs, 12% or 372 described themselves as 'ministers in secular employment' or 'worker priests'. Those so doing were the proportion of SSMs who saw the workplace rather than the parish as the primary focus of their ministry. Nearly all of them were in white collar jobs, many in education, the helping or legal professions, and a good number in middle management positions.

In 2011, 54 Methodist presbyters and deacons who were self-supporting were exercising a similar form of work-focused ministry (*Minutes of the Methodist Conference*, 2011). Though, in Methodism, such ministers are often called 'sector ministers', here they are designated, along with those having similar roles and status in other denominations, as ministers in secular employment or MSEs.

Only one body exists in the UK to represent 'Christians in Secular Ministry', though the large majority of its members are ordained. It is currently known as CHRISM. Its origins lie in a group of MSEs who first met in London in the 1970s. It was helped on its way by the first national conference of MSEs held in 1984 at Nottingham University, with about 150 people attending. After other national gatherings, CHRISM, or Christians in Secular Ministry, was formed in 1993. In 2011, CHRISM had 170 individual members, 21 members representing institutions and 43 institutional members. Individual membership represented 5.5% of all SSMs. Membership is dominantly Anglican though it also includes members from other denominations, especially the Methodist and United Reformed Churches. CHRISM publishes a quarterly journal entitled *Ministers-at-Work* and occasional pamphlets. CHRISM'S annual conference has in recent years somewhat dwindled in numbers. Its annual reflective week-end continues to be been well attended.

I have described more fully elsewhere how the position of ministers in secular employment and of sector ministers came into being (Clark, 2005, pp. 210-214). Here the focus is on how their ministries are currently attuned to the stance and practicalities of the Kingdom at Work Project. In particular, the same question as that addressed to chaplains is of immediate relevance. How well placed is this not inconsiderable cohort of ministers to undertake the role of mentor to lay people engaged in the workplace?

Categories and models of ministry in secular employment

Unlike chaplains, MSEs are predominantly employees of secular organizations with similar credentials and status as lay people. They are not appointed or recognized by the employing organization because of the authority given them by the church. As employees many constraints are placed on their role as priests and ministers which do not apply to chaplains.

Because MSEs are engaged in a wide spectrum of occupations, the *categories* of chaplaincy noted in *Diagram 10* are of little relevance to their situation. However, the five *models* of practice identified in the diagram can be applied to the roles that MSEs seek to play as an important aspect of what is sometimes referred to as their 'bi-vocational' stance (*Spiritual Direction for Ministers in Secular Employment*, January 2011, pp. 1-3).

MSEs certainly see themselves as **pastors**, seeking to offer support, encouragement, comfort (Fuller and Vaughan, p. 27) and friendship to colleagues at work, though in a personal not formal capacity. In this context, MSEs are responsive rather than pro-active. They need to be careful not to encroach on the role of those officially appointed by the organization, for example under the auspices of a human resources department, to act as counsellors to the workforce. However, Patrick Vaughan (2011) argues that, in the 1970s, by labelling non-stipendiary ministry as Auxiliary *Pastoral* Ministry rather than Auxiliary *Parochial* Ministry, the bishops of the Church of England never formally adopted ministry in secular employment as a recognized strategy for *mission* (p. 17). They thus locked expectations of ministry in secular employment into a pastoral model.

MSEs themselves would seem to be somewhat ambivalent about employing the model of **priest** to describe their role within the workplace. In interviews conducted by Fuller and Vaughan (pp. 9-54), for some MSEs the word 'priest' was very prominent in the conversations, a number of them explicitly building their identity at work around the concept of priesthood (p. 13). Not a few MSEs receive requests to officiate at baptisms, marriages or funerals of work colleagues and at public services such as those held at Christmas (p. 11). However, for many other MSEs the traditional role of priest was less important, at least within the workplace, some wanting to present an image to work colleagues other than that typical of priesthood within a Christendom model of church.

All MSEs strongly embrace the model of **'presence'**. Trevor Pitt (in Francis and Francis, p. 298) describes this model as follows:

> In order to undertake such a ministry, the minister in secular employment needs to be secure enough in God not to need to be constantly talking about God or sharing Christian things;

needs to have no anxiety about being successful; needs to have no unrealistic goals about making converts; needs simply to be able to wait for God to disclose his purposes in the situation.

The model of presence seems to have two facets for MSESs. One is summed up in what CHRISM calls its 'vision' statement: 'To help ourselves and others to celebrate the presence of God and the holiness of life in our work and to see and tell the Christian story there'. The other aspect of presence is the conviction that God speaks through the words and deeds of MSEs simply by their 'being there'. One MSE sums up this second understanding of presence as follows. 'My greatest reason for being an MSE... is to be an outward sign that "God in the Mass on Sunday is the same God in the Mess on Monday".' (*Reflections on Ministry in Secular Employment*, p. 27)

MSEs are even less than chaplains inclined or able to emulate the model of ***prophet***. John Davis (in Fuller and Vaughan) takes MSEs to task for this failure because, as he sees it, the organizations many of them are helping to maintain 'in good order' are 'mammon-dominated' (p. 77). He comments that 'amongst the MSE revelations (as stories in Fuller and Vaughan) there were few indications of the Christian worker (priest) as an enthusiast for justice' (p. 76). Davis found not 'a single clear vision of a prophetic character' (p. 78). Jill Robson, reflecting on the same stories in the same symposium, asks 'Why are not these MSE's speaking out against injustice, working for the poor, concerned with "kingdom" issues: why are they not hungering and thirsting after structural righteousness?' (p. 80) Although the stories referred to were recounted in the 1980s, there is little evidence that those told today would be very different.

Some of the reasons why the role of MSE does not reflect a prophetic model of practice are suggested by Jill Robson herself. One is that most MSEs work in organizations where critical questions and the pursuit of truth are not an integral part of a culture in which the prophet can flourish (p. 83). Another reason is that many MSEs are in middle management positions and were appointed as, and assumed to be guardians not critics of their workplace culture. Their investment in the company, economically, socially or personally, does not encourage a prophetic ministry (pp. 84-85). Jill Robson, though only referring to this implicitly, is also concerned that MSEs are neglecting their potentially prophetic role in relation to the church, where there should be far fewer constraints on them than in the workplace (pp. 87-88).

The role of ***partnership builder*** is more accessible to MSEs. There is evidence (in Fuller and Vaughan, p. 27, and CHRISM publications) of MSEs fulfilling the role of mediator, negotiator or reconciler. Here their management status becomes a potential asset, giving them the opportunity, formally and informally, to engage in the resolving of conflicts and disagreements. Having this status, they are in a good position to give expression to the meaning of dialogue [Stage 8(3)] in a secular context.

MSEs and the Kingdom at Work Project

A kingdom theology?

To what extent does a theology of the kingdom community, and its gifts of life, liberation, love and learning, underpin and shape the models of ministry which MSEs adopt?

Much of the early literature concerning MSEs is grounded in a kingdom theology. Peter Baelz and William Jacob, writing in 1985, though here including MSEs in a remit embracing all forms of 'non-stipendiary ministers', entitle their book *Ministers of the Kingdom*. Even more to the point, John Fuller and Patrick Vaughan's symposium, published a year later, and focused specifically on MSEs, is called *Working for the Kingdom*. The authors' approach to an understanding of what they call 'the "muddy" nature of life in that kingdom' (p. 206), is through reflection on a diverse range of stories told by MSEs. However, what their reflections lack is a distilling out of the common ground linking these stories and, on that basis, offering a kingdom theology of practical relevance to all ministries within the workplace. Fuller and Vaughan seem to become aware of this omission when, at the end of their book, they comment that 'there is… still very little theological guidance for those engaged in the complexities of the secular realm' (p. 211).

After these early publications, and perhaps reflecting the institutional church's continuing ambivalence about the work-focused priorities of MSEs, in-depth theological reflection on the latter's role has been notable by its absence. The kingdom theology espoused at the outset has become ever more implicit then explicit. Even so, through its journal and pamphlets, CHRISM has tried hard to keep theological reflection on the role of MSEs to the fore. In 2010, MSEs in the Coventry Diocese produced a booklet entitled *Reflections on Ministry in Secular Employment*. In this, Dawn Waterton, a MSE working in the construction industry, uses her experience to link building with the work of God the Creator (life being one of the gifts of the kingdom community). She comments: 'Good building can bring new life to a community if it is done sensitively and well' (p. 17). Richard Dobell, a music teacher, writes that through 'treating mistakes as learning opportunities' (the gift of learning) and expressing 'loving care for each person, each student in the school' (the gift of love), the latter 'is trying to express the values of God's kingdom in today's life' (p. 23).

MSEs have made notable attempts to explore a spirituality for the workplace. Trevor Pitt (in Francis and Francis) likens the experience of MSEs to being 'desert explorers' often in 'bleak places… institutions or spheres where there is no obvious Christian presence' (p. 297). However, he argues that such a situation 'should be welcomed and embraced as the… place for patient looking, listening and contemplating' (p. 298). Chris Knights has written about 'Work as a spirituality activity' drawing on the Rule of St Benedict for help and guidance (*Ministers-at-Work*, April 2009). In the same issue of that journal, Felicity Smith touches on 'Sacraments at work', identifying the shared lunch and 'rites of passage' like retirement, or even redundancy, as potentially visible signs of grace. In 2011, CHRISM produce a pamphlet entitled *Spiritual Direction for Ministers in Secular Employment*. Contrary to Pitt's view of work as a spiritual desert, one MSE believes that it can be 'a spiritual oasis' (pp. 15-16). It is recorded that another MSE is following a rule of life (again linked to the Benedictine Rule) using a cell-phone to remind himself of set times for prayer each day (p. 17). In addition, CHRISM has produced a useful pamphlet on *Worship Resources* (2005).

Ecclesiology

Because the implications for MSEs of espousing a kingdom theology are not explored at any great depth, their ecclesiology continues to reflect that of a Christendom rather than diaconal church (Clark, 2005, 2008). Jill Robson's view, noted above, that MSEs are largely silent when it comes to any critique of the life and mission of the inherited church here strikes home.

Above all, however, as with chaplains, the major weakness of the ecclesiology embraced by MSEs is a failure to affirm with clarity and conviction that it is lay people who are the church's primary resources for mission within the world of work. Robin Bennett (in *Ministers of the*

Kingdom, p. 46) writes: 'In so far as non-stipendiary ministers are those who "go before" the Christian, as a sign and a forerunner of the Christian people, they are doing a valuable job. In as far as they are acting in place of the Christian lay person, they are causing confusion and making it harder for others to accept authority for their own fundamental ministry as God's people.'

In the literature relating to MSEs the latter rather than the former state of affairs is dominant. Few MSEs seem to be exercised as to what it means to be 'a sign and a forerunner of the Christian people' in the world of work. Indeed, if anything, MSEs appear to be more concerned with finding an identity which enhances their status in the eyes of the gathered church. In relation to the emergence of 'fresh expressions of church', for example, their main lament is not the neglect of lay ministry within the workplace (which 'fresh expressions' has done little to change), but that the ministry undertaken by MSEs as such hardly gets a mention (*MSE and Fresh Expressions*. CHRISM, 10, April 2009, p. 18). If, as the Bishop of Salisbury argues (in Fuller and Vaughan, p. xi), 'the minister in secular employment is the key figure' in enabling Christians to live out their faith in daily life, there is little evidence that this responsibility has been addressed as a priority by most MSEs.

The mainstream denominations, still shaped by a Christendom model of church and by clericalism in particular, continue to do little to encourage MSEs to use their experience of the world of work to equip lay people for mission in that sector. Teresa Morgan, reporting three years later on the response of the Church of England to the survey of self-supporting ministries (SSMs) she carried out in 2010 (*Church Times,* 1/2/2013 and mentioned at the outset of this section), appears greatly encouraged by the way in which dioceses are responding in an increasingly pro-active way to using the resources and skills that SSMs (and presumably also MSEs, though the latter do not get a mention) can offer to assist parish and diocesan ministries. However, in her report there is no reference to ways in which the church might employ the experience of SSMs, and especially of MSEs, to further mission within the world *of work*, either through their own endeavours or by equipping lay people at work for that task. Yet again it seems that it is mainly for the sake of the church rather than of the world of work that these new forms of ministry have been welcomed.

MSEs as mentors

As with chaplains, there is every reason for MSEs to reclaim a kingdom theology and become engaged in the communal transformation of the places where they work. The resources offered by this project could help them in that task. However, as noted in the context of chaplaincy, the church will continue to make only a limited impact on the communal transformation of the workplace until its lay members are educated and enabled to engage more effectively in mission at work. Yet again the need for mentors to assist lay people in that task comes to the fore. MSEs are potentially a key resource for the development of that role.

In 1968 and 1970, a commission set up by the Methodist Conference to explore 'the church's ministries in the modern world' produced two reports which remain a landmark in the development of what Methodism then called 'sector ministry' (ministers in secular employment). The 1968 report stated (p. 3) that, 'The church in the sector will depend largely on the skills and experience of its laymen and women. Here the minister will be the servant, bringing the gifts and skills of his own ministry and training... (to) enable the abilities and understandings of his lay colleagues to be fully released and co-ordinated.' The role of mentor developed by the Kingdom at Work Project seeks to make that commitment, long unfulfilled, a reality. What could MSEs bring to that endeavour?

Anthony Russell (in Fuller and Vaughan, p. 197) believes that the MSE should and could be 'the *animateur* of the people of God'. Eric Forshaw (in Fuller and Vaughan, p. 71) argues that 'the role of enabler or catalyst... is a key one for the MSE because it puts him closer to the role already being exercised by a committed lay teacher, technician or trade unionist.' In a few places throughout the literature about or by MSEs, a similar chord is struck. Phil Aspinall, for example, believes that 'the MSE is in a place to help others articulate events - there is Good News to be told' (*Reflections on Ministry in Secular Employment*, p. 21). However, neither the role of *enabler* nor that of *educator* of lay people engaged in the world of work is given consistent attention. It would seem, therefore, that if MSEs are to fulfil the role of mentors, a radical change of priorities will need to occur in their ministry *beyond* the workplace. That this is not happening is extremely disappointing because they would be able to bring to that role, perhaps even more fully than chaplains, first-hand knowledge and experience of what it means, in a mission context, to be a Christian at work.

Summary

MSEs are not numerous. Nevertheless, they form a notable body of those ordained which continues to remind the church that mission within the world of work is of vital importance. CHRISM, the organization which represents their concerns, has worked hard over the years to develop a deeper understanding by MSEs of their ministry and to make the church more aware of their existence. However, that task remains unfinished.

MSEs as secular employees stand in a different relationship to the world of work from chaplains. However, many of the models of practice which identify the latters' roles are applicable to the ministry of MSEs. Pastor and priest are models clearly reflected in the life of many MSEs. However, it is the model of presence which seems to be universally acknowledged, not least because MSEs are in a similar position to lay employees. MSEs have not been prominent in expressing the prophetic model, not least because the culture of the workplace is especially hard to challenge by those who depend upon it for their livelihood. The model of partnership builder is more in evidence.

Most MSEs would appear to be committed to a kingdom theology in principle. The problem is that it is a theology which has remained more implicit than explicit and its practical implications have not been developed. There have been some attempts by MSEs to develop a spirituality of the workplace. However, the ecclesiology with which they operate remains one shaped by a Christendom rather than diaconal model of church. This has led to most MSEs paying little attention to the role of mentor and the task of equipping lay people for their own ministry in the world of work.

As in the case of chaplains, all this means that a Copernican scale revolution will be required if MSEs (and SSMs) are to escape the ever-present danger of clericalism and employ their considerable experience to inform and develop the role of mentor to lay people within the workplace. To kick-start this radical change, the recommendation of this project is that *MSEs (and where appropriate SSMs) should undertake in-service training which equips them with the expertise for mentoring Christians at work and with the skills to enable the gathered church to support the latter.*

Part 4
Review

Stage 12
Reflection and review

This brief section is concerned with reflection on and review of the usefulness and importance of the Kingdom at Work Project *as a project*. It is suggested that reflection and review are undertaken in the following sequence.

1. The reflection and review process should start by looking at the heart of the project: the usefulness or otherwise of Stages 7 and 8, discernment and intervention, in enabling the workplace to manifest the gifts of the kingdom community. The emphasis should be on the value of the discernment and intervention process in general, not on any particular attempt at discernment and intervention.

The review should consider whether or not a convincing case for the importance of human scale initiatives has been made [Stage 6].

In relation to Stage 7 which is focused on discernment, the reflection and review process should be concerned with the value of signs and/or critical incidents in identifying possible mission tasks. The review should also enquire into how useful the approaches to intervention described in Stage 8 have proved to be. In relation to both stages, the importance of the roles identified by the project as typical of servant leadership should be reviewed.

2. The reflection and review process should consider whether the communal principles on which the project is built have proved relevant and helpful [Stages 1 to 5]. Issues of how fully and/or in what form these foundations need to be an integral part of the portfolio of Christians seeking to engage in mission at work should be discussed.

3. The quality of facilitation and support needed to sustain and resource the project [Stages 9 to 11] should be reviewed. Especially important is the issue of whether or not the role of mentor has proved viable and useful in giving the project direction and impetus [Stage 9]. In this context, a review of the actual and potential contribution of chaplains and ministers in secular employment to the role of mentor should be undertaken. The extent to which it has been possible, and in future might be feasible to engage the gathered church more fully in furthering the mission of the church in the world of work should be addressed [Stage 10].

385

4. There should be a review of the adequacy and usefulness of the material set out in the Bibliography.

Glossary

Authority – achieved	The authority a worker has because of their work-related experience and expertise and/or their social skills and personal qualities
Authority – ascribed	Authority bestowed on a worker because he or she occupies some formally recognised leadership position
Collective	See 'social collective'
The communal dilemma	The problem social collectives face when attempting to become increasingly open to one another without undermining or weakening their own sense of community or that of others
Communal imperative	The need to create a global community of character which embraces and bonds together many diverse communities of character
Communities of character	Social collectives that clearly manifest one or more of the kingdom community's universal and inclusive gifts of, life, liberation, love and learning. They may include secular as well as religious communities, from the local to the global.
Community of character – global	A world transformed by the kingdom community's gifts of life, liberation, love and learning
Communities of practice	Occupational groups which engage in the sustained pursuit of a shared enterprise
Context	The physical, material and environmental aspects of the workplace
Contract	A task-focused, functional and formal agreement

Covenant	A person-centred and often informal agreement based on mutual respect and trust.
Critical incident	Critical incidents are unscheduled or unexpected happenings within the workplace which reveal the gifts of the kingdom community at work
Diaconal church	A church which is the servant of the kingdom community
A diaconal ecclesiology	The main characteristics of a church which seeks to be a servant of the kingdom community
Dialogue	A conversation in which participants share their concerns in a spirit of mutual inquiry and reflective response
Discernment	The spiritually reflective process of identifying the gifts of the kingdom community
Ecumenical imperative	The need to approach any mission task as a holistic Christian endeavour
The 4Ls	The kingdom community's gifts of life, liberation, love and learning
The 4Ss	A sense of security, of significance and of solidarity developed through a process of socialization – key components of a sociological understanding of the concept of community
Gifts of the kingdom community	The gifts of life, liberation, love and learning
The gift of life	The gift of God as Creator
The gift of liberation	The gift of Christ as Liberator
The gift of love	The gift of the Holy Spirit as Unifier
The gift of learning	The gift of the Trinity as a learning community

Intervention	Any initiative which seeks to advance the mission task (see below)
Intervention – implicit	Intervention where no overt reference is made to Christian faith or Christian concepts
Intervention – explicit	Intervention involving the overt use of concepts, language or symbols which are derived from and informed by a communal theology, spirituality, economy and the nature of diaconal structures.
Intervention – individual	Intervention by the Christian at work which does not necessitate involving others as active partners in that undertaking. It is often of an informal nature and short-term.
Intervention – collective	Intervention by the Christian at work which is intentionally undertaken in partnership with others. Such intervention is usually deliberately planned and of some duration.
Initiator	A Christian who intervenes in the workplace to further a specific mission task
The Kingdom at Work Project	A project to help create workplaces transformed by the gifts of the kingdom community
Kingdom community	The divine community which manifests the Trinity's universal and inclusive gifts of life, liberation, love and learning
Learning - double-loop	Learning that questions assumptions and/or received wisdom within a secular frame of reference
Learning - single-loo	*p*Learning that docs not question assumptions and/or received wisdom

389

Learning - triple-loop	Learning that questions assumptions and/or received wisdom within a frame of reference which regards secular *and* spiritual interpretations of reality as important and complementary
Mentor	A person who facilitates the personal and professional development of another by the mutual sharing of knowledge, experience and insights
Mission task	See *Task - mission*
Model	A representation, image or picture which brings together key features from a range of sources, theoretical and practical, to offer an overview of the phenomenon under consideration.
Relationships at work	The relationships between all those associated with the work task and/or workplace
Servant leadership	That form of leadership which seeks to create social collectives that manifest the kingdom community's gifts of life, liberation, love and learning
Servant leadership - complementary roles	Visionary (envisions the 4Ls), strategist (earths the 4Ls), animator (advances the gift of life); enabler (advances the gift of liberation); intermediary (advances the gift of love); educator (advances the gift of learning)
Servant leadership team	A team which incorporates the six complementary servant leadership roles
Signs	Ongoing or recurrent features of the workplace discerned as revealing one or more of the gifts of the kingdom community at work

Social collective	Any identifiable and ongoing group or larger body usually within the world of work.
Socialization	The process of induction into a culture through nurture, instruction and training
Social system	See *Social collective*
A theology of community – a communal theology	A theology founded on the concept of the kingdom community and its four gifts
Task – mission (overall)	The universal task of creating a world of work transformed by the gifts of the kingdom community: life, liberation, love and learning
Task – mission (specific)	The specific task chosen to enable the workplace to be transformed by the gifts of the kingdom community
Work	Paid employment
Working relationships	Interpersonal relationships between those at work
Workplace	That network of relationships which links people involved in a shared occupational endeavour usually focused on or emanating from some identifiable location
Work task	The task which an employing body engages its workers to undertake
World of work	Those spheres of life across all sectors of society where people are in paid employment. It is a world consisting of myriads of workplaces.

Bibliography

About our Father's Business (2010) Birmingham: St Peter's Saltley Trust and Diocese of Birmingham

Adam, D. (1992) *Power Lines - Celtic prayers about work.* London: SPCK

Ambler, R. (2002) *Light to Live By - an exploration of Quaker spirituality.* London: Quaker Books

Andrew, R., 'An impoverished catholicity; theological considerations for a Methodist future' in Marsh, C., Beck, B., Shier-Jones, A. and Wareing, H. (eds.) (2004) *Unmasking Methodist Theology.* London: Continuum

Argyris, C. and Schön, D. (1974) *Theory in Practice – Increasing professional effectiveness.* San Francisco: Jossey-Bass

Argyris, C. and Schön, D. (1978) *Organizational Learning: A theory of action perspective.* Reading, MA: Addison-Wesley

Atherton, J. (2003) *Marginalization.* London: SCM Press

Atherton, J and Skinner, H. (2007) *Through the Eye of a Needle – Theological Conversations over the Political Economy.* Peterborough: Epworth

Atkins, M. (2010) *Discipleship…and the people called Methodists.* London: Methodist Publishing House

Baelz, P. and Jacob, W. (eds.) (1985) *Ministers of the Kingdom. Exploration in Non- Stipendiary Ministry.* London: CIO Publishing.

Bagshaw, P. (1994) *The Church Beyond the Church – Sheffield Industrial Mission 1944-1994.* Sheffield: Industrial Mission in South Yorkshire

Bakewell@Work Prayer Booklet (2009). Bakewell: Bakewell Association of Christians

Bakewell Community Project (2012-2014). Bakewell: Bakewell Association of Christians

Bakewell Methodist Church@Work (various dates). Bakewell: Bakewell Methodist Church

Bakewell@Work Newsletter (various dates). Bakewell: Association of Bakewell Christians

[All the Bakewell material available from David Clark - david@clark58.eclipse.co.uk]

Bakhtin, M. M. (1984) *Problems of Dostoevsky's Poetics*, trans. by C. Emerson. Minneapolis: University of Minnesota Press

Barkway, L. in *An Anthology of the Love of God - from the writings of Evelyn Underhill* (1953) London: Mowbray

Bauman, Z. (2001) *Community*. Cambridge: Polity

Bauman, Z. (2004) *Identity*. Cambridge: Polity Press

Beeson, T. (2013) *Priests and Politics - the Church Speaks Out*. London: SCM Press

Berger, P. L., Berger, B. and Kellner, H. (1974) *The Homeless Mind*. Harmondsworth: Penguin

Berger, P. and Luckmann, T. (1984) *The Social Construction of Reality*. Harmondsworth: Penguin

Bohm, D. (1996) *On Dialogue*. London: Routledge

Boswell, J. (1990) *Community and the Economy: the Theory of Public Co-operation*. London: Routledge.

Bradley, I. (1993) *The Celtic Way*. London: Darton, Longman and Todd

Braley, B. (ed.) (1996) *Touching the Pulse: Worship and Where We Work*. London: Stainer and Bell

Breadon, J. 'Reflections on Chaplaincy in Further Education' in *Epworth Review* (2010) (see below)

Britton, A. 'Readers at Work' in *Bridging the Gap - Reader ministry today*. (2002) London: Church House Publishing

Brodrick, J. (1940) *The Origin of the Jesuits*. London: Longmans

Brown, M. and Ballard, P. (2006) *The Church and Economic Life*. Peterborough: Epworth

Buber, M. (2nd ed., 1958) *I and Thou*. Edinburgh: T. and T. Clark

Bunting, M. (2005) *Willing Slaves*. London: Harper Perennial

Burchell, M. and Robin, J. (2011) *The Great Workplace*. San Francisco, CA: Jossey-Bass

Butland, C. (1985) *Work in Worship*. London: Hodder and Stoughton

Cadbury, D. (2010) *Chocolate Wars*. London: Harper Press

Called to Love and Praise: A Methodist Conference Statement on the Church (1999) Peterborough: Methodist Publishing House

Caritas in Veritate - Charity in Truth (2009) Pope Benedict XVI. San Francisco: Ignatius Press

Chaplaincy Feasibility Study - Research Report (1) (2009) London: The Methodist Church

Chester, T. (2006) *the Busy Christian's Guide to Busyness.* Nottingham: Inter-Varsity Press

Choosing the Common Good (2010) Bishops' Conference of England and Wales. Stoke-on-Trent: Alive Publishing

CHRISM pamphlets (various numbers and dates) (2014, Secretary: margaret.joachim@london.anglican.org)

Christians in Public Life Programme (CIPL) (various dates). Birmingham: Westhill College [A selection of these papers are published in Clark, D. (1997) *Changing World, Unchanging Church?* (see below)]

Clark, D. (1969) *Community and a Suburban Village.* University of Sheffield: unpublished Ph.D. thesis

Clark, D. (1970) 'Local and Cosmopolitan Aspects of Religious Activity in A Northern Suburb', in Martin, D and Hill, M (eds.), *A Sociological Yearbook of Religion in Britain* 3, London: SCM Press

Clark, D. (1971) 'Local and Cosmopolitan Aspects of Religious Activity in a Northern Suburb: Processes of Change', in Hill, M. (ed.), *A Sociological Yearbook of Religion in Britain* 4, London: SCM Press

Clark, D. (ed.) (1971-1986) *Community*. Journal of the National Centre for Christian Communities and Networks. Birmingham: NACCCAN

Clark, D. (August, 1973a) 'The Concept of Community – a Re-examination' in *The Sociological Review* 3 (21) Keele: University of Keele

Clark, D. (June, 1973b) 'Social Education: An Experiment with Early School Leavers' in *The Journal of Moral Education*, **2** (3)

Clark, D. (June, 1975) 'Group Work with Early School Leavers in *The Journal of Curriculum Studies*, **7** (1)

Clark, D. (1976) 'The Academic, the Interpersonal and the Role of the Teacher in Social and Moral Education'. *Journal of Moral Education*, **2** (5). London: Pemberton Publishing

Clark, D. (1977) *Basic Communities – Towards and alternative society*. London: SPCK

Clark, D. (1984) *The Liberation of the Church. The role of basic Christian groups in a new re-formation*. Birmingham, Westhill College: The National Centre for Christian Communities and Networks

Clark, D. (1987) *Yes to Life*. London: Collins

Clark, D. (January, 1992) 'The journey in and the journey out'. Position paper B5. Birmingham: Christians in Public Life Programme (see above)

Clark, D. (1992) 'Education for Community in the 1990s: A Christian Perspective' in Allen, G and Martin, I. (eds.) *Education and Community – the Politics of Practice*. London: Cassell

Clark, D. (1993) *A Survey of Christians at Work and its implications for the Churches*. Birmingham: Westhill College (Christians in Public Life Programme)

Clark, D. (1996) *Transforming Education - The school as a learning community*. London: Cassell

Clark, D. (1997) *Changing World, Unchanging Church?* London: Mowbray

Clark, D (2005) *Breaking the Mould of Christendom: Kingdom community, diaconal church and the liberation of the laity*. Peterborough: Epworth

Clark, D. (2007) *Breaking the Mould of Regeneration - the legacy, role and future of the Human City Institute* (available from Trident Housing Association, 239 Holliday Street, Birmingham B1 1SJ)

Clark, D. (ed.) (2008a) *The Diaconal Church - beyond the mould of Christendom.* Peterborough: Epworth Press

Clark, D. 'Setting up "Faith at Work" programmes' in Nelson, J. (ed.) (2008b) *How to Become a Creative Church Leader.* Norwich: Canterbury Press

Clark, D. (2008c) *The Lord's Prayer* (Unpublished prayers)

Clark, D. (2009) 'Discerning the gifts of the kingdom community at work'. *Worksheets* (2009) Methodist Diaconal Order's Faith and Work Group. Download from - www.methodist.org.uk/businessworksheets)

Clark, D. (2010) *Reshaping the mission of Methodism*. Oldham: Church in the Market Place (pp. 167-191)

Clark, D. (2012) *Building the Human City - the Origins and Future Potential of the Human City Institute (1995 - 2002)*. Birmingham: Human City Institute (available from HCI, 239 Holliday Street, Birmingham B1 1SJ or download free from www.humancity.org.uk)

Clark, D. (2013) 'The hallmark of the Methodist Diaconal Order - its life as a religious order - and some implications the future of Methodism' in *Theology and Ministry - An Online Journal*. (Vol. 2) University of Durham: St John's College - www.durham.ac.uk/theologyandministry

Clark, S. and Myers, M. (2007) *Managing Difficult Conversations at Work*. Cirencester: Management Books 2000

Coffey, I. (2008) *Working it Out*. Nottingham: Inter-Varsity Press

Cohen, A.P. (1985) *The Symbolic Construction of Community*. London: Ellis Harwood and Tavistock

Cohen, A.P. (1985) *The Symbolic Construction of Community*. London: Ellis Harwood and Tavistock

Collins, J. N. (2002) *Deacons and the Church*. Leominster: Gracewing

The Common Good and the Catholic Church's Social Teaching (1996) London: Catholic Bishops' Conference of England and Wales

Compendium of the Social Doctrine of the Church (English edition, 2005), London: Continuum

Cope, P. and West, M. (2011) *Engaging Mission – the lasting value of Industrial Mission for today*. Guildford: Grosvenor House Publishing

Copeland, G. (2001) *Prayers that avail much for the workplace*. Tulsa, Oklahoma: Harrison House Inc.

Cosden, D. (2004) *A Theology of Work: Work and the new creation*. Bletchley: Paternoster

Cosden, D (2006) *The Heavenly Good of Earthly Work*. Milton Keynes: Paternoster Press

Costa, K. (2007) *God at Work*. London: Continuum

Courses on Faith at Work - see Stage 9

Crucible - Work (January-March, 2011) London: Hymns Ancient and Modern

Crucible – Chaplaincy (October-December, 2011) London: Hymns Ancient and Modern

Cunningham, D. S. (1998) *These Three Are One: The Practice of Trinitarian* Theology. Oxford: Blackwell

Cutts, N. (2010) *Love at Work*. Pool-in-Wharfedale: Fisher King Publishing

Dawson, P. (1981) *Making a Comprehensive Work*. Oxford: Blackwell

DeBerri, E. P., Hug, J. E. with Henriot, P. J. and Schultheis. M. J. *Catholic Social Teaching Our Best Kept Secret* (2003, 4th edition). Maryknoll, New York: Orbis Books

de Waal, E. (1996) *The Celtic Way of Prayer*. London: Hodder and Stoughton

de Waal, E. (ed.) (2001 revised edition) *The Celtic Vision*. Liguori, Missouri: Liguori/Triumph

Diaconal Reflections: How we experience our diaconal calling in our diversity (1998). A paper produced for DIAKONIA

Dollard, K., Marrett-Crosby, A. and Wright, T. (2002) *Doing business with Benedict – the Rule of Saint Benedict and business management: a conversation*. London: Continuum

Drucker, P. F. (1993) *Post-Capitalist Society*. Oxford: Butterworth-Heinemann

Ecclestone, A. (1975) *Yes to God*. London: Darton, Longman and Todd

Ecclestone, A. (compiled by Cotter, J.) (1999) *Firing the Clay – Articles and Addresses*. Sheffield: Cairns Publications

Echelin, P. E. (1971) *The Deacon in the Church: Past and Future*. New York: Alba House. *Epworth Review* 24.2

Elliott, C. (1985) *Praying the Kingdom*. London: Darton, Longman and Todd)

Engaging for success: enhancing performance through employee engagement (2009) MacLeod, D. and Clarke, N. A report to the Department for Business. London

Employee Engagement - the evidence (November, 2012) Prepared by Rayton, B. Bath: Bath University School of Management

Epworth Review (Vol. 37, No. 4, December 2010) 'Chaplaincy Special Edition'. London: Methodist Publishing

Faith, Work and Economic Life (January 2011) General Synod of the Church of England: Education Division and Mission and Public Affairs Division

Fitzgerald, W. (1903) *The Roots of Methodism* (London: Epworth)

For such a time as this. A renewed diaconate in the Church of England (2001). London: Church House Publishing

Fox, M. (1994) *The Reinvention of Work*. San Francisco: Harper: San Francisco

Fox, R. (2011) *Coaching Church Leaders -An Introduction to Coaching*. MODEM Occasional Paper No. 4 (www.modem-uk.org)

Francis, J. M. M. and Francis, L. J. (1998) *Tentmaking*. Leominster: Gracewing

Fuller, J. and Vaughan, P. (eds.) (1986) *Working for the Kingdom. The Story of Ministers in Secular Employment*. London: SPCK

Galbraith, J. K. (1992) *The Culture of Contentment*. Harmondsworth: Penguin

Gibbs, M. and Morton, T. R. (1964) *God's Frozen People*. London: Fontana/Collins

Gibbs, M. and Morton, T. R. (1971) *God's Lively People*. London: Fontana/Collins

Global Workforce Study (2012) New York: Towers Watson

Good Business - Ethics at work (2000) London: The Quakers and Business group

Good Work and Our Times (July 2011) Report of the Good Work Commission. Prepared by Parker, L. and Bevan, S. London: The Work Foundation

Gore, A. (2013) *The Future*. London: W. H. Allen

Great Workplaces (2011, 2012, 2013, 2014) London: Great Place to Work Institute UK

Green, J. *Open Source Chaplaincy* (2011 and 2012) (www.opensourcechaplaincy.org.uk)

Green, L. 'The Two Cultures' in Clark, D. (1997) *Changing World, Unchanging Church?* London: Mowbray

Greene, M. (2001) *Supporting Christians at Work*. London: LICC

Greene, M. (2004a) *Pocket Prayers for Work*. London: Church House Publishing

Greene, M. (2004b) *Pocket Prayers for Teachers*. London: Church House Publishing

Greene, M. (2005, 3rd ed.) *Thank God it's Monday*. Bletchley: Scripture Union

Greene, M. and Cooling, T. (2008) *Supporting Christians in Education*. London: LICC

Gregg, M. (2011) *Work's Intimacy*. Cambridge: Polity

Grey, M. (1993) *The Wisdom of Fools?* London: SPCK

Hammersley, J. (undated) *Psalms of Life*. Milton Keynes: Stantonbury Parish Print

Hanson, D. (Spring 2006) *Confronting the Realities of Work*. The Bible in Transition. Swindon: The Bible Society

Harkness, Georgia (1957) *Christian* Ethics. www.religion-online.org

Hart, P. (2012) *Can Chaplains provide missional leadership in the world of work?* Unpublished MA thesis, Manchester University

Harvey, R. (ed.) (1999) *Wrestling and Resting – Exploring stories of spirituality*. London CTBI

Hauerwas, S. (1981) *A Community of Character*. South Bend, IN: University of Notre Dame Press

Hauerwas, S. (1986) (3rd edition) *The Peaceable Kingdom: a Primer in Christian Ethics*. Notre Dame and London: University of Notre Dame Press

Haughton, R. (1982) *The Passionate God*. London: Darton, Longman and Todd

Helms, D. (2013) M.A. thesis (unpublished). Calver, nr Sheffield: Cliff College (University of Manchester)

Hesketh, W (2007) *Lever: Port Sunlight and Port Fishlight*. Development Trust Association

Higginson, R. (2012) *Faith, Hope and the Global Economy*. Nottingham: Inter-Varsity Press

Howard, S. and Welbourn, D. (2004) *The Spirit at Work Phenomenon*. London: Azure

Hoyland, J. S. (1964) *Silent Dawn - an anthology of prayers*. London: Friends Home Service Committee

Hughes, J. (2007) *The End of Work – Theological Critiques of Capitalism*. Oxford: Blackwell Publishing

Hull, J. M. (1993) *The Hockerill Lecture. 1993*. London: Hockerill Educational Foundation

Hull, J. (2006) *Mission-shaped Church: a Theological Response*. London: SCM Press

Hutson, S. (2009) *Faith and Work*. London: Mission in London's Economy

Hutton, W. (2010) *Them and Us. Changing Britain – Why we need a fair society*. London: Little Brown

Hymns and Psalms (1983). London: Methodist Publishing House

IMAgenda (2014) (Moderator and Editor: Randell Moll – (randellmoll@yahoo.co.uk)

Industrial Mission - an Appraisal (1988) London: Board for Social Responsibility (Church of England)

Jenkins, D. (1968) *The Glory of Man*. London: SCM Press

Jenkins, D. (1976) *The Contradiction of Christianity*. London: SCM Press

Jenkins, D. (2000) *Market Whys and Human Wherefores*. London: Cassell

Jenner, J., 'The Society of Friends as a learning community: the Quaker experience' in Clark, D. (ed.) (2008) *The Diaconal Church - beyond the mould of Christendom.* Peterborough: Epworth Press

Jensen, D. H. (2006) *Responsive Labor.* Louisville, Kentucky: Westminster John Knox Press

Jones, M. 'Growing in Grace and Holiness' in Marsh, C., Beck, B., Shier-Jones, A. and Wareing, H. (eds.) (2004) *Unmasking Methodist Theology.* London: Continuum

The Joy of the Gospel: Evangelii Gaudium, Pope Francis (2013). CreateSpace Independent Publishing Platform via Amazon UK

Kane, M. (1986) *What kind of God?* London: SCM Press

Kingdom at Work Project - Bulletin (February, 2014) from www.saltleytrust.org.uk

Kirkpatrick, F. G. (2001) *The Ethics of Community.* Oxford: Blackwell

Korten, D. C. (1996) *When Corporations Rule the World.* Connecticut: Kumarian Press

Kraemer, H. (1958; 2005 edition) *A Theology of the Laity.* Vancouver: Regent College Publishing

Laborem Exercens (1981) London: Catholic Truth Society

Lakeland, P. (2003) *The Liberation of the Laity.* London: Continuum

Larive, A. L. (2004) *After Sunday: A Theology of* Work. New York: Continuum

Brother Lawrence (2008) *The Practice of the Presence of God.* Radford VA: Wilde Publications

Lewin, A. (1987) *Unfinished Sentences.* Winchester: Optimum Litho

Lewin, A. (1988) *Between the Lines.* Winchester: Optimum Litho

Lewis, C. S. (reissue ed., 1998) *Surprised by Joy.* London: Collins

MacIntyre, A. (1985, 2nd edition) *After Virtue – a study in moral theory.* London: Duckworth

MacIver, R.M. and Page, C.H. (1950) *Society.* London: Macmillan

Macquiban, T. S., A. 'Dialogue with the Wesleys: Remembering Origins' in Marsh, C., Beck, B., Shier-Jones, A. and Wareing, H. (eds.) (2004) *Unmasking Methodist Theology*. London: Continuum

McFayden, A. I. (1990) *The call to personhood - a Christian theory of the individual in social relationships*. Cambridge: Cambridge University Press

Maddocks, A. 'City centre chaplaincy' (G1) in Methodist Diaconal Order (MDO) (2009) *Worksheets*. Methodist Diaconal Order's Faith and Work Group (see below)

Mason, P. (2012) *Why it's Kicking off Everywhere*. London: Verso

Masumoto, S. (1983) 'A Critique of British Industrial Mission as a Response of the Church to Modern Industrial Society' in Brown, M. and Ballard, P. (2006) *The Church and Economic Life*. Peterborough: Epworth

Matthews, H. (2013) *Faith and Work in Theological Education and Training: an Enquiry*. Birmingham: The Saltley Trust

Mauzy, J. and Harriman, R. (2003) *Creativity Inc.: Building an Inventive Organization*. Harvard: Harvard Business Review

Megginson, D. and Clutterbuck, D. (2005) *Techniques for Coaching and Mentoring*. (2005) London: Elsevier

Megginson, D., Clutterbuck, D., Garvery, B., Stokes, P. and Garrett-Harris, R. *Mentoring in Action*. (2006, second edition). London: Kogan Page

Messer, N. (2006) *Christian Ethics*. London: SCM

Methodist Diaconal Order (MDO) (2009) *Worksheets*. Methodist Diaconal Order's Faith and Work Group. Download from: www.methodist.org.uk/businessworksheets

Methodist Prayer Handbook [MPH] (various years). Peterborough: Methodist Publishing

Ministers-at-Work: Theology Resource Book (1999). CHRISM at www.chrism.org.uk

Ministers-at-Work - The Journal for Christians in Secular Ministry, CHRISM. (Editor, 2014: Rob Fox - rob.fox36@gmail.com)

The Ministry of the People of God. Methodist Conference (1988)

The Ministry of the People of God in the World. Methodist Conference (1990)

Mission-shaped Church (2004) London: Church House Publishing

Morgan, T. in the *Church Times* (1/4/11; 8/4/11; 1/2/13). London: Church Times

Munson, J. (1991) *The Nonconformists - In search of a lost culture*. London: SPCK

Newbigin, L. (1980) *Your Kingdom Come*. Leeds: John Paul The Preacher's Press

Oliver, D. (2005) *Love Work - Live Life!* Bletchley: Authentic Media

Our Best Kept Secret (2003) (4th ed.). DeBerri, E. P. et al. Maryknoll, NY: Orbis Books

Palmer, P. (1987) *A Place Called Community*. Pennsylvannia: Pendle Hill.

Parry (Abbot) and de Waal, E. (1990) *The Rule of Saint Benedict*. Leominster: Gracewing

Pawley, M (1991) *Prayers for Pilgrims*. London: SPCK - Triangle

Pikkety, T. (translated by Goldhammer, A.) (2014) *Capital in the Twenty-First Century*. MA, USA: Harvard University Press

Poole, E. (2010) *The Church on Capitalism: Theology and the Market*. London: Palgrave Macmillan

Prayers New and Old (1966) London: Lutterworth Press

Preston, R.H. (1991) *Religion and the Ambiguities of Capitalism*. London: SCM Press

Quaker Faith and Practice (QFP) (third edition) (2005) London: Religious Society of Friends

Reed, E. (2010) *Work! For God's Sake – Christian Ethics in the Workplace*. London: Darton, Longman and Todd

Reflections on Ministry in Secular Employment (2010) (2nd edition - first published 2000). Diocese of Coventry: Coventry MSE Group

Rhymes, D. (1967) *Prayer in the Secular City*. London: Lutterworth Press

Rice, A. K. (1965) *Learning for Leadership*. London: Tavistock

Sacks, J. (2011) *The Great Partnership - God, Science and the Search for Meaning*. London: Hodder

Sandel, M (2012) *What Money Can't Buy*. New York: Farrar, Straus and Giroux

Sandercock, L. (1998) *Towards Cosmopolis*. Chichester: John Wiley and Sons

Saval, N. (2014) *Cubed - A Secret History of the Workplace*. New York: Doubleday

Schon, D. (1991) *The Reflective Practitioner*. Aldershot: Ashgate Publishing

School Improvement Butterflies (1995) Birmingham: Birmingham City Council Education Department Schools Advisory Service

Schumacher, E. F. (1973) *Small Is Beautiful: A Study of Economics as if People Mattered*. London: Blond & Briggs

Schumacher, E. F. (1980) *Good Work*. (London: Sphere Books, Abacus edition)

Sedgewick, P. (2008) *The Market Economy and Christian Ethics*. Cambridge: Cambridge University Press

Selby, P. (1997) *Grace and Mortgage: The Language of Faith and the Debt of the World*. London: Darton, Longman and Todd

Senge, P.M. (1990) *The Fifth Discipline*. New York: Currency and Doubleday

Shaping the Future - Sustainable Organization Performance. What really makes the difference? (January 2011) London: CIPD

Singing the Faith (2011). London: Hymns Ancient & Modern

Skidelsky, R. and Skidelsky, E. (2012) *How Much is Enough?* London: Allen Lane

Snyder, H. A. (1991) *Models of the Kingdom*. Eugene, Oregon: Wipf and Stock

Social Responsibility, ISO Focus+ (March 2011), Vol. 2, No. 3. Geneva: ISO

Spiritual Direction for Ministers in Secular Employment. CHRISM 11 (2011): at www.chrism.org.uk

The Spiritual Exercises of Saint Ignatius Loyola. Hughes, G. and Ivens, M. (translator) (2004) Leominster: Gracewing

Spufford, F. (2012) *Unapologetic*. London: Faber and Faber

Stamp, G. (January 1992). '*Stealing the Churches' Clothes?*' CIPL Paper G3. Birmingham: Westhill College

Stevens, R. P. (1999) *The Abolition of the Laity*. Carlisle: Paternoster Press

Tanner, K. (2005) *Economy of Grace*. Augsburg, MN: Fortress Press

Taylor, C. (2007) *A Secular* Age. Cambridge, MA: Harvard University Press

Temple, W. (1956 - first published 1942) *Christianity and the Social Order*. Harmondsworth: Penguin Books

Theology of Work Project (2014) Boston, USA (www.theologyofwork.org)

Thompson, W. D. (2006) *On-the-job Prayers*. Skokie, IL: ACTA Publications

Threlfall-Holmes, M. and Newitt, M. (2011) *Being a Chaplain*. London: SPCK

Tolle, E. (2001) *The Power of Now*. London: Hodder and Stoughton

Tolle, E. (2002) *Practising the Power of Now*. London: Hodder and Stoughton

Tolle, E. (2005) *A New Earth*. London: Penguin Books

Torry, M. (2010) *Bridgebuilders - A Workplace Chaplaincy*. Norwich: Canterbury Press

Turner, J. M. (2005) *Wesleyan Methodism*. London: Epworth

Unemployment and the Future of Work (1997). London: CCBI

Underhill, E. (1934) *The School of Charity*. London: Longmans, Green and Co.

Underhill. E (1937) *The Spiritual Life*. London: Hodder and Stoughton

Underhill, E. (1953) *An Anthology of the Love of God*. London: Mowbray

Valler, P. (2008) *Get a Life*. Nottingham: Inter-Varsity Press

Vaughan, P. (September 2011) *Challenging Clerical Stereotypes - reflections on the genesis of NSM*. CHRISM 12 (www.chrism.org.uk)

Vocation of the Business Leader - a Reflection (2012) Pontifical Council for Justice and Peace, USA. Saint Paul, Minnesota: University of St. Thomas

Volf, M. (1991) *Work in the Spirit: Toward a theology of work*. Eugene, Oregon: Wipf and Stock

Wakefield, G. S. (1999) *Methodist Spirituality*. Peterborough: Epworth

Walcot, K. 'Mission as dialogue' in Clark, D. (1997) *Changing World, Unchanging Church?* London: Mowbray

Wallis, J. (2013) *On God's Side - what religion forgets and politics hasn't yet learned about serving the common good*. Oxford: Lion Hudson

Walton, R. (2012) *The Reflective Disciple*. SCM Press: Norwich

Ward, G. (2009) *The Politics of Discipleship*. Grand Rapids, MI: Baker Acedemic

Webley, S. (2003) *Developing a Code of Business Ethics*. London: Institute of Business Ethics

Wenger, E. (1998) *Communities of Practice*. Cambridge: Cambridge University Press

Wenger, E., McDermott, T. and Snyder, W. M. (2002) *Cultivating Communities of Practice*. Boston, MA: Harvard Business School Press

What is a Deacon? (2004) Methodist Conference Report

Whipp, M. J. (2008) *Speaking of Faith at Work: towards a Trinitarian hermeneutic*. (Unpublished Ph. D. thesis). Glasgow: University of Glasgow

Wilkinson, R. and Pickett, K. (2010) *The Spirit Level*. London: Penguin

Williams, C. (1960) *John Wesley's Theology Today*. London: Epworth Press

Williams, R. (2012) *Faith in the Public Square*. London: Bloomsbury

Wink, W. (1984) *Naming the Powers: The Language of Power in the New Testament*. Philadelphia: Fortress Press

Wink, W. (1986) *Unmasking the Powers: The Invisible Forces That Determine Human* Existence. Philadelphia: Fortress Press

Wink, W. (1992) *Engaging the Powers: Discernment and Resistance in a World of Domination.* Philadelphia: Fortress Press

Wink, W. (1998) *The Powers That Be: Theology for a New Millennium.* New York: Doubleday)

Worship Resources (2005) Chrism 9. Christians in Secular Ministry

Wright, J. (2009) *Reclaiming Business for the Kingdom of God* in 'Faith in Business Quarterly' Vol.10, No.2

Wuthnow, R. (1994) *Sharing the Journey – Support Groups and America's New Quest for Community.* New York: The Free Press

Wynne, J. (2009) *Working without Wilting.* Nottingham: Inter-Varsity Press

Younge, G. (2011) *Who are we?* London: Penguin Books

Yuill, C. (2011) *Moving in the Right Circles - Embracing the discipleship adventure.* Nottingham: Inter-Varsity Press

Web sites

After Sunday - www.aftersunday.org.uk

Alpha in the Workplace - www.alphafriends.rog/workplace

Business in the Community (BITC) - www.bitc.org.uk

Catholic Online - www.catholic.org/prayers

CHRISM (ministers in secular employment) - www.chrism.org.uk

Christian Association of Business Executives (CABE) - www.cabe-online.org

Chartered Institute of Personnel and Development (CIPD) – www.cipd.co.uk

Christians at Work - www.christiansatwork.org.uk

Diocese of Chelmsford - www.chelmsford.anglican.org/CITW

Diocese of Peterborough - www.peterborough-diocese.org.uk/workingdisciple

Economy for the Common Good Association - www.gemeinwohl-oekonomie.org

Engage for Success - www.engageforsucess.org

FTSE4Good Index – www.ftse.co.uk/Indices/FTSE4Good_Index_Series

God at Work (Ken Costa) - www.godatwork.org.uk

The GoodCorporation - www.goodcorporation.com

Great Place to Work Institute UK - www.greatplacetowork.co.uk

Human City Institute - www.humancity.org.uk

Industrial Christian Fellowship - www.icf-online.org

Industrial Mission Association (IMA) - www.industrialmission.org.uk

Institute of Business Ethics (IBE) - www.ibe.org.uk

International Organization for Standardization (ISO) - www.iso.org

Investors in People - www.investorsinpeople.co.uk

London Institute for Contemporary Christianity -
www.licc.org.uk/engaging-with-work

Methodist Church - worksheets -
www.methodist.org.uk/businessworksheets

MODEM - www.modem-uk.org

New Economics Foundation - www.neweconomics.org

OD and Christian Organisations Learning Group -
www.developingchurches.ning.com

Ogden, John - www.cavhmc.org.uk

Open Source Chaplaincy (Methodist Church) -
www.opensourcechaplaincy.org.uk

Quakers and Business Group - www.qandb.org

Ridley Hall Foundation - www.ridley.cam.ac.uk

St James, Piccadilly - www.st-james-piccadilly.org

St Paul's Institute - www.stpaulsinstitute.org.uk

St Peter's Saltley Trust - www.saltleytrust.org.uk

Schumacher Society - www.schumacher.org.uk

Self-supporting ministries (Church of England) - www.1pf.co.uk/SSM

STETS - www.stets.ac.uk

Street Pastors - www.streetpastors.co.uk

Theology of Work Project - www.theologyofwork.org

Together for the Common Good –
www.togetherforthecommongood.co.uk

Transforming Presence - www.transformingpresence.org.uk

Transform Work UK - www.transformworkuk.org

Workplace Matters (Chaplaincy) –
www.workplacematters.org.uk/chaplaincy-team

Worktalk - www.worktalk.gs

Young Christian Workers - www.ycwimpact.com

Organizations Index

411